The Sagebrush Trail

The Modern American West
David M. Wrobel and Andrew G. Kirk, Editors

Carl Abbott
The Metropolitan Frontier: Cities in the Modern American West

Richard W. Etulain
Re-imagining the Modern American West: A Century of Fiction, History, and Art

Gerald D. Nash
The Federal Landscape: An Economic History of the Twentieth-Century West

Ferenc Morton Szasz
Religion in the Modern American West

Oscar J. Martínez
Mexican-Origin People in the United States: A Topical History

Duane A. Smith
Rocky Mountain Heartland: Colorado, Montana, and Wyoming in the Twentieth Century

William G. Robbins and Katrine Barber
Nature's Northwest: The North Pacific Slope in the Twentieth Century

R. Douglas Hurt
The Big Empty: The Great Plains in the Twentieth Century

Robert L. Dorman
Hell of a Vision: Regionalism and the Modern American West

Donald L. Fixico
Indian Resilience and Rebuilding: Indigenous Nations in the Modern American West

Richard Aquila
The Sagebrush Trail: Western Movies and Twentieth-Century America

The Sagebrush Trail

Western Movies and Twentieth-Century America

Richard Aquila

The University of
Arizona Press
Tucson

The University of Arizona Press
www.uapress.arizona.edu

Printed in the United States of America
20 19 18 17 16 15 6 5 4 3 2 1

ISBN-13: 978-0-8165-0105-2 (cloth)
ISBN-13: 978-0-8165-3154-7 (paper)

Cover designed by Carrie House, HOUSEdesign llc
Cover image © Silvia Bukovac

Library of Congress Cataloging-in-Publication Data
Aquila, Richard, 1946–
The sagebrush trail : western movies and twentieth-century America / Richard Aquila.
pages cm — (The modern American West)
Includes bibliographical references and index.
ISBN 978-0-8165-3154-7 (pbk. : alk. paper) — ISBN 978-0-8165-0105-2 (cloth edition)
1. Western films—United States—History and criticism. I. Title. II. Series: Modern American West.
PN1995.9.W4A67 2015
791.43'65878—dc23
2014037296

♾ This paper meets the requirements of ANSI/NISO Z39.48–1992 (Permanence of Paper).

For Mom

Contents

Illustrations

Acknowledgments

Many people have helped with this project. First, I would like to thank Richard Etulain, who invited me to write this volume for the University of Arizona Press's Modern American West series. He provided encouragement and expert advice about the manuscript. I'd also like to thank the other editor of the series, David Wrobel, as well as Kristen Buckles of the University of Arizona Press, for their support and insights. Penn State University provided me with a sabbatical and funds for research. My family offered additional help and encouragement. My son, Stephen, his wife, Meredith, my daughter, Valerie, and her husband, Jeff, served as my focus group and always listened enthusiastically whenever I talked about western movies. And my wife, Marie, proved to be an excellent companion on the "sagebrush trail." She watched hundreds of westerns with me, most of which never would have made her Netflix queue. She listened patiently to my comments, and then graciously read and helped edit the final manuscript. I'm sure she is as happy as I am that this book is finally completed, but perhaps for different reasons. I can remember back in the 1950s when my parents bought me a cowboy hat and six-shooters, and my brother, Phil, and I used to sit on the floor every day in front of the TV watching Hopalong Cassidy, The Lone Ranger, Cisco and Pancho, and other cinematic cowboys galloping across the screen. Who would have guessed . . . ?

The Sagebrush Trail

PROLOGUE

The Sagebrush Trail

The Sagebrush Trail is a history of western movies but also a history of twentieth-century America. The book's title is based on a 1933 film that starred John Wayne as an innocent man convicted of murder back east. He breaks out of jail and heads for the American West to find the real killer. One movie poster features the tall and lean twenty-six-year-old actor wearing a black cowboy hat, black pants, and tight red shirt, with a jaunty bandanna around his neck. A tooled-leather holster clings to his hips. His gun is drawn and pointed directly at the viewer. A tagline emblazoned in red across the top reads: "HE WROTE THE CODE OF JUSTICE WITH A BLAZING SIX-GUN!"

Wayne's character—a rugged individual named John Brant—is the quintessential western hero. Strong and silent, he lets his fists and guns do the talking. He fights for truth and justice, righting every wrong and helping those in need. Before he's through, the determined westerner not only locates the real killer, but he finds romance with the beautiful Sally Blake (Nancy Shubert) and manages to outsmart, outride, and outshoot a gang of cutthroat desperadoes (led by actor/stuntman extraordinaire Yakima Canutt). Wayne's character accomplishes his goals by posing as an outlaw to infiltrate the bad guys' gang. When one of the crooks witnesses Brant evading a posse, he invites him back to their hideout. "You're a pretty smart hombre, and you got plenty of nerve," he tells Brant. "It strikes me that the boss could use somebody like you." When Brant refuses to reveal his name, the gang member says with a smile, "Smith, ain't it? That's the handle most of you fast travelers use. Aw, it's as good a name as any. Mine's Jones!"

Figure 1. Sagebrush Trail (Lone Star Pictures, 1933) featured a young John Wayne playing a good guy who plays a bad guy to win the day, not to mention the girl.

Just as Wayne's character in *Sagebrush Trail* was not what he appeared to be, western movies are also more than they seem at first glance. For more than one hundred years, moviegoers have sat on the edge of their seats, mesmerized by great train robberies, Indian attacks, cavalry charges, and shootouts at high noon. Yet, they have never grown tired of watching cowboys and Indians gallop across Big Sky country. Audiences have cheered on movie versions of Buffalo Bill, Annie Oakley, Wyatt Earp, George Armstrong Custer, Crazy Horse, and other historical westerners. And they have embraced fictional heroes like Shane and Hopalong Cassidy, as well as "real" film cowboys like Gene Autry and Roy Rogers.

Westerns have always been great fun and entertainment, but these films—like John Wayne's character in *Sagebrush Trail*—hold deeper secrets and meanings. Clues about America are scattered along the "sagebrush trail" of western movies, which winds through the twentieth century and beyond. They reveal that for more than a century, western movies have reflected—and sometimes have helped shape—American history and culture.

Movies and the Mythic West

The cinematic West was always more myth than reality. It was part of a long cultural tradition that went back hundreds if not thousands of years. By the time colonists made their way to American shores, the notion of a mythic West had already taken root in the European mind. For centuries, Europeans had been dreaming and talking about fabled lands somewhere to the west where they might find riches and happiness. Powered by tales of early historians and poets or later exploits of explorers such as Christopher Columbus and Juan Ponce de León, the mythic West took root in the popular imagination.[1]

The West was a dream long before it became a reality, promising a new beginning for anyone with the courage and determination to take on the "howling wilderness." Some Americans believed the West was an actual place; others viewed it as a concept or hope. George Catlin, who journeyed to the Trans-Mississippi West in the 1830s to paint portraits and lifestyles of American Indians, understood the difficulties in trying to locate a West situated between myth and reality. "Few people even know the true definition of the term *West*," he noted, "and, where is its location?—phantom-like it flies before us as we travel, and on our way is continually gilded, before us, as we approach the setting sun."[2]

Later writers came no closer to defining the West. In 1893, historian Frederick Jackson Turner suggested in his seminal frontier thesis that the "West" or "Frontier" (he used the terms interchangeably) was a process of westward movement rather than just one place. Ever since, historians have debated the *place* versus *process* approach to the American West. In 1992, a survey asked historians and other western experts to define the West. While most said that the West was a place or region rather than a process, they could not agree on a specific location. Some wanted a broad definition that would cover earlier frontiers in the east. Others argued that the West should include only the region west of the Mississippi River. Still others insisted on a more narrow definition, frequently suggesting that the West should be limited to the territory bounded by the one hundredth meridian (the western plains) in the East and the Sierra Nevada and Cascade ranges in the West. Significantly, one out of every six rejected any spatial or temporal definition, maintaining that the West was simply "a state of mind," a "myth," an "idea," or a "mental construct." Literary scholars Frank Bergon and Zeese Papanikolas suggest, "More than other American regions, the West eludes definition, because it is as much dream as a fact, and its locale was never geographical. Before it was a place, it was a conception."[3]

Regardless of definition, the West evokes numerous images in the American mind. It is often described as a Garden of Eden, a land of abundance with a climate so vibrant, healthy, and rejuvenating that it must truly be God's country. In this idyllic view, the West is a land of opportunity where Americans can realize the pursuit of happiness. This mythic West offers a new beginning and better life for individuals who are self-reliant and hardworking. In the West, one can find freedom, equality, opportunity, economic success, universal brotherhood, spiritual regeneration, harmony, contentment, and more. Images of the mythic West as a land of milk and honey contributed to the American Dream and the belief that a better future was always just around the bend. During hard times, Americans saw the West as a possible escape route. They might never actually break free from the chains of economic or political oppression, but the western Garden of Eden at least gave them hope and allowed Americans to feel as though they were in control of their destinies. "Whether or not such hope is justified is beside the point," suggests western historian Robert G. Athearn. "The fulfillment has always been less important than the anticipation, the dream."[4]

Many Americans were fascinated by the West's image as a remote, romantic, and strange land. Frequently, the mythic West was viewed as a place of adventure and thrills, rife with excitement and danger. Those brave enough to head in the direction of the setting sun had to cope with natural threats from hostile climates, wide open spaces, and foreboding mountains, and then fend off wild beasts, savage Indians, and vicious desperadoes. On the plus side, the mythic West promised rewards beyond belief. It told of legendary cities of gold; spoke of fame, fortune, and glory; and guaranteed romance and excitement. The mythic West was a land of hope and second chances, a place where common-man heroes such as Kit Carson, Wild Bill Hickok, and Buffalo Bill stood up for the American way of life, always defeating the evil designs of bad guys, renegades, and villains. The western story became an exciting morality play that taught Americans how to succeed through traditional values, rugged individualism, and, when necessary, aggressive behavior. If the mythic West offered potential for astounding success, it also presented the possibility of abject failure through broken dreams, unfulfilled promises, financial ruin, or tragic death. The dark side of the myth powered well-known tales about the Donner party, Jesse James, and Custer's Last Stand.

The mythic West with its tremendous potential for glorious victory or catastrophic defeat reflected the tensions in American culture between civilization and wilderness, realism and romance, the past and progress, and ultimately between good and evil. This was the stuff of legends. No wonder the West became a profitable and ideal subject for early pop culture products, including captivity narratives, popular histories and literature, art, melodrama, dime novels, and Wild West shows. The power, drama, excitement, and commercial track record of the "Pop Culture West" eventually made it an ideal subject for western movies.

From the early 1900s onward, western films offered powerful images of the mythic West, providing exhilarating tales, positive memories, and an unambiguous national identity for nostalgic Americans caught up in rapid social, cultural, and political change. Even if most Americans were tied down by their lives and families in cities, towns, and rural areas, they could always roam the mythic West in pop culture dreams readily available in movie theaters across the land. The cinematic West glorified spectacular western landscapes, celebrated colorful characters, and marveled at the majesty and mystery to be found on the American frontier. It offered vicarious thrills and escape from contemporary life or immediate economic, political, and social concerns. And its legendary tales reflected and reinforced American beliefs in democracy, freedom, self-reliance, morality, nationalism, and heroism. Though the movies' mythic West changed with the times, it remained an immensely popular and profitable enterprise. Equally important, it retained its historical significance as it yielded important information about American life and thought of the twentieth century and beyond.

Following the Sagebrush Trail

This book comprises a cultural history of western movies during the twentieth century. It covers both the silent and the sound eras and includes classic feature westerns such as *Stagecoach* (1939), *A Fistful of Dollars* (1964), and *Unforgiven* (1992), as well as low-budget "B-Westerns," which starred film cowboys like Tom Mix and Gene Autry. It is hard to say for certain how many western movies were produced during the 1900s and beyond. The data, particularly for the silent-film era, is sketchy at best, and the numbers cited by various catalogers do not always jibe. It appears that at least 2,000 silent westerns were made prior to 1929, and the total number of sound westerns made after that date exceeds 3,700 (with most of them released between 1930 and 1959). After 1960, the number dropped off precipitously. Yet, westerns never went away completely. The lure of the West on the big screen continues to attract enthusiastic audiences in the twenty-first century.[5]

Each section of *The Sagebrush Trail* focuses on a distinct era in western movie history. Part I traces the birth and growth of westerns from the late 1800s through the end of World War II. It spotlights silent westerns by Edwin S. Porter, Thomas H. Ince, and other pioneering directors, as well as early cowboy stars such as Broncho Billy Anderson and William S. Hart. Produced in an era characterized by urbanization, industrialization, and immigration, these early westerns offered a much-needed reminder about Americans' self-identity. They reaffirmed traditional values and beliefs associated with the nation's white Anglo-Saxon Protestant culture, and they assured Americans that they would triumph over modern technology and contemporary problems. The popularity of these westerns reflected in part the nation's ambivalence about the transition from the old rural America to a modern industrial, urban nation. They offered temporary escape from modern times as they simultaneously picked up on currents of change in American politics and society. The earliest westerns celebrated America's story. They justified westward expansion, reinforced American imperialism and patriotism, and endorsed the spirit of Progressivism and the rise of the Social Gospel movement. After 1920, silent westerns evolved to keep pace with the changing times. Reflecting post–World War I trends and the nation's desire to "return to normalcy," patriotic westerns praised the American character and celebrated the nation's Manifest Destiny that conquered the Old West. The rise of low-budget B-Westerns, starring glitzy new stars like Tom Mix, marked the turn toward a laissez-faire approach in politics, society, and culture, as well as the era's emerging consumer culture associated with the Roaring Twenties.

Western movies changed considerably between 1929 and 1945 with the emergence of new movie-making technologies, particularly the development of talkies. Hollywood cranked out big-budget westerns such as *In Old Arizona* (1929) and *Cimarron* (1931), as well as hundreds of B-Westerns, featuring action stars such as Buck Jones or singing cowboys like Gene Autry. Because these years included the Great Depression and World War II, the action on the screen was often connected directly or indirectly to the troubled times. If westerns offered some viewers temporary escape from daily concerns, they showed others how to deal with life's problems.

Westerns offered familiar images of the mythic West, which reminded Americans about their proud heritage and national destiny. The movies pointed out that Americans had always defeated bad guys in the past and assured viewers that the results would be the same in the future. Patriotic Americans could overcome the Great Depression and triumph over the Axis powers as long as they remained true to the heroic actions and traditional values that had won the mythic West.

Part II focuses on a transitional period in western movie history during the two decades following World War II. The United States emerged from the war a changed nation, as evidenced by new types of westerns. As B-Westerns faded from view, more sophisticated westerns began exploring social, cultural, and political concerns. Many films, including *High Noon* (1952) and *The Searchers* (1956), reflected the rise of a Cold War culture. Most reveal consensus behavior, increased patriotism, and adherence to traditional values, but other westerns, such as *Johnny Guitar* (1954) and *Sergeant Rutledge* (1960), suggest that conflict over gender, race, and other issues was brewing just below the surface of Cold War America.

Part III of the book shows how western movies reflected the social and cultural changes that transformed America in the last four decades of the twentieth century. After 1963, conflict would bubble up to the top in both western movies and American society. Some films, such as *True Grit* (1969) and *Silverado* (1985), continued to promote traditional values and attitudes. Revisionist westerns, including *The Wild Bunch* (1969) and *Dances with Wolves* (1990), addressed concerns about the Vietnam War, violence, or social change involving race, gender, and youth culture. Westerns, like other forms of popular culture, mirrored the tumult and polarization that threatened to tear the nation apart in the late sixties and seventies. By the eighties and beyond, a weary nation settled into an uneasy calm after the storms of the sixties had passed. For a time, westerns appeared played out, but like the nation, they too would rise again. The cinematic West still had much to offer as America approached a new millennium. As in earlier days, the mythic West evolved with the times. By century's end, the West on the silver screen was more multicultural and diverse than ever, but it still offered excitement, escape, and the opportunity for a nation to address its hopes, dreams, and fears.

* * *

The Sagebrush Trail tracks changing images of the mythic West in western movies throughout the twentieth century. It explains how westerns evolved to keep pace with corresponding changes in American history and culture, and it provides new evidence and fresh interpretations of westerns and American history. Significantly, western movies demonstrate that the "New Western History" that emerged among professional historians in the last few decades of the twentieth century was neither as new nor as revolutionary as some have suggested. Much of what revisionist historians began writing about in the eighties and beyond, including topics such as race, class, gender, environment, and the role of government in the West, can be found decades earlier in revisionist western movies of the fifties, sixties, and seventies.

Along with providing a much-needed chronological overview of western movies, *The Sagebrush Trail* explains how westerns have reflected—and sometimes helped shape—American history and culture since 1900. It shows that all westerns—from the sophisticated films of John Ford to more formulaic B-Westerns—are historically important. The result contributes to our understanding of not just film history but also the mythic West and American history.

The mythic West beckons but eludes. Yet, glimpses of its utopian potential can always be found, even if for just a few hours, in the realm of western movies. There on the silver screen, the mythic West—like John Wayne—continues to ride tall in the saddle along a "sagebrush trail" that reveals valuable clues about American life and thought.

PART ONE

The Rise of Western Movies
1900–1944

CHAPTER ONE

The Great Train Robbery

Or How Early Western Movies Stole America's Heart

In 1893, Frederick Jackson Turner delivered a talk entitled "The Significance of the Frontier in American History" at a history conference in Chicago. The young scholar began with a quote from the bulletin of the superintendent of the U.S. census, announcing that the frontier was officially closed. He went on to explain how the frontier and free land had played a major role in the development of America.[1]

Ironically, just a few miles away from where Turner was analyzing the end of the frontier at a gathering of historians, Buffalo Bill Cody's Wild West show was doing banner business right next door to the World's Columbian Exposition. Cody's colorful company of cowboys, Indians, and other frontier types attracted more than three million customers eager to experience the American West.[2] If the actual frontier in the Trans-Mississippi West had ended, the imaginary frontier of the Pop Culture West was still very much alive. The popularity of the mythic West would continue to grow, not just through Buffalo Bill's Wild West but also in popular writing, stage drama, art, and other forms of popular culture.

Given the ubiquity of western images in popular culture, it is not surprising that motion pictures—the newest pop art form emerging at the turn of the century—would strike gold with the American West. A western film released in 1903—Edwin S. Porter's *The Great Train Robbery*—would steal the hearts of people everywhere and make celluloid cowboys the latest and greatest stars of the Pop Culture West. Over the next decade, silent western films would continue to grow in popularity, reflecting—and sometimes shaping—not just the tastes of moviegoers but also American life and thought in the early twentieth century.

The Coming of Moving Pictures and Western Films

The Great Train Robbery has been called the first western movie, the first narrative film, even the first full-length motion picture. Actually, it was none of those. It was, however, a major step in the development of not just westerns, but the entire movie industry.

Ever since the early 1890s, moving pictures had been attracting viewers. Early devices such as Thomas Edison's Kinetoscope enabled individuals to look through a viewfinder at flickering images for a penny a peep that lasted around thirty seconds. By 1896, projectors such as Edison's vitascope and the Lumière brothers' *cinématographe* (from which the term *cinema* was derived) allowed early theaters (called *nickelodeons* because of their five-cent admission price) to spring up in cities across the United States.

At first, customers were thrilled just by the novelty of "moving" pictures. They eagerly plunked down their coins to watch "actualities" (short films that featured actual people, events, or places). Audiences marveled at strongman Eugen Sandow flexing his muscles; they were amazed by Carmencita as she danced in a fancy Mexican costume; and they applauded flickering images of acrobats, trapeze artists, boxers, and wrestlers. Moviegoers were also fascinated by shots of Niagara Falls or travelogues that provided glimpses of Venice, India, or other faraway lands. They were even mesmerized by flickering images of mundane events, such as a man sneezing or girls having a pillow fight.

Film makers soon realized that funny or unusual films would attract even larger audiences. Early comedies portrayed a gardener losing control of his hose and a woman trying to give a dog a bath. Not surprisingly, sex sold, as evidenced by popular films such as *Dolorita's Passion Dance* (1894) and *The Kiss* (1896). Audiences were also intrigued by "trick films," such as Edison's *Vanishing Lady* (1898) and Georges Méliès's *The Conjurer* (1899), which used stop-action shots to make people appear and disappear. Some films added simple story lines. Audiences marveled at Georges Méliès's science fiction/fantasy film *A Trip to the Moon* (1902), and they cheered as they watched Edwin S. Porter's *Life of an American Fireman* (1903), which depicted the exciting rescue of a mother and daughter.

Many early films showcased the mythic West, already a proven moneymaker for dime novels and live entertainment. In 1894, Edison produced

Kinetoscopes of performers from Buffalo Bill's Wild West, including bits of Annie Oakley shooting at targets and a cowboy riding a bucking bronco. In addition, there were snippets of a Wild West parade, as well as a short that showed Buffalo Bill and Indians galloping into an arena to perform. Other films told stories set in the West. The Edison Manufacturing Company's brief *Poker at Dawson City* (1899) depicted card players during the Alaska gold rush getting into a fight over cheating. Edison followed up with *Cripple Creek Bar-Room Scene* (1899), a slightly more sophisticated vignette that some experts have called the first western. Less than a minute long, the film told a story about cowboys getting thrown out of a saloon. Three years later, Edison's company released Edwin S. Porter's *Capture of the Biddle Brothers*, a two-minute-long film that depicted a shootout between good guys and bad guys.

The American Mutoscope and Biograph Company got in on the action with a pair of story films about the West directed by Wallace McCutcheon. *The Pioneers*, a fifteen-minute-long drama released in October 1903, opens with an Indian attack on a settlers' cabin. The invaders brutally kill a man and his wife, and then skulk back into the woods, taking with them the victims' young daughter as a captive. Shortly thereafter, trappers come upon the sight of the massacre and vow revenge. They track down the war party, kill the warriors, and rescue the girl. Biograph followed up that same month with a twenty-one-minute historical drama, *Kit Carson*, spotlighting the western hero. The producers boasted that the expensive film was "enacted with the greatest possible fidelity" and included "hand-to-hand conflicts with savage Indians" and other exciting adventures of one of "the greatest of all the American scouts and pathfinders."[3]

Neither *Kit Carson* nor *The Pioneers* was distributed to theaters until early 1904. By that time, another western story film was already playing in theaters and had become the box office champ. *The Great Train Robbery*—directed by Edwin S. Porter and released by the Edison Manufacturing Company in December 1903—may not have been the first film about the West or even the first western with a story line, but it would become a game changer not just for westerns but for the entire motion picture industry.

The Great Train Robbery

In late 1903, people of all ages rushed out to theaters across America to watch *The Great Train Robbery*. Almost twelve minutes long, the movie combined familiar elements from dime novels, Wild West shows, popular books such as Owen Wister's *The Virginian* (1902), and other areas of the Pop Culture West, with a story line based loosely on a real train holdup in 1901 by the Wild Bunch gang led by Butch Cassidy and the Sundance Kid. Not only did Edwin S. Porter's movie tell an exciting tale about the mythic West, but it promised a *totally* new viewing experience. Advertising brought the excitement to fever pitch. One ad called the film "thrilling" and "exciting." Edison's film catalog of 1903 promised distributors: "This sensational and highly tragic subject will certainly make a decided 'hit' whenever shown. In every respect we consider it absolutely the superior of any moving picture ever made."[4]

A colorful movie poster that looked like a cover of a dime novel announced the film's arrival in cities across the land. Across the top was the title in brilliant red letters set against a vivid gold background. Beneath the banner, a powerful locomotive screeches to a stop as an explosion blows out the side of a train car. One bandit opens fire with his pistol, while another orders the train men to reach for the sky. Lawmen in cowboy hats approach with rifles drawn. For added shock value, two Indians wielding tomahawks are crouched low, ready to pounce (even though no Indians are included in the movie). The bottom line of the poster reads like a yellow journalism headline: "SENSATIONAL AND STARTLING 'HOLD UP' OF THE 'GOLD EXPRESS' BY FAMOUS WESTERN OUTLAWS."

The movie did not disappoint. It begins with bold outlaws staging the robbery; a posse is then rounded up; and an exciting chase ensues. The tension builds, climaxing in a violent shootout, with lots of gun smoke and melodramatic deaths. The fast-paced story kept audiences on the edge of their seats. For almost twelve minutes, viewers were awestruck by the flickering images on the screen. They marveled at the nonstop action as it jumped back and forth in time or switched seamlessly from indoor scenes to on board the moving train, to outdoors in the wilds of the legendary West (they did not know that Porter actually filmed the movie along the Delaware and Lackawanna Railroad tracks in New Jersey). Audiences gasped at spectacular effects, resulting from Porter's innovative use of dissolves, pans, mattes, crosscutting, stop-action shots, and other cutting-edge camera techniques. Those lucky enough to see the special edition version, which included tints and hand-colored frames, could not believe their eyes when they witnessed an explosion with a pink cloud of smoke, women dancing in bright yellow or red dresses, or colorized gun smoke during shootouts between the posse and outlaws. Viewers were equally wowed by action shots that included holdups, fisticuffs, gunfights, explosions,

Figure 2. This movie poster for *The Great Train Robbery* (Edison Manufacturing Company, 1903) attracted audiences by evoking the blood and gore of popular western dime novels.

dancing, chases on horseback, and shootouts. And they were horrified yet fascinated by the film's gratuitous violence, cold-blooded murders, and brutal retribution.

One scene in particular impressed viewers. Devised as a freestanding shot that theater operators could insert either at the beginning or the end of the film, it was most often used at the conclusion for shock value or dramatic effect. Following the film's climatic shootout between the good guys and bad guys, a huge close-up of the outlaw leader fills the entire screen. Wearing a black cowboy hat and a wild bandanna that partly covers his western-style shirt, he glares momentarily at the audience. His callous eyes are framed by dark hair, bushy eyebrows, and a drooping mustache. All of a sudden, the menacing cowboy lifts his six-shooter, points it directly at the audience, and fires repeatedly. From all accounts, audiences were stunned. A few startled viewers screamed or flinched in their chairs. Even the strong were taken aback by the hideous sight of the larger-than-life villain shooting a gun directly at them.

Audiences had never seen anything like *The Great Train Robbery*. They might have read about outlaws and gunfights in dime novels or *The Virginian*. Perhaps they had even seen a live stage play or attended a Wild West show where good guys and bad guys took potshots at each other. But

Figure 3. The outlaw in *The Great Train Robbery* (Edison Manufacturing Company, 1903), played by Justus D. Barnes, caused a sensation by firing directly at the audience.

The Great Train Robbery went further than any of those. The movie made the mythic West come alive as it blurred the line between the real and imaginary West. More vivid than a book and more dramatic and intimate than live entertainment, the western film elevated the mythic West to a new level. Audiences could now see the West, experience it, and become part of the drama as they witnessed events unfold on a large screen. The close-up of the outlaw leader was an excellent metaphor for the relationship between the movie and the audience. It personified all the trappings, excitement, thrills, danger, and violence of the mythic West. When that bad guy in the black hat shot at audiences from point-blank range, they became personally involved. The West was no longer just an abstraction.

The Great Train Robbery became the first blockbuster film of the twentieth century. In the process, Porter's seminal film demonstrated the tremendous potential for movies about the West, and it established a western formula that included holdups, gunfights, posses, chases, cowboys shooting at a guy's feet to make him dance, and a climactic showdown where the good guys defeat the bad guys. The movie's phenomenal commercial and artistic success made it a prototype for future narrative films, which copied its camera techniques, action sequences, and approach to storytelling.[5]

The Great Train Robbery was a success not only because of its subject matter and innovative approach to film making, but also because it struck a responsive chord with many Americans at the turn of the century. The movie picked up on the nation's uneasiness about the transition from the old agrarian, rural America to a modern industrial, urban nation. The tension played out in the contest between the outlaw gang, representing the old untamed West, and the great train, the symbol of modern industrial America. Initially, the bad guys used old-fashioned tactics to defeat the forces of modernity, but ultimately, the film demonstrates that traditional values would triumph over both evil and modern technology. The posse (representing ordinary Americans and time-honored notions of right and wrong) rides horses (the old-fashioned means of transportation) to overtake the outlaws. Good defeats evil when the posse opens fire with six-guns and repeating rifles (thereby harnessing the era's most advanced personal weapons).

The Great Train Robbery tapped into the era's rising Progressive movement. Just as middle-class reformers were going after the corruption and vice associated with robber barons, machine politicians, and other threats to America's social, political, and economic well-being, the ordinary townspeople in Porter's film rise up in opposition to greedy train robbers. Their swift retaliation was in step with one of President Theodore Roosevelt's favorite sayings, "Speak softly, but carry a big stick." Prior to the holdup, the townsfolk were minding their own business and doing the types of things that ordinary Americans do every day: working at their jobs, taking care of children, and enjoying social activities. But when threatened, they struck back with overwhelming, deadly force.

For a nation in the midst of all the rapid changes associated with urbanization, industrialization, and rising immigration, *The Great Train Robbery* was a much-needed reminder about America's self-identity. The western setting and portrayal of ordinary Americans springing into action in defense of traditional values underscored all the things that made America great. It reinforced two of the nation's most popular myths—the West and the superiority of the common man. And it simultaneously provided nostalgic escape into an earlier frontier America as it celebrated modernity through amazing images of a powerful locomotive and the breathtaking new medium of motion pictures. Ultimately, both native-born Americans and new immigrants could relate to Porter's movie, which glorified the American character, reaffirmed the nation's identity, myths, and values, and mirrored the country's conflicting attitudes about the myriad social, economic, political, and cultural changes occurring at the turn of the century.

The Great Train Robbery would forever change how movies were made. It would also help western films become a staple of popular culture. Porter's innovative film gave moviegoers everything they wanted in one neat package: good guys, bad guys, drama, excitement, action, violence, even the hint of men and women carousing in a dance hall. From that moment on, audiences could not get enough of big-screen images of the mythic West.

The Winning of the Western

The phenomenal success of Edwin S. Porter's film opened the door for numerous other westerns and blazed the trail for the entire movie industry. "*The Great Train Robbery* marked the birth of the motion picture industry, which from its beginnings was preoccupied with westerns," suggest historians Robert V. Hine and John Mack Faragher. "Over the next sixty years at least a third of all the films made in the United States were westerns."[6]

Hoping to capitalize on the phenomenal success of Porter's film, copycat westerns such as *The Hold-Up of the Leadville Stage* (1904) and *Holdup of the Rocky Mountain Express* (1906) were soon playing in nickelodeons across the country. The most blatant imitation was Siegmund Lubin's *The Great Train Robbery* (1904), which used the original's exact title and copied all the scenes, action, and sets. Even Edwin S. Porter copied his earlier film with a bizarre remake called *The Little Train Robbery* (1905), which featured children and a miniature train.

European filmmakers likewise tried to capitalize on the popularity of westerns. The Great Northern Film Company out of Denmark found success with *Texas Tex* (1908). French film producer Jean Hamman chimed in with *Cowboy* (1907) and *The Adventures of Buffalo Bill* (1909). Another French company—Pathé Frères—also tried to crack the American market. Their first western came out in 1904 with *Indiens et cow-boys* (*Indians and Cowboys*), but subsequent Pathé films, like European westerns in general, lacked authenticity for American audiences. After viewing Pathé's 1909 release, *A Western Hero*, an exhibitor noted that somebody needs to tell European filmmakers that Indians do not wear "checked gingham shirts," live in huts "made of cornstalks," or camp in the middle of "apple orchards."[7]

Foreign studios were hard pressed to keep up with American film makers. American westerns, by definition, had an authenticity that European films could not match. In addition, American studios had easier access to western locations, and their writers and directors had a better grasp of the mythic West. As a result, American companies set the pace for both the quality and the quantity of western films. The Edison Manufacturing Company, Vitagraph, Polyscope, Biograph, Essanay, Lubin, Bison, and other American companies streamlined their production processes and began releasing one western after another in assembly-line fashion. Two Chicago-based companies—Polyscope and Essanay—emerged as the most prolific and profitable of them all. Both routinely dispatched film crews westward to shoot on location, and their releases typically featured top-notch stories, fast-paced action, and solid production values.

Selig Polyscope Company, established in 1897 by William N. Selig, was the first to find success. Selig's earliest efforts at western story films included two one-reelers shot in Colorado, *A Lynching at Cripple Creek* (1904) and *The Hold-Up of the Leadville Stage* (1904). The company's western film production got a big boost when Selig hired Francis Boggs, a former stage actor and director, who shared Selig's vision of producing the best westerns possible. Soon thereafter, Boggs headed west and began shooting movies throughout Colorado and the Southwest, including *The Indian's Gratitude*, *The Cattle Rustlers*, and several other westerns in 1908. No sooner were they in the can than Selig began promoting them with descriptions such as "real western drama" or the "greatest western picture ever turned out." Boggs's initial success led him to Los Angeles so he could continue making films during the winter of 1908–09. Impressed with the climate, topography, and working arrangements, he convinced his boss to set up a permanent studio in Edendale, just north of downtown. The move proved far more eventful than either man could have imagined. Selig's Edendale would be the first permanent film studio in California. Before long, other film companies would set up shop nearby, making Hollywood and the West Coast the headquarters of the film industry.[8]

While Boggs was establishing the Selig Polyscope Company's foothold in California, Selig was back in Chicago working on ways to improve his company's product. Like other producers, Selig had to deal with increasing pressures and complaints from journalists, exhibitors, reformers, politicians, and concerned citizens who believed motion pictures were undermining public morality. No doubt, Selig took notice when the mayor of New York City, on Christmas Eve 1908, responded to ministers' complaints by revoking the licenses of 550 nickelodeons that were exhibiting objectionable movies. Several months later, Selig watched intently as the Motion Picture Patents Company (of which Polyscope was a member) established a National Board of Censorship to safeguard traditional middle-class values in movies. Much of the vitriol was aimed at sensational westerns, because they tended to attract working-class crowds, especially young males accustomed to the sensationalism, gore, and action associated with dime novels, as well as immigrants who were drawn to cheap amusements with an American bent. Selig was convinced that better quality films would attract larger audiences and contribute to a better image for the film industry. Perhaps he took his cue from Buffalo Bill's Wild West or similar shows, which grew in popularity after they began presenting elaborate historical spectacles aimed at middle-class audiences. In similar fashion, Selig aimed to produce "the very best films [to] educate the people up to the highest class picture entertainment." To accomplish that, he brought in veteran stage director Otis Turner, and following the lead of Wild West shows, he hired Indians as actors and incorporated historical events into story lines. Some of his westerns even used cowboys and equipment from the Miller Brothers 101 Ranch Real Wild West show.[9]

Selig's new approach resulted in some of the most popular westerns of the day, including *On the Little Big Horn; or, Custer's Last Stand* (1909) and *Across the Plains* (1910). The movies were essentially Wild West reenactments on film, albeit with more dramatic flair. The Selig films used the same action scenes, cowboy stunts, and staging found in Wild West show performances, including cowboys doing rope tricks, Indians circling the wagons, and cavalry riding to the rescue. For added authenticity, Selig incorporated stock footage of real cowboys at work, which his crews shot in 1909 at the Miller Brothers' 101 Ranch in Oklahoma. Not only did Selig's westerns look like Wild West shows, but they followed the spectacles' lead in glorifying westward expansion. Just as Buffalo Bill and other Wild West show impresarios justified their use of violence by linking it to American expansion, Selig's films portrayed brave westerners resorting to violence to protect the American way of life. In effect, unlike the gratuitous violence of many dime novels and cheap western movies, Selig's violence had a worthwhile purpose, which made it more acceptable to middle- and upper-class audiences. One movie reviewer called the violence in Selig westerns "valid" because it was necessary in America's struggle against "nature" and "Indians."[10]

Selig's main competitor was another Chicago-based company, Essanay, cofounded by Gilbert M. Anderson and George K. Spoor in 1907. Within five years, Essanay replaced Selig's company as the number one producer of western films, and Anderson became the most famous western star in the country, acting in, writing, directing, editing, and producing some of the most successful westerns of the early 1900s.

Gilbert M. Anderson—who was born Max Aronson and later achieved fame as G. M. "Broncho Billy" Anderson—got his first big break playing several bit parts in *The Great Train Robbery*. He was the outlaw who had trouble getting on his horse and then was the first to be killed by the posse; he was the train passenger shot down by the bandits; and he was the tenderfoot dude forced to dance by cowboys shooting bullets at his feet. When Anderson saw the phenomenal reaction to Porter's film, he knew what he wanted to do with his life. "That's it," he recalled years later. "It's going to be the picture business for me. The future had no end."[11]

Following *The Great Train Robbery*, Gilbert Anderson went to work in 1904 as a production assistant for the Vitagraph Company. That experience helped him land a position in 1906 with Selig's Polyscope. Anderson convinced Selig to send him to Colorado, so he could make westerns on location with "rugged scenery and cowboys." Three films were released in 1907, but when none did well at the box office, Anderson and Selig parted company. Later that year, Anderson and Spoor, the Chicago film producer, distributor, and co-inventor of the Magniscope projector, formed their own motion picture production company, which they named the Essanay Film Manufacturing Company. Essanay (the phonetic spelling of their initials) made it big, producing numerous westerns, as well as most of the early films by Charlie Chaplin, Gloria Swanson, Francis X. Bushman, Wallace Beery, and other silent film stars.[12]

Essanay's first westerns were directed by E. Lawrence Lee, who shot the movies in Chicago and nearby Michigan using Wild West show performers for authenticity. Two 1908 releases attracted considerable attention: *The James Boys in Missouri* and *The Younger Brothers*. Lee's movies followed the lead of earlier ballads, melodramas, and dime novels that glorified outlaws who robbed railroads, banks, and other big businesses. The rise of these antiheroes reflected the era's social, economic, and political divisions. Historian Richard White points out that romantic images of western outlaws often began as folk traditions. "Driven outside the law because of some act sanctioned by local conventions but regarded as criminal by the state or local authorities, the social bandit was forced to become an outlaw," explains White. "Members of the community, however, still considered him an honorable man." Lee's outlaw films were applauded by audiences, but moral reformers were not pleased. Many complained that the movies glorified criminal activity, undermined family values, corrupted youth, and threatened social order. *The James Boys in Missouri* was even banned in numerous cities.[13]

Although Gilbert Anderson was pleased with the commercial success of Lee's westerns, he knew that if he did not placate the critics, Essanay could lose its foothold in the lucrative western movie market. Unlike the Selig Polyscope Company, which began producing more elaborate historical westerns to counter similar criticisms, Anderson decided on a simpler and less expensive solution. At first, he simply toned down the illegal behavior of Essanay's good badman heroes. Eventually, he would take it a step further and produce movies featuring a clean-cut western hero beyond reproach. Anderson's tactics were actually not that different from Selig's. Both men copied strategies that Wild West shows had used to gain respectability. Buffalo Bill Cody, for example, enhanced his show's reputation by adopting a middle-class persona for himself and featuring programs billed as historically accurate spectacles that would entertain and educate audiences.

Gilbert Anderson was well aware of the public demand for westerns and convinced that Essanay could be a leader in the field. Anderson already had a track record based on his own experiences making westerns and the commercial success of Lee's films. He also had a solid game plan. Anderson intended to film on location in Colorado, Montana, California, and anywhere else that offered excellent scenery and an authentic western feel, and he was confident that Essanay had the creativity and resources to succeed. His first batch of westerns was filmed on location in California. "No western type produced in the East can possibly compare to an Essanay western," he boasted. Filming on location gave Essanay westerns "the true spirit, the life color, and the touches that make for vivid character delineation." In addition, Essanay films featured "real cowpunchers," who knew how to ride, rope, and shoot. Anderson took charge of the entire production process, including writing, filming, editing, and even starring in successful westerns such as *The Ranchman's Rival* (1909) and *The Cowboy and the Squaw* (1910).[14]

Although Gilbert Anderson sometimes played a nonwhite hero in films, such as *A Mexican's Gratitude* (1909) or *An Indian's Sacrifice* (1910), his greatest success came with a series of films that focused on a recognizable white cowboy hero named Broncho Billy. He developed the character partly to counter the critics and social reformers who condemned violence and immorality in westerns, but Anderson also believed that the character would allow Essanay to develop a special niche in a market already saturated by westerns. He first played the character in a 1908 film entitled *The Bandit Makes Good*, based on Peter B. Kyne's recent story in the *Saturday Evening Post*, "Broncho Billy and the Baby." Anderson's character

Figure 4. G. M. Anderson's Broncho Billy was America's first well-known cowboy hero. His western outfit copied the look of cowboys popularized by dime novels and Wild West shows. Richard Aquila Collection.

begins the film as a bank robber but ends up a hero when he goes straight and helps the sheriff retrieve the stolen money. "The fan response was so great," reported the *New York Times*, "that Mr. Anderson started a series around the Robin Hood type of bandit."[15]

Between 1908 and 1915, G. M. "Broncho Billy" Anderson produced and starred in approximately 375 Broncho Billy films. Each was ten to twenty-four minutes long, with a simple descriptive title, such as *Broncho Billy's Redemption* (1910), *Broncho Billy's Christmas Dinner* (1911), or *Broncho Billy's Love Affair* (1915). Each was made to stand alone. The films did not have a continuing story line, and Anderson's character varied from film to film. Sometimes Broncho Billy was a good guy, other times a bad guy who turns out good. He even got killed off in at least one movie only to return unharmed in the next.

Two films issued in 1914 and 1915 demonstrate the diversity of the character. *Broncho Billy and the Greaser* (1914) featured him as a good-natured, lovable mailman. It opens with Billy riding up to a general store on his horse. As he dismounts, he notices a lovely young woman arriving in her buckboard. He flashes a charming boyish grin and then gets back to work. The girl enters the building, says hello to various customers, and asks the clerk to refill a bottle. When Billy brings in the mailbags, the clerk begins sorting the letters while the girl queues up with the other customers waiting for the mail to be handed out. Just then, a swarthy-looking hombre—the Greaser—saunters in, shoves the girl aside, and steps to the head of the line. Broncho Billy rushes to her defense. He pulls out his six-shooter and escorts the villain outside, forcing him to back down and skulk off into the woods. From a distance, the Greaser glares at Broncho Billy and vows revenge. He follows Billy back to his cabin, breaks in when he falls asleep, and ties him up. Luckily for Billy, the girl from the post office arrives on the scene to thank him for his gallantry at the general store. When she witnesses the dastardly deeds taking place, she rushes back to town and forms a posse. They arrive just as the Greaser is about to knife Broncho Billy. The bad guy is led away, and Billy winds up with the girl.

Though the plot is ordinary, several things stand out. Broncho Billy comes off as a goofy, big-hearted, lovable palooka. For example, when he says good-bye to the girl after the initial scene in the general store, he rides on his horse backwards so he can wave to her. Hardly the no-nonsense hero one would expect to find in a western film. Still, the good-natured Billy is tough when he has to be. He does the right thing and stands up to the bully even though ultimately he is unable to defeat him. Equally interesting is the girl that Broncho Billy defends. Her decisive actions allow her to save him rather than vice versa. If Billy and the girl reflect positive gender attributes of the day, the Greaser villain mirrors the era's negative stereotypes of Mexicans.

The Broncho Billy character that appears at the beginning of *Broncho Billy's Sentence* (1915) is a stagecoach robber. After he absconds with money from a lockbox, he forces his way into the home of a farmer and his daughter to hide from a posse. As soon as the coast is clear, Billy decides to leave, but first he kisses the young woman against her will while holding off the father at gunpoint. He then tries to escape into the woods, but the farmer's daughter grabs her father's rifle and shoots the fleeing bandit in the head. Billy staggers through the woods, hides his loot in a tree, and then breaks into a nearby church. The minister and his wife find him and nurse him back to health, praying for him and reading the Bible to him all the while. Touched by their Christian charity, the bad man repents. While they participate in a Sunday service, Billy writes them a note: "Dear Friends, I lied to you. You have made a man of me. I am going to suffer the penalty of my crime." He then picks up a Bible and leaves the sanctuary.

His first stop is the tree where he hid the loot. He then heads to the sheriff's office, turns himself in, and hands over his gun and the stolen money. The surprised lawman locks him up in a cell, where the remorseful Billy drops down on a cot and begins to read the Bible. The next scene takes place years later. A prison guard leads a group of inmates into the chapel. At their head is a reformed Broncho Billy, carrying his Bible. At that very moment, the warden is back in his office reading a letter ordering Billy's release. The camera cuts back to the chapel with a close-up of pious Billy reading from the Bible and looking more like a preacher than a felon. He looks toward heaven, closes his eyes, and preaches salvation and repentance to his fellow prisoners. Just then, Billy is summoned to the warden's office. He enters still clutching his Bible. The warden takes the book and hands Billy the release papers. The stunned Billy starts to cry and is so grateful he almost collapses. The next scene shows Billy once again in the warden's office, this time dressed in a suit and tie. He thanks the warden and begins to walk out the door. Suddenly, he stops, turns around, and walks back toward the warden's desk. He points to the Bible that he had left on the desk, and the warden gives it to him. They shake hands once more, and Billy walks out, stopping briefly to shake a prisoner's hand just as the film ends. The movie's obvious message struck a responsive chord with moviegoers during the Progressive Era. Just as good works and Christian belief saved Broncho Billy, so too would they lead American society toward redemption and perfection.

Those two films suggest how the Broncho Billy character changed considerably from one movie to the next. Audiences never quite knew what to expect. Would Anderson's character show up as a sheriff or a desperado? An Indian fighter or an Indian lover? A drifter, prospector, cowboy, or something else? Perhaps the uncertainty was part of the fun. In any case, audiences went with the flow and cheered on Broncho Billy no matter what. A writer for *Bioscope* in 1914 summed up audience response: "The picture theatre public has now had an opportunity of beholding that immortal personage, Broncho Billy, in almost every sort of situation, under almost every sort of circumstance, and yet in spite of everybody's familiarity with every aspect of this many-sided character, his popularity increases daily." Showing the immediacy of mass media even in the movie industry's infancy, the writer added, "We have ceased to think of him as an imaginary figure. . . . He has become for us a personal friend and comrade."[16]

While the Broncho Billy stories varied from film to film, other things remained constant. Billy was always earnest and ultimately likable. He was the common man made good. Though not always perfect, he would eventually overcome his problems and do the right thing. Broncho Billy's distinct multidimensional personality shone through every film: at various times he was funny, serious, compassionate, bad but good, strong yet tender, and always moral. And Billy always had a distinctive look. He was handsome in a rugged way, and his face and body language exuded character. Tall with a stocky build, he had an unforgettable face. His prominent nose, penetrating eyes, high cheekbones, and square jaw were enhanced by an unruly shock of long, wavy brown hair pushed to the side, giving him a boyish quality even though Anderson was in his thirties when he made most of the Broncho Billy films. Although Billy looked frumpy in his baggy shirt, he had an identifiable style. He wore his gun cross-draw, and his outfit was patterned after Wild West show cowboys, with a white flat-brimmed, Montana-peak hat, cowboy boots, and a studded leather belt with matching gauntlets and holster.

Broncho Billy westerns were always well done, characterized by authentic scenery, realistic acting, interesting scripts, and excellent production values. Early movies were filmed throughout California. In 1912, Anderson established a West Coast studio for Essanay, headquartered in Niles, California. The California sun allowed year-round filming, and the topography was perfect for westerns. Anderson's fine acting made the Broncho Billy character come alive for audiences, who could relate to his sense of humor, personality flaws, struggles between good and evil, and basic human frailty. There was always an element of pathos surrounding Broncho Billy, making him the western hero equivalent of another Essanay star—Charlie Chaplin. Audiences were also fascinated by other characters in Broncho Billy westerns, including independent females and memorable Indians and Mexicans.

Broncho Billy greatly influenced the western genre. He pointed the way for series westerns and action films set in authentic locales. He became the movie cowboy archetype, influencing later stars from Tom Mix to John Wayne. Significantly, Anderson did not create the character from scratch. He borrowed heavily from cowboy images found throughout the Pop Culture West, particularly in Buffalo Bill's Wild West show, where cowboys in broad-brimmed hats, fancy boots, and decorative leather accessories could shoot six-guns with deadly accuracy and fend off desperadoes, wild Indians, or other stereotypical bad guys. Even his nickname evoked the alliteration of the Pop Culture West's most famous hero, Buffalo Bill. Though Anderson didn't invent the cowboy's image, he certainly helped transfer it to the motion picture screen, thereby exposing it to even larger audiences.

Broncho Billy continued the "frontier hero" tradition that can be traced back at least to James Fenimore Cooper's Leatherstocking Tales. Like other good guys of the Pop Culture West, Billy was a rugged individual with the courage of an Arthurian knight. A skilled fighter and determined opponent, he was kind to women and children and a defender of God, country, and family. Anderson's noble character was the ideal hero in an era when middle-class Progressive reformers were convinced they could solve every social problem and save every sinner through rational means and Christian principles. Billy could have been their poster boy. At his best, he was Broncho Billy—*Progressive Reformer Extraordinaire*—defeating villains and making the world safe for democracy. At his worst, he was a testimonial to Progressivism's curative power. Billy—the quintessential good badman—sometimes strayed from the straight and narrow path, but audiences knew that in the end, he would always be redeemed. Ultimately, Broncho Billy was the perfect American, who was ethical, religious, and always willing to lead the crusade against evil, even if it meant sacrificing his own needs to help others.

Broncho Billy's positive image was no accident. Essanay marketed Anderson's westerns as "uplifting" entertainment. Billy was the very model of a model American—a defender of motherhood, children, and the innocent, as well as an advocate for Christian beliefs and Victorian values. "Broncho Billy has been grinding out the better sort of Wild West Indian pictures," noted one observer. Despite all the shooting, holdups, fights, chases, and Indian massacres, he added, "it's all been a jolly Peter-Pannish lark, sweetened by a moral at the end and with Billy's bright eyes and hypnotic smile shining at you through the rifle smoke."[17]

Broncho Billy was a perfect fit for audiences in the early twentieth century. His potent blend of traditional American values, nonstop action, and images of the mythic West appealed to all social classes. Such universal appeal helped him become one of the era's most successful stars. At his peak, Anderson earned $125,000 per year and was one of the most popular actors in the country. In 1911, he almost caused a riot when fans in New York City rushed toward him as he walked down the street to a restaurant. The following year, *Variety* magazine named him one of the most famous "picture actors" in the country.[18]

Gilbert M. Anderson was a true film pioneer. He acted in, directed, wrote, and/or produced more than five hundred movies, most of which were westerns. His greatest success came prior to 1916. Then his star faded. His simple one-and-two-reel westerns were eventually replaced by longer feature films, designed to hold the attention of larger crowds in the bigger movie palaces that were beginning to pop up across the country. At that point, the film industry's first western hero, Broncho Billy, rode off into the sunset. Anderson retired in 1916 after he sold his share of Essanay. Afterwards, he made only occasional appearances, the last of which was a cameo role in a 1965 western entitled *The Bounty Killer*.

Essanay and Polyscope were not the only companies producing profitable westerns in the early 1900s. New York Motion Picture, Vitagraph, Lubin, Pathé, Biograph, Kalem, Pocahontas, and others were also churning out popular cowboy and Indian movies. Some of the more interesting films came from the New York Motion Picture Company, founded in 1909 by Adam Kessel, Charles O. Baumann, and Fred J. Balshofer. The NYMP found a niche with offbeat westerns that combined the most sensational aspects of dime novels with more nuanced images of Native Americans.

Fred Balshofer headed up Bison films, the NYMP unit charged with making westerns. His first successful western was *Davy Crockett—In Hearts United* (1909). He followed up with two more Indian movies, *The Squaw's Revenge* (1909) and *The True Heart of an Indian* (1909). The latter starred white actor Charles Inslee as an Indian clad most of the time in a skimpy loincloth. The box office appeal of Inslee's virile warrior became evident when fan letters came pouring in addressed simply to "The Indian" or "The Lone Indian." "The ladies simply went gaga over him," recalled Balshofer, "whenever he appeared on screen in one of his naked Indian hero roles."[19]

Balshofer soon found an even better star for his Indian movies. James Young Deer, who also appeared in *The True Heart of an Indian*, seemed like a perfect choice. The handsome actor had striking features and long jet black hair. Plus, he claimed to be a real Indian and was married to a Winnebago actress named Lillian Red Wing (aka Lillian St. Cyr). Balshofer boasted that the Indian couple would bring "realism" and "color" to Bison films, which had always been more successful commercially than artistically. The situation improved after Young Deer and Red Wing began contributing fine acting skills, as well as valuable creative advice. Even the titles of Bison westerns, such as *Young Deer's Return* (1910) and *For the Love of Red Wing* (1910), spotlighted the Indian stars. Audiences liked what they saw, and the Indian couple came to represent the authenticity of Bison films.[20]

Audiences were not the only ones impressed. Job offers were soon pouring in from other film makers. The Pathé Frères company, in particular, saw Young Deer as the answer to their problems. The French company had been plagued by complaints that their westerns were unrealistic. Desperate to improve, Pathé hired Young Deer in 1910 to head up their new studio in Edendale, California, hoping that the experienced Indian director and actor would give their movies instant authenticity. Pathé was not disappointed. Under Young Deer's supervision, the company began releasing more credible westerns, many of which starred Young Deer and his wife. Young Deer depicted Indian life-styles as accurately as possible and used Wild West show performers and equipment. Audiences were impressed by Young Deer's sympathetic portrayals of Native Americans. Most early westerns followed the lead of dime novels and treated Indians as bloodthirsty savages. But Young Deer/Red Wing films often represented Native Americans as moral and courageous heroes who were the equals of whites.[21]

Young Deer's movies also offered new perspectives on interracial romance. Before the Indian director arrived on the scene, pop culture usually depicted Indians as either savage beasts (reflecting negative frontier attitudes toward Indians) or noble savages (in keeping with the approach made famous by French *philosophes* who saw Indians as untainted children of nature). Romance between Indians and whites was viewed as either taboo or doomed. More often than not, the Indian in the relationship was a female, and she usually wound up dead, either from tragic circumstances or by choice as the supreme sacrifice. Several Young Deer films pushed the interracial story line in different directions, often questioning the alleged superiority of the white culture. *For the Papoose* (1912) starts out in typical fashion with a marriage between a white man and an Indian woman, but it quickly veers away from the formula. The white husband is clearly inferior to the Indian wife. He gets drunk, tries to force the child to drink whiskey, and then abandons his wife, running away with the child and a white woman. After his Indian brother-in-law tracks him down and kills him for his despicable actions, the child is returned safely to the Indian mother, and they live happily ever after as Indians.

Although Young Deer was innovative in his treatment of Indians, his overall approach to film making was fairly standard. Like most directors of his era, he relied on melodramatic story lines, violent action, and uninspired production techniques. The uneven quality of Young Deer's films is even apparent in *White Fawn's Devotion* (1910), one of the "landmark movies" included in the Library of Congress's National Film Registry. On the plus side, the movie offers a new twist on the hackneyed storyline found in Edwin Milton Royle's popular play *The Squaw Man* (1905). At first glance, it appears to replicate Royle's play. The white protagonist is married to an Indian woman (played by Red Wing) and has a child. When he learns that he has to return east to claim his inheritance, his wife, White Fawn, refuses to go along. Not wanting to stand in the way of her husband and child's happiness, the noble Indian plunges a knife into her chest, just as the Indian wife had done in Royle's play. From that point on, though, the film heads off in a totally different direction than *The Squaw Man*. The woman's Indian relatives are convinced that the white man attacked her and chase him over hills, through valleys, down cliffs, and across a river, finally capturing him and bringing him back to the village for justice. Just as he is about to be executed, White Fawn recovers from the knife wound and saves her beloved by confessing that she was the one responsible for her wound. Unlike *The Squaw Man*, which treated white culture as superior and neatly solved the interracial romance dilemma through a gracious act by a noble savage—that is, the Indian wife taking her own life—*White Fawn's Devotion* is far more ambiguous. By film's end, the audience is aware of antipathies on both sides of the racial divide and is left not knowing for certain the fate of the interracial couple and their child.

Despite its quirky plot, the film suffers from mediocre camera work, poor staging, bad acting, and trite characters. The white husband looks like a Buffalo Bill Cody impersonator, wearing long hair and a goatee, a broad sombrero, a buckskin jacket, and knee-length boots. Even the Indian characters come off badly. Unlike many Young Deer films that portray Indians in positive ways, *White Fawn's Devotion* reverts to clichéd images of savage Indians. Red Wing's character is overly dramatic from the moment she attempts her ill-conceived suicide to the final scene, where she throws her body onto her husband's for protection in a scene all too reminiscent of Pocahontas and Captain John Smith. And White Fawn's father, the Indian chief, comes across as a manic savage, who pursues his human prey like a frenzied dog. Even the ending is unclear and unsatisfying. After chasing down the white man and almost killing him for a crime he did not commit, the Indian leader simply points off screen when he learns the truth, apparently banishing his daughter, white son-in-law, and granddaughter.

Industry demands and the public mood sustained Young Deer's career for a brief time, but conditions soon changed. When westerns began to decline in popularity, studios turned toward longer feature films or more sensational westerns that relied on images of bloodthirsty Indians. By 1913, Young Deer's career began to slide. Although his career was relatively brief, James Young Deer left his mark on early westerns as both a director and an actor. Not only is he generally recognized as the first Native American film director, but many of his movies featured images of Indians that were more nuanced and sophisticated than those typically found in westerns. His movies often treated racism, interracial romance, and other social issues in original ways, resulting in some of the most interesting one-reel westerns produced in the early 1900s.[22]

* * *

By the early 1910s, westerns were well established as one of the movie industry's most important genres, but declining revenues and more frequent attacks by critics, who maintained that sensational westerns were bad influences on young audiences, forced industry insiders to rethink their approach to cowboy and Indian pictures. Westerns were about to undergo major changes. Before long, D. W. Griffith, Thomas H. Ince, and other new directors would be crafting more complex and sophisticated movies, blazing a trail for feature films and new western stars.

CHAPTER TWO

Blazing the Trail

New Directors and the Rise of Feature Westerns

Blazing the Trail, a two-reel western directed by Thomas Ince, was released on April 15, 1912. The plot is simple. Ethel Grandin's character heads west and is captured by Indians. After many trials and tribulations, she is rescued by the hero, played by Francis Ford, the older brother of John Ford. The movie ends poignantly with the couple visiting the graves of pioneers killed by Indians. The film might not sound that much different from other westerns of the day, but it attracted considerable attention because it was marketed by the New York Motion Picture Company as a Bison 101 film—a totally new type of western.

Audiences had first read about Bison 101 films just a few months earlier. At the time, most westerns were anything but exciting. Throughout the first decade of the twentieth century, studios had been cranking out westerns in almost assembly-line fashion. A writer in *Variety* noted that the westerns made in 1908 and 1909 were competent but hardly original, explaining, "It has all been done so often before, and usually better." So the NYMP decided to try something new. On December 6, 1911, the company took out an ad in the *New York Dramatic Mirror*. Across the top a banner proclaimed, "IMPORTANT ANNOUNCEMENT." The text explained: "Realizing that the day of the ordinary cowboy and Indian picture has passed from public favor, a radical change has been made in the Bison company, and in the future nothing but SENSATIONAL—SPECTACULAR—WESTERN—HISTORICAL—MILITARY SUBJECTS will be released." The ad explained that Bison had hired new directors and signed a deal with the Miller Brothers 101 Ranch Real Wild West show to employ "350 people (riders, actors

Figure 5. This scene from *Blazing the Trail* (Bison Motion Pictures/New York Motion Picture Company, 1912), which appeared on the cover of *Film Fancies* (March 2, 1912), depicts a white woman captured by Indians, a popular story line that can be traced back to captivity narratives in colonial America. Reproduced from Andrew Brodie Smith, *Shooting Cowboys and Indians: Silent Western Films, American Culture, and the Birth of Hollywood* (Boulder: University Press of Colorado, 2003).

and Indians), together with their horses, equipment and paraphernalia." The result would be "massive productions" that feature "Dare-Devil and Sensational Feats of Horsemanship." Moviegoers took note and rushed out to buy tickets as soon as *Blazing the Trail* hit the theaters. They were not disappointed. One reviewer gushed, "I have never seen action more vivid and realistic."[1]

Thomas Ince and the New York Motion Picture Company were not the only ones trying to take westerns in a new direction. Other new film makers, including D. W. Griffith, Cecil B. DeMille, William S. Hart, James Cruze, and John Ford, were trying sophisticated approaches that would lead to the rise of feature western films. Still others began crafting full-length action westerns that starred Tom Mix and other early B-Western cowboys. All of these efforts would blaze a new trail for westerns during the 1910s and 1920s.

The Changing Western

Studios began releasing more elaborate westerns at the beginning of the second decade of the twentieth century. "It is just simply the case of a gold mine that has been worked to the limit," explained an editor at *Nickelodeon* in 1911. One way to jumpstart the market for western films was to replace hackneyed plots with fresh stories powered by complex characters, historical accuracy, and sophisticated film-making techniques. Film makers hoped that a new approach would not only revitalize the tired western but expand the market.[2]

The proliferation of high-end movie theaters added to the demand for longer and more sophisticated feature films. New York City impresario Samuel L. "Roxy" Rothafel played a major role in convincing exhibitors to build more elegant theaters designed specifically for movies. His management of enormous New York movie theaters such as the Regent and Strand, which could seat more than two thousand people, attracted large crowds by giving them the royal treatment, replete with uniformed ushers and upscale surroundings, which included oversized lobbies, crystal chandeliers, ornate walls and ceilings, thick carpets, plush seats, and even fancy restrooms. Roxy's formula quickly caught on. A manual for building theaters published in 1917 recommended structures that were "palatial in design, of colossal dimensions." Patrons could feel like royalty when they entered these cinematic dreamlands. To attract larger crowds to these expensive movie palaces, owners pressured film companies to deliver longer, higher-class films that would appeal to broader audiences and justify the higher cost of admission.[3]

The growing demand for elaborate westerns offered new opportunities for small studios and independent film makers. The established movie studios, which formed the Motion Picture Patents Company (aka the Trust) in 1908—Edison, Vitagraph, Selig Polyscope, Essanay, Biograph, Kalem, Lubin, Pathé, and Méliès—saw no reason to change since the Trust already controlled almost 100 percent of the film production and importation in the United States. Furthermore, some members of the Trust were determined to produce only short films of two reels or less, which were less expensive and more profitable. As a result, the market was wide open for independent studios to produce a variety of innovative westerns, including features of three reels or more. By 1912, the independents were producing almost half of all films in the United States, including all of the longer feature films.[4]

Economics was not the only reason to switch to more stylish westerns. Creative young film makers such as Thomas Ince and D. W. Griffith were eager to experiment with the innovative filming and editing techniques that were being used by European studios to produce longer and more artistic films. And many studio heads realized that better-crafted westerns that appealed to more refined audiences would counter critics who associated the film industry with working-class tastes and condemned movies as cheap amusements that were harmful to society.[5]

The Western Films of D. W. Griffith

One of the individuals who would play a major role in reshaping westerns was D. W. Griffith. The legendary director—best known for his later epics *The Birth of a Nation* (1915) and *Intolerance* (1916)—began his directing career at Biograph. Between 1908 and 1913, Griffith cranked out more than four hundred films, mostly one-reel melodramas about Indians, Zulu, Chinese, and other exotic subjects or short films based on novels. Included were more than fifty westerns. The Biograph films featured many of the same themes as his later movies. There were historical dramas and films about social problems, moral dilemmas, and racial strife, as well as exciting chases, pitched battles, and dramatic rescues.[6]

The novice director learned by trial and error as he devised new approaches or borrowed techniques from other successful directors. While he was not the first to use innovative techniques such as crosscutting, pan shots, flashbacks, or different shooting perspectives like close-ups, medium shots, long shots, and panoramic shots, he was the first to integrate them seamlessly into the story line. He also used images to leap through time and space. At one point, his bosses at Biograph questioned whether audiences could understand all the different shots and scene shifts. Griffith brushed off the criticism, asking "Doesn't Dickens write that way?"[7]

Griffith's films were unique in other ways. He placed furniture and other backdrops strategically to create an illusion of depth. He used natural light and shadows for effect. And he was the first director to make use of electric lighting. Griffith also assembled a stock company of talented players, which included Mary Pickford, Lillian and Dorothy Gish, and Lionel Barrymore, and instructed them to substitute more subdued and natural facial expressions and body movements for the more exaggerated acting styles commonly used in live stage performances. While other directors simply barked out impromptu orders to actors during filming, Griffith held rehearsals to make sure the scene would play out the same way that he saw it in his head.

Griffith brought movie making to a new level. If not yet art, it was closing in on it fast. His innovative techniques and inimitable style breathed new life into the western. Of course, Griffith's westerns—like all his Biograph films—varied greatly in quality. Many were simply mass produced to meet his two-films-per-week quota, but others featured dynamic stories, creative staging, outstanding acting, and imaginative camera work and editing. Films such as *The Red Girl* (1908) and *Ramona* (1910) were powered by unusually sympathetic portrayals of Native Americans, while *In the Days of '49* (1911) and *Fighting Blood* (1911) offered introspective views of male-female relationships.

Griffith's best western is *The Battle at Elderbush Gulch* (1913), which featured Lillian Gish, Mae Marsh, and Robert Harron in starring roles with Lionel Barrymore and Harry Carey in the supporting cast. The plot follows two orphaned sisters who head west to live with relatives. One of the sisters is almost killed when she rescues the girls' runaway puppies from hungry Indians. The incident touches off an Indian war. Eventually, the cavalry arrives, drives off the marauding Indians, and all the settlers live happily ever after.

Though the film includes stereotypical images of savage Indians, Griffith's superb skills as a movie maker and storyteller make *The Battle at Elderbush Gulch* exceptional. Close-ups, panoramic shots, and cross-cutting are used extensively to build tension, while Griffith serves up unforgettable images of innocent children playing with puppies, Indians attacking a frontier settlement, and graphic violence that includes scalping. He offers a couple of surprises for western fans accustomed to heroics by white cowboys. One of the young girls, for instance, emerges as the hero when she saves a baby during the Indian attack, and it is a brave Mexican who rides through enemy lines to bring the cavalry to the rescue. The movie includes several prototypical scenes that will reappear later in Griffith's monumental *The Birth of a Nation* (1915): a cabin under siege, innocent women and children cowering in fear, and male settlers ready to kill their womenfolk to save them from a fate worse than death at the hands of savage racial enemies. Even the basic premise of *The Battle at Elderbush Gulch* influenced the plot of *The Birth of a Nation*. Both films climaxed with a "ride to the rescue" scene, although the one in the later classic was done on a much grander scale. "Instead of saving one little Nell of the plains," explained Griffith, "this ride would be to save a nation."[8]

Griffith was just coming into his own as a director when he made *The Battle at Elderbush Gulch*. Like other top directors of the day, he was eager to make feature films, but Biograph would not grant permission, insisting that he had to stay within the two-reel limit imposed by the Motion Picture Patents Company. Griffith balked and eventually wound up signing with the Mutual Film Corporation. He would go on to write and direct numerous feature films, most notably *The Birth of a Nation*, a sprawling historical drama about the South during the Civil War and Reconstruction.[9]

Although D. W. Griffith is best known for his pioneering feature films, he clearly left his imprint on westerns. Early on, Griffith rode point for western film directors, blazing the trail for more elaborate westerns through sophisticated film making, creative plots, and heightened drama.

Thomas Ince and Bison 101 Films

Like D. W. Griffith, Thomas H. Ince was eager to direct excellent westerns. Ince had started out in theater and vaudeville before switching to motion pictures in 1910, first at Biograph and then at Carl Laemmle's Independent Moving Pictures Company. In September 1911, Ince was hired by the New York Motion Picture Company to head up their Bison film unit in California. The NYMP was convinced that better quality westerns would attract a broader audience and greater profits, and might also calm critics who blasted the sensationalism of most cheap westerns.[10]

The NYMP provided Ince with all the resources needed for success. The company acquired eighteen thousand acres of land in the Santa Ynez canyon north of Santa Monica. The rugged terrain with its beautiful vistas, steep canyon walls, mesas, sagebrush, and creeks was perfect for shooting westerns. The NYMP also struck a deal with the Miller Brothers 101 Ranch Real Wild West Show. "Our arrangement gave us the use of about seventy-five cowboys, twenty-five cowgirls, and about thirty-five Indians and their squaws," explained one of the company's owners. "We also had the use of twenty-four oxen, some bison, and many horses complete with trappings, as well as prairie schooners and stage coaches."[11] The president of the NYMP compared the company's earlier Bison westerns to unrealistic dime novels but pledged that the new westerns would be different. They would have bigger budgets, be longer at two reels instead of one, and reflect "the actual life and experiences of the early settlers in the Far West, the Indian tribes, the gold prospectors, the cattle herdsmen, etc." To emphasize the new approach as well as the connection with the Miller Brothers' Wild West show, the New York Motion Picture Company adopted the name Bison 101 for its new western films.[12]

Ince was hired to make the NYMP's promises a reality. He sprang into action as soon as he arrived in California, demonstrating organizational ability by building from scratch a superb outdoor studio on the Santa Ynez site. Within a short time, he planned and supervised construction of a western town set and an Indian village. "When the actors . . . discovered that large numbers of insects and rattlesnakes also resided on the movie ranch and slithered and crawled into the canvas tents used as dressing rooms, log cabins were quickly built," points out historian Michael Wallis. Ince added an electrical power plant, telephone lines, a water system, a two-story school, and a working farm to provide for the five hundred workers who eventually worked year-round in the studio town, which came to be known as Inceville.[13]

Ince's rustic studio provided the perfect backdrop for realistic Bison 101 westerns. Other directors had employed Wild West performers in earlier movies, but none did it with as much flair as Ince. He focused on cowboys' riding and shooting skills and spotlighted Indians' exotic appearances and militaristic lifestyles, all the while showcasing spirited horses, shaggy bison, and authentic western gear, covered wagons, buckboards, and stagecoaches. Ince's cinematic versions of Wild West shows duplicated the way outdoor dramas staged action scenes and Indian fights. Bison 101 films even echoed the nationalistic ideology found in Wild West shows. Just as Buffalo Bill's Wild West justified the use of violence to protect settlers from Indians, Mexicans, or other enemies that threatened the American way of life, Ince's movies portrayed gunfights and battles as acceptable means to promote the nation's westward expansion.

Bison 101 westerns took Wild West shows to the next level. While retaining the historical details and nationalistic pride found in the outdoor spectacles, they cranked the excitement up a notch by adding dramatic plots and thrilling adventures. For example, Ince's three-reel epic *Custer's Last Fight* (1912) offered audiences a fresh approach to a familiar subject. Rather than relying on stereotypical images of savage Indians overrunning heroic American soldiers, Ince places the battle in historical context, treating it as a tragic chapter in an ongoing struggle between equal adversaries over land and other valuable resources. The exciting docudrama breathed new life into the well-known event through historically accurate details, rugged scenery, realistic staging, and natural performances by Indians and Wild West show actors. As late as the thirties, the silent film was still being exhibited as "the greatest Indian frontier spectacle ever shown." Other Ince westerns also got rave reviews. A writer in the *New York Dramatic Mirror* noted that the Bison 101 movies "are so far in advance of the general run of cowboy and Indian pictures that they mark a distinct and independent step in motion picture development." Moviegoers voted their approval at the box office, enabling Ince's westerns to set new attendance records in some theaters.[14]

Bison 101 films were successful for a variety of reasons. The use of real cowboys and Indians from a Wild West show provided authentic ethnographic details and depth to the movies. Inceville's rustic setting added to the realism, while panoramic scenes of colorful characters shot against rugged western landscapes created spectacular visual effects. Watching a Bison 101 film, said one critic, was like "standing upon the edge of a high cliff, gazing over leagues of virgin forest lands, and witnessing . . . a savage drama." Bison 101 westerns were well-crafted, with solid production values, strong story lines, and memorable scenes. Ince gave audiences uncomplicated plots and lots of action and pageantry without getting bogged down in characters' motives. The results were always exciting, explained one critic, even though audiences knew that "the Indians are going to have a war dance and attack the settlers, that some hero or heroine will go through all sorts of perils to reach the military post, and that the troops will arrive in the nick of time."[15]

Most Bison 101 westerns plugged into themes that resonated with audiences. Following the lead of Wild West shows, Ince's westerns defended traditional values and reinforced American patriotism and imperialism. Bison 101 protagonists—whether they were soldiers, settlers, cowboys, or Indians—always acted in accordance with established moral principles. And ultimately, the action in the films justified American progress and westward expansion.

Despite Ince's success as a director, he soon began concentrating more on film production. "If [D. W.] Griffith was the film's first real director," suggests film historian Gerald Mast, "Ince was its first important producer." He introduced numerous innovations, including detailed shooting scripts, specialization of labor, a step-by-step production breakdown, and a rigid shooting schedule, all of which allowed him to supervise the production of several films at once. Ince became the Hollywood equivalent of Frederick W. Taylor, the era's most influential efficiency expert, who gained fame applying studies "of how quickly the various kinds of work . . . ought to be done." Inceville became a motion picture factory, minimizing production costs while maximizing profits. One observer noted that subordinate directors were given scripts three weeks in advance. By the time filming began, everything was in place: costumes were hanging on the hooks; sets were completed; props were on hand; and everybody was familiar with the script. He explained, "With the cogs of the big Ince machine oiled to the smallest gear and the entire plant running as smoothly as an automobile in the hands of a salesman, the picture travels from beginning to end without delays."[16]

Ince all but stopped making westerns by the end of 1914. After that, he was increasingly preoccupied with the production end of the business, as well as other business interests. Ince eventually left NYMP to produce and direct for Triangle Pictures and other companies. He continued making films right up until his death in 1924, which occurred under suspicious circumstances at a Hollywood party on William Randolph Hearst's yacht.[17]

Thomas Ince helped chart a new direction for both westerns and the entire film industry. Ince introduced a Wild West show sensibility to western movies; he wrote the book on how to make epic outdoor westerns; and he invented the studio system. En route, he provided breaks to several individuals destined to leave their own marks on western movies, including director John Ford and William S. Hart, one of the earliest and most popular western stars.

Western Docudramas

While Thomas Ince westerns were mimicking Wild West shows, the actual father of the Wild West phenomenon—William F. "Buffalo Bill" Cody—was preparing to launch his own movie epic. For years, Cody had been toying with the idea of bringing his Wild West show to the silver screen. In the 1890s, he arranged to have Edison make Kinetoscope recordings of some of the acts in his show. An early film was made of Buffalo Bill's Wild West parade, and the American Mutoscope and Biograph Company shot footage of Cody's troupe entering an outdoor arena for a performance. When western movies became the rage in the early twentieth century, Buffalo Bill formed a production company and released a one-reeler entitled *The Life of Buffalo Bill* (1912). The film begins with the sixty-six-year-old

Cody riding along a trail. After displaying his tracking skills, he gets off his horse and settles down for a nap. The film then cuts to the old scout dreaming about his youth, at which point an actor playing the part of the young Buffalo Bill reenacts some of the most famous episodes of Cody's life. As the dream sequence ends, the real Buffalo Bill wakes up, climbs back on his horse, and rides off into the sunset.[18]

All of those early films were simply a prologue for Cody's biggest cinematic adventure. In 1913, Buffalo Bill attempted his boldest stroke yet to transfer his Wild West magic to the silver screen. By then, he was sixty-seven years old and nearing the end of the show business trail. The past few years had not been kind to the old scout. His image had been tarnished by a messy divorce, and his once-considerable fortune had been squandered through bad business decisions. The irrepressible Cody was down, but not out. He devised what promised to be his grandest scheme ever in a career built on grand schemes. Buffalo Bill had watched closely as western movies patterned on his own Wild West show became box office smashes. Not only were movie directors borrowing freely from Wild West shows' staging of battles, but they engaged Wild West performers to give their movies an air of authenticity. Several directors blatantly used Cody's persona in their films. Thomas Ince, for example, used Buffalo Bill look-alikes in both *Blazing the Trail* (1912) and *The Heart of an Indian* (1912). Inspired by western movies—which ironically had been inspired by him—Cody developed what seemed to be a surefire plan to restore his fame, fortune, and glory. Who better to star in and produce a historically accurate western than Buffalo Bill himself?

In 1913, William F. Cody decided to make the definitive motion picture about the Indian wars. He would star in the film alongside other historical figures who had taken part in the battles, including soldiers such as General Nelson A. Miles and Indian warriors like Short Bull. The grand enterprise promised to be "the greatest film ever made, a lasting pictorial history." With financial backing from two Denver businessmen and help from Essanay, Cody formed the Colonel Wm. F. Cody (Buffalo Bill) Historical Picture Company. Next, he secured permission from the U.S. government to employ real Indians and actual soldiers in the film. He then hired veteran western-movie director Theodore Wharton, and together they worked on the script and made arrangements to film on location near Denver and on the western plains. The planned epic was shot between September 26 and November 1, 1913.[19]

Buffalo Bill's high hopes were soon dashed. It quickly became apparent that the camera was not treating the aged scout kindly. The 1913 version of Buffalo Bill hardly resembled the more rugged and youthful Buffalo Bill who had taken the "first scalp for Custer" at the Battle of Warbonnet Creek back in 1876. With his long gray hair, gray goatee, slight paunch, and slowed movements, Cody looked like the sixty-seven-year-old man that he was. Sadly, he looked too old to compete against the dashing celluloid heroes that could be found in other movie westerns. His appearance was not the only problem. Cody soon realized that reenacting Indian battles in his Wild West show was far easier than trying to duplicate them in front of cameras. At times, it seemed as if everybody on the set wanted to be the director. General Miles repeatedly locked horns with his old friend about where and how the army scenes should be shot.[20]

Cody ran into similar problems with Indians. It was difficult enough getting them to follow the script when they filmed early skirmishes such as Warbonnet Creek, but the situation turned outright tense when they had to recreate the more recent fighting at Wounded Knee (1890). Neither Cody nor the Indians realized beforehand how difficult it would be for them to return to the site of the massacre. "According to one account, Indian women chanted death songs and wept when they returned to the scene of the slaughter," writes historian Joy S. Kasson, "and it was reported that some of the young men vowed to use live ammunition in the battle scene to avenge their fathers."[21] While actual shots were never fired, the film shots took a toll on all the participants.

Lacking continuity and focus, the star-crossed film never came together properly. Cody and his production team shot more than thirty thousand feet of film. Eventually, it was edited down to at least three different versions, giving exhibitors a choice of five-, six-, or eight-reel movies. Adding to the confusion, the films were released under a variety of titles, including *The Last Indian War, The Indian Wars Refought, Indian War Pictures, Last Indian Battles, Indian Wars, Indian Wars Refought by United States Army*, and *Buffalo Bill's War Pictures*. But all lacked the excitement, drama, and charismatic characters that audiences had come to expect from Buffalo Bill's Wild West. Even the final scene in all the versions was a disappointment. To secure the government's permission to employ Indians, Cody had to conclude the movie with a scene showing Indians working toward assimilation on modern reservations. Moviegoers accustomed to western films with climactic battle scenes or cavalry riding to the rescue could only yawn as they watched contemporary Indians working in factories or attending vocational schools.[22]

When the movie flopped at the box office, Cody returned to the live entertainment circuit and continued touring until his death in 1917. In a blatant attempt to capitalize on the passing of the frontier hero, the film was re-released, and Essanay followed up with a new movie, *The Adventures of Buffalo Bill,* that incorporated some of Cody's original footage. Neither garnered much attention. Sadly, the original Cody film disappeared almost without a trace. Eventually, all the known copies deteriorated due to heat, mildew, or chemical reactions that ate away the film. Only a few fragments and stills remain from Buffalo Bill's attempt to bring the mythic West to the movie screen, but even though Cody failed to produce his own epic western, the spirit of Buffalo Bill lived on, influencing countless westerns throughout the twentieth century and beyond.[23]

Like Buffalo Bill, a photographer named Edward S. Curtis dreamed of producing a full-length motion picture that would accurately depict Indians and the West. The experience that changed Curtis's career came in 1899 when he met anthropologist George Bird Grinnell, who suggested that Curtis photograph the rapidly vanishing life-styles of Indians.[24]

Soon thereafter, Curtis blocked out an idea for a project that would dominate his life for the next thirty years. His plan was to document Native American culture through a multivolume photographic history of every major tribe in the United States. Knowing the venture would be time consuming and expensive, Curtis decided to raise money by lecturing, selling Indian photographs, and securing funding from donors. When he received an invitation to take photographs at President Theodore Roosevelt's inauguration in 1905, he used the opportunity to lobby the president for support. Roosevelt—an amateur historian and devotee of the American West—thought it was a bully idea and wrote a letter of endorsement, which the photographer then used to gain an audience with wealthy financier John Pierpont Morgan. When Morgan agreed to provide the necessary funds, Curtis began photographing Indians throughout the West.[25]

The first volume in the series was published in 1907. The disappointing sales prompted Curtis to drum up support through continued lecturing and writing. He even toured with a sophisticated multimedia lecture called *The Indian Picture Opera: A Vanishing Race,* which featured lantern slides, field recordings, and film clips backed by a small orchestra. He followed up with an even bigger idea to attract the attention of both the public and potential donors. Aware of the growing popularity of western movies, Curtis formed the Continental Film Company in 1912 to make a historically accurate feature film about the Kwakiutl Indians of the Pacific Northwest. He attracted investors with a proposal promising that the dramatic film would have it all—"vision quest, love, witchcraft, war, ceremony, revenge, capture, rescue, escape, and triumph!" Even the movie's sensational title—*In the Land of the Head Hunters*—was designed to attract moviegoers accustomed to blood-and-thunder westerns.[26]

Curtis envisioned the movie as the perfect blend of Hollywood drama and historical accuracy, featuring real Indians, authentic reenactments of Native American rituals, and detailed reconstructions of Kwakiutl villages and artifacts. Released in 1914, the epic film had a plot based loosely on Henry Wadsworth Longfellow's poem *The Song of Hiawatha*.[27] Shot on location in British Columbia, the film offered beautiful scenery and meticulous re-creations of Indian costumes, ceremonies, and artifacts that were visually stunning. Curtis used a special tinting process to enhance the images and commissioned the famous composer John J. Braham to write an original score based on authentic Indian songs. The movie was then promoted with a glitzy marketing campaign that included brightly colored posters and billboards.[28]

All the elements seemed to be there to make *In the Land of the Head Hunters* an excellent feature film: the melodramatic story line promised thrills and entertainment; the accurate depictions of Indian life-styles guaranteed authenticity; and Curtis had the photographic skills and knowledge to produce an excellent movie. Yet, the whole never equaled the sum of its parts. The feature-length film debuted on December 7, 1914, with simultaneous showings in Seattle, Washington, and New York City. Although newspaper reviews were positive, audiences were not impressed. Despite all the hoopla, the movie flopped at the box office for one simple reason—it was boring. The four-reel film seemed more like a slow-moving museum documentary than a fast-paced cowboy and Indian picture.

The disheartened Curtis wound up selling his film to the American Museum of Natural History for a fraction of what it cost to make. Subsequently, he returned to his magnum opus book project, publishing all twenty volumes of *The North American Indian* by 1930. The multivolume set shared the positives and negatives of the movie. Both were praised stylistically for the impressive and dramatic effect of the visuals, yet the books—like the film—were viewed as tedious versions of Native American life that appeared staged and ultimately uninteresting.

Despite its lack of commercial success, *In the Land of the Head Hunters* left its mark. The movie inspired Robert Flaherty to do a similar but more successful film in 1922 entitled *Nanook of the North*. Curtis's movie also preserved, albeit in romanticized form, elements of Kwakiutl culture, including rituals, dances, clothing, war paraphernalia, and other aspects of daily life. As testimony to the movie's historical and cultural importance, it is now included as one of the landmark films in the Library of Congress's National Film Registry.

The Rise of Feature Westerns

Where Edward S. Curtis and William F. Cody both failed in their attempts to produce western film features, other film directors would succeed. The breakthrough came in 1914 with the release of Cecil B. DeMille's six-reel epic *The Squaw Man*. Though not the first feature film or even the first feature western, it was the first feature-length movie to be filmed in Hollywood, and its phenomenal success set the pace for subsequent westerns. The movie, which marked DeMille's directorial debut, was the first venture by the Jesse L. Lasky Feature Play Company, which was formed in 1913 by DeMille, Lasky, and Lasky's brother-in-law, Samuel Goldfish (aka Goldwyn). Hoping to make quality films for middle- and upper-class audiences, the Lasky Company signed renowned stage actor Dustin Farnum to star in the film version of the era's most famous play, Edwin Milton Royle's *The Squaw Man* (1905).[29]

DeMille's film remained faithful to the play as it told the tragic tale of the "Squaw Man," that is, a white man married to an Indian woman. The story opens in England on the estate of Sir Henry Wynnegate, the Earl of Kerhill. When his cousin Captain James Wynnegate (Dustin Farnum) learns that Sir Henry has embezzled funds that their military regiment had collected for widows and orphans, he decides to take the blame—not to save his gambling-addict cousin or even the family name, but because he is in love with his cousin's wife, Lady Diana. James escapes to America, changes his name to Jim Carston, and buys a ranch out West, "where folks keep their hands in their own pockets."

The expatriate nobleman soon tangles with the dastardly Cash Hawkins, who is trying to swindle a naïve Ute Indian chief named Tabywana. Jim's intervention wins the admiration of Nat-U-Ritch (the chief's daughter, played by Lillian Red Wing) as well as Hawkins' enmity. When the cowardly villain attempts to murder the good guy, Hawkins is shot and killed by Nat-U-Ritch. Shortly thereafter, the chief's daughter saves Jim again after he gets lost in a snow storm. Jim and Nat-U-Ritch then become romantically involved, resulting in marriage and the birth of a son. A few years later, Jim's first love, Lady Diana, arrives on the scene, announcing that her husband has died, but not before confessing that he was the thief who embezzled the funds. Though the path is now clear for Jim to return to England where he can reclaim his name, position, and even his first love, he feels compelled to do the honorable thing. Jim decides to send his son back to England, while he remains on the frontier with his Indian wife. At that point, Nat-U-Ritch steps forward to save her husband for the third time. The noble Indian woman makes the ultimate sacrifice. She commits suicide so that her husband and child can return to England, enabling Jim to become the new Earl of Kerhill and marry Lady Diana, and allowing the boy to claim his rightful heritage.

DeMille's movie version of *The Squaw Man* became a huge hit due in part to splendid acting, excellent production values, and an authentic feel. Equally important, the film was powered by a superb story line, with an exotic setting and fascinating characters who tested the limits of cultural boundaries. The plot picked up on the mythic American West, as well as colorful images of cowboys and Indians made popular by dime novels, Wild West shows, and early western films. The story also capitalized on the enormous popularity of titillating tales about interracial romance in popular culture.[30]

Although DeMille's *The Squaw Man* was a movie version of Edwin Milton Royle's popular 1905 play, the story line had much deeper roots that can be traced back to at least the previous century. Pierre Loti's *Madame Chrysantheme* (1887) and John Luther Long's *Madame Butterfly* (1898) both dealt with interracial romance between a white man and a Japanese woman. Long's short story led to David Belasco's play of the same name in 1900, which in turn inspired Giacomo Puccini's 1904 opera *Madama Butterfly*. When Royle wrote his *Squaw Man* stage play the following year, he simply substituted an Indian woman in the American West for the Asian woman in Japan, but he resolved the interracial romance the same way: Nat-U-Ritch—like Madame Butterfly—commits suicide so her white husband and mixed-blood child can live out their lives in the white man's world. DeMille's movie, like its predecessors, reflected generally accepted notions of race, class, and gender. In each instance, the gentleman and the white race triumph over lower-class nonwhites in keeping with the era's attitudes toward race and belief in Social Darwinism.

The Squaw Man became a model for subsequent westerns. Studios tried to duplicate DeMille's success by producing their own feature-length films. DeMille even copied himself, remaking *The Squaw Man* in 1918 and then again as a talkie in 1931. Throughout the rest of the decade and into the twenties, all the major westerns were at least five reels long; only films produced on the skimpiest of budgets were shorter. Feature westerns would follow two distinct approaches. Some would focus on a main character, leading to the rise of new western stars such as William S. Hart and Tom Mix. Others, often with big budgets, would stress plot and setting, resulting in sprawling epics like *The Covered Wagon* (1923). No matter what the approach, one thing was certain—feature westerns were here to stay.

William S. Hart as the New Cowboy Hero

By the mid-1910s, a new type of western star was on the rise. Broncho Billy was giving way to cowboys who were a better fit for the "star system" that was taking over the film industry. Initially, the Motion Picture Patents Company did not want films to include credits, because they knew that "stars" would want to be paid more. Audiences, however, quickly developed favorites, writing fan letters to "the Biograph Girl" or "the Indian" at Bison Pictures. Carl Laemmle, the owner of the Independent Moving Pictures Company (IMP), understood what audiences wanted. In 1909, he instituted the star system by hiring Florence Lawrence—the "Biograph Girl"—away from Biograph. He then launched a marketing campaign to promote her as IMP's new "movie star." The following year Laemmle lured away Biograph's other popular actress, Mary Pickford, by doubling her salary. Other stars were soon born, including comedians like Charlie Chaplin and sex goddesses such as Theda Bara and Gloria Swanson.[31]

William S. Hart emerged as the biggest western star. Unlike most western movie actors, Hart was an accomplished thespian. By the mid-1890s, his natural laconic style won praise from numerous critics who saw him in Shakespeare plays. When theater companies began abandoning Shakespeare to attract larger audiences with more popular fare, Hart was forced into other roles. In 1905, he landed the villain's part in Royle's stage play *The Squaw Man*. Over the next several years, he appeared in other popular plays, including a stage version of *The Virginian*. Hart's career took a sudden turn in January 1914, when he saw his first western movie. He came away convinced that he could do better. Raised in the West, he had first-hand experience with cowboys and Indians, and his training as an actor provided him with the skills needed to communicate an authentic western feel to audiences. No doubt, the money to be made in the growing film industry also appealed to the struggling stage actor.[32]

When Hart arrived in Los Angeles as part of a touring theatrical group, he rushed off to look up an old friend, Thomas Ince, who had become one of Hollywood's most influential directors. Ince initially refused to help Hart break into westerns, because the market was already "flooded," but the phenomenal success of DeMille's *The Squaw Man* (1914) changed Ince's mind, and he hired Hart to make two feature-length westerns for the New York Motion Picture Company. When one of them, *The Bargain* (1914), began attracting crowds at a local theater, Ince signed Hart to a long-term contract.[33]

At first, Hart directed and starred in a series of nondescript two-reel westerns. His character was patterned mostly on Broncho Billy, but Hart added a touch of realism. While none was a success, films such as *The Passing of Two-Gun Hicks* (1914) enabled Hart to develop a fan base as he learned the craft of film making. Things began to click in 1916 when Hart started making feature-length films aimed at more sophisticated audiences. The actor and his writers, C. Gardner Sullivan and J. G. Hawks, found success with characters and plots that picked up on the era's reform movements. The stories "are not merely western pictures," explained Hart, "but in every instance there is some motive behind the story that has weight and depth and meaning that makes people think, and creates a profound impression."[34]

The serious westerns appealed to audiences at a time when Progressivism and the Social Gospel movement were at high tide. President Woodrow Wilson and other reformers were not only solving a variety of domestic problems by advancing the values of white Anglo-Saxon Protestant America, but they were about to embark on the grandest reform of them all—a world war to make the world "safe for democracy." Underlying all the reforms was the "Social Gospel" of Protestant ministers such as Washington Gladden and Charles Monroe Sheldon, who believed that Jesus's teachings should be applied to everyday life. "What would Jesus do?" asked Sheldon in his 1897 novel, *In His Steps*. Hart's films answered that question in the context of the American West, depicting the white cowboy hero as a moral crusader who triumphed over corrupt institutions, criminals, political bosses, nonwhite villains, and other varmints. Benevolent ends always justified Hart's violent means.

A good example of Hart's "Progressive" approach to westerns is *Hell's Hinges* (1916), which established him as the most popular western star of his day. Hart's character—Blaze Tracey—is a bad hombre who works as a hired gun for Silk Miller, a dastardly villain "mingling the oily craftiness of a Mexican with the deadly treachery of a rattler." Their domain is an evil town known as Hell's Hinges. Tracey is ordered to run the new minister out of town. He attempts to do so but is stopped in his tracks when he comes face-to-face with the minister's beautiful and pious sister, the aptly named Faith. A title card explains the scene: "One who is evil, looking for the first

Figure 6. William S. Hart is in the center holding two guns in this still from *The Gunfighter* (Kay-Bee Pictures/New York Motion Picture Company, 1917). Hart's serious approach and plain clothes injected realism into westerns.

time on that which is good." Blaze's transformation is rapid. "I reckon God ain't wantin' me much," he explains to Faith, "but when I look at you I feel I've been ridin' the wrong trail." Demonstrating what Jesus would do in the wicked town of Hell's Hinges, Blaze becomes an avenging angel, killing Silk Miller, driving his evil minions away, and setting the town ablaze. As Hell's Hinges burns to the ground like a western version of Sodom and Gomorrah, a title card flashes on the screen—"Hell's Crown." At film's end, Blaze and Faith walk off toward the mountains and a new life together.

Hell's Hinges left viewers spellbound. The apocalyptic images, racial stereotypes, struggle between good and evil, and redemption of a sinner fighting for justice, love, and God's kingdom on earth resonated with Progressive Era audiences accustomed to moral crusades, personal salvation, and the "white man's burden." Subsequent feature films, such as *The Aryan* (1916) and *The Toll Gate* (1920), followed similar paths to success and solidified William S. Hart's reputation as the greatest western star of his day.

The Toll Gate was Hart's biggest box office hit. In typical fashion, he played a good badman named Black Deering. Although the boss of an outlaw gang, he follows his moral compass to eventual redemption. The wily and courageous outlaw eludes law enforcement officials and kills off bad guys and evil Mexicans, but winds up sacrificing his own future to save a good woman and her innocent young son. The film reinforced popular notions about good ultimately defeating evil, every individual's potential for self-improvement, and the superiority of white Anglo-Saxon Protestant culture. Hart's serious approach and flawed but righteous characters impressed both audiences and critics. One viewer suggested that the cowboy star was doing "missionary work as surely and as successfully as the clergy." Even President Woodrow Wilson took notice, citing *The Toll Gate* as evidence that motion picture producers could serve as leaders in "patriotic and religious educational life."[35]

William S. Hart reached the peak of his career between 1916 and 1920. But then the mood of the country changed. Following World War I, Progressivism and moral reforms died out and were replaced by new laissez-faire attitudes in politics and society. Hart's earnest characters with their Victorian values and moral reforms now seemed terribly old-fashioned, causing his career to plummet. He came back briefly in 1925 with *Tumbleweeds*, but Hart's approach and the film's subject—the passing of the West—were merely nostalgic by the mid-twenties. Hart's serious cowboy hero was no longer in step with the times. Even movie palaces were reluctant to show the film, fearing that audiences would not show up to see an aging star riding the range in an old-fashioned western. At one point in the film, Hart and other cowboys are sitting on horses looking out over the plains, witnessing the retreat of the cattle frontier. A title card quotes the old-looking Hart saying wistfully, "Boys, it's the last of the West."

Tumbleweeds served as an epitaph not only for the Old West, but also for Hart's career. Though he never made another major western, Hart would not be forgotten. The accomplished actor and talented director produced some of the silent era's finest films, powered by sophisticated story lines, compelling characters, and excellent production values. The stylish westerns demonstrated that the genre could change with the times and appeal to middle-class audiences during the Progressive Era. Hart's cowboy figure was a moral reformer, who exemplified the era's traditional values and notions of masculinity. Hart introduced a new type of western hero to movies—a tall, lean, laconic, rugged individual who could be counted on to do the right thing in the end. Hart's hero rang true, because of his manliness and values as well as his distinct appearance. The handsome

Hart had striking features and stood six feet two. He rode tall in the saddle, wore two guns on his hips, and looked rugged in his dusty clothes, boots, and hat. But he also had a gentler side. He protected women and children, was kind to animals, and even was the first cowboy star genuinely fond of his horse—a pinto named Fritz.

William S. Hart's charisma, vision, unique style, and realistic approach to film making rejuvenated the western genre in the late-1910s and had a lasting impact on the film industry. His enigmatic cowboy hero became the prototype for John Wayne and other rugged western stars. Hart's love of the mythic West was evident in his final appearance on the silver screen. When his silent movie *Tumbleweeds* was re-released in 1939 with music and sound effects, it included a poignant eight-minute prologue delivered passionately by the aged cowboy star. "My friends, I love the art of making motion pictures. It is as the breath of life to me," he said. "The rush of the wind that cuts your face, the pounding hoofs of the pursuing posse," recalled Hart, "and then, the clouds of dust. . . . Oh, the thrill of it all!"

From Features to Epics

William S. Hart was not the only film maker of his day producing major feature-length westerns characterized by serious plots, solid production values, and relatively big budgets. Although two of the greatest western movie pioneers—Thomas Ince and D. W. Griffith—were no longer major western film directors by the late-1910s, they never completely abandoned the genre. Ince continued to supervise NYMP westerns such as *The Bugle Call* (1916) and *The Deserter* (1916), while Griffith occasionally directed westerns, such as *Scarlet Days* (1919), and provided advice to subordinate directors who were making serious westerns.

Quality western films often built on earlier traditions. The westerns of Harry Carey (directed by John Ford) followed the realistic approach of William S. Hart. King Vidor's *The Sky Pilot* (1921) recalled *Hell's Hinges* with its grim tale about a minister who tries to bring religion to a Wild West town. Feature films such as *Hiawatha* (1913), *The Last of the Mohicans* (1920), and *Nanook of the North* (1922) continued the emphasis on Native Americans. And Franklyn Farnum's *The Fighting Grin* (1918) and Fatty Arbuckle's *The Round-Up* (1920) took a lighter approach, blending comedy with western story lines in the tradition of Broncho Billy.

Some of the most popular big-budget westerns starred actors who had established their careers in other genres. Douglas Fairbanks first gained popularity with a series of romantic comedies in the late 1910s. His best western feature was a swashbuckler entitled *The Mark of Zorro* (1920), directed by Fred Niblo and based on Johnston McCulley's pulp fiction story "The Curse of Capistrano." The film became a box office smash around the same time that stories about the Mexican bandit Pancho Villa and corrupt Mexican politicians were grabbing headlines throughout the United States. At the center of the action was Fairbanks's character, Zorro (aka Don Diego Vega), a lone caballero who eventually becomes the leader of a citizens' revolt against tyranny. Audiences cheered wildly as the graceful and wily Zorro matched swords and wits with Mexican villains. Featuring a large cast of settlers, soldiers, priests, and Indians dressed in authentic-looking costumes, it was set against historically accurate presidios, pueblos, and haciendas. The fast-paced film set the bar for future westerns about Old California, as it mixed the excitement of traditional westerns with the latest trends in comedy films and movie making.

Despite the success of films such as *The Mark of Zorro*, westerns as a whole were decreasing in popularity by the early twenties. The release in 1923 of the first epic western—*The Covered Wagon*, directed by James Cruze—revitalized the genre. Even President Warren G. Harding was impressed. "Not long ago I saw *The Covered Wagon* in the moving picture. I sat entranced," he explained. "Everywhere aflame was the soul of unalterable purpose."[36]

The Covered Wagon was a cinematic experience. The plot was simple. As a wagon train heads west on the Oregon Trail, a love triangle develops, entangling the hero, heroine, and villain. En route the travelers encounter savage Indians, dangerous bad guys, hazardous river crossings, prairie fires, blizzards, buffalo hunts, runaway horses, gold fever, and a variety of colorful frontier characters, including famous scouts like Kit Carson and Jim Bridger. But it was not the story line or characters that caught the public's attention. It was the movie's magnificent theme, spectacular effects, and stunning visuals.

Cruze's film, based on Emerson Hough's novel of the same name, plugged into one of America's most potent creation myths—westward movement. Prior to *The Covered Wagon*, this "glorious period of American history received but little recognition," noted reviewer Robert E. Sherwood. "This is the period of expansion which commenced about 1846, and which resulted in the settlement of the Pacific Coast. It was then that the pioneers—men, women and children—struggled across the prairies and over the mountains in their trains of covered wagons, passing through incredible hardships and cordons of belligerent Indians."[37]

Figure 7. The size of the wagon train and the never-ending wide-open spaces depicted in *The Covered Wagon* (Famous Players, Lasky Corporation/Paramount Pictures, 1923) captured the enormous challenge of America's westward movement.

The way the story of America's westward movement was told was as important as the story itself. James Cruze later recalled his initial reaction to the script. "I saw it as just another Western with a few wagons and so on—or a big special. I talked with Mr. Jesse Lasky [the head of Paramount Pictures] and . . . he gave me orders to go ahead [with the epic approach]." The finished product was indeed a spectacle to behold. Starring J. Warren Kerrigan as hero Will Banion, Lois Wilson as heroine Molly Wingate, Ernest Torrence as Banion's trustworthy friend and grizzled scout Jackson, and Alan Hale as villain Sam Woodhull, the movie featured a supporting cast of thousands, breathtaking visuals, and dazzling effects.[38]

The Covered Wagon was shot on location in Nevada, Utah, and California, providing stunning images of dusty trails, expansive vistas, blinding blizzards, ravaging floods, parched deserts, and rugged mountain terrain never before captured on film. To the core group of 127 actors and film crew, the director added 800 to 1,100 extras recruited from the region, including real cowboys, settlers, and original forty-niners. For added authenticity, Cruze brought in 750 Indians. The souvenir program bragged that some of them had even fought against Custer. Researchers provided details about daily life on the Oregon Trail, as well as information used to create accurate period garments for plainsmen, Indians, emigrants, and other characters. Advice from historians enabled Cruze to reconstruct Fort Bridger and build hundreds of authentic covered wagons. To complete the wagon train outfit, the director secured all the necessary trappings, including yokes, harnesses, and saddles. In various scenes, he used one thousand horses and oxen, two hundred mules, and other animals, including dogs, cattle, and a large herd of buffalo.[39]

The action was likewise breathtaking. The souvenir program proclaimed: "Thrills? Well, take all the wild west shows and combine them and you get some idea of what it was like [making this film]." The Indian attack on the wagon train included almost one thousand warriors. The scenes of five hundred wagons fording a swollen river "were made at great risk, for men and horses and oxen actually had to swim for their lives." At one point, the wagon train was filmed during an actual blizzard, "which providentially appeared just when needed." Various scenes of natural disasters and animal hunts were real not staged, often with little or no regard for the ecological impact. "Nine square miles of waste prairie were burned up for the great Prairie Fire scenes," bragged a film publicist. Several bison were actually killed during the hunt scene despite the fact that the once great herds were almost extinct by the early twenties.[40]

Cruze was proud of the movie. "It was in every way pioneering in picture work," he said. "We blazed new trails all the time. . . . And it was an experience that will never be forgotten, never." The film was equally memorable for audiences. Most were spellbound by the look and feel of the spectacular film. Critics called it "the first real American epic of the screen." Others described it as "monumental," "magnificent," and "gripping." "Just think of the film which has given you the biggest thrill you ever had. No matter which one it may happen to have been, *The Covered Wagon* eclipses it completely," gushed a reviewer in the *New York Evening Telegram*.[41]

The Covered Wagon became a blockbuster hit. The epic cost $782,000 to make—an extraordinary sum of money at a time when most big-budget films averaged $250,000 and low-budget (or B) movies could be produced for as little as $10,000—but it pulled in more than $3,800,000 at the box office. Halfway through the project, James Cruze realized who the real star of the film was. "The wagon train curiously became the star," he explained, "with a personality all its own." On screen, the wagon train was a sight to behold. Long shots revealed a long line of five hundred wagons that stretched out for three miles. Close-ups captured the sturdy wood frames and crisp canvas covers, as well as all the dangers faced by the wagons on the trek westward. Movie posters spotlighted the prairie schooners, elevating them as western icons that were the equal of cowboys, horses, and six-guns. The souvenir program equated the wagon train with the story of America. "They were dreamers, these pioneers; they saw visions and they had dreams," it explained. "They laid down their lives in toil; they suffered without complaint; from nothing they created our glorified states; honor, reverence and glory be everlastingly theirs."[42]

The sprawling, patriotic epic was in sync with the times. Not only did it tap into popular memories of the mythic West, but it underscored the nation's patriotism in the early twenties. The United States had emerged from World War I as a global power. Refusing to join the League of Nations, the nation turned inward, priding itself on its heroism, patriotism, and military might. The rising tide of xenophobia that contributed to the Red Scare, the Sacco and Vanzetti trial, and the rebirth of the Ku Klux Klan added to the surge of flag-waving patriotism. Americans cheered as President Warren G. Harding, Senator Henry Cabot Lodge, and other national politicians espoused an independent internationalism that would promote American interests through summits, such as the Washington Naval Conference (1921–22), and economic investments throughout the world. The nationalistic mood of the nation all but guaranteed a positive public response to *The Covered Wagon*. Appealing to patriotic Americans in both urban and rural areas, the film spotlighted a relatively neglected chapter in the nation's history and made Americans proud of their heritage. To underscore the movie's link to American history, the souvenir program proclaimed that the film was dedicated to Theodore Roosevelt, the former president and author of *The Winning of the West*.[43]

From sea to shining sea, reviewers heaped praise on the American epic. "Perhaps it is because the blood of pioneers is in our veins that we acclaim *The Covered Wagon* as America's greatest motion picture," said a reviewer in *The New York Commercial*. "It is an enduring record of the greatness of our American heritage. It should be shown to every citizen of this republic." Others suggested the "heroic" movie would "stimulate patriotism" and give audiences "a deeper appreciation of the land in which [they] live." Another critic pointed out, "There is a rhythm of empire building about the whole [film] which is impelling."[44]

The phenomenal popularity of *The Covered Wagon* rejuvenated the western genre. Within a year, production of westerns almost tripled. For the rest of the decade, Hollywood pulled out all the stops to cash in on the surging demand, producing epics and big-budget westerns such as *The Iron Horse* (1924), *The Great Divide* (1925), *The Winning of Barbara Worth* (1926), and *The Wind* (1928).

The best of the batch was *The Iron Horse*. Directed by John Ford, the sprawling, two-hour and forty-minute epic called attention to the role of the transcontinental railroad in westward expansion just as Cruze's movie had spotlighted the importance of covered wagons on the Oregon Trail. Starring George O'Brien and Madge Bellamy, with a supporting cast of thousands, the spectacular film earned rave reviews and over two million dollars. The director expertly weaves into the main story line a variety of subplots about Indian attacks, the pony express, cattle drives, saloon brawls, and colorful western characters such as Buffalo Bill Cody and Wild Bill Hickok, as well as broader themes involving labor and ethnic strife, tensions between capitalists, presidential and local politics, and westward expansion. "The final scene at Promontory Point, where the Union Pacific is finally joined with the Central Pacific, reproduces in tableau form the scenes recorded by photographers at the time," notes film historian Edward Buscombe, "thus justifying, if little else in this boisterously inventive film does, the claim in the opening titles to be 'accurate and faithful in every particular.'"[45]

The Iron Horse was not the only film inspired by *The Covered Wagon*. After Paramount Pictures struck gold with Cruze's film version of Emerson Hough's popular novel, other studios began producing movies based on western novels. One of the most successful was *The Vanishing American* (1925), based on a Zane Grey novel. The tale spanned two thousand years, beginning with ancient cliff dwellers of the American Southwest and ending with Indian veterans after World War I. Filmed on location in Monument Valley a decade before John Ford arrived to film *Stagecoach*, the movie offers a sympathetic portrayal of Native Americans in keeping with the era's reformist attitudes, which culminated in the granting of citizenship to Indians in 1924. From beginning to end, the movie depicts different generations of Indians, some strong, some weak, but the tragic outcome is always the same. Even when Indians win, they ultimately lose their lands, culture, and lives. Basically a tale of survival of the fittest, *The Vanishing American* reflected the era's beliefs about the superiority of white civilization.[46]

Hollywood stars jumped on the western film bandwagon with films such as Clara Bow's *The Scarlet West* (1925) and Charlie Chaplin's *The Gold Rush* (1925). In addition there were parodies of *The Covered Wagon* and *The Iron Horse*, including Hal Roach's *The Uncovered Wagon* (1923) and Mack Sennett's *The Iron Nag* (1925). More important, the commercial success of *The Covered Wagon* gave rise to the increased production of low-budget action films that would transform the western movie landscape.

Tom Mix and Other Shooting Stars

During the twenties, William S. Hart and other actors in big-budget westerns were eclipsed by the appearance of new stars on the western horizon. Tom Mix blazed the trail for a new cohort of cowboy stars who found success with low-budget action films that came to be known by a variety of names, including B-Westerns, series westerns, shoot-'em-ups, oaters, and horse operas. Regardless of what name they went by, these low-budget pictures followed the formula made famous by dime novels, pulp fiction, and Wild West shows. "Action, action, action is the thing. So long as you keep your hero jumping through fiery hoops on every page you're all right," explained western fiction writer Max Brand. "There has to be a woman, but not much of one. A good horse is much more important."[47]

Tom Mix began his career as a cowboy with the Miller Brothers 101 Ranch and their Wild West show. In 1909, the young wrangler caught the eye of William N. Selig, the western film maker who had come to the Miller Ranch to shoot some footage for his movies. Selig knew instantly that the charismatic cowboy was a natural for the silver screen, so he recruited the good-looking and athletic cowhand for some bit parts and eventually began featuring him as the star in western shorts, including a film version of B. M. Bower's best-selling western novel *Chip of the Flying U* (1914). Mix's movie career took off after he switched over to the Fox Film Corporation in 1918 and began making feature westerns such as *Cupid's Roundup* (1918).[48]

Tom Mix became the most popular western star of the twenties. Adults and children alike were captivated by the cowboy's action-packed films, which featured amazing daredevil stunts. Tom Mix could outride, outfight, outshoot, and outsmart any villain. Glitzy outfits were part of the Mix formula. The charismatic cowboy became known for his broad-brimmed Stetson, flashy bandannas, fancy boots and spurs, and stylish western shirts and pants. Unlike earlier celluloid cowboys, he did not drink, smoke, or swear, and he used violence only as a last resort. Usually, Tom would defeat the bad guy with his fists or capture him by lassoing him or shooting the gun out of his hand. Mix never wound up on the losing end, and he always did the right thing, defending the innocent and traditional values. To top it off, Mix had the greatest horse that ever galloped onto the silver screen. Tony the Wonder Horse was smarter than most of the bad guys. He could bow, count by pawing at the ground, come when called, and even untie the ropes that villains occasionally used to bind the hero's hands and feet.

Figure 8. Tom Mix, B-Western cowboy extraordinaire. Richard Aquila Collection.

Tom Mix's superhero character offered sharp contrast to William S. Hart's somber and realistic westerner. "Mix was everything Hart was not. He wore a frilly cowboy suit and flamboyant ten-gallon hat which made Hart's simple leather trousers seem ragged in comparison," explains film historian Buck Rainey. "Hart would cinematically shoot to kill . . . but Mix only grazed the bad guys . . . so they 'fainted' long enough to bring them in for a fair trial. Mix being a tough-as-nails westerner himself, his performance naturally carried authority, but otherwise his films were breezy, cheerful, streamlined, aimed at a wide audience, careful not to contain elements that might disturb children, and free of romantic entanglements."[49]

With Mix leading the charge, other charismatic cowboy heroes soon galloped onto the silver screen. Each had something different to offer. Ken Maynard was the flashiest, wearing a white cowboy hat and fancy outfits as he rode his palomino, Tarzan. Hoot Gibson was known for his humor. Fred Thomson was a top-notch rider and athlete. Tim McCoy and Harry Carey offered slightly older and more realistic heroes. The youthful Bob Steele was a tough fighter and fast on the draw. Arguably, the most impressive was Buck Jones, who combined the good looks and glamour of Ken Maynard with the toughness and realism of Tim McCoy and Harry Carey.[50] Most B-Western heroes were white Anglo-Saxon Protestant males, in keeping with traditions established by Wild West shows and earlier films, as well as the expectations of the dominant culture. But there were some exceptions. Heroines such as Texas Guinan (who was billed as the female William S. Hart) and Ruth Mix (Tom's daughter) starred in several B-Westerns. Buzz Barton demonstrated that young boys could also make it as celluloid cowboys. On occasion, minorities also appeared as stars of western films. An Indian protagonist was featured in *Braveheart* (1925), while Bill Pickett and other African American cowboy heroes could be found in all-black westerns such as *The Bull-Dogger* (1921) and *The Crimson Skull* (1922).

Given racial and gender prejudices of the day, it was actually easier for animals to make it big in western films. The trusty steeds of numerous B-Western heroes became stars in their own right. Whether fans were fast or slow on the draw, they could quickly name all the cowboy stars and their horses, for example, Tom Mix (Tony); William S. Hart (Fritz); Ken Maynard (Tarzan); Buck Jones (Silver); Fred Thomson (Silver King). One equine—Rex the Wonder Horse—even starred in his own film, *The King of the Wild Horses* (1924). Westerns also featured canine stars such as Rin Tin Tin, Dynamite, Peter the Great, Napoleon Bonaparte, and Strongheart. Rin Tin Tin—a German shepherd known affectionately as Rinty—was the Tom Mix of the pack. "Rinty was more than just a well-trained dog and a beautiful animal; he was an actor," insist film historians George N. Fenin and William K. Everson. "Rin Tin Tin was as good a Western star, in his own way as any [B-Western cowboy], and a good deal more intelligent than some."[51]

Most B-Western fans had favorite stars. They would argue about which cowboy was the best rider and best fighter. Who was fastest on the draw? Or, who had the best horse? Best hat? Despite the distinct traits of movie cowboys, their films actually had much in common. All were shot quickly and cheaply. By the twenties, overproduction of westerns had resulted in a new strategy for film makers. Although it became increasingly harder to book westerns in top-tier movie palaces, studio heads realized there was still big demand in neighborhood theaters across the country and abroad. Standardization became the key to success. Studios lowered production costs and maximized profits through low-budget series westerns that featured identifiable stars, simple plots, and few innovations. Tom Mix movies provide an excellent example. Mix's westerns seldom played in top-tier theaters, where ticket prices were higher and bookings longer, but Mix made up for that by appearing regularly in smaller venues, where every week for a small admission charge audiences could see a new Tom Mix western. The emphasis on quantity rather than quality resulted in the same profits. By the mid-twenties, Mix ranked alongside big-budget movie stars such as Douglas Fairbanks, Mary Pickford, Charlie Chaplin, and Rudolph Valentino as one of the most popular and highest-paid actors in the country.[52]

B-Westerns attracted large and diverse crowds to local theaters across America. The exact composition of the audiences is hard to pin down. Some experts have argued that moviegoers were primarily young males; others insist that low-budget westerns targeted working-class audiences. In any case, B-Westerns appealed to a variety of viewers—young and old; rich and poor; urban and rural; black and white; even male and female—who were interested in the mythic West, traditional values, fast-paced action, and simple story lines.[53]

These low-budget films were a perfect fit for the times. As the twenties decade opened, millions of Americans wanted to distance themselves from prewar reform movements and wartime fears. They had had more than enough reality during the war, and they needed a break. They just wanted to be left alone so they could return to individual pursuits of happiness. Warren G. Harding rode those sentiments all the way to the White House, promising "a return to normalcy." For many Americans, that meant adhering to traditional behavior, values, and beliefs.

B-Westerns served up a cinematic version of normalcy that focused on one of America's most cherished and potent traditions—the mythic West. Unlike William S. Hart's dark and moralistic films, B-Westerns were light and carefree. They offered audiences nostalgic visions of a glorious past, as well as uncomplicated plots with no ties to moral reforms or serious issues. The action-packed movies offered lots of fun, as well as the opportunity for audiences to escape from the demands and stresses of modern American life, even if just for an hour or so. The B-Western formula included nonstop thrills set against a mythical western backdrop, where rugged individuals always found happiness fighting for truth, justice, and the American Way. The never-ending frontier drama played out in film after film and included exciting shootouts, chases on horseback, fistfights, and daredevil stunts, as well as all the expected images of the mythic West—spectacular scenery and iconic cowboys, Indians, good guys, and bad guys.

Completing the motif were all the familiar props, including cowboy hats, saddles, spurs, guns, and horses. The formula not the plot determined success. That is why Tom Mix could joke about the sameness of his stories. "I ride into a place owning my own horse, saddle, and bridle," he explained. "It isn't my quarrel, but I get into trouble doing the right thing for somebody else. When it's all ironed out, I never get any money reward. I may be made foreman of the ranch and I get the girl, but there is never a fervid love scene."[54]

The specific locale of the escapist entertainment was particularly important. Throughout history, people have turned to an idealized or nostalgic past to cope with stress or rapid social, cultural, and political change. B-Westerns served as a time machine, transporting viewers from the tumultuous twenties back to a simpler Old West. The low-budget films recalled earlier pop culture forms such as dime novels, melodramas, and Wild West shows.[55]

Western themes, scenery, and iconic images underscored the mythic location. The good guy galloping across the rugged terrain was instantly recognizable as a traditional American hero. Some have argued that the cowboy was just an update of the European knight. Like Lancelot of old, the celluloid cowboy was a lone rider on horseback, wore easily identifiable garb, and was expert with his chosen weapons, but despite those similarities, the cowboy was first and foremost an American original. A western version of Daniel Boone or other frontiersmen made famous by pop culture, the cowboy was a distinct American hero—a common man with uncommon skill. Hollywood polished his rough frontier edges to fit the times. The B-Western movie cowboy built on the tradition of earlier fictional heroes of American pop culture, such as Frank and Dick Merriwell or the Rover Boys. He was an excellent athlete, who could ride like the wind or defeat any villain with his fists or guns. He did not smoke or drink. And he always protected those in need and righted all wrongs. Tom Mix, Buck Jones, and other clean-cut cowboy stars set the stage for Charles Lindbergh. They personified how American heroes of the twenties should look, act, and think. Ironically, even though movie cowboys were cinematic creations, they came across as authentic heroes. Many had real work experiences on ranches or in rodeos or Wild West shows, and their family roots often ran deep in western soil. Just as Lindbergh's midwestern heritage would later be emphasized, film studios advertised Tom Mix as "a native-born son of the great southwest," and Ken Maynard was described as "a Texan with a drawl, a real cowboy" (even though he actually hailed from Indiana).[56]

B-Westerns reaffirmed traditional values. Like an old friend, the movie cowboy was a constant reminder of America's past, providing comfort, continuity, and stability throughout the Roaring Twenties. As public opinion divided over the Sacco and Vanzetti case, the Scopes monkey trial, the behavior of flappers, or the coming of Prohibition, B-Westerns offered common ground. Americans might debate the rightness of Woodrow Wilson's policies compared to Henry Cabot Lodge's, but they would always agree that Tom Mix should triumph over the bad guy in his latest film. There was no ambiguity on the B-Western frontier. Cowboy pictures became morality plays, clarifying right and wrong for Americans in a time of great social change. Cowboy heroes were moral and patriotic; they believed in democracy and individual freedom; and they were always strong men who were true to their principles and defenders of the innocent and oppressed.

Tom Mix and other movie cowboys helped B-Westerns become a popular and profitable western subgenre. "All I have to do is put Mix's name out front and [audiences] come back like prodigal sons," explained a theater manager in 1928. "There's affection and trust in their eyes again when they lay down their dough. They take for granted that Mix will never go up against less than twenty guys. There's a man for 'em."[57]

* * *

By the end of the twenties, feature western movies were well established. Two main patterns emerged: big-budget westerns relied on sophisticated story lines and refined production techniques; B-Westerns featured lots of action and big-name stars appearing in low-budget series westerns. Film makers were confident that both approaches had the potential to attract audiences in the future. But first they had to deal with a basic question that threatened the very survival of the genre: Could western movies adapt to the coming of talkies?

CHAPTER THREE

The Big Trail

Tracking Feature Westerns Through Depression and War

The Fox Film Corporation had high hopes for *The Big Trail*, their epic western released in 1930. The "all talking" picture seemed to have all the ingredients for success. With a two-million-dollar budget, the spectacular film was shot on location throughout the West, using an experimental 70 mm wide-screen format called Fox Grandeur. It featured a plot reminiscent of *The Covered Wagon* and was directed by Raoul Walsh, who just one year earlier had earned kudos for directing the first western sound film, *In Old Arizona*. To top it off, *The Big Trail* introduced a handsome new actor with huge box office potential—John Wayne.

A movie poster proclaimed that *The Big Trail* was "THE MOST IMPORTANT PICTURE EVER PRODUCED." Evoking a painting of the Southwest done in earth tones of orange, brown, and rust, the hand-drawn poster depicts a wagon train heading west. On the right is a young couple standing in front of a Conestoga wagon. The tall pioneer man is wearing fringed buckskins and a broad cowboy hat, with a rifle strapped to his muscular back. Close to him stands a petite young woman. Her dress is blowing gently in the breeze, clinging to her shapely legs and torso. As she leans ever so slightly against him, the powerfully built young man holds her with one arm and points westward with the other. The entire scene recalls Emanuel Gottlieb Leutze's *Westward the Course of Empire Takes Its Way*, the iconic mural commissioned by the U.S. House of Representatives in 1861. Like the famous painting, the poster celebrates Manifest Destiny, a seminal chapter

Figure 9. This movie poster for *The Big Trail* (Fox Film Corporation, 1930) glorified America's westward movement.

in American history. It shows families in covered wagons, teams of horses straining to pull heavy loads on the Oregon Trail, and optimistic pioneers bound for a new future in a new land. Even the red streaks in the orange sky capture the feel of westward movement toward the setting sun.

The Big Trail promised a frontier tale of revenge and romance set against a mythic western backdrop. The young trapper played by John Wayne seeks revenge against villains who killed his best friend. When he learns that the murderers are headed west on a wagon train bound for Oregon, he signs on as a scout with the outfit. The plot thickens when Wayne falls in love with a beautiful young woman (Marguerite Churchill), who is traveling with her brother and sister to Oregon. By trail's end, the hero defeats the bad guys and gets the girl. But that's only a small part of the story. The real drama involves the action and dangers along the Oregon Trail. Audiences must have felt like eyewitnesses to history as they observed covered wagons rolling across the Great Plains and through spectacular mountain passes; witnessed wagons fording raging rivers or getting lowered by ropes down craggy cliffs; or saw pioneers fighting off Indians and surviving blizzards.

Fox's high hopes for the epic came crashing down when *The Big Trail* flopped at the box office. The timing of the film's release could not have been worse. As America's economy worsened during the first year of the Great Depression, only two theaters in the entire country—one in New York City, the other in Los Angeles—could afford to purchase the new projectors and wide screens needed to show the 70 mm film. Everyone else had to settle for the standard 35 mm version, which lacked the stunning wide-screen visuals of the wagons moving west. Adding to the problem, the film plodded along more slowly than the Conestoga wagons it portrayed. *Variety* was not impressed by "the simple romance and the silly melodrama." Neither the leading man nor the leading lady helped the situation. The nineteen-year-old Marguerite Churchill was "so unimpressive," says film historian Daniel Eagan, "that she could only find later parts in B movies." Eagan gives Wayne equally bad marks: "[He] often seems stiff, frozen in poses, with an awkward awareness of the camera." Wayne's mediocre performance nearly finished his career before it began, relegating him to B movies for almost the next ten years. He would not land a starring role in another big-budget western until *Stagecoach* in 1939.[1]

Though *The Big Trail* disappointed at the time, its reputation has grown over the years. Along with introducing Wayne as a leading man, the film offered stunning images of the Old West. The excellent cinematography, breathtaking scenery, and unforgettable re-creations of wagons winding their way across the plains and through the Rockies eventually helped the film earn a place on the Library of Congress's National Film Registry.

The film's title serves as an excellent metaphor. Between 1929 and 1945, almost two thousand westerns would follow their own "big trail," finding a path through new technologies, the Great Depression, and World War II. Regardless of whether they were big-budget productions or less expensive B-Westerns, they offer fascinating glimpses of changing times.

The Coming of Western "Talkies"

No one was more disappointed by *The Big Trail*'s failure at the box office than its director. Just one year before, Raoul Walsh was being heralded as one of Hollywood's leading directors after he codirected (with Irving Cummings) the first talking western picture, *In Old Arizona* (1929). The movie became a huge commercial and artistic success, garnering five Oscar nominations, including a Best Actor win for Warner Baxter.

Prior to the success of *In Old Arizona,* many producers doubted that westerns could make the transition from silent films to talkies because of the difficulties of recording outdoors. Indoor studios compensated for noisy cameras by introducing soundproof cabinets, or *blimp* covers, for cameras. Filming indoors also allowed sound technicians to place microphones close to actors by hiding them in plants or other stage props. Moving outdoors compounded the production problems, which creative sound engineers solved by introducing innovations such as insulated cameras, boom microphones, and directional microphones.[2]

In Old Arizona proved once and for all that sound westerns could succeed. The film was based on the Cisco Kid character from O. Henry's short story, "The Caballero's Way." Unlike O. Henry's pathological outlaw, who "killed for the love of it," the movie version of the Cisco Kid (played by Warner Baxter with gusto and a thick Mexican accent) is a charming, happy-go-lucky bandit with a five-thousand-dollar reward on his head. Baxter's Kid is a likable rake who avoids violence and champions common folks. During a stage holdup early in the movie, the gallant Robin Hood of the Old West grabs the money box but assures passengers, "I never rob the individual."[3]

The plot stays fairly close to O. Henry's original story. The Cisco Kid commits robberies and lavishes affection and presents on his sexy girlfriend, Tonia Maria (Dorothy Burgess), but the promiscuous Mexican spitfire is insatiable. She flirts with the handsome U.S. cavalry sergeant (Edmund Lowe) who wants Cisco dead or alive. She even conspires with the lawman to ambush the Kid for the reward, but the wily outlaw outsmarts them both, tricking the soldier into shooting and killing Tonia instead. As Cisco rides off into the night, he says with charm and irony, "Her flirting days are over, and she's ready to settle down."

Sound was a large part of the film's appeal. A movie poster boasted that the film was "100% ALL-TALKING" and promised "YOU HEAR WHAT YOU SEE WHILE ENJOYING IN OLD ARIZONA." The film did not disappoint. The opening credits set the tone with a Mexican-influenced theme song performed by full orchestra. Audiences sat back in their seats and marveled at what came next. Sights of horses, stagecoaches, cattle, and other familiar western images suddenly came alive through the added dimension of sound. When the stagecoach first appears, the audience can hear the horses galloping, the wagon wheels rolling on the dirt road, and even the harness bells tinkling. Gunshots, colorful dialogue, and original music add to the sonic mix. One

Figure 10. Movie poster for *In Old Arizona* (Fox Film Corporation, 1928) shows the Cisco Kid on the left and a lawman on the right. Cisco's girlfriend stands in between, suggesting various ways she might help Cisco's cause.

of the songs in the movie—the Cisco Kid's ballad for his girl, "My Tonia"—was so popular it even became a hit record for pop singer Nick Lucas.

In Old Arizona struck a responsive chord with twenties audiences. Unlike most films that offered negative stereotypes of Mexicans, this one portrayed the Cisco Kid as a striking olive-skinned swashbuckler, in keeping with the era's Latin lover image, popularized by exotic film stars such as Rudolph Valentino and Lupe Velez. The film polished Cisco's ethnicity by describing him as half Portuguese and half Old Californian. The screenwriters continued other ethnic stereotypes: an Italian is depicted as a barber; Chinese men do the laundry; the Irish are soldiers; and most of the Mexicans are hot tempered.

The movie mirrored liberal sexual attitudes of the Roaring Twenties. The film's "Ham and Eggs" scene, which focuses on the Cisco Kid romancing Tonia, is a perfect example. Tonia sits on a bed high atop a loft. The Kid is standing on a ladder, caressing her bare legs. Suddenly, they are interrupted by the cook. Witnessing the couple's passionate kiss, the old woman asks Cisco, "How do you like *it*, then? Turned over?" For emphasis, she motions suggestively with her hand, first laying it flat, then turning it slowly on its back. "Turned over?" asks an embarrassed Cisco. "The eggs," she replies mischievously, reminding him that she's cooking ham and eggs. As the couple begins to climb down from the loft, Tonia stops halfway down and spreads her bare legs apart, allowing Cisco to lean in toward her. She asks playfully, "You got something for me?" He laughs, kisses her stomach, and with the top of his head touching her breasts ever so slightly, he repeats her line "You got something for me?" After the two climb down from the ladder, he gives her jewelry, talks briefly to the cook, and then returns to Tonia, who has poured two glasses of wine. Cisco offers a toast "to my flower of love." They clink their glasses together and drink. "That hits the spot," he says. She moves closer to him and says coyly, "Makes you warm, eh?" He replies lasciviously, "I don't need anything to make me warm," and then falls into a chair and pulls her onto his lap. They embrace, and he professes his love. As his right hand caresses the side of her breast, he speaks glowingly about her beauty and laughter. Having gone about as far as one could go on the screen in 1929, Cisco stops suddenly and says with a laugh, these "words [are] too damn beautiful for that old woman [cook] to hear." Tonia laughs like a delighted schoolgirl, and the scene ends.

If the film's risqué scenes, double entendre, and glorification of criminal behavior attracted some moviegoers, they also caught the attention of critics. The 1929 movie may have even contributed to the adoption of the Motion Picture Production Code in 1930, designed in part to stop the production of movies "which will lower the moral standards of [viewers]" or cause audiences to sympathize with "crime, wrong-doing, evil or sin." Also known as the Hays Code (after Will H. Hays, the official in charge of enforcing the rules), much of the production code would remain in effect until the 1960s. For most audiences, though, *In Old Arizona* was not an immoral film. It was just an enjoyable western with fascinating characters and an interesting plot. Baxter's Cisco Kid comes across as a loveable rogue, while Dorothy Burgess's Tonia Maria is a flawed señorita justifiably punished for her indiscretions and betrayals. The western tale was a thoroughly entertaining experience, enhanced by sound, music, and numerous plot twists that delighted moviegoers right up until the final scene.

In Old Arizona was one of the most popular films of 1929. Before the year was out, other feature westerns were also breaking the sound barrier.

Gary Cooper delivered a sensational performance, for example, in an epic sound version of Owen Wister's classic novel, *The Virginian*. The catch phrase—"You wanna call me that, *smile*!"—caught on across the land as Cooper's soft-spoken but rugged hero became immortalized as America's quintessential cowboy. As the thirties decade opened, sound westerns were on the threshold of even greater successes, as well as serious dangers.

Heading West in Troubled Times

No sooner did Hollywood solve the problems associated with making talkies than it had to deal with two new threats. The arrival of the Great Depression and the gathering storm of World War II threatened the existence of not just the film industry but the nation itself. The economic downturn hit the movie industry hard. Major studios teetered on the brink of bankruptcy. Hundreds of theaters went out of business. Film budgets were slashed, and salaries for actors, production crews, and film executives plummeted. The industry responded in various ways. As Hollywood producers and directors searched for film ideas that would appeal to Americans during troubled times, theater operators devised new gimmicks to attract customers. Theaters ran double features; cut ticket prices; offered two tickets for the price of one; held lotteries; gave away free glasses, dishes, and other premiums; and relied more heavily on selling candy, popcorn, and soda drinks to increase profits.[4]

Hollywood moguls were convinced they could weather the troubled times with violent gangster movies, screwball comedies, dreamy musicals, or other escapist fare that allowed viewers to forget their troubles for at least an hour. Studios also saw the value of old-fashioned films that promoted traditional values and beliefs. Such movies would counter critics who decried sex and violence in movies and would enable film makers to tap into the changing public mood brought about by the Depression, as well as by President Franklin Roosevelt's policies and rhetoric. "The New Deal Administration was seeking to boost the morale of a confused and anxious people by fostering a spirit of patriotism, unity, and commitment to national values, a political goal that coincided with similar tendencies within the movie industry," notes historian Robert Sklar. Hollywood producers realized that patriotism and profits often went hand in hand. By 1934, Will Hays of the Motion Picture Producers and Distributors Association could brag, "No medium has contributed more greatly than the film to the maintenance of the national morale during a period featured by revolution, riot and political turmoil in other countries."[5]

Westerns had particular appeal as America's economy sputtered and the nation drifted toward war. These movies offered audiences escape to a simpler, more attractive time. Novelist Will Henry understood the public's fascination with the Old West. "Let [the audience] keep his illusions," he said. "Don't tell it like it was. Tell it like it ought to have been . . . a better life in a better land that never really existed, but should have." If westerns represented escape for some, they showed others how to cope with life's daily problems. Western movies celebrated American exceptionalism, reminding troubled viewers about their national heritage, the American character, and traditional values associated with the mythic West. Equally important, they offered simple solutions to complex problems and suggested that Americans would always triumph as long as they remained true to the values that made America great.[6]

Hollywood produced numerous westerns that resonated with audiences experiencing the Depression and World War II. Among the more popular were films that glorified major triumphs in American history, including westward movement and empire building on the cattle, mining, and transportation frontiers. For example, movies like *Fighting Caravans* (1931) and *Union Pacific* (1939) celebrated America's westward movement, while films of classic novels such as *Last of the Mohicans* (1936), *Drums Along the Mohawk* (1939), and *Northwest Passage* (1940) glorified courageous Americans fighting against brutal enemies.[7] By depicting the winning of the West, these movies became veritable pageants of American progress.

Cimarron (1931), based on Edna Ferber's novel, is an excellent example of the era's patriotic westerns. Directed by Wesley Ruggles and starring Richard Dix as the charismatic Yancey Cravat and Irene Dunne as his determined wife, Sabra, the epic was a box office smash and critical success. It won three Oscars, for Best Picture, Best Writing/Adaptation, and Best Interior Decoration, and picked up four additional Academy Award nominations, for Best Director, Best Actor, Best Actress, and Best Cinematography. No western movie would win an Oscar for Best Picture again until *Dances with Wolves* in 1990.

The melodrama offered a love story as big as the wide open West itself. Set in Oklahoma, the sprawling epic tracks the Cravat family and friends through four glorious decades of American history, beginning with early pioneers on the wild frontier and ending in the twentieth century with skyscrapers, statehood, and national politics. The spectacular opening scene catches the viewer's attention immediately as thousands of people on horseback, in wagons, on foot, and even one riding on a high-front-wheel bicycle race to claim the best homesteads in the Oklahoma land rush of 1889. Shortly thereafter, Yancey Cravat, a crusading newspaper editor and sometime lawyer who is also fast on the draw, brings his wife and family west to settle in the Oklahoma boom town of Osage. Yancey tangles with numerous desperadoes in the Wild West. His first nemesis is Lon Yountis, a thoroughly evil bad guy played brilliantly by Stanley Fields. After Yountis shoots Yancey's white Stetson off his head, Cravat retaliates by shooting part of the bad guy's ear off. Several more tense showdowns occur until finally Lon draws on Yancey in the middle of a church service. With both God and quicker reflexes on his side, Cravat shoots faster and more accurately, allowing Yountis the dubious honor of being the first resident of the town's boot hill. "Did you have to kill him like that?" asks Sabra afterwards. "No, I could have let him kill me," replies Yancey matter-of-factly. Later, when he is alone, Yancey proudly carves another notch on his white-handled six-shooter, marking the sixth time he has taken another person's life in the name of justice.

Typical westerners abound, including cowboys, Indians, gunslingers, ranchers, gamblers, saloon girls, corrupt politicians, and even upper-class ladies who work diligently to civilize the lawless western town. The film also spotlights nontraditional players in the western saga: Sol Levy, a Jewish merchant, starts out in 1889 as a poor tinker with a mule and ends in 1929 as a wealthy department store owner; Isaiah, a young black servant who accompanies Yancey's family westward, can visualize a glorious future just like that of his namesake in the Bible; and Jesse Rickey, a printer with a severe stutter but lots of grit and determination, helps the Cravat family newspaper become a major force in the boomtown.

At the heart of the saga is a big theme—the triumph of American civilization, represented by westward expansion. A patriotic foreword provides a tantalizing glimpse of what lies ahead: "A nation rising to greatness through the work of men and women . . . new country opening . . . raw land blossoming . . . crude towns growing into cities . . . territories becoming rich states." As the story moves forward, audiences witness pioneers heading West for opportunity and freedom, a town established, problems and hardships overcome, economic and political growth, and the expansion of human rights as a new western state takes its rightful place in the union. The sprawling saga recalls historian Frederick Jackson Turner's famous description of westward movement, with various stages of settlement rolling across America like waves on an ocean.[8]

Yancey Cravat clearly understood his role in history. He was the pioneer, laying the foundation for the next chapter in America's glorious story. "We're going into new things, a new empire," he tells his wife as they head west, "and I want to help build it for you." Throughout his life,

Yancey remains true to the American Way. The crusading newspaper editor, sometime lawyer, budding politician, courageous citizen, and charismatic leader always stands on the side of liberty, justice, and equality. He expands the American Dream to include women, Indians, minorities, and others who are less fortunate, all the while promoting the traditional values that made America great. Like Daniel Boone and other early frontiersmen, Cravat blazes the trail and then sets off for new frontiers, leaving others behind to reap the harvests of civilization. Then, like Davy Crockett, he dies a martyr, sacrificing his life to save an Oklahoma oil-drilling crew from an explosion. But before Yancey exits the stage, he fulfills his promise. He helps build a new western empire for his wife, who by film's end is a wealthy businesswoman elected to the U.S. Congress by the citizens of Oklahoma. Sabra's accomplishments anticipated the hopes and dreams of other independent women in 1930s America.

At one point in the movie, the merchant Sol Levy assures Sabra that courageous pioneers and visionaries such as her husband will never be forgotten. "It's men like [Yancey] that build the world," he explains. "The rest of them, like me, we just come along and live in it." Levy's prediction is right on the mark. Following Yancey's death at the end of the movie, Oklahoma unveils a statue "to commemorate the Oklahoma pioneer" who settled the frontier. As the camera zooms in, the inspiration for the sculpted pioneer becomes evident. Wearing a broad Stetson and western-style clothes that recall Yancey's signature look, the figure brandishes Colt .45s in the two-gun holster slung low on his hips. As a symbol of heroic accomplishments in the West, he stands tall with his right hand ready to draw his peacemaker on bad guys throughout eternity.

Cimarron resonated with audiences staggered by the stock market crash and the worsening American economy. The epic's celebration of national progress and the winning of the West delivered a timely reminder about America's greatness and ability to overcome all problems whatever the odds.

The Winning of the Westerner

Cimarron was not the only feature western that found success with traditional images of the mythic West. Rugged individuals fighting for liberty, justice, and other American values were spotlighted in a series of westerns that starred Errol Flynn: *Dodge City* (1939), *Santa Fe Trail* (1940), *Virginia City* (1940), *They Died with Their Boots On* (1941), and *San Antonio* (1945). The promise of redemption in the mythic West powered movies such as *Texas* (1941) and *The Desperadoes* (1943). Even Cecil B. DeMille revisited the theme in 1931 with a sound version of his 1914 classic, *The Squaw Man*, which reminded Depression-weary audiences that America always offered determined individuals second chances.

Traditional western heroes such as Buffalo Bill Cody, Wild Bill Hickok, and Annie Oakley were glorified in numerous big-budget films.[9] The 1944 film biography of Buffalo Bill Cody demonstrates how contemporary movies celebrated western heroes. Directed by William A. Wellman and starring Joel McCrea as Buffalo Bill and Maureen O'Hara as the tempestuous Louisa Frederici Cody, the epic was filmed in Technicolor, capturing brilliant visuals of colorful cowboys, picturesque Indians, and gaudily dressed show people, as well as the magnificent scenery of Montana's Big Sky country.

Released during World War II, *Buffalo Bill* offered dazzling images of the mythic West that reinforced patriotism and unity. Though the film plays loose with historical facts, it celebrates America's heritage, assuring viewers that the country will succeed as long as Americans stick to their principles and guns, and they remain vigilant against evil foes, corrupt politicians, greedy capitalists, and ineffectual military leaders. At one point, the movie inaccurately depicts the dime novelist Ned Buntline (Thomas Mitchell) as the originator of Buffalo Bill's Wild West show. "If the East won't go to the West," says Buntline, "we'll bring the West to the East." Cody responds enthusiastically, realizing that the show will educate easterners about the ways in which they have mistreated Indians and squandered natural resources. Not exactly good history, but it certainly gets across the point that Americans have much to learn from the mythic West.

The movie ends with a spectacular re-creation of Buffalo Bill's Wild West, replete with exotic westerners caught up in patriotic fervor. The performance begins with an Indian waving an American flag as he gallops into the arena. He is followed by cowboys shooting their guns, a racing stagecoach, marauding warriors, cavalry troops riding to the rescue, all climaxed by Buffalo Bill riding triumphantly into the arena on his spirited horse as he tips his broad-brimmed cowboy hat to the crowd. Suddenly, a voice-over sounding like God himself proclaims: "Almost overnight, Buffalo Bill's Wild West Show captured the imagination of the public; he brought the western frontier and the Indians to the sidewalks of New York; the city folks saw for themselves the true pioneer spirit of the West. . . . [Buffalo Bill] came to typify to all of us frontiers and freedom, adventure and fair play, the Spirit of the West." As the Voice of God speaks, the movie flashes images of bucking broncos, cowboys shooting their six-guns, and riders on horseback, while in the stands spectators are cheering, and kings, queens, dignitaries, and even President Teddy Roosevelt are applauding and smiling with approval.

The final scene shows an aged Buffalo Bill Cody alone in the spotlight of the darkened arena, with the crowded stands draped with American flags. Sitting tall in the saddle on his white horse, he begins his farewell address by stating that he and his wife "hand in hand" are returning "to the sunset," to their home in the West. "Good-bye and God bless you," he tells the crowd, at which point a young boy on crutches stands up in the stands and yells out, "And God bless you, too, Buffalo Bill!" Cody tips his hat, blows a kiss to the boy and crowd, gives his horse a nudge, then gallops away. As "The End" flashes up on the screen, a graphic comes on telling moviegoers that they can buy U.S. war bonds in the theater today.

Along with spotlighting traditional heroes, western movies reshaped the images of notorious outlaws such as Billy the Kid and the James brothers to meet the needs of American audiences during the thirties and early forties.[10] *The Return of Frank James* (1940), directed by Fritz Lang and starring Henry Fonda, is a good example of the new western outlaw hero who became a fixture in Depression-era films. The movie was a follow-up to the box office smash of the previous year, *Jesse James*, which featured Tyrone Power as Jesse and Henry Fonda as his brother, Frank. The brothers are forced to take the law into their own hands when a corrupt railroad agent kills their mother and steals their land. The sequel begins with the James boys hiding out from the law on separate farms in Missouri. When Frank learns that Jesse has been shot in the back by Bob and Charlie Ford for a ten-thousand-dollar reward offered by the St. Louis Midland Railroad Company, he is confident that the government will punish the cowardly murderers. But when news arrives that the governor pardoned the killers and granted them the reward, Frank turns to vigilante justice.

To obtain traveling money, Frank robs the railroad company's express office, reasoning that since railroad reward money got Jesse killed, it was only fitting that railroad money should pay the cost to bring the killers to justice. When a security guard is killed by a stray bullet fired by one of the sheriff's men, Frank is charged with both robbery and murder. Accompanied by his young ward, Clem (Jackie Cooper), Frank heads west to settle the score with the reprehensible Ford brothers. The younger Ford, Charlie, is killed when he falls off a cliff during a shootout, but the other one escapes. Before Frank can track him down, he learns that authorities back home are about to hang his African American field hand and friend, Pinky, who was wrongly blamed for taking part in the robbery. Putting morality over vengeance, Frank abandons the hunt for his brother's killer and returns to his hometown—the ironically named Liberty—to give himself up in order to save Pinky.

In the ensuing trial, Frank's lawyer, Rufus Cobb, emphasizes that his client is a decent man and a good citizen who has been railroaded by one injustice after another inspired by the villainous St. Louis Midland Railroad Company. Frank committed the robbery as a means to justifiable ends, that is, righting the wrongs committed by the greedy railroad company, the dastardly Ford brothers, and the ineffectual governor who issued the pardon. "So in desperation and only as a last resort did Frank turn to robbery," explains Cobb to the jury. "Did he rob a bank containing the thrifty savings of the poor? No. Did he rob an honest shopkeeper? No. He took money from the railroad. The railroad that has caused the death of his mother and brother. The railroad that stole your lands and drove you from your farms. The railroad."

The jury, made up of decent middle-class farmers who despise greedy railroads and all perfidy, quickly finds Frank James not guilty. Bob Ford, who had come to the courthouse hoping to witness a death sentence for Frank, flees into the street, where he becomes involved in a shootout with Frank's ward, Clem. Leaving the boy for dead, the critically wounded Ford manages to hide out in a nearby livery stable. Frank picks up Clem's gun and follows the cowardly killer into the barn for a showdown. After Ford attempts to shoot Frank in the back, he hides in the loft, but before Frank can move in for the kill, Ford dies from the earlier wound inflicted by young Clem. Both of Jesse James's murderers have now been brought to justice, but significantly, Frank James did not kill either. Shortly thereafter, Cobb writes an editorial demanding a full pardon for Frank James, who has always acted "in full accordance with the wishes of the people." By the end of the film, Frank has been transformed from a fugitive wanted dead or alive to a folk hero celebrated by the residents of Liberty, Missouri.

Of course, not all westerns of the thirties and forties treated outlaws as heroes. A good example is *The Outlaw* (1943), produced and directed by Howard Hughes. Dropping all pretense of historical accuracy, the sensational film depicts Billy the Kid as a pathological killer entangled in sadistic relationships with the deadly gunfighter Doc Holliday; a neurotic lawman, Pat Garrett; and a sexy young woman named Rio McDonald (played by Jane Russell). Film censors were not pleased. At first, the administrator responsible for enforcing the Motion Picture Production Code refused to grant a seal of approval. In 1940, Joseph I. Breen complained to Howard Hughes that the final script depicted Billy the Kid as a "major criminal who goes unpunished." He also condemned the film for suggesting "illicit

Figure 11. Jane Russell poses seductively in *The Outlaw* (Hughes Productions/United Artists, 1943). Richard Aquila Collection.

sex between Billy and Rio," depicting a "trick marriage," and showing "undue brutality and unnecessary killings."[11]

When the film was finally released in 1943, an advertising campaign pulled out all the stops. A titillating theatrical trailer promised "savage love," "primitive emotions," and "trigger fast action combined with sensation too startling to describe." Movie posters and publicity shots spotlighted Jane Russell, often with a movie still that showed her reclining seductively in the hay. The long barrel of the six-shooter in her hand is pointed suggestively toward her thighs, while her flimsy peasant-style blouse clings to her breasts, and her loose skirt is pulled up, exposing her legs. Another poster asked suggestively in letters just above her chest: "What are the two reasons for Jane Russell's rise to stardom?"[12]

Despite all the publicity, the film flopped. Viewers found the characters unlikable, the plot bizarre, and the acting abysmal. One film critic called the movie "strictly second-rate," explaining it was "long and tedious and crudely acted for the most part." The combination of bad reviews and continued controversy over the content caused *The Outlaw* to disappear quickly from movie theaters. The film's negative portrayal of outlaws and gratuitous use of sex and violence made it totally out of step with the times.[13]

The western outlaw films that gained the most popularity during the thirties and forties were those like *The Return of Frank James* (1940), which treated outlaws as benign if not benevolent heroes who reinforced traditional values. To an extent, these western movies glorifying social bandits were patterned after *The Public Enemy* (1931), *Little Caesar* (1931), and other successful gangster films that used criminals as symbols for the common man's struggle against social and political injustice.[14] But feature films about western outlaws were not just copies of the era's gangster films. Indeed, *Billy the Kid* (1930), directed by King Vidor and starring Johnny Mack Brown as the Kid and Wallace Beery as Deputy Sheriff Pat Garrett, actually predated the popular gangster movies of the thirties. The notion of social bandits, such as Billy the Kid and Jesse James, who—like Robin Hood—stole from the rich to give to the poor had a long history in westerns, dating back to at least nineteenth-century folklore and dime novels. Western movies of the thirties and forties continued that approach, turning the outlaws into bona fide folk heroes who were every bit as moral and patriotic as previous western heroes.

The new, sanitized version of western outlaws was quite appealing during the Depression and war years. When cleaned up, these desperadoes looked outright heroic to audiences. Sometimes it was impossible to distinguish them from conventional good guys. They dressed the same, with six-guns, cowboy hats, boots, and spurs. They could outdraw and outfight any rival. And they believed in America's most cherished values: they were rugged individuals; they were determined and hardworking; they protected the innocent; and they righted all wrongs. Even their legal indiscretions could be rationalized as mere peccadilloes that highlighted their basic humanity. After all, America has always loved underdogs. Perhaps this love can be attributed to Americans' belief in liberty and justice for all. Or maybe it had something to do with notions of equal opportunity or Americans' belief in second chances and redemption.

In any case, western outlaws found new life in the mythic West throughout the thirties and forties. The magic of Hollywood transformed these desperadoes into symbols of the common man. They became champions in the era's struggle against shady bankers, crooked railroad agents, corrupt politicians, ineffectual leaders, and other enemies of the common man. These new versions of Jesse James and Billy the Kid served notice that ordinary people were not going to be pushed around. Cinematic social bandits proved that even in hard times, the common man could succeed. In the depths of despair, when no one else was willing to stop corruption or help those in need—whether it was on the old frontier or in Depression America—these western Robin Hoods came through. Sometimes the pragmatic movie outlaws helped audiences solve problems by suggesting that the ends justified the means. Other times, they simply allowed audiences to strike back vicariously at injustice or social, political, and economic constraints.

Western outlaws became working-class heroes in movies rife with class conflict. Desperadoes were the perfect outsiders for the time. Standing tall beyond traditional social and legal boundaries, they were freer and more able to fight against the Establishment. During the Depression and war years, notions of right and wrong were not always clear, so social bandits could ride an ambiguous trail, holding up stagecoaches, banks, and trains or committing other crimes for the good of society. If outlaws went too far over the line and their criminal actions became self-serving, they had to pay the ultimate cost, just as the tragic heroes of gangster films did. Even when they remained true to their cause, they sometimes still wound up getting shot dead in the streets of Laredo or saloons in Dodge City. The desperadoes' deaths, however, were learning opportunities for Depression-era audiences. Not only did the paybacks reaffirm traditional conventions of morality and justice, but they underscored the consequences of civil disobedience. The tragic outlaws in westerns about Billy the Kid or Jesse James were simply the latest citizens who had to pay a hefty price for their principles.

If western outlaws were outsiders in some ways, they were mainstream in others. These social bandits adhered to American ideals and were cloaked in a New Deal sensibility. Following FDR's lead, movies about desperadoes espoused patriotic rhetoric and took the side of average Americans against banking and big business interests. Westerns about outlaws became parables, teaching important lessons about the American character. They demonstrated the importance of standing up for one's rights no matter what the odds, and they reminded Americans that they had to remain determined and true to their principles to make it through hard times. Just as the James boys became folk heroes in *Jesse James* (1939) and *The Return of Frank James* (1940) by fighting for what was right against an evil railroad company, contemporary Americans could accomplish heroic acts by standing up to corrupt powers and malevolent forces in the Great Depression and World War II.

Westerns and Social Change

Big-budget westerns used the mythic West in other ways to address specific problems and issues facing the nation during the thirties and early forties.

Stagecoach (1939) offered subtle social commentary about the troubled times. Directed by John Ford and based on a story by Ernest Haycox, the film earned four Oscar nominations for Best Picture, Best Director, Best Cinematography, and Best Supporting Actor (which Thomas Mitchell won for his dazzling portrayal of an alcoholic doctor).

Stagecoach focuses on a motley group of passengers riding through dangerous Apache territory. The movie is a journey into the mythic West itself. It stars John Wayne as the Ringo Kid—a quintessential western hero who believes in traditional values and justice for all. The handsome, powerfully built Ringo is a deadly shot with the rifle and just as accurate when it comes to judging peoples' characters. Wayne's character makes what may be the grandest entrance in movie history. As a gunshot brings the stagecoach to a sudden stop, the camera cuts to John Wayne. The tall, rugged-looking cowboy twirls his rifle with one hand and holds a saddle in the other. Wearing blue jeans and suspenders and a cavalry-style bib shirt

Figure 12. John Wayne makes what may be the grandest entrance ever in a western movie in *Stagecoach* (Walter Wanger Productions/ United Artists, 1939).

with a bandanna tied around his neck, his determined look is accented by the backlighting of the golden sun in a Monument Valley sky, which creates a halo effect around his broad-brimmed hat. This cowboy archangel is America personified in all his frontier glory.

Stagecoach plugged into well-established images of the mythic West. The movie showcases panoramic views of rugged western landscapes and makes effective use of western formulas involving Indian attacks, cavalry riding to the rescue, and a showdown with desperadoes. It spotlights iconic images of cowboys, Indians, dusty towns, Winchesters, six-shooters, saloons, and, of course, the stagecoach itself. Ford's film becomes a morality play as it treats the West as a land of opportunity, justice, and redemption. Even the name of the town to which the passengers are traveling—Lordsburg—suggests that the journey will end with a judgment day, a moment of reckoning for all the weary travelers. Only those who follow their moral compasses will be saved.

John Ford's excellent direction makes this an extraordinary western. He frames scenes like an artist, using close-ups for emphasis and employing dialogue (or sometimes no dialogue at all) for dramatic effect. The director's decision to shoot in black and white underscores the dark mood of the film. The authentic feel of the movie is enhanced by spectacular cinematography, stunning Monument Valley vistas, and a powerful musical score based on American folk songs. Ford adds numerous little touches that make a good movie great. One scene, for example, demonstrates how early settlers tied logs to a wagon's wheels to float it across a river. Another accurately depicts Spanish influences on Apache clothing. In a barroom scene just before a fight takes place, saloonkeepers remove a mirror hanging behind the bar (a scene Ford reprised from his 1924 silent *The Iron Horse*). The ninety-six-minute film rushes forward with never a dull moment, matching the frenetic pace of the stagecoach racing through the wilderness.

Stagecoach was a commercial and an artistic success not only because it had plenty of western action and thrills, but also because it fit in perfectly with the times. The movie addressed social tensions and class conflicts caused by the Great Depression. Its depiction of the three upper-class passengers, for example, reflected the era's mistrust of the powerful and wealthy. First on the scene is Mrs. Lucy Mallory (Louise Platt), the well-bred and standoffish wife of an army captain. Though seemingly benign, she repeatedly displays her true colors by snubbing Dallas, the lower-class saloon girl/prostitute played convincingly by Claire Trevor.

Mrs. Mallory's initial contact with Dallas occurs at the beginning of the film, when she witnesses the blond saloon girl being given a one-way ticket out of town at the insistence of the community's upper-class women. Good wife Mallory does nothing to ease Dallas's humiliation and assures friends that she will not interact on the stage with the woman of ill repute. True to her word, Mrs. Mallory keeps a social distance. When the coach stops at a way station, she balks at sitting next to Dallas at the dining table and moves to the other end, allegedly to be closer to a window. Even at the end of the journey—after Dallas has literally saved her life by helping her through childbirth—Mrs. Mallory still cannot overcome rigid social boundaries. "If there's ever anything I can do," she begins to say to Dallas, but she never finishes her sentence. Realizing that the upper-class woman did not really mean what she was saying, Dallas simply replies, "Yeah, I know," at which point other upper-class ladies arrive to escort Mrs. Mallory to the upscale comfort of her new home, leaving Dallas alone in the street.

Mrs. Mallory is joined on the stage by another upper-crust character—an effete gambler named Hatfield (John Carradine). Hatfield looks and often acts like a gentleman, but his gambling habit, reputation for shooting men in card games, and lecherous actions suggest otherwise. The mutual attraction between the gambler and the married lady is evident from the moment their eyes first meet. Hatfield confides to his card-playing acquaintances that she looks "like an angel in a jungle." When one of them laughs, he says patronizingly, "You would not understand, cowboy. You've never seen an angel or a gentlewoman, nor a great lady." After several flirtatious exchanges, Hatfield decides to go along on the stage allegedly to protect her. The lecherous lion in sheep's clothing tries to establish his credentials as a gentleman by assuring her that he served in the Confederate army under her father.

Throughout the journey, Hatfield fawns over Mrs. Mallory, treating her like royalty even as he shows disrespect toward Dallas and other lower-class passengers. When she is thirsty, he offers her water from his own personal silver cup. When the coach stops at a way station, he gallantly offers his arm and escorts her to dinner, insulating her from social contact with lower-class passengers. And when Indians are threatening to overrun the stagecoach, he contemplates the ultimate chivalrous act to protect the lady's honor. In a scene reminiscent of D. W. Griffith's *The Birth of a Nation*, where a father plans to shoot his daughter to ensure she does not fall into the hands of ex-slaves, Hatfield saves one last bullet in the chamber of his fancy pistol. Just as he is about to shoot Mrs. Mallory in the head to save the gentlewoman from being ravished by savages, he himself is mortally wounded. As he breathes his last breath, he says to the lady, "If you see Judge Greenfield. . . ." In a flash, she realizes that Hatfield, the roguish gambler, was actually the son of one of Virginia's finest families.

The final upper-class passenger on the stage is the town's banker, Henry Gatewood (played by Berton Churchill, who bears more than a slight resemblance to President Herbert Hoover). Early in the film, Gatewood displays his sense of self-importance by declaring, "What's good for the banks is good for the country." As soon as he boards the coach, he says pompously to his fellow travelers, "I don't know what the government is coming to. . . . Why, they're even talking now about having bank examiners. As if we bankers don't know how to run our own banks." Though the other travelers have no way of knowing it, the hypocritical banker is clutching a valise with embezzled money at the very moment he is alleging government wrongdoing. "The government must not interfere with business!" he exclaims. "What this country needs is a businessman for president!"

While *Stagecoach* depicts the upper-class passengers as self-absorbed, snobbish, and hypocritical, it portrays middle- and working-class passengers as the salt of the earth. John Wayne's Ringo Kid is clearly a hardworking, moral individual who is facing hard times through no fault of his own. Framed by the Plummer brothers, who murdered his father and brother, Ringo breaks out of jail and heads toward Lordsburg for a showdown with the killers. When he is warned that he will be killed if he tries to take on all three brothers, Ringo replies, "There are just some things a man can't run away from." Even if he manages to win the gunfight, Ringo realizes that he will wind up back in jail. "I used to be a good guy, but things happen," he confides to Dallas, who replies knowingly, "Yea, things happen."

Dallas knows only too well that bad things often happen to good people. After her parents were killed in an Indian massacre, the young girl was forced to fend for herself in the streets of wild western towns. "You gotta live no matter what happens," she tells Ringo. In her case that meant becoming a saloon girl and prostitute. Though life forced her to sell her body, she refused to sell her soul. When upper-class women insist that she leave town on the stage bound for dangerous Indian territory, she agrees to go, reasoning, "There are worse things than Apaches." Dallas's innate goodness shines throughout the hazardous stagecoach journey. She turns the other cheek when insulted by upper-class passengers, provides aid and comfort to the Ringo Kid, and selflessly helps Mrs. Mallory, nursing her back to health and caring for her baby.

The other passengers are all hardworking, moral characters. Sheriff Curley Wilcox (George Bancroft) is a fair and compassionate man who hopes to save Ringo by sending him back to jail in order to stop him from being killed in a gunfight with the Plummer gang. Buck, the stage driver (played marvelously by Andy Devine), is a jovial hard worker, who goes well beyond the call of duty in dangerous conditions. The mild-mannered whiskey salesman, Samuel Peacock (played by the aptly named Donald Meek), is a solid family man with a wife and five children back home in Kansas City. Last but not least is Thomas Mitchell's character—Josiah "Doc" Boone, a doctor who has been banished from town because of his constant drinking. The alcoholic Doc clearly has his faults, but even he comes through admirably when duty calls.

The true character of each of the nine passengers rises to the surface during the journey to Lordsburg. The stagecoach becomes a veritable WPA project on wheels, providing the opportunity for individuals from all walks of life to work together toward a common goal. The middle-class and working-class passengers are able to meet most of the challenges head on, with little or no help from the upper-class ones, but ultimately, they lack the resources to survive against the greatest threat. When Apaches launch a full-scale attack against the stage, Ringo and his common-man comrades fight back gallantly, but they soon run out of ammunition. Just when all appears lost, the U.S. Cavalry rides to the rescue! The brave and determined people on the stagecoach were saved by government intervention, just as New Deal assistance would rescue average Americans from economic disaster in the thirties.

Even the ruthless Apaches probably seemed familiar to audiences aware of the gathering war clouds on the horizon of 1930s America. Geronimo and the Apaches appear every bit as brutal, warlike, and untrustworthy as any modern-day European fascist. Audiences came away from the film assured that American liberty, determination, and military strength could triumph against contemporary foes just as they had against Indian enemies in the Old West.

After the Apaches are defeated, the military escort the stagecoach to Lordsburg. The day of reckoning finally arrives for the weary passengers, who have traveled a long way—literally and figuratively—since their journey began. Tested by hardships and hardened by gunfire, they arrive at their moment of truth. The potentially adulterous and still snobbish Mrs. Mallory is reunited with her husband, not necessarily a good thing for either. The corrupt banker is arrested and jeered by a mob that disdains corrupt businessmen. The immoral gambler, the wayward son of a wealthy family, is hauled off in a coffin. The other passengers—all worthy common men and women who remain loyal to their principles—also get what they deserve. Both the stage driver and whiskey salesman recover from their wounds and return home to their families. Sheriff Wilcox and Doc Boone are congratulated for meeting their professional responsibilities with compassion and courage. And Ringo and Dallas find themselves and each other.

One challenge remains, though—the Ringo Kid's showdown with Luke Plummer and his two brothers. Making the odds even worse, Ringo has only three bullets left in his gun. Bidding good-bye to Dallas, he heads toward the saloon and his rendezvous with destiny. As residents scatter in anticipation of deadly gunfire, the Plummer brothers appear. The enemies walk slowly toward each other and suddenly open fire. Ringo hits the dirt and gets off three quick shots with his Winchester. Each hits its mark.

Following the shootout, Ringo returns to an anxious Dallas. As they embrace and talk about their future, Sheriff Wilcox and Doc Boone pull up in a buckboard to take Ringo away to jail. The lawman asks Dallas if she would like to ride along next to Ringo for a bit. A long camera shot shows the couple sitting side by side in the wagon, its white wheels shimmering in the dark, with a team of two beautiful painted horses in front. Suddenly, the sheriff throws a rock at the horses as he and Doc yell to chase them away. As the buckboard lunges forward, Doc says sarcastically, "Well, they're saved from the blessings of civilization."

Audiences felt good about the upbeat ending. As Ringo and Dallas ride off into the sunset, the words "The End" flash on the screen, but everyone knows this is really the beginning, because the young couple has earned redemption in the mythic West through hard work, determination, and traditional American values. Very likely, many members of the Depression audience could identify with the couple's victory against overwhelming odds, as well as the sheriff's decision to let Ringo go free. After all, Americans during the thirties were fighting desperately for survival against economic and political forces beyond their control. They or their relatives and friends were struggling to make ends meet as heartless bankers foreclosed on mortgages and callous creditors seized assets. Given the hard times and the many innocent victims of the Depression, moviegoers could understand why a good sheriff like Curley Wilcox would bend the law for the sake of fairness and true justice.

Stagecoach was an allegory for the times. The passengers' journey across the hazardous frontier became a metaphor for the Depression itself, while the overland stage represented the means by which individuals could work together to reach safety on the other side. John Ford's movie offered hope that all threats could be overcome, whether they came from corrupt bankers, effete snobs, and hostile enemies, or were the result of impersonal economic and social forces. The film made it clear that Americans could triumph, but only if they remained determined, hardworking, and true to their values, just like pioneers in the mythic West.

Stagecoach was not the only western to take aim at issues that concerned Americans in the thirties and forties. Some films set in the West reflected attitudes toward success in Depression-era America. *Ruggles of Red Gap* (1935) reinforced the notion of America as a land of opportunity, while *The Grapes of Wrath* (1940) offered a bleaker assessment. Numerous movies explored the changing roles of women. Throughout the Depression and war years, President Roosevelt supported greater opportunities for women through political appointments and programs that provided direct assistance. Eleanor Roosevelt also worked energetically for women's rights, writing a daily newspaper column, holding press conferences limited to female journalists, and promoting day-care centers and other issues of interest to women. During the Depression, the percentage of women in the workforce actually grew slightly, and labor shortages during World War II created even more opportunities for women to land jobs outside the home and to play leadership roles on the home front.

Reflecting the changing times, westerns often depicted independent frontier women. Following the lead of *Cimarron* (1931), which showcased Irene Dunne as a determined and talented woman who runs a newspaper and gets elected to Congress, westerns began featuring strong female lead characters. *Belle Starr* (1941) starred Gene Tierney as the Bandit Queen, who was the equal of any man with a six-shooter. Barbara Stanwyck played intelligent, liberated women in numerous westerns, including *Annie Oakley* (1935) and *The Great Man's Lady* (1942). Stanwyck's heroines "exercised personal agency, even to the point of giving up a man or life itself," suggests historian Glenda Riley. They "often experienced redemption, heretofore reserved for western male heroes," and they "exhibited strength of mind, character, and will."[15]

Loretta Young also portrayed liberated western women. *The Lady from Cheyenne* (1941) featured Young as a shrewd Quaker schoolmarm who aids the rise of women's suffrage in Wyoming. *Along Came Jones* (1945) starred Young as an independent woman who was as fast with a gun as she was with her wits. The film begins with Melody Jones (Gary Cooper), a bungling cowboy who can't shoot straight, riding into town. The initials "M. J." carved on his saddle cause people to mistake him for the notorious outlaw Monte Jarrad (Dan Duryea). Jarrad's girl, Cherry de Longpre (Loretta Young), helps perpetuate the misunderstanding so the posse will pursue Melody instead of her lover, but Jones refuses to go along with the ruse, because he falls in love with Cherry.

A showdown occurs when the evil Monte returns to get rid of Melody. Just when the outlaw is going to kill the helpless Jones, along comes Cherry, who has fallen for Melody. The female sharpshooter fires her rifle and grazes Jarrad in the head. Initially, Jones thinks his friend shot the outlaw, because he can't imagine a "girl" making such a fabulous shot. Cherry points out, "It ain't no disgrace to be saved by a woman." Still, Melody refuses to believe her. The indignant Cherry calls Jones a "butter-fingered gun juggler." To prove her point, she pulls out a six-gun and does some fancy shooting near his head, even firing a bullet through the crown of his hat. When the startled but convinced Melody rushes up to kiss her, she melts in his arms and says demurely, "My goodness, you don't have to be so rough about it."

Even though the movie ends with the courageous and talented Cherry feigning submissiveness to a clearly inferior man, the movie's feminist message wasn't lost on viewers. The film made it clear that the soon-to-be "Mrs. Jones" was smarter and more skilled than Mr. Jones. Even the title—*Along Came Jones*—which alluded to the "man-saves-woman" cliché found in melodramas, was an ironic reminder that in this case, the woman saved the man.

While *Along Came Jones* was spotlighting changing roles of women, *The Ox-Bow Incident* (1943) addressed questions involving race, ethnicity, law and order, civil liberties, and the responsibilities of citizens in a democracy. At a time when lynchings of blacks in the South were in the headlines, fears about totalitarianism abounded, and fairness issues permeated all levels of a society wracked by Depression and war, William Wellman's film version of Walter Van Tilburg Clark's novel offered moviegoers a shocking civics lesson. Filmed in black and white on a stark if not surrealistic set, the bleak movie dealt with vigilante justice and mob violence. Henry Fonda stars as a reluctant participant in the posse's chilling rush to judgment, which results in the hangings of three innocent men.

As *The Ox-Bow Incident* unfolds, issues of ethnicity and race come into play. In an attempt to clear himself by placing the blame on another prisoner who is Hispanic, one of the accused blurts out, "The Mexican did it!" Ironically, a black preacher named Sparks, whose younger brother was lynched by a mob, is a member of the posse. Sparks prays for the accused and tries to convince the vigilantes not to hang them. "His most important moment comes, however, when the mob votes on whether or not to hang the men," explains film historian R. Philip Loy. When one of the vigilantes asks all those who are opposed to the hanging to step to one side, Sparks is the first to move. "He clearly is the conscience of the mob," notes Loy, "a remarkable role for a black man in 1943."[16]

The three accused men go to their deaths insisting they are innocent. Shortly thereafter, the sheriff arrives with evidence that proves the three had committed no crimes. Henry Fonda then reads a farewell letter that one of the victims had written for his widow: "My Dear Wife, Mr. Davies will tell you what's happening here tonight. He's a good man and has done everything he can for me. I suppose there are some other good men here, too, only they don't seem to realize what they're doing. They're the ones I feel sorry for 'cause it'll be over for me in a little while, but they'll have to go on remembering for the rest of their lives. A man just naturally can't take the law into his own hands and hang people. . . . [The Law is] everything people ever have found out about justice and what's right and wrong. It's the very conscience of humanity. There can't be any such thing as civilization unless people have a conscience, because if people touch God anywhere, where is it except through their conscience? And what is anybody's conscience except a little piece of the conscience of all men that ever lived? I guess that's all I've got to say except kiss the babies for me and God bless you. Your husband, Donald."

Not surprisingly, the dark western received a mixed reception. The film was "lofty in its purpose, stark in its realism and slashing in its savagery," noted a perceptive critic in *Life* magazine, "but it is likely that these very distinctions will make it unpopular." Audiences, accustomed to escapist fare and patriotic films during World War II, stayed away from theaters in droves. Though it flopped at the box office, *The Ox-Bow Incident* earned an Oscar nomination for Best Picture of 1943, but lost out to a film that was a better fit for the times, *Casablanca*.[17]

Westerns focused on other topics and issues that concerned Americans during the thirties and forties. With bombastic fascist leaders on the rise in Europe, and populist firebrands such as Huey Long and Father Charles Coughlin stirring up trouble at home, western films took potshots at demagogues of the Old West. *The Westerner* (1940), starring Gary Cooper as Cole Harden and Walter Brennan as Judge Roy Bean, focuses on a charismatic populist judge who turns out to be a megalomaniac. *Dark Command* (1940) stars John Wayne as a marshal who opposes the histrionics of an alleged patriot named Will Cantrell, patterned after the Civil War–era demagogue William Quantrill. *Santa Fe Trail* (1940) features Errol Flynn and Ronald Reagan as U.S. Cavalry officers Jeb Stuart and George Armstrong Custer, who are ordered to stop the homicidal John Brown as he uses fiery rhetoric and violence to undermine American democracy. At the end of the film, with Brown on the gallows and the "Battle Hymn of the Republic" playing in the background, Robert E. Lee, still a U.S. Army officer, says patriotically: "So perish all such enemies of the union, all such foes of the human race."

In the lead-up to World War II, westerns alluded to national concerns about policies and preparedness. Two Errol Flynn movies suggested that corruption could undermine American interests: *Virginia City* (1940) portrayed an unpatriotic villain who smuggled gold to the Confederacy during the Civil War; *They Died with Their Boots On* (1941) blamed war profiteers for the defeat of Custer and the 7th U.S. Cavalry. A James Stewart film released in 1939, *Destry Rides Again*, reflected the national debate over the best way for the United States to respond to fascist aggression abroad and provided insights about dealing with evil on the eve of world war.

Destry Rides Again features Stewart as Deputy Sheriff Tom Destry, a pacifist who believes that reason is the best solution to problems. The lawman even refuses to wear a gun, because he believes it won't stop violence and might even provoke it. Destry was the personification of the independent internationalist if not isolationist forces in the nation that supported the Neutrality Acts and opposed President Roosevelt's interventionist position prior to World War II. Whereas the president believed that the best way to stop aggression was through military preparedness and assistance to those who needed it, independent internationalists warned that such actions might provoke the very war with Nazi Germany that the nation was seeking to avoid. The United States, they insisted, should not go to war unless attacked first.

The movie points out the flaws in the independent internationalist approach. At first, Destry tries to coexist with the bad guys. He tries to reason with them. He appeases them when they make demands, and he won't fight when they make fun of him. Not only will he not carry a gun, but he refuses to take up arms to defend innocent homesteaders when their lands are invaded by the bad guys. His pacifist and rational approach to violence is eventually a total failure. Destry's friend and boss, Sheriff Dimsdale, winds up dead after he is shot in the back by the bad guys. Only then—after the enemy attacks—does Destry grab his guns and lead an all-out effort to defeat the dastardly villains.

No doubt, many moviegoers viewed *Destry Rides Again* as simply an offbeat western, perhaps even a light musical comedy that joked about a pacifist deputy sheriff who refused to wear a gun and ordered milk at the bar instead of whiskey. But those in the audience who followed news headlines were more apt to pick up on the movie's serious moments. They might have noticed that Frenchy—the foreign-sounding saloon girl played by Marlene Dietrich—initially collaborated with the mustachioed villain, or that one of Destry's allies was a bumbling Russian named Boris (Mischa Auer), who feared imprisonment in the "salt mines" and needed direction to stand up to the bad guys. Very likely, they understood the film's main message: one cannot reason with evil people—whether they are bad guys in the Old West or fascist dictators in the modern world—because they cannot be trusted and will shoot you in the back every time. Like Destry, Americans eventually would have to grab their guns and fight.

Not all westerns took a serious approach to the era's problems. Some were simply escapist fare, following the lead of popular Hollywood musicals and screwball comedies, which used pure fantasy to help Americans forget their troubles during the Depression and war years. There were western comedies, such as Jack Benny's *Buck Benny Rides Again* (1940) and Abbott and Costello's *Ride 'Em Cowboy* (1942), as well as numerous musical westerns, including Bing Crosby's *Rhythm on the Range* (1936) and Nelson Eddy and Jeanette MacDonald's *Rose-Marie* (1936), which showcased what would become the duo's signature song, "Indian Love Call."

* * *

Regardless of whether feature westerns were traditional or nontraditional in their subject and approach, they all had tremendous appeal for Americans experiencing the Great Depression and World War II. They offered comforting and familiar images of the mythic West, which reminded audiences about the nation's unique heritage and destiny. Westerns showed that Americans had always defeated desperadoes and other dastardly foes in the past, and suggested that the future would be no different. Americans could overcome the Great Depression and triumph over the Axis powers as long as they remained true to the heroic actions and traditional values that had won the West. That message would also echo across the wide open spaces throughout the West portrayed in the low-budget films of Hopalong Cassidy, Gene Autry, Roy Rogers, and other B-Western stars in the thirties and forties.

CHAPTER FOUR

Tumbling Tumbleweeds

Guns, Guitars, and B-Western Cowboys

Audiences knew from the moment *Tumbling Tumbleweeds* began that this was no ordinary B-Western. Most moviegoers were accustomed to the shootouts and fistfights found in the action-packed films of Tom Mix and Ken Maynard. They had even heard a few cowboy songs in early B-Western talkies such as John Wayne's *Riders of Destiny* (1933) or Maynard's *The Fiddlin' Buckaroo* (1933). But audiences had never experienced anything quite like *Tumbling Tumbleweeds*. The 1935 movie had an unusual sound, style, and story line. Its mystical theme song was at once familiar and new. The film's star—a newcomer named Gene Autry—had had a hit record the previous February singing "Tumbling Tumbleweeds." The powerful instrumental version used to open the movie immediately evoked the mythic West, casting a sonic spotlight on opening credits superimposed on images of tumbleweeds and cacti. The song continued its relentless march as cowboys and covered wagons appeared on the screen. An opening crawl provided context that resonated with Depression-era audiences: "In the old West, there was no law. Men came, saw good land and took what they wanted—the stronger divided empires. Later arrivals asked only for water and a plot of ground where they might live in peace. These were the Nesters. And the great land lords hated them. From this hatred came bitter range warfare." Then, the music ended and the story began—not with a bang, but with lots of gunshots, explosions, and galloping horses, creating a collage of violence between farmers and cattlemen.

Tumbling Tumbleweeds was more important than audiences could have imagined when they first saw it back in 1935. Not only did it mark

Figure 13. Gene Autry holds a guitar instead of a gun on this movie poster for *Tumbling Tumbleweeds* (Republic Pictures, 1935).

Autry's first feature film, but it helped create a new subgenre of western movies—musical westerns that featured singing cowboys. Cowboy picture fans were witnessing a major turning point in the history of B-Westerns. From that point on, low-budget cowboy movies would usually follow one of two paths. Some were traditional action westerns that starred rugged movie cowboys such as Buck Jones or Ken Maynard. Others were innovative cowboy musicals that featured Gene Autry, Roy Rogers, or other singing cowboys. Whether B-Western heroes used guns or guitars, they drifted across America's cultural landscape like tumbleweeds, offering glimpses of American life in the thirties, forties, and beyond.

Riding the B-Western Trail

Hollywood cranked out approximately two thousand B-Westerns between 1930 and the mid-1950s. Unlike major feature films, which typically had budgets over one million dollars, B-Westerns usually cost just a few thousand dollars and were shot in seven days or less. "The B Western formula plots romanticized and glorified the American West, depicting the struggle between a hero and his sidekick and villains who stole cattle, lands, and gold mines or who tried to take over valleys, towns, banks, and watering holes," explains historian Ray White. "The heroes always triumphed over the villains and departed the screen ready for action the following week."[1]

By the early thirties, almost every Hollywood studio had a western movie production unit. Production values varied greatly depending on budget. The major studios—Columbia, Fox, MGM, Paramount, RKO, United Artists, Universal, and Warner Brothers—had better resources and more technical know-how, which enabled them to produce some of the finest B-Westerns of the era. Independents such as Republic, Monogram, PRC, and many of the smaller shoestring operations located in the Poverty Row section of Hollywood, had to make to do with less. Yet, even they often produced some top-notch films.

B-Westerns were featured at Saturday matinees or evening shows in theaters across the country. The films were geared mostly to adolescent males but were never just for kids. Many older viewers flocked to B-Westerns because they found the antiurban subtext of the films appealing. Others identified with the movies' common-man heroes and working-class messages. Still others loved the action and stories set in the West. B-Western fans were often partial to a particular cowboy star. Some favored the rugged Buck Jones. Others loved to see Ken Maynard doing daredevil stunts. Still others preferred the songs and humor found in the films of Gene Autry or Roy Rogers or the look and style of some other movie cowboy.[2]

The coming of television in the late forties and early fifties was a double-edged sword for B-Westerns. On the plus side, a whole new generation of fans was introduced to movie cowboys through reruns of old B-Westerns on Saturday morning television, but the ubiquity of cowboys on TV eventually undercut the market for low-budget westerns in movie theaters, so production dropped off. Most fans found it easier and cheaper to watch cowboy pictures at home than at local cinemas. Higher costs and the production shift from movie westerns to TV westerns in the fifties also contributed to the demise of B-Westerns. Some experts insist that the last B-Western was *Two Guns and a Badge* (1954), which starred Wayne Morris and Beverly Garland. Others point out that independent studios produced low-budget westerns throughout the rest of the decade. Film historian Ray White explains that these cheap westerns of the late fifties, though not B-Westerns in the strictest sense of the term, shared the same shoestring budgets and low production values as earlier series westerns. They were sold to drive-ins and small town theaters to fill twin bills.[3]

B-Western Action Pictures

B-Western action pictures of the thirties and forties followed the same basic formula popularized by silent cowboy pictures of the early twentieth century—lots of gunfights, fistfights, chases, and other action featuring cowboys galloping across the rugged western countryside. The only real difference was the addition of sound. The first B-Western "talkie" was *Overland Bound* (1929), directed by and starring Leo D. Maloney. Had fate not intervened, Maloney might have become the first successful cowboy star of the sound era. Instead, he died of a heart attack shortly after the film's release. The commercial success of *Overland Bound* encouraged others to try their hand at sound westerns. Not surprisingly, the first generation of sound cowboys came out of silent films. Within a short time, audiences could hear Tom Mix and other popular silent movie cowpokes galloping across the silver screen.[4]

Tom Mix was retired from movies when he got a lucrative offer from Carl Laemmle's Universal Pictures in 1932 to make a series of talking western pictures. Both Mix and Universal were confident that Tom could recapture the magic that had made him the most popular movie cowboy of the twenties. Back then, audiences couldn't get enough of Mix's style and action-packed films. He dressed in flamboyant western garb. The crowning touch was a magnificent cowboy hat with a five-inch brim and seven-inch crown. The oversized hat became so identifiable that the Stetson Company began producing a Tom Mix signature model in 1925, which came to be known as the ten-gallon hat. The Tom Mix look soon could be seen everywhere, not just on other celluloid cowboys but also on young fans, country musicians, rodeo riders, and even working cowboys. Mix rode like the wind on his smart and speedy horse, Tony; he whipped off one daredevil stunt after another, completing each dangerous maneuver with the grace of an acrobat; and he created a memorable persona as the silver screen's first western superhero—a clean-cut, virtuous all-American boy who always triumphed over villains and varmints.[5]

Mix's nine sound westerns for Universal in 1932 and 1933 would follow the same formula for success as his earlier silents, but this time around, fans would get to hear their hero talk. His 1932 comeback film, *Destry Rides Again* (not to be confused with James Stewart's 1939 movie of the same name), was based loosely on a Max Brand novel and featured enough action to lure fans back to the theater for eight subsequent movies. Despite moderately good reviews, Tom Mix's comeback fell short. "The only trouble with [Mix's] voice was that it was a 50-year-old voice," explains B-Western expert Don Miller. "Tom Mix was no longer a young man."[6] Though Mix never made it back to the top as a movie cowboy, his legacy lived on. Tom Mix's showmanship, action sequences, and sartorial splendor would influence a new generation of cowboy stars in the thirties, forties, and beyond.

Other movie cowboys from the silent era had an easier time making the transition to sound westerns because they were a generation younger than Mix.[7] Movie fans particularly loved Buck Jones, who began his career as a cowboy with the Miller Brothers 101 Ranch and Wild West show. He made his first silent western in 1920 and would appear in sixty more before the decade was out. Buck's films had everything moviegoers craved: believable plots, fast-paced action, thrilling romance, even touches of humor. The thirty-nine-year-old Jones made the transition to sound westerns with well-received movies such as *The Dawn Trail* (1930) and *The Fighting Sheriff* (1931). By mid-decade, his popularity was at an all-time high. Buck looked every inch the rugged cowboy. He had a handsome face, square jaw, and powerful build, and his taste in clothes came in somewhere between the gritty realism of William S. Hart and the more fanciful style of Tom Mix. His only concessions to B-Western conventions were his white cowboy hat, ornate gun and holster, and beautiful white horse, Silver. Buck became the quintessential cowboy hero, who didn't smoke, drink, or swear. He came across as a strong, silent, no-nonsense type, who excelled at fighting, shooting, and riding. His westerns featured believable plots and lots of action, and his eclectic approach attracted a wide range of moviegoers. Youngsters enjoyed the exciting fistfights, loud shootouts, daring stunts, and western humor; older viewers appreciated the action, humor, and romance. At one point, Jones was even getting more fan mail from adults than Clark Gable.[8]

Just when Buck Jones was at the top of his game, his career faltered. His first misstep came in 1937 when he left Universal and signed with Columbia Pictures' Coronet Production Company. The new films suffered from poor scripts and production values. His career continued to decline until 1941, when he signed with Monogram Pictures to costar in the Rough Riders series. Audiences cheered on Buck and the Rough Riders in eight films. Then tragedy struck. On November 28, 1942, Buck Jones was attending a function at the Cocoanut Grove night club in Boston when suddenly the crowded club erupted in flames. Almost five hundred people died, including Jones.[9] Millions of Americans mourned Buck Jones's tragic end, believing they had lost a true hero. For parts of three decades, Buck's adventures on the silver screen had thrilled generations of moviegoers and served as cinematic reminders of the values that made America great.

Ken Maynard was another silent-film cowboy who struck gold with sound westerns. A former trick rider for circuses and Wild West shows, he earned star billing in the twenties with action-packed westerns such as *Señor Daredevil* (1926) and *The Red Raiders* (1927). Six feet tall and strikingly handsome, with wavy black hair and piercing black eyes, Maynard dominated every scene. Taking his fashion cue from Tom Mix, Ken wore ornate cowboy shirts, fancy pants, and pointed-toe boots with jingling spurs. Accessories included an oversized white Stetson and two pearl-handled six-guns ready for action in a leather-tooled holster. Maynard's good looks were enhanced by his graceful, fluid movements. The young cowboy could leap like an acrobat from building to building and mesmerize viewers with daredevil stunts while riding his palomino, Tarzan, at breakneck speed.

The coming of talking motion pictures opened new doors for Maynard. After signing a lucrative contract with Universal Pictures, he began making excellent sound westerns in 1930, such as *Mountain Justice* and *Song of the Caballero*. Not only did the films have strong production values and plenty of action, but they helped establish Maynard's claim as the first singing cowboy. Maynard started singing in his films from the very beginning, as evidenced by westerns like *Sons of the Saddle* (1930). Later on, he added even more songs, accompanying himself on the guitar or fiddle in movies such as *The Fiddlin' Buckaroo* (1933) and *Strawberry Roan* (1933), but audiences weren't impressed by his nasally twang, so the singing was eventually phased out. Despite Maynard's commercial success, the star's relations with his bosses at Universal rapidly deteriorated. "[Maynard] was temperamental and demanding, he wanted things done his way and flew into tantrums when they were not," explains film historian Tony Thomas, "and he was one of those unfortunate men who become frightening when drunk—and Maynard drank heavily." After several cost overruns and numerous profane arguments, the cowboy star and the major movie studio parted ways.[10]

In 1934, Nat Levine and Mascot Pictures decided to take a chance on the unruly Maynard. The initial outing—*In Old Santa Fe*, which starred Ken and introduced a young radio singer named Gene Autry—opened to good reviews. But Levine was soon fed up with the star's drinking and abusive behavior. Instead of using Maynard as originally planned in a 1935 serial entitled *The Phantom Empire*, Levine offered the part to Autry. Maynard's career then went steadily downhill. His drinking worsened, he put on weight, and he was no longer the agile cowboy that moviegoers came to see. From 1935 until 1940, the aging performer cranked out B-Westerns with increasingly bad production values for independent producers and studios on Poverty Row. When job offers dried up, he went on the road as a trick rider with a circus. His career improved briefly in 1943 when Monogram signed him to costar in the Trail Blazers series, but Maynard was let go after only six pictures because of disruptive behavior. After that, Maynard made ends meet by touring with circuses and through personal appearances. By the 1960s he was living in poverty. He died in 1973 after a long illness, still battling alcoholism.[11]

During his heyday, Ken Maynard was pure magic on the silver screen. Tall, dark, and handsome, he rode his beautiful horse with wild abandon, performing astounding stunts with the greatest of ease while shooting six-guns out of the hands of bad guys or lassoing varmints as they tried to escape. He even sang an occasional song, pointing the way for later singing cowboys. The tragedy of Ken Maynard is that even though no hombre could come close to defeating him on screen, off screen he was done in by personal demons.

Another silent film cowboy who made a successful transition to sound westerns was Tim McCoy. After the coming of talkies, McCoy signed with Universal, where he made two western serials in 1930 and 1931. Throughout the rest of the decade and into the early forties, McCoy would make approximately seventy-five feature films and serials, most of which were westerns. The action-packed films would establish him as one of the leading western stars in the country.[12]

McCoy's distinct look and no-nonsense approach distinguished him from other movie cowboys. Arguably, no B-Western cowboy was as quick on the draw as McCoy. Sometimes, just his steely glare was enough to melt the resolve of the most dastardly foe. Unlike most cowboy stars, he dressed plainly, often in black, and didn't have a special horse. What impressed moviegoers most was McCoy's authenticity. The former U.S. Cavalry officer and experienced working cowboy had a deep love of western lore and firsthand knowledge about Indians, which came through loud and clear in movies such as *End of the Trail* (1932). Although McCoy's western star began to fade in the late thirties, when younger heroes and singing cowboys took center stage, he made a comeback in the early forties, when he costarred with Buck Jones and Raymond Hatton in Monogram's Rough Riders series. McCoy's service in World War II all but ended his film career, although he later won an Emmy for a children's TV show about the American West that he hosted for five years on KNX-TV in Los Angeles.[13]

Tim McCoy's legacy includes not only every later cowboy hero who ever dressed in black and was fast on the draw, but also every youngster who learned the difference between right and wrong by watching Tim fight a never-ending battle against bad guys in the Wild West. McCoy remained self-effacing to the very end. A year before his death in 1978, an interviewer asked him about his future plans. The humble movie cowboy smiled and then recalled the punch line of an old vaudeville joke: "I have a bright future behind me."[14]

While Tim McCoy was known for his serious demeanor and lightning-fast draw, another former silent western film star, Hoot Gibson, attracted attention with his winning personality and warm sense of humor. With his common-man image and average build, Gibson seemed more like the guy next door than a glamorous movie cowboy, but he lit up the screen with his comedic style and excellent riding skills. Before he was through, Gibson would appear in more than two hundred westerns, many of which, such as *The Hard Hombre* (1931) or Monogram's Trail Blazers series, featured him as a lovable character who would rather make jokes than fight. The success of his light-hearted approach paved the way for later performers to use comedy in westerns, including James Stewart in *Destry Rides Again* and James Garner in TV's *Maverick*.

One of the veteran silent-film cowboys who appeared alongside Hoot Gibson in the Trail Blazers series was Bob Steele. Although Steele was never as famous as Tom Mix or Ken Maynard, he made a smoother and ultimately more successful transition to talking pictures. Born Robert Adrian Bradbury in 1907, Bob began appearing in movies while still in his early teens. In 1920, his father, movie director Robert North Bradbury, featured Bob and his twin brother in a serial called *The Adventures of Bob and Bill*. By the end of the decade, he was starring as "Bob Steele" in silent westerns such as *The Mojave Kid* (1927) and *The Cowboy and the Outlaw* (1929). Steele was well positioned to make the leap to sound westerns. His fine acting ability, youthful appearance, and scrappy image attracted numerous fans, who loved to watch the five-foot-five cowboy take on taller but less good-looking bad guys in fistfights or gun battles. Steele became one of the most popular B-Western cowboys of the thirties and forties. By the end of World War II, he had appeared in more than 110 films. While most were westerns, he also earned rave reviews for his performances in feature films, such as *Of Mice and Men* (1939). His film career continued into the seventies, with roles in westerns and other movies, as well as parts in TV westerns such as *Gunsmoke*, *Have Gun—Will Travel*, *Maverick*, and *F Troop*.

As the thirties progressed, a new generation of B-Western cowboys rode onto the silver screen. John Wayne became the most successful. Wayne's acting career stalled after he appeared in *The Big Trail* (1930), a big-budget western that flopped at the box office. For the next few years, he bounced around, making low-budget films for Fox, Columbia, Mascot, and Warner Brothers. His luck turned when he signed with Monogram, where his first release, *Riders of Destiny* (1933), established him as a B-Western star. Written and directed by Robert North Bradbury, the film opens with Wayne's character, Singin' Sandy Saunders, riding a white horse and singing as he strums his guitar. Though Wayne was only lip-synching to songs prerecorded by William Bradbury (the director's son), the performance helped pave the way for Gene Autry and other singing cowboys.

The plot in *Riders of Destiny* is nothing special. Like many B-Westerns produced during the Great Depression, it shows good guys coming to the aid of ordinary folks exploited by evil businessmen. In this case, Singin' Sandy is a Secret Service agent dispatched from Washington, DC, to investigate claims that a local businessman, James Kincaid, has used nefarious means to monopolize water rights in the valley. Before he even makes it to town, Saunders rescues a sheriff who has been shot in the back and gallops down a steep hill on his white horse to save a beautiful blond named Fay Denton (Cecilia Parker). When he gets to town, Saunders quickly resolves all the problems at hand. He outshoots Kincaid's hired gunslinger; outsmarts the despicable Kincaid and gets water flowing in all directions; and snuffs out evil once and for all, when he shoots the fleeing Kincaid, who dies appropriately enough when he plunges into a watery grave. Singin' Sandy's heroics even help him get the girl.

Despite the ordinary story line, *Riders of Destiny* was a cut above most B-Westerns. The film helped establish Wayne's persona as a B-Western cowboy known for his unique voice, swagger, and appearance. From the moment he rides onto the screen, he grabs the audience's attention and never lets go. Tall and lean, the strapping young cowboy looks as rugged as he is handsome. Wayne dresses simply in tight jeans, a plain shirt, and a black hat. His dark clothes are complemented by a fancy holster, a pearl-handled six-gun, and a white horse. The supporting cast is impressive. George "Gabby" Hayes, in his first movie with John Wayne, sparkles as Fay Denton's father. Earl Dwire, dressed in black and sporting a tiny mustache, is picture perfect as an evil gunslinger, and stuntman Yakima Canutt is extraordinary. In one scene, he leaps on the backs of a team of

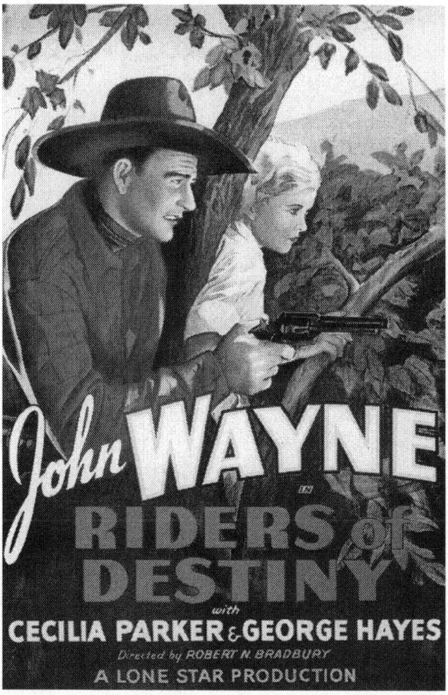

Figure 14. The rugged cowboy hero, John Wayne, protects a woman on this movie poster for *Riders of Destiny* (Monogram Pictures, 1933).

horses and then falls underneath the wagon before pulling himself up to the driver's seat—a dangerous but dramatic trick that he would reprise six years later in John Ford's *Stagecoach*. Sandy's showdown with the gunslinger is also marvelous. As they begin the traditional walk toward each other, Wayne's character suddenly starts to sing. "Why, that's Singin' Sandy, the most notorious gunman since Billy the Kid," says a startled onlooker. The hero draws his gun with lightning speed and shoots both of the gunslinger's wrists, ending the bad guy's career. The conclusion is equally memorable. The sexual tension between Sandy and Fay is finally resolved when the tall cowboy sweeps the petite blond into his arms and kisses her with a breathtaking passion that leaves her helpless. Promising to return, he jumps on his white horse and rides off, waving his hat in a gallant salute.

Riders of Destiny had it all—action, music, romance, humor, and a good-looking cowboy riding in on a white horse to rescue a beautiful damsel and desperate townsfolk. As an added dividend, the Depression-era film, released just as President Roosevelt's New Deal was taking hold, depicted Wayne as a federal government agent sent out West to help ordinary people break the power of an unfair business monopoly.

Throughout the rest of the decade, John Wayne starred in numerous low-budget westerns, even portraying Stony Brooke in Republic Pictures' successful series, the Three Mesquiteers. By the mid-thirties, he was one of the most popular movie cowboys in the country. But then Wayne received an offer that would change his career. John Ford hired him to play the Ringo Kid in a big-budget western that would launch him to superstardom, *Stagecoach* (1939). After Ford's film was released, Republic issued four more John Wayne Mesquiteer movies. The title of the final one—*New Frontier* (1939)—foreshadowed Wayne's future. After 1939, he would never again star in a B-Western. John Wayne was about to conquer a new frontier in feature films. Before he was through, he would become not just a popular movie cowboy, but an American icon.

John Wayne was the only movie cowboy able to make the leap from B-Westerns to big-budget films. However, numerous movie cowboys who arrived on the scene in the thirties and forties made it big by following the traditional B-Western formula. Each had a unique quality that attracted loyal fans. There were former star athletes such as Johnny Mack Brown, Buster Crabbe, and Don "Red" Barry; World War II heroes like Audie Murphy; rodeo performers such as Wild Bill Elliott and Sunset Carson; seasoned actors like William Boyd; and handsome newcomers such as Allan "Rocky" Lane and Tim Holt. Their rise to fame was often aided and abetted by funny sidekicks, such as Max Terhune, Raymond Hatton, Andy Clyde, Fuzzy Knight, and George "Gabby" Hayes. Of all of the cowboy heroes, none would have greater success than William Boyd, who became a film legend playing Hopalong Cassidy.

Boyd made sixty-six Hopalong Cassidy movies between 1935 and 1947. All were loosely based on Clarence E. Mulford's popular Bar 20 novels, which featured a grizzled cowboy named Bill Cassidy. Nicknamed Hopalong because of a limp that resulted from a gunfight, the tough cowpoke was fond of drinking, smoking, and swearing. But Boyd's version of Hoppy was nothing like Mulford's original. The cinematic Cassidy drank only sarsaparilla and never smoked or uttered a profane word. He fought for truth and justice and helped those in need. Boyd's moral character came across as a friendly father figure who could be trusted and counted on for advice and protection. When bad guys crossed him or mistreated others, he would always right the wrong. Hoppy had a tender side, as well.

Figure 15. William Boyd as Hopalong Cassidy. Richard Aquila Collection.

He was easily moved by the plight of others. And his wonderful sense of humor featured a loud, jovial laugh that rolled across the prairie like thunder.

Unlike most B-Western good guys, Cassidy usually dressed in black, which made him stand out even more against his magnificent white horse, Topper. Fans noticed other things about their hero: he frequently wore just one glove so his right hand was always ready for a fast draw; and his spurs jangled loudly when he walked. Even Hoppy's age contributed to his distinct appearance. His white hair underscored the fact that he was older than most cowboy stars, and it added to his image as an authority figure. Hopalong was the cowboy equivalent of Franklin D. Roosevelt. Both were elder statesmen whose leadership qualities, affable personalities, and compassion for ordinary folk attracted devoted followers throughout the thirties and forties.

The Cassidy movies featured excellent character development, interesting plots, innovative filming techniques, and a creative use of music that added to the excitement. The trailer for the initial *Hop-Along Cassidy* (1935) includes a frenetic opening with countless riders, chases, and Hopalong galloping across the plains, while the fast-paced "Dance of the Furies" plays in the background. With breathtaking speed, the promo serves up film clips that show gunfights, fistfights, and other action. It closes with the promise that the film version of Clarence E. Mulford's *Hop-Along Cassidy* is a "Thrill-Spiked Saga of the Real Old West!"[15]

Boyd's Hopalong Cassidy was successful in part because he played off two characters who became regular saddle pals—a young cowboy and a comic sidekick. Not all Hopalong films featured the same young cowboy or comic sidekick, but the approach remained the same. The young cowboy was always impetuous, liked girls, and got into trouble; the older sidekick cracked jokes, frequently looked scared, and got into trouble. Hoppy—positioned between the two—was the experienced leader, the brains of the outfit, and the one who mentored the young cowboy, laughed at the old-timer, and bailed them both out of trouble.

Hopalong Cassidy became a phenomenon, attracting millions of fans of all ages. From the late thirties through the fifties, William Boyd consistently ranked at or near the top of various lists of popular western stars. Boyd had the foresight to purchase the rights to his films, and he later made millions of dollars by recycling them on television in the late forties and early fifties, which paved the way for a new *Hopalong Cassidy* TV show. His tremendous popularity led to endorsements, personal appearances, and innumerable Hopalong Cassidy products, including gun and holster sets, cowboy hats, clothing, boots, clocks, radios, mugs, plates, and myriad toys.[16] The opening line to Hoppy's theme song—"Here he comes, here he comes"—proved prophetic as Hoppymania swept across the country. Hoppy became a role model who taught generations of young people the difference between right and wrong. He also became a pop culture icon, who personified the spirit of the Old West and America itself.

The success of the Hopalong Cassidy films, which resulted in part from the entertaining and exciting interaction between Hoppy and his two sidekicks, contributed to the rise of what came to be known as *trigger trios*. Republic Pictures jumped in first with *The Three Mesquiteers* (1936), based on characters from William Colt MacDonald's western novels, which were inspired by Alexandre Dumas's *The Three Musketeers*. Between 1936 and 1943, Republic cranked out fifty-one films featuring nine different Mesquiteer trios, although in most cases the movies retained MacDonald's original characters: Tucson Smith, Stony Brooke, and Lullaby Joslin. The initial outing starred Ray Corrigan as tough Tucson Smith, Bob

Livingston as the good-looking Stony Brooke, and Syd Saylor as the comic sidekick, Lullaby Joslin. The sequel—*Ghost Town Gold* (1936)—had Max Terhune replacing Saylor. That trio remained intact for the next thirteen films and became the most popular Mesquiteer team. Subsequent films in the series included replacements such as John Wayne (as Stony Brooke) and Duncan Renaldo (his Rico Rinaldo briefly replaced Tucson Smith; Renaldo later gained fame as TV's Cisco Kid).

The Three Mesquiteers' success inspired other movie studios to develop trigger trio series. Monogram produced three series westerns: the Range Busters (1940–43); the Rough Riders (1941–42); and the Trail Blazers (1943–44). PRC Pictures got in on the action with two trigger trio series, the Texas Rangers (1942–45) and the Frontier Marshals (1942).

Studios came up with other ideas to make films stand out in a crowded field. Some B-Westerns featured masked heroes, including The Lone Ranger (played first in the movies by Lee Powell in 1938, followed by Bob Livingston in 1939); Zorro (played by Douglas Fairbanks in the 1920s, then by Bob Livingston and Reed Hadley in the 1930s and Tyrone Power in 1940); the Durango Kid (Charles Starrett); the Phantom Rancher (Ken Maynard); and the Masked Phantom (Monte Rawlins). Other films starred good guys who used whips (Lash LaRue and Whip Wilson), or they showcased offbeat heroes such as the Cisco Kid and Red Ryder. In addition, there were all-black westerns such as *Harlem on the Prairie* (1937) and *The Bronze Buckaroo* (1939). One B-Western, *The Terror of Tiny Town* (1938), featured an "All-Midget Cast," Shetland ponies, and small-scale furniture. Film studios also showcased cowboys with pedigrees, such as Kermit Maynard (brother of Ken) and Tim Holt (son of western star Jack Holt). They starred actors who used famous names, for example, Buffalo Bill Jr., Buddy Roosevelt, Bill Cody, and Bob Custer. Or they enlisted the help of celebrities: baseball star Lou Gehrig played a rancher in the 1938 film *Rawhide*, while football legend Sammy Baugh starred in the 1941 Republic serial *King of the Texas Rangers*. But the most successful innovation of them all was the musical western, which featured a brand new type of B-Western buckaroo—the singing cowboy.

Singing Cowboys

Tumbling Tumbleweeds altered the B-Western landscape forever. Gene Autry's 1935 film touched off a singing cowboy craze. Approximately half of the B-Westerns made between 1935 and 1954 were musical westerns.

B-Western authority Douglas B. Green (aka Ranger Doug of the country and western group Riders in the Sky) points out that these films "featured a singer as a hero, or had singing leads, or singing ranch hands to provide that dreamy, romantic, exquisitely beautiful music we now think of as western." A less sympathetic observer summed up the genre this way: "Them bandits have beaten my mother, ravished my girl, burned down my house, killed my cattle and blinded my best friend. I'm goin' to get 'em if it's the last thing I do. But first, folks, I'm going to sing you a little song."[17]

The use of music in westerns dates back to the silent-film era, when musical scores regularly made use of western-style songs for mood and effect. The first talking western, *In Old Arizona* (1929), furthered the tradition when Warner Baxter's Cisco Kid strummed on the guitar while singing "My Tonia" to his treacherous girlfriend. That performance inspired other movie cowboys to try their hand at singing. Ken Maynard sang in several westerns of the early thirties. Johnny Mack Brown and others contributed songs to *Montana Moon* (1930). Bob Steele got in on the action when he sang in *The Oklahoma Cyclone* (1930). And in *Riders of Destiny* (1933), John Wayne lip-synched to songs prerecorded by Steele's twin brother, William Bradbury. Despite those early attempts, musical westerns did not take hold until Autry arrived on the scene.

Gene Autry began his career as a singer on a Tulsa radio station. After one of his records, "That Silver Haired Daddy of Mine," became a regional hit in 1931, he became a regular on *The National Barn Dance*, a popular country and western show broadcast over Chicago's WLS radio. By 1933, Autry's producer at the American Record Corporation (ARC), Art Satherley, and WLS announcer Ann Williams convinced the singer that he could become even more popular if he focused on western music. So Gene started singing cowboy songs and wearing western costumes on stage, while WLS promoted him as "Oklahoma's Singing Cowboy."[18]

Autry's career was powered by continued exposure on radio, concert tours, and numerous hit records. Convinced that Gene had the potential to become a major star, Art Satherley convinced his boss at ARC, Herbert J. Yates, to set up a meeting between Gene and Yates's friend Nat Levine (the owner of Mascot Pictures). Levine offered Autry a small singing part in Ken Maynard's *In Old Santa Fe* (1934). Though Maynard was the star, Gene's performance attracted the attention of theater operators and moviegoers.[19]

Recognizing a good thing when he saw it, Levine starred Autry in Mascot's next scheduled serial, a strange sci-fi/western hybrid entitled *The Phantom Empire* (1935). The quirky serial's absurd blend of cowboys and aliens, music and action, horses and airplanes, and science fiction and the American West was so bad it was almost good. Good enough at least for Levine to sign Autry to do some full-length B-Westerns. As fate would have it, several weeks later Mascot Pictures was absorbed by a new film company, Republic Pictures, whose owner was none other than Autry's boss at ARC, Herbert J. Yates. Realizing that both Autry and Republic would profit tremendously if the singing cowboy could become a star in two entertainment fields—movies and records—Yates quickly moved forward with Levine's plan to star Gene in a full-length B-Western.[20]

Tumbling Tumbleweeds arrived in movie theaters in the autumn of 1935. The first glimpse of Autry on screen gave audiences pause. Following action scenes of a range war, the camera cuts to young Gene sitting comfortably in a ranch house, strumming his guitar and singing softly, "I'll yodel my troubles away." His father, a rugged rancher and owner of a large spread, is none too pleased that his musician son refused to take part in the battle. So, he banishes the lad, who picks up his guitar and rides off. Five years later, Gene returns home as a successful radio singer and performer in a traveling medicine show. Autry soon learns that the ranchers and farmers are still fighting, and one of his old nester friends has been framed for killing Gene's father. The rest of the movie follows Autry as he sets out to prove that the real killer is an evil rancher who is trying to grab all the land and water rights in the region. To say that Gene Autry rises to the occasion is an understatement. En route to solving the murder of his father and making peace between the nesters and cattlemen, Gene manages to sing several songs and puts his guitar down long enough to win some fistfights and woo a beautiful young woman.

Tumbling Tumbleweeds made Autry a B-Western star and put Republic Pictures on the movie map. It also helped establish singing cowboys as a distinct western movie category. In some ways, Gene was simply continuing traditions established by earlier celluloid cowboys such as Tom Mix: he rode a beautiful horse and wore fancy duds, including a white hat, ornate boots, and snappy cowboy shirts with elaborate piping. But unlike previous cowboy stars, Autry was as good with a guitar as he was with his guns and fists. *Tumbling Tumbleweeds* demonstrated that the movie industry and music business could profit by working together. Not only would hit records help sell movie tickets, but successful movies could help make hit records.

Despite the film's unique qualities, *Tumbling Tumbleweeds* still fit squarely in the realm of B-Westerns. Produced for approximately $12,500 (at a time when feature films often cost over $1,000,000), the low-budget film relied on the same basic formula and props as other B-Westerns. While *Tumbling Tumbleweeds'* musical component was more extensive than those of previous westerns, the music did not alter the film's basic approach to the mythic West. The good guys still wore white hats, rode horses, and shot it out with varmints. The only difference was that every once in a while, they took a break in the action to sing a cowboy song. Somehow, for B-Western fans, it all seemed to fit.[21]

Gene Autry went on to become one of the most popular movie cowboys of all time. Straddling the Old West and modern America, his updated cowboy hero revitalized the B-Western formula. His easygoing manner helped calm Americans during dark days of economic depression and world war. The affable young man came across as nonthreatening. The fact that he was neither a great actor nor great singer underscored his authenticity, as did his tendency to use his own name in movies. Unlike most movie cowboys who played fictional characters, Autry usually just played himself, further blurring the distinction between reality and fantasy.

Moviegoers of all ages flocked to theaters, confident that Gene's films would always deliver excellent stories, solid production values, good acting, enjoyable music, and entertaining comedy. To a large extent, Gene represented a nostalgic vision of America. In typical B-Western fashion, he wore a white hat, dressed in fancy western garb, and was fast on the draw, a crack shot, and a good fighter. He even had a smart horse named Champion. Gene personified the American character as he promoted individualism, fairness, honesty, and, of course, liberty and justice for all. Eventually, he codified those values into a Cowboy Code for youngsters, which was basically a B-Western equivalent of the Ten Commandments.[22]

Even though Autry represented continuity with earlier B-Westerns, he also offered a fresh approach. He became the big screen's first movie cowboy who was successful because of his singing. Gene's heartfelt music resonated during the Depression. Many listeners simply liked his voice or the simple melodies and harmonies. Others might have been attracted by something deeper. Autry insisted that his music was the sound of "America's true pioneers."[23] He helped transform "hillbilly music" into modern country and western. He broadened the music's base by offering a slick blend of pop, country, and folk. His polished vocals, pop-sounding melodies, and western garb gave the music a glitzy new shine, while down-home lyrics and western instrumentation retained an authentic feel that reminded listeners that the heart of this music was still pure folk. Before long, Autry's influence could be seen all over the pop charts, even influencing pop hits such as Bing Crosby's "I'm an Old Cowhand" (1936).

Autry's films refined the B-Western practice of mixing disparate elements from different periods into one seamless time-warped western. Although earlier movie cowboys such as Ken Maynard and Hoot Gibson occasionally crossed paths with cars and other modern devices, Gene made it commonplace. Many of Autry's westerns were prototypes for postmodernism. They featured—sometimes even in the same scene—stagecoaches and automobiles, rocket ships and horses, smoke signals and telephones, or Indian attacks and television transmissions. In retrospect, one cannot help but ask, what the heck was going on there? What possessed Autry and other film makers to combine elements from the Old West with modern times? And why were audiences so willing to accept B-Westerns that jumped back and forth between different periods? From the film studio's perspective, the modern trappings offered audiences a fresh approach to an old subject. As early as 1929, an editorial in *Photoplay* insisted that westerns had to change if they wanted to be relevant in modern America. "[Charles] Lindbergh has put the cowboy into the discard as a type of national hero," opined the writer, "Tom Mix, Hoot Gibson and Ken Maynard must swap horses for aeroplanes or go to the old actors' home." Placing Gene in a contemporary setting updated the genre, opening up all sorts of new ideas for scripts, which included everything from modern crooks and evil Nazis to high-tech cars and machine guns. Of course, there was also a practical reason for placing Gene in a modern setting. Republic Pictures wanted to take full advantage of Autry's reputation as a radio performer and singer, so they decided to have Autry play himself in most films. Since Autry could not exist in two different periods at once, the films had to have a contemporary setting.[24]

Most moviegoers apparently had no problem with the innovative approach. After all, Autry's films were set in the thirties and forties, so why not include cars, airplanes, telephones, radio, and other modern trappings? Perhaps the blend of the Old West and modern times resonated with audiences who were at once nostalgic for the past but acutely aware of rapid cultural and technological change. Or maybe the approach worked because it reminded viewers about American exceptionalism, demonstrating that traditional values and the frontier experience could still solve problems in contemporary America.[25]

Autry movies reflected modern times in other ways. They picked up on social change involving minorities. Although older stereotypes of Native Americans, African Americans, Hispanics, and other minorities abound in Autry movies, more positive images began appearing with greater frequency as the thirties progressed into the forties. Autry westerns also promoted the era's "new woman," not just by depicting females in new ways but also by employing women script writers. Heroines in Autry movies were usually smart and confident: they ran businesses; made decisions; even made their own mistakes. For good or bad, they were independent. These leading ladies "were not just there for decoration or to point out which way the bad guys went," explains Gene in his autobiography. "They gave me a lot of anything-you-can-do-I can-do-better sass. . . . That may have been due, in no small part, to the presence of [female] screenwriters."[26]

Gene's movies dealt with thirties' and forties' issues involving the government, the economy, and the environment. They addressed class warfare, and they focused on crooked politicians, corrupt businessmen, and other threats to the nation. "I did not engage, for the most part, in such mundane activities as saving the old homestead or chasing bank bandits," explained Autry in his autobiography. "While my solutions were a little less complex than those offered by FDR, and my methods a bit more direct, I played a kind of New Deal Cowboy who never hesitated to tackle many of the same problems: the dust bowl, unemployment, or the harnessing of power. This may have contributed to my popularity with the 1930s audiences." Autry's reaction to the coming of World War II underscored his support of the government and country. He stressed patriotism in his films and on his radio show. Over the objections of his movie studio, he even volunteered for the U.S. Army Air Corps at the age of thirty-five and was sworn in during a live broadcast of his radio show. "Every movie cowboy ought to devote time to the Army winning or helping win until the war is won—the same as any other American citizen," insisted Autry.[27]

Autry's success cut across movies, radio, records, music publishing, live performance, and eventually even television. He became the first major motion picture star to try his hand at weekly acting on television when *The Gene Autry Show* debuted on July 23, 1950. The popular show inspired Autry to form Flying A Productions, which produced other TV westerns, such as *The Range Rider* and *Annie Oakley*. Autry's myriad accomplishments were recognized when he became the only entertainer in history to receive five stars on the Hollywood Walk of Fame—one for each of his achievements in movies, radio, recording, live performances, and television. The shrewd businessman amassed a fortune through investments in oil, ranches, hotels, and other enterprises, and by the nineties he regularly appeared on *Fortune* magazine's list of the wealthiest Americans. "Autry used to ride off into the sunset, now he owns it," quipped movie sidekick Pat Buttram. Gene became one of the country's top philanthropists, contributing millions to various charities and establishing the Autry Museum of Western Heritage in Los Angeles. Autry's last major pop culture venture came in 1961, when he launched one of professional baseball's first expansion teams, the Los Angeles Angels.[28]

Despite his many achievements in entertainment, business, philanthropy, sports, and other fields, Gene Autry will always be remembered foremost as the genial singing cowboy who galloped into the American imagination astride his beautiful horse, Champion. Perhaps the brief inscription at the top of the bronze plaque on Gene Autry's grave in Forest Lawn Cemetery in Los Angeles describes him best—"America's Favorite Cowboy."

* * *

Gene Autry's phenomenal success inspired rival studios to introduce their own crooning cowboys and singing cowgirls.[29] Although each had his or her own fan base, one in particular emerged as a potential rival for Autry—Tex Ritter. Born in Texas in 1905, Ritter grew up listening to western music. By 1928, he had a weekly program singing authentic cowboy songs on a Houston radio station. His big break came in the early thirties when he landed a part on Broadway in *Green Grow the Lilacs* (which later became the musical *Oklahoma*). His authentic Texas drawl, pleasing personality, and strong singing voice impressed theatergoers and led to numerous other bookings. Tex's growing reputation attracted the attention of ARC's Art Satherley, who had helped spearhead Autry's recording career, and Ed Finney, an independent producer eager to sign a singing cowboy to make movies for Grand National Films, a small Poverty Row movie studio. Ritter signed deals with both and headed for Hollywood.[30]

Tex made his movie debut in *Song of the Gringo* (1936) and over the next two years starred in eleven more Grand National westerns. Ritter's cowboy persona resonated with B-Western fans, who liked his down-home personality. He came across on screen as fast on the draw, good with his fists, and expert in the saddle (few viewers knew that his stunts were actually performed by Yakima Canutt). Ritter seemed like an authentic Texas cowboy. Even his songs had more of a folk quality than Autry's pop-sounding ditties. Depression-era audiences watching *Trouble in Texas* (1937), for instance, could relate to Ritter's deep, expressive voice and plaintive sound on traditional ballads such as "The Cowboy's Lament." Plus, Ritter's songs usually fit into the story line, whereas Autry would sometimes burst into song for no apparent reason.

Between 1936 and 1945, Tex Ritter appeared in more than sixty motion pictures for Grand National, Monogram, Columbia, Universal, and PRC.

Figure 16. From the left, Yakima Canutt, Rita Cansino (aka Rita Hayworth), and Tex Ritter from *Trouble in Texas* (Grand National Pictures, 1937).

He closed out his movie cowboy career by costarring in PRC's Texas Rangers trigger trio series. Moviegoers during the Great Depression and World War II identified with Ritter's working-class cowboy: they shared his traditional values; they admired his courage and skills; they enjoyed the honest music and light-hearted comedy; and they applauded Ritter's patriotism, often demonstrated by his character's willingness to work with the government to counter corruption and defeat bad guys and cheats. Toward the end of his career, Tex concentrated almost exclusively on singing and performing on TV, although he did make occasional movie appearances. In 1952, he wound up back in the national spotlight when he recorded the theme song for *High Noon*, which won an Oscar for Best Song. In 1965, he became a regular on the *Grand Old Opry* and four years later was inducted into the Country Music Hall of Fame. Tex Ritter died from a heart attack in 1974, leaving a legacy as a successful B-Western star, recording artist, and performer on radio, TV, and stage.

One of Tex's last triumphs on the national stage came decades after his initial successes as a B-Western movie cowboy. In 1961, Ritter earned a top twenty hit record with "I Dreamed of a Hillbilly Heaven." The nostalgic song reminded millions of fans about the qualities that helped make Tex one of the most beloved B-Western cowboys of all time: his soft Texas drawl, traditional values, and sincerity, as well as his enthusiasm for the music he loved so much. The song reinforced the public's perception that Ritter was just a regular guy, who could not believe his good fortune. The lyrics explain how Tex dreamed of visiting "hillbilly heaven," where he sees all the greatest stars in the history of country and western music. He asks his heavenly guide who else would be arriving in the next hundred years and is shocked to learn that he would be one of the inductees. "That's when I woke up, and I'm sorry I did," explained the modest singer and B-Western star, "because I dreamed I was there in hillbilly heaven. Oh, what a beautiful sight."[31]

* * *

Ironically, the greatest threat to Gene Autry's status as America's favorite singing cowboy did not come from Tex Ritter or anyone else at a rival movie studio. Instead, the threat rose up from within. The man who would be "King of the Cowboys"—Roy Rogers—began as one of Autry's stablemates at Republic Pictures.

Born Leonard Sly (his family later added an "e" to the last name) in Cincinnati, Ohio, in 1911, Roy first found success with a Los Angeles country and western trio that also included Tim Spencer and Bob Nolan. By 1934, the three young singers were appearing regularly on radio and attracting lots of attention with their smooth harmonies and multipart yodels. Nolan and Spencer's original compositions added to the group's western image, and by early 1935, the trio had added a fiddler and a guitarist and were calling themselves the Sons of the Pioneers. Their following grew when a station manager recorded and marketed their songs to various stations across the country. The national exposure led to offers to sing in several films, including Bing Crosby's feature western *Rhythm on the Range* (1936). By the mid-thirties, the Sons of the Pioneers were one of country and western music's top acts, with numerous radio performances, movie appearances, live performances, and even a top twenty hit record, "Tumbling Tumbleweeds" (1934), written by Bob Nolan.[32]

In 1937, Len Slye auditioned for a role as a singing cowboy at Republic Pictures. When he got the job, he and the Sons of the Pioneers went separate ways. The group signed on to sing in B-Westerns for Columbia, while he headed off for his new job with Republic. Yates's studio put Len to work immediately with small parts in *Wild Horse Rodeo* (1937) and *The Old*

Barn Dance (1938). When Gene Autry balked at doing a movie because of a contractual disagreement, Republic responded by changing Slye's name to the more alliterative Roy Rogers and giving him Autry's starring role in *Under Western Stars* (1938). The movie was a huge success. Set in the modern West, it features Rogers as a singing congressman trying to pass federal legislation that will secure water for his parched home district in the midst of the dust bowl. (This was Mr. Rogers going to Washington one year before James Stewart's Mr. Smith went!) Congressman Rogers outmaneuvers politicians, outsmarts the powerful water company, and prevents radicals from taking the law into their own hands. In between all the politicking, action scenes, and comic relief provided by Smiley Burnette, Roy finds time to romance the big businessman's daughter and sing several songs, including "Dust," which earned an Academy Award nomination.[33]

The contemporary western hit home with Depression-era audiences fed up with economic woes and bad news. Despite its bleak dust bowl images, the movie left viewers feeling upbeat. It offered hope to Americans wanting a New Deal to protect them against greedy businessmen and corrupt politicians, and it suggested that the federal government could shield Americans from callous economic forces and natural disasters. The film's likable young star added to the optimistic message. Rogers flashed across the silver screen on his golden palomino, Trigger, like a beacon of light cutting through the dark mood of Depression America. Not only did his inner strength, quiet determination, and traditional values appeal to viewers, but the fact that he could sing even when life appeared darkest was a life lesson in itself.

Movie critics were impressed. "This new cowboy, Roy Rogers, who joined Republic while Gene Autry was battling with the studio, is the nearest thing to Gary Cooper the screen has yet produced," gushed a reviewer in the *Schenectady Gazette*. Rogers' success inspired Autry to resolve his labor dispute with Herbert J. Yates. Shortly thereafter, Gene was back in the saddle again, picking up where he left off as Republic's number one singing cowboy. At the same time, Republic had no intention of letting Roy Rogers go. Yates devised a game plan that would provide distinct identities to the Rogers and Autry westerns. Most of Rogers's subsequent films were set in the historical past, unlike Autry's contemporary westerns. Rogers's movies also had more action and fewer songs than the Autry films. Plus, Rogers's budgets were smaller.[34]

Between 1938 and 1942, Roy Rogers established himself as one of Hollywood's top movie cowboys with fast-paced films set in the Old West, such as *Billy the Kid Returns* (1938) and *Days of Jesse James* (1939). The handsome and likable Rogers was scrappy in fights, fast on the draw, and had a distinctive look. Whether he was striding along wooden sidewalks in tailored western outfits with spurs jingling or leaning forward in the saddle of his galloping palomino—"Trigger, the smartest horse in the movies"—Roy Rogers was an original. Fans enjoyed his singing, too, particularly after he reunited with the Sons of the Pioneers, beginning with the film *Red River Valley* (1941).[35]

After Autry enlisted in the army, Republic Pictures began promoting Roy as their number one cowboy. He slipped effortlessly into Autry's slot, benefiting from better production units, bigger budgets, and scripts that featured contemporary settings and more songs and comedy. His first big-budget release was *Heart of the Golden West* (1942), which portrayed Roy as a modern cowboy protecting local cattlemen from a ruthless trucker named Ross Lambert. The movie appealed to viewers on numerous levels. It had a contemporary plot, interesting characters, and lots of action, romance, comedy, and music. Roy and the Sons of the Pioneers performed several outstanding songs, sometimes accompanied by black gospel singers. Even the hero's powerful palomino was amazing. Trigger was fast, smart, and as smooth as his master. The story line—small businessmen oppressed by a callous corporation—resonated with Depression-era audiences. After Rogers defeats Lambert and negotiates an agreement between the ranchers and a steamship company, the newspaper headline proudly proclaims: "Stranglehold of Truckers Broken." A sidebar adds that the trucking magnate had been arrested on fifteen criminal counts.

In early 1943, Republic released *King of the Cowboys*, which confirmed their rising star's new status and bestowed on him a new moniker. Rogers plays a contemporary singing cowboy and rodeo star hired by the governor to track down a gang of saboteurs responsible for blowing up buildings and undermining industries vital to American security in World War II. The action-packed movie ends at a rodeo, where the governor presents Roy with an official proclamation that reads: "To the King of the Cowboys, in grateful recognition of services rendered." The mounted cowboy smiles modestly and thanks the governor, as Trigger rears back on his hind legs and Roy waves his hat to the cheering crowd.

After 1943, Rogers's movies often seemed more like Broadway musicals than B-Westerns. Around that time, Herbert J. Yates saw *Oklahoma!* on Broadway and was inspired to make his own western musicals. Republic soon began pumping more money into Roy Rogers films, such as *Lights of Old Santa Fe* (1944) and *Utah* (1945). Roy's cowboy outfits became fancier, with sequins, embroidery, fringes, and tight pants fashioned by Nudie's of Hollywood. Sets became more elaborate, casts grew larger, and

Figure 17. An uncomfortable-looking Gabby Hayes with Dale Evans and Roy Rogers, as well as a bevy of chorus cowgirls in the musical finale of *Utah* (Republic Pictures, 1945).

costumes more ornate. Lavish musical reviews were added, and films often ended not with the customary showdowns, but with extravagant musical numbers, replete with orchestras, dancing girls, and lots of singing. *Lights of Old Santa Fe* is a good example. Set in the contemporary West, the film opens at a charity benefit with nightclub dancers performing on stage. Leading lady Dale Evans then croons "Amor," a syrupy Latin ballad. A ballet scene featuring young girls in tutus is next, causing a befuddled Gabby Hayes to exclaim, "Jumpin' jackrabbits. What kind of jigity you call that?" Shortly thereafter, Gabby joins Roy and the Sons of the Pioneers performing "The Cowpoke Polka." The entire sequence eats up almost the first ten minutes of the film. Throughout the rest of the movie, action continues to take a back seat to music and comedy.

While some B-Western purists were appalled by the turn of events, most fans could not get enough of Rogers's glitzy B-Western musicals. A reviewer in the *New York Times* called Roy "a Sinatra in a Sombrero." More important, between 1943 and 1954, Roy Rogers was ranked the number one western star on the annual top ten lists issued by the industry's two most important trade papers. Rogers's success was not limited to films. He earned numerous hit records and performed frequently on the radio, even hosting shows such as *Radio Rodeo* (1940), *The Call of the West* (1942), and *The Roy Rogers Show* (1944–45). Roy also became a top attraction at rodeos, parades, concerts, and other live performance venues. His phenomenal popularity led to numerous endorsements and marketing opportunities, which enabled fans to buy a variety of Roy Rogers products, including cereal, furniture, cowboy hats, cap pistols, holsters, shirts, and lunch boxes. There were even Roy Rogers and Trigger comic books.[36]

By the mid-forties, Roy Rogers was riding high as a successful star of screen, radio, records, rodeos, and more. Then suddenly, his world turned upside down. His wife of ten years, the former Arline Wilkins, died on November 3, 1946. Over the next year, the distraught cowboy star grew closer to Dale Evans, who starred alongside him in twenty films made between 1944 and 1947. They married on December 31, 1947, and would remain husband and wife for more than fifty years, until Roy's death in 1998. The marriage marked a turning point in Roy's career as well as his personal life. Even though Rogers and Evans had costarred in numerous films prior to their marriage, Herbert J. Yates initially believed that moviegoers would not buy tickets to see a married couple in westerns, so he yanked her out of Rogers's movies. When fans complained loudly, she was quickly reinstated. Republic then began promoting the duo as the "King of the Cowboys" and the "Queen of the West." From that point on, their careers were intertwined. Roy and Dale would make numerous films together, sing on record albums together, costar on radio and TV programs, and make joint personal appearances.[37]

After World War II, Roy Rogers's movies remained extremely popular, even though they were toned down somewhat, with less singing and glitzy costumes. Eventually, Rogers, like Gene Autry before him, clashed with Yates over money. The final straw came in the early fifties when Roy tried to follow Autry and William "Hopalong Cassidy" Boyd into television. When Yates said no, fearing that free exposure on the small screen would make Rogers less of a draw at the movie box office, Roy refused to renew his contract and bolted to TV, where he and Dale found success with *The Roy Rogers Show*, which ran weekly on NBC from 1951 until 1957.

If Roy Rogers personified the all-American boy, Dale Evans offered girls a perfect role model in an era of social change. Dale combined traditional feminine traits—beauty, grace, singing ability, and support for her man—with the attributes of the new woman of the forties, who was independent, intelligent, career minded, and often the equal of any man. The liberated cowgirl was good with a six-gun, an expert rider, and could stand up to the most dastardly villains the West had to offer. The King of the Cowboys and Queen of the West became two of the most popular B-Western stars of the forties and fifties. Roy's many achievements were later recognized when he was awarded four stars on the Hollywood Walk of Fame—one each for movies, radio, and television, and one for recording with the Sons of the Pioneers.

After retirement, Roy looked back at his career with pride. "Over the years I've taken some good-natured ribbing about the old Westerns: about those six-shooters that never needed reloading, about the fancy outfits and 'rigs' that real cowboys would never have worn, and so on. And, I can assure you we never kidded ourselves that we were making 'realistic' or 'historically accurate' pictures," explains Rogers. "But we *did* try to get across certain themes and messages to our audience: Fair play, justice for all, love of animals, respect for the environment, faith in God and country. And, if you'll allow my saying so, I think we did a pretty good job. . . . It seems our old Westerns made more of an impression than we thought, and that they've become part of our American folklore." No doubt, Roy Rogers's fans would agree. To this day, they still remember the King of the Cowboys fondly whenever they hear his TV show's signature theme song, written by Dale Evans: "Happy trails to you, until we meet again."[38]

B-Westerns and American Culture

B-Westerns had great appeal during the thirties and forties. Although elite critics routinely dismissed the low-budget films, moviegoers nationwide enthusiastically rushed out to theaters to see the latest releases. B-Westerns offered audiences inexpensive entertainment that spotlighted colorful western characters, picturesque ranches and towns, and panoramic views of majestic mountains and prairies. They also featured plenty of exciting adventures and fast-paced action. Some even offered comedy and western music.

For many moviegoers, B-Westerns were more than just entertainment. Cowboy movies offered temporary escape, maybe even catharsis, during the Depression and World War II. The frontier tales transported audiences to the mythic West, a land of hope and redemption. The cowboy hats, six-shooters, and spurs, along with the sights and sounds of heroic good guys galloping across wide open spaces, evoked simpler days in a magical place. Mythic cowboy heroes could be counted on to right every wrong and overcome any obstacle, and they never succumbed to villains or hard times. Audiences could relax in the fantasy world of the Wild West, which provided temporary sanctuary from the hostile world outside the darkened cinema.

If B-Westerns offered some viewers escape, they showed others how to cope with troubled times. They recalled America's glorious past, reaffirmed long-held principles, and taught moviegoers how to overcome trials and tribulations that came their way. "Without recognizing it at the time, these black-and-white films, with their black-and-white values, played an important role in shaping who and what we are—both as individuals and as a nation," notes film historian Richard W. Bann. "How many of us learned more, from just watching these films, about honesty, chivalry, respect, and the difference between right and wrong, than from anything we heard in church or were taught in school?"[39]

Movie cowboys became role models and kindred spirits who could offer solutions to even the most difficult problems. These western morality plays assured viewers that good would always win out in the end. Cowboy stars taught youngsters traditional values by their words as well as actions, as evidenced by Gene Autry's Cowboy Code of Honor, Hopalong Cassidy's Creed for American Boys and Girls, and groups like the Buck Jones Rangers or Roy Rogers Riders Club. B-Westerns such as Ken Maynard's *Drum Taps* (1933) and Tex Ritter's *Tex Rides with the Boy Scouts* (1937) even featured cowboy heroes teaming up with the Boy Scouts to stop evil doers. Cowboy movies featured heroes who did not drink, smoke, or swear, and they made it clear that individuals who remained true to God, country, and American principles would always triumph no matter what the odds. These cinematic parables reaffirmed American values at a critical time in the nation's history.[40]

B-Westerns of the Depression and World War II years demonstrated that Americans had the right stuff to overcome any problem or threat. These films were built on the rock of American exceptionalism. Movie cowboys exhibited all the traits of the American character noted in Frederick Jackson Turner's frontier thesis. They were independent, egalitarian, hardworking, innovative, mobile, and nationalistic. These rugged individuals celebrated westward movement as they promoted life, liberty, and justice for all. Movie cowboys personified American capitalism. Not only did they defend the right of ordinary Americans to own ranches, farms, gold mines, and other private property, but they linked conspicuous consumption to the Old West. Many cowboy heroes wore glitzy cowboy hats, ornate leather holsters, hand-tooled cowboy boots, and silver spurs;

they owned expensive pearl-handled six-shooters; and they rode beautiful horses, trimmed in silver-studded, fine-leather harnesses, collars, and halters. Some even endorsed commercial products, including cowboy hats, toys, and cereal.

B-Westerns underscored Americans' fondness for pragmatic solutions. "The speed with which the B-Western hero outsmarted and dispatched the villains also expressed the American appreciation for action," explains historian Ray White. "These fast-paced horse operas fit what most Americans conceived to be the proper method of problem solving: do something, and do it quickly. If one solution does not work, try something else, be pragmatic." Some B-Westerns even suggested that the end justifies the means. "The hero, in his zeal and determination to . . . bring the villains to justice, sometimes winked at the law and occasionally violated it outright, with no explanation for his action," notes White. Movie cowboys suggested that individualistic Americans should cooperate during times of crisis. Reflecting the mood of a nation that was willing to work together to end the Great Depression or combat Axis aggression, cowboy heroes frequently joined forces to defeat villains or resolve serious economic or social issues. The Three Mesquiteers and other trigger trios became B-Western equivalents of the New Deal's WPA or CCC, as individualistic cowboys worked in concert to accomplish larger goals that would benefit society. Other Depression-era westerns, such as *Billy the Kid Returns* (1938) and *Colorado Sunset* (1939), focused on corrupt businessmen and unfair business practices that hurt the community. In each case, good guys cooperated to overcome threats to society.[41]

B-Westerns provide fascinating glimpses of life in twentieth-century America. Numerous movies reveal social tensions during the Depression. B-Western heroes defend ordinary people from wealthy cattle barons, greedy businessmen, and corrupt politicians. Gene Autry's *Tumbling Tumbleweeds* (1935) and Roy Rogers's *Under Western Stars* (1938) focus on social conflict between haves and have-nots, while *Wyoming Outlaw* (1939) features the Three Mesquiteers coming to the aid of a destitute man who stole a cow to feed his hungry family. Cowboy pictures also show concerns about threats from abroad. The fear of Axis spies on the home front during World War II set the stage for *Texas to Bataan* (1942) and *Wild Horse Rustlers* (1943). Other B-Westerns reflect the rise of the Cold War. Roy Rogers's *Bells of Coronado* (1950) features the King of the Cowboys working with the federal government to stop traitors from smuggling uranium to foreign enemies. Rogers followed up with *Spoilers of the Plains* (1951). As Roy thwarts a spy trying to steal American rocket secrets, he evokes McCarthyism: "You never can tell [who might try to hurt America], it might be your next-door neighbor."[42]

B-Westerns provide other clues about American society at mid-century. The images of women in B-Westerns reflect changing gender roles. At first glance, western women seem quite conventional. They appear to be passive and dependent on the heroes. But there was always another side to B-Western heroines. Cowgirls often displayed skills and ambitions worthy of prototypical frontier feminists such as Annie Oakley and Calamity Jane. The heroines in Tex Ritter's *Trouble in Texas* (1937) and *Riders of the Rockies* (1937), for example, were undercover government agents who helped defeat bad guys.

By 1938, executives at Grand National Pictures were convinced that the time was right for a female counterpart to Gene Autry. They tapped actress and radio singer Dorothy Page to become "the screen's first Lady Buckaroo" and featured her in *The Singing Cowgirl* (1938) and two other films. Page's western career was short-lived, but other cowgirls were soon galloping across the movie screen. Grand National Pictures even considered making an "all-girl Western." Although that never came to pass, many B-Westerns did feature smart, tough, and independent women, many of whom wielded six-guns.[43]

Just as Rosie the Riveter proved that women could do men's jobs during World War II, the images of forceful females in B-Westerns before, during, and after World War II suggested that women could hold their own against men in the Old West. *Target* (1952), which starred Tim Holt and Mary Jo Tarola (aka Linda Douglas), featured a liberated female character named Terry Moran. She becomes marshal of Pecos, Texas, because town officials wrongly believed they were hiring her famous lawman father with the same name. When the all-male hiring committee learns the truth, they refuse to give her the job. Terry threatens to sue for breach of contract and insists she has the skills needed for the job. To prove her point, she whips out her six-gun and shoots jars off a shelf. Impressed by her shooting and fearing a lawsuit, the men reluctantly agree to hand over the badge. The female marshal then hires Tim Holt as a deputy, and together they clean up the town, with Marshal Moran doing her fair share of the shooting and fighting.

Resourceful women also appear as shrewd and forceful villains in B-Westerns such as *The Hawk of Powder River* (1948) and *The Dalton Girls* (1957). The latter is particularly interesting, because it focuses on four young women who violate both moral and gender rules. After the girls' father and uncle (the notorious Dalton brothers) are killed by a posse, fate drives the four Dalton girls to continue the family business of robbing banks and stages. Even though the film portrays the Dalton girls as expert gunslingers and accomplished outlaws, it shows what happens when women wander too far from prescribed gender roles and morals. Arguably, the Daltons were driven to a life of crime by forces beyond their control. Even the gambler who falls in love with one of the sisters, Columbine, realizes there were mitigating circumstances behind the girls' actions. "You and the three other women held up a stagecoach," he says. "So what? You had to make your way on the frontier. It's more honorable than some others. And a lot braver." Yet, in the end, their life of crime was one of choice not necessity. Each of the four sisters eventually has to make a personal decision whether to stay the course as an outlaw or go straight. The three sisters who refuse to change their ways wind up dead or in jail. Only Columbine, who renounces her evil ways and decides to settle down with the man she loves (thereby following prescribed morality and gender roles), finds redemption. Arguably, the Dalton girls were treated the same as B-Western bad guys. Typically, the villain who eventually does the right thing can be saved, but the one who remains bad is punished.

Some of the most liberated women in B-Westerns can be found in films produced by Republic Pictures. "My leading ladies were hardly helpless females," explained Gene Autry. "[They] were spirited young women with minds of their own." Heroines in Roy Rogers's movies made in the forties, especially those played by Dale Evans, Jane Frazee, and Penny Edwards, were equally independent. "The war required women to alter traditional social roles as they assumed jobs vacated by the men in uniform. Evans, Frazee, and Edwards reflected the changing times," explains Ray White. The three actresses appeared in nontraditional roles such as ranch owners, newspaper reporters, businesswomen, and law enforcement officials. Dale Evans, in particular, earned her spurs by standing up to some of the toughest villains that Hollywood had to offer. She often wore the requisite cowboy hat, carried a six-shooter, and repeatedly proved that she could outride, outshoot, and outsmart most of the guys in the picture.[44]

Of course, not all B-Westerns portrayed independent women in progressive ways. Some spotlighted strong-willed women merely to profit from gratuitous sex. *Outlaw Women* (1952) tells a story about a town controlled by Iron Mae McLeod (Marie Windsor) and her gang of female gunslingers. One movie poster features a beautiful dance-hall woman loading her six-gun, barely clothed in a skimpy costume and fishnet stockings. "THIS IS WHY COYOTES HOWL," says the poster, "Six Gun Sirens Who Shoot to Thrill!" Other films were equally provocative. A poster for *Jesse James'*

Women (1954) depicts two women with their breasts barely covered, fighting and pulling each other's hair, while men in a barroom cheer wildly. The tagline reads: "Women WANTED him more than the law."[45]

Sexploitation films were the exception rather than the norm. Most B-Westerns treated women in positive ways. The emergence of cowgirls who played important roles in B-Westerns mirrored the times. During the Depression and World War II, women often became wage earners to help out during financial hard times or to replace male workers who had gone off to war. Movie cowgirls demonstrate that the era's females were also ready to assume their rightful places in the mythic West. Although independent cowgirls still were not the equal of cowboys, their emergence in the thirties and forties suggested that change was in the western wind.

Minorities had a more difficult time in B-Westerns. Reflecting the dominant culture, cowboy pictures usually marginalized anyone who was different. A good example is *The Terror of Tiny Town* (1938), which was exactly like any other B-Western of the day with one obvious difference—it featured an all-midget and dwarf cast riding ponies and downsized stagecoaches. The film, like carnival side shows of the day, treated the small actors and actresses as oddities.[46]

B-Westerns proved equally unsympathetic to other outsiders. Cowboy pictures—like the culture as a whole—assumed that whites were superior to people of color. Not surprisingly, the most successful cowboy stars were white males with Anglo-Saxon Protestant names such as Wayne, Rogers, or Jones. Even though there were actually thousands of African Americans who lived and worked in the Old West as cowboys, soldiers, ranchers, farmers, or prospectors, one would never know it by viewing B-Westerns. Blacks were either omitted entirely from scripts, included as subordinate or dependent heroes, or treated in stereotypical ways. For example, Fred "Snowflake" Toones played bit parts in numerous B-Westerns, usually in a menial job as a cook, janitor, or servant. His high-pitched voice and childish mannerisms were played for comedic effect in films such as John Wayne's *The Lawless Nineties* (1936) and the Three Mesquiteers' *Riders of the Black Hills* (1938). Even when blacks were cast as good guys, they were caricatured, as evidenced by Eugene Jackson's role as Eightball, a song and dance man who helps Gene Autry fight bad guys, in *Tumbling Tumbleweeds*.[47]

Such stereotypes were avoided only by Herb Jeffries (aka Herbert Jeffrey), an African American singer and bandleader, who starred in four "all-black" B-Westerns: *Harlem on the Prairie* (1937); *Two-Gun Man from Harlem* (1938); *The Bronze Buckaroo* (1939); and *Harlem Rides the Range* (1939). The films, written and directed by whites, featured all-black casts and were aimed at black audiences. They played only in black neighborhoods, but all turned a profit. A movie poster for *Harlem Rides the Range* suggests that the film followed the basic B-Western formula. It shows Jeffries wearing a white hat and riding a white horse as he fights off a bad guy in a black hat.[48] Jeffries's separate but equal westerns were able to avoid racial stereotypes only because they stayed within the accepted bounds of the era's segregated society.

Images of Asians in B-Westerns also reflected the era's prejudices. On the few occasions when Asians appeared, they were usually typecast as subservient cooks, houseboys, laundry workers, or sneaky villains.[49] Stereotypes got nastier after Pearl Harbor. The Asian cook in the Range Busters' *Texas to Bataan* (1942), for instance, turns out to be a Japanese spy. Significantly, the most positive image of an Asian in a B-Western came from Tim McCoy's sympathetic portrayal of a Chinese man in *Six-Gun Trail* (1938). McCoy comes across as a cowboy version of Charlie Chan, as he unravels a mystery involving jewel thieves.

Although Hispanics had a higher profile in B-Westerns, they also suffered from stereotypes. The stage was set by two early blockbusters. *The Mark of Zorro* (1920) featured Douglas Fairbanks as the charming Don Diego Vega (aka Zorro) and Noah Beery as the cruel and incompetent Mexican sergeant, Pedro Gonzalez. Set in Old California, the story introduced cinematic characters destined to become Hispanic archetypes, including the dashing hero, a beautiful señorita, genteel landowners, comedic sidekicks, oppressed peasants, and smiling but sadistic villains. *In Old Arizona* (1929) added additional images. Warner Baxter's Cisco Kid (who was half Portuguese and half Old Californian) pointed the way for later happy-go-lucky Mexican bandits, while Dorothy Burgess's Tonia Maria was the quintessential Mexican spitfire.

Subsequent B-Westerns portrayed Hispanic males as banditos, buffoons, and sidekicks, or alternately as distinguished governors, courtly ranchers, or gallant caballeros. Often speaking broken English and sporting mustaches, they dressed in tight pants and fancy jackets and wore large sombreros. Hispanic females were usually depicted either as elegantly dressed blue bloods or hot-blooded coquettes wearing peasant blouses with flowing skirts covering bare legs. For example, *Arizona Terror* (1931) included a conniving Mexican bandit, replete with an oversized sombrero, bullet belts adorning his chest, and a sinister sense of humor. His lusty Mexican girlfriend coveted good guy Ken Maynard. *The Cisco Kid Returns* (1945) marked the beginning of a long run for Duncan Renaldo as O. Henry's famous Robin Hood of the Old West. Both films followed the B-Western convention of portraying lower-class Hispanic characters as Mexican and more refined ones as descended from Europeans or the Spanish in Old California. Such stereotypes suggest that mainstream America was willing to accept Hispanics as long as they had a European background and shared traditional American values.[50]

Given the era's acceptance of white supremacy, it is not surprising that Indians wound up outsiders in B-Westerns. Although the First Americans initially outnumbered whites on the frontier, they were usually absent from B-Westerns, which implies that Indians were not important in history. Contrary to popular belief, most B-Westerns did not deal with cowboys and Indians. Instead, they focused on battles between good guys and bad guys, who were almost always white. When B-Westerns did include Indians, the images usually were not flattering. Indians were depicted as bloodthirsty warriors, drunkards, dullards, buffoons, exotic creatures, noble savages, and more, but they seldom were equals of white Americans.

One of the first B-Westerns to treat Native Americans in an even-handed manner was *End of the Trail* (1932), which starred Tim McCoy as a military officer sympathetic to the Indian cause. "Remarkably for its time, the film pleads the Indians' cause with fervor and conviction," notes western writer Ted Sennett. McCoy's character condemns the government, because it "has never kept a single treaty," and he denounces the military for "burning teepees, killing men, women, and children." *End of the Trail* not only offers a pro-Indian view of history, but it includes accurate depictions of Plains Indian culture. Shot on location at an Arapaho reservation in Wyoming, the movie provided stock footage for later westerns.[51]

Even when B-Westerns attempted to treat Indians in positive ways, the results could be negative. *Massacre* (1934), which starred white actor Richard Barthelmess as an acculturated Indian named Joe Thunder Horse, is a good example. Though sympathetic toward Native Americans, the film perpetuated racial stereotypes. The "bad" Indians are just as evil as the white Indian agent. Even the "good" Indians are problematic. The movie portrays Joe Thunder Horse as an aberration. He is college educated, wealthy, handsome, athletic, and far superior to the rest of his tribe (not to mention most of the whites in the movie). Most of the other "good" Indians in the film are passive, poor, uneducated, and childlike. They get cheated and mistreated, but they just take it. When they finally spring into action to help Joe, who is being persecuted by the Indian agent, they resort to savage behavior, screaming war cries as they burn down the courthouse. Joe intervenes, explaining Indians cannot survive if they break the white man's laws. Only then, do they cease and desist. In the end, none of these Indians can fend for himself. The bad ones are defeated, and the good ones need help from an acculturated Indian. But even Joe Thunder Horse cannot succeed without help from powerful whites and the federal government.

Along with relying on conventional images of "good" and "bad" Indians, *Massacre* plays off long-established fears of miscegenation. White women find the dark-skinned, powerfully built Thunder Horse irresistible. An attractive brunette says, "I'll be that big chief's squaw, anytime." A blond looks at the erect feather in his hair and says brazenly, "Hey, Chief, how about a feather for a souvenir?" Thunder Horse's black employee is the source of additional racial stereotypes. The wisecracking servant pokes fun at both Indians and whites, but whites quickly put him down when he gets too uppity. One irritated white man even kicks him like a dog. Most moviegoers of the thirties had no problems with the film's racial messages. One review praised the movie for its poignant portrayal of the slaughter of the "Red Men" but accepted the film's Indian stereotypes. "[Thunder Horse] was the last of the great warrior chiefs—and he was a civilized, much sought after, cultivated, young American," wrote the reviewer, "Yet under his polished exterior beat the heart of a savage Indian."[52]

Native American heroes were neutralized in other ways. Sometimes, the Indian hero turned out to be a white man. The movie poster for Buck Jones's *White Eagle* (1932) depicts the star as a proud and powerful warrior wearing a war bonnet and riding an Indian pony.[53] The film tells a complicated tale about a brave warrior who falls in love with a white woman and protects her when racial violence erupts on the frontier. Moviegoers eventually learn that White Eagle is really a white man raised by Indians. The pat ending conveniently sidesteps racial issues, allowing White Eagle (aka John Harvey) to wind up with the girl.

Of course, not all Indian heroes were white men. B-Westerns depicted numerous brave Native Americans, but usually they were just sidekicks for white heroes. Tonto is the classic example. Patterned after Chingachgook, Natty Bumppo's loyal friend in *Last of the Mohicans*, Tonto is the staunch ally and confidant of The Lone Ranger, who first appeared on radio in 1933. Chief Thundercloud (aka Victor Daniels) played Tonto to Lee Powell's masked man in both the popular Republic serial, *The Lone Ranger* (1938), and the edited version, *Hi-Yo Silver*, released in 1940 as a feature film. Thundercloud reprised the role in *The Lone Ranger Rides Again* (1939), with Robert Livingston replacing Powell. *The Lone Ranger* eventually became a popular TV show, running from 1949 until 1957, starring Clayton Moore as the masked man (except for the fourth season, when he was replaced by John Hart) and Jay Silverheels as Tonto.

Though cast members of Lone Ranger films and television shows changed over the years, the main elements remained constant. "A fiery horse with the speed of light, a cloud of dust and a hearty 'Hi-Yo Silver! Away!'" explained the TV show. "With his faithful Indian companion Tonto, The Lone Ranger, daring and resourceful masked rider of the plains, led the fight for law and order in the early West. Return with us now to those thrilling days of yesteryear. The Lone Ranger rides again!" The Masked Man, who handed out silver bullets as his calling card and rode his snow-white horse, Silver, was aided every step of the way by his Indian sidekick, but in the end, The Lone Ranger got all the glory, while the equally brave Tonto simply provided backup for "Kemo Sabe." Whether the friendly Indian was portrayed by a real Native American such as Jay Silverheels or by a white actor such as Yakima Canutt, who played John Wayne's Indian pal in *The Star Packer* (1934), the result was the same. No matter how positive the image, Indian characters usually wound up subordinates to the primary heroes, who were always white.[54]

The Tonto syndrome was common in B-Westerns, but neither it nor other cinematic images of Native Americans were new. These stereotypes can be traced back hundreds of years and demonstrate continuity in American life and thought. That so few B-Westerns offered sympathetic portrayals of Indians does suggest change, but not in a positive direction. Given that some silent films of the early 1900s did treat Indians in realistic and compassionate ways, it is striking that most B-Westerns of the 1930s and 1940s did not. Perhaps the explanation lies in the fact that cowboy movies were simply continuing the tradition of dime novels and Wild West shows, which typically appealed to audiences by featuring plenty of blood-and-thunder action involving stereotypical Indians. Or maybe it was because B-Westerns were produced in an era that demanded solidarity against economic hardships and foreign enemies. In any case, it is ironic that Native Americans, who played dominant roles in the real West, were treated as supporting players in B-Westerns. Stereotypes of Indians, like those of Mexicans, Asians, and African Americans, not only reinforced the notion that the mythic West was the exclusive realm of white Anglo-Saxon Protestants, but reminded America about its Manifest Destiny.

* * *

B-Westerns stand as testimony to the dreams, hopes, and fears of Americans during the Great Depression and World War II. They offer fascinating glimpses of a nation staggered by economic, political, and social crises yet determined to defeat enemies at home and abroad. Movie cowboys who invariably triumphed over desperadoes, corrupt businessmen, Indians, or other bad guys taught moviegoers an important lesson. As long as patriotic citizens adhered to the traditional beliefs and actions associated with the mythic West, the American way of life would always win out in the end. Low-budget cowboy pictures—like their big-budget counterparts—would change considerably after 1945 as Hollywood tried to keep pace with new developments in Cold War America. Although B-Westerns would ride off into the sunset by the end of the fifties, they would never be forgotten. "The reel cowboys of B-films left a great legacy to millions upon millions of young boys," insists B-Western expert Buck Rainey. "They 'done themselves proud,' providing the best entertainment ever given a youngster and teaching simple moral lessons that would sustain a world."[55]

PART TWO

Transitional Westerns on New Frontiers

1945–1963

CHAPTER FIVE

The Searchers

Cowboys and Containment on the Cold War Frontier

The Searchers is one of the greatest westerns ever made. Directed brilliantly by John Ford, the movie was filmed in vivid Technicolor and panoramic VistaVision on locations that included Utah's breathtaking Monument Valley, the majestic Colorado Rockies, and the rolling prairies and mountains of Canada. "I wouldn't make a western on a back lot," explained Ford. "I think you can say that the real star of my westerns has always been the land."[1] The sprawling epic features John Wayne as the quintessential cowboy hero in a tragic yet telling tale that touches on almost every major theme found in westerns released between 1945 and 1963.

The movie opens with a woman homesteader looking out her cabin door. Far off in the distance, she sees a lone rider. Her husband, Aaron, joins her, and together they watch the rider come ever closer. Martha soon realizes that the stranger is her brother-in-law, Ethan Edwards, returning home to Texas after the Civil War. By the time Ethan reaches the cabin, most of the Edwards family is outside to greet him. Ethan shakes his brother's hand, gives Martha a gentle kiss, and is pleased to see his nieces and nephew, Lucy, Debbie, and Ben. He is less enthusiastic when Martin Pawley shows up. The part-Cherokee young man was raised by the Edwards family after Ethan found him orphaned by an Indian attack. As the family gets reacquainted, it becomes clear that Ethan and Martha have deep feelings for each other.

Figure 18. This movie poster suggests that John Wayne's character will never quit in *The Searchers* (C. V. Whitney Pictures/ Warner Brothers Pictures, 1956).

The family reunion is cut short the next day when a posse of Texas Rangers and deputized neighbors arrive. Ethan and Marty join them to track down the culprits who stole cattle from a neighboring farm. After following the trail for miles, the men suddenly realize they have been duped by Comanches, who lured them away so they could attack a defenseless ranch. Ethan and Marty desperately rush back home but arrive too late. They find the cabin burned to the ground and no survivors. As Ethan walks through the rubble, he suddenly stops and picks up Martha's torn dress from the ground. A few steps away in a shed, he discovers her body. The anguished look on his face reveals the horror of her death. A barking dog catches Ethan's attention. When he investigates, he finds Debbie's doll next to the family dog. He realizes that the nine-year-old and her teenaged sister, Lucy, have been abducted by the brutal Comanches. The rest of the movie focuses on the seven-year odyssey of Ethan and Marty—the searchers—as they travel the West in pursuit of Chief Scar and the war party that captured the young girls. Along the way, they conquer their enemies and fears, finding redemption in the mythic West.

Early in the search, Ethan discovers Lucy's body and realizes that Debbie will be raised as an Indian and married off as a squaw. He pledges not to quit until he finds the girl and gets revenge on the Comanches. Marty insists on going, too. He wants to rescue his adopted sister and fears that the Indian-hating Ethan will kill Debbie for surrendering herself to Chief Scar. Ethan's obsession became the tagline of movie posters: "He had to find her, he had to find her."

The Searchers epitomizes the sophisticated westerns that emerged after World War II. In the thirties and forties, westerns surged in popularity by offering audiences clear-cut morality plays that could get them through economic hard times and political crises. After the war, westerns grew increasingly more complex. They changed rapidly with the times, evolving to deal with Cold War issues and social change. John Wayne's Ethan Edwards was just one of many complicated cowboy heroes who traveled the mythic West searching for answers on the Cold War frontier. Their battles against enemies and quests for freedom, redemption, and opportunity offer insights into American life and thought in the decades following World War II.

The Searchers and Postwar America

John Ford called *The Searchers* his "psychological epic."[2] The moving tale about a troubled Civil War veteran no doubt resonated with millions of veterans after World War II, who could relate to Ethan Edwards's cynicism, anxieties, and feelings of alienation, isolation, depression, and rage—symptoms that modern psychologists might now diagnose as combat-related post-traumatic stress disorder (PTSD).

As John Wayne's character battles his psychological demons, he must also confront a dangerous external threat—the Comanches. Cold War audiences of the fifties who lived in constant fear of brutal Communists at home and abroad could relate to the menace posed by the Indians. Ethan leaves little doubt about the enemy's cruelty. When Lucy's beau, who was part of the initial search for the captured girls, thinks he caught a glimpse of the girl in a nearby Indian village, Ethan snaps. "What you saw was a buck wearin' Lucy's dress. I found Lucy back in the canyon. Wrapped her in my coat, buried her with my own hands. I thought it best to keep it from you." When the shaken young man stammers, "Did they . . . ? Was she . . . ?" an angry Ethan shouts, "What do you want me to do? Draw you a picture? Spell it out? Don't ever ask me! Long as you live, don't ever ask me more!" The point was not lost on many moviegoers. The evil enemy—whether Indians in the Old West or Communists of the Cold War Era—threatened hearth, home, and the American way of life. "Better dead than red" was the conclusion in both instances.

Historians suggest that a Cold War culture emerged in the United States by the fifties. "The search to define and affirm a way of life, the need to express and celebrate the meaning of Americanism, was the flip side of stigmatizing Communism," explains Stephen J. Whitfield.[3] Ford's western mirrored the culture of the Cold War as it celebrated patriotism, the family, community, religion, and other established American values as ways to combat evil. Ethan and other members of the community, for example, volunteer as citizen-soldiers to help the Texas Rangers defend their families and homes against external threats. The story highlights the important role ranchers, homesteaders, and families played in the winning of the West. Indeed, the need to protect and preserve families is the movie's unifying theme. Throughout the film, aggressive frontiersmen provide protection, determination, and grit, while nurturing womenfolk offer stability, support, and continuity, in keeping with traditional gender roles of the fifties.

Other traditional American values abound in Ford's frontier saga. A mistrust of big government is evident in the frontiersmen's determination to solve their own problems and not rely on the U.S. Army. Religion is ever present in the tough and feisty character of Reverend Samuel Clayton (played with gusto by Ward Bond), who, when not officiating at funerals and weddings, doubles as the head of the local militia and captain of the Texas Rangers. When Clayton gives orders to prepare for an imminent Indian attack, one of his men loads a weapon and says, "That which we are about to receive, we thank thee, O Lord." Of course, there are limits to what religion can accomplish even in Cold War America. Wayne's character clearly understands the old adage that God helps those who help themselves. When the reverend's prayers run long at the Edwards's family funeral, Ethan, eager to hit the trail in pursuit of the Indians, shouts: "Put an Amen to it!"

Ethan Edwards personifies the traditional western hero, a rugged individual who joins with others in times of trouble to defend his family, friends, and community. In keeping with the spirit of westward expansion, Ethan is independent, strong, innovative, and unwilling to give up. The hero's words and actions were particularly relevant to a generation that had just come together to defeat the Axis powers and was now involved in a worldwide struggle against communism. At one point, Ethan assures a disheartened Marty that they will succeed because they will never quit. "Injun will chase a thing till he thinks he's chased it enough. Then he quits. Same way when he runs," explains Ethan. "Seems like he never learns there's such a thing as a critter that'll just keep comin' on. So we'll find 'em in the end, I promise you. We'll find 'em."

If *The Searchers* reflects America's Cold War culture and the continuing belief in the mythic West as a land of redemption, liberty, justice, and opportunity, it also mirrors rapid social change after World War II. *The Searchers* picked up on the era's rising civil rights movement and changing racial attitudes. Although no African Americans appear in the film, another minority group is spotlighted—Indians. For authenticity, John Ford hired Native Americans to play most of the Indian roles. Although the Comanches are the bad guys, they ultimately are portrayed with dignity and sympathy. No mere savages, they mourn their dead, take care of families, and struggle to defend their homes and lands against white aggression. Even the hated war chief, Scar, winds up more than just a one-dimensional villain. When he shows Ethan all the white scalps he has taken, he notes with great satisfaction that they are retribution for the death of his sons at the hands of white men. Scar's racial hatred and acts of vengeance are the mirror images of Ethan's.

The movie takes on racism in other ways. The mixed-blood Marty (Jeffrey Hunter), who initially is the target of racial insults uttered by Ethan, eventually wins his respect if not admiration. Marty's character provides Ford with an opportunity to address contemporary attitudes toward miscegenation. In one scene, Marty accidentally winds up married to a young Indian woman, who is peaceful, well meaning, and sensitive to her new husband's needs. But Marty's true love is the girl next door, Laurie Jorgensen (Vera Miles), who, like Ethan, frequently displays hatred of Indians. In an attempt to convince Marty to abandon his search for Debbie, Laurie points out the absurdity of trying to rescue the girl. "Fetch what home?" she asks. "The leavings a Comanche buck sold time and again to the highest bidder, with savage brats of her own?" Laurie adds, "Do you know what Ethan will do if he has a chance? He'll put a bullet in her brain. I tell you, [her mother] would want him to." By the end of the film, however, Laurie has overcome her racist views. Not only is she eager to marry the mixed-blood Marty, but she accepts the redeemed Debbie into her family as well.

Significantly, even Ethan overcomes his hatred of all things Indian. Throughout the movie, he seeks revenge against the savages who butchered

Martha and other members of his family. From all indications, Ethan even intends to kill Debbie when he finds her, because she has become Scar's squaw and accepted "Injun" ways. His racial hatred turns him into an avenging angel who kills Indians with pleasure, desecrates a native grave, and shoots the eyes out of a dead Indian's skull because he knows that a Comanche believes that if he "ain't got no eyes, he can't enter the spirit-land. [He] has to wander forever between the winds."

During the climactic attack on Scar's Indian village, Ethan comes across the dead body of Scar, the hated war chief killed by Marty during his daring rescue of Debbie. Not willing to let Scar's death interfere with his own need for vengeance, Ethan scalps the corpse as payback for the deaths of his loved ones. Then, Ethan turns to his final task—settling the score with Debbie, who flees in terror at the sight of the man she used to call uncle. He chases her on horseback, but instead of killing her, he sweeps her into his arms and says simply, "Let's go home, Debbie." By film's end, Ethan has been redeemed as much as Debbie. "The story is a morality play," explains film historian Douglas Brode, "in which the rugged American individualist Ethan—and, subsequently, America itself—works himself free of racism, which ultimately centers around a fear of miscegenation."[4]

Indians are not the only minority group treated sympathetically. The movie's portrayal of Hispanics is benign. Unlike many westerns that offered only stereotypical smiling yet cutthroat Mexican banditos, *The Searchers* features a wealthy comanchero named Emilio Gabriel Fernandez y Figueroa, who for a price leads Ethan and Marty to Scar's camp. Once Figueroa realizes that Scar is aware of the searchers' plans, he gives Ethan his money back, explaining that his principles will not allow him to keep blood money. The dignified Hispanic businessman then shakes Ethan's hand and wishes him *Vaya con Dios*.

Along with reflecting shifting attitudes toward race and ethnicity, *The Searchers* mirrored other social change in postwar America. The movie is designed in part to appeal to the era's emerging youth culture. By the fifties, teenagers and rising baby boomers became the frequent subjects of magazine stories, TV shows, movies, and other mass media. *The Searchers* appealed to youth on a variety of levels. It costarred one of Hollywood's newest heartthrobs, Jeffrey Hunter, as Wayne's young sidekick, and featured the beautiful young actress Natalie Wood (who received an Oscar nomination in 1955 for *Rebel Without a Cause*) as the girl captured by the Indians. One of the subplots involves generational conflict between the middle-aged Ethan and his upstart nephew, Marty. Equally important is the story line involving young love between Marty and Laurie. Even the marketing campaign took direct aim at young people. Several movie posters spotlighted the young romance angle; publicity people at Warner Brothers recommended that theaters launch The Searchers for Safety youth clubs to cut down on teenage automobile accidents; and Warner Brothers rushed out Game Mats for Kids, as well as a full-length Dell comic book to coincide with the movie's release. Not only did the film succeed in attracting a young audience, but two young viewers in Lubbock, Texas—Buddy Holly and Jerry Allison, who would later gain fame as the cofounders of the rock & roll group, the Crickets—were so taken by a catchphrase that John Wayne used in the movie that they used it as the title for their number one rock & roll record in 1957, "That'll Be the Day."[5]

The Searchers spotlighted changing gender roles. By the mid-fifties, an increasing number of married women were working outside the home, preparing the way for later feminists. The women in Ford's western anticipate the changing roles of females in postwar America. Though the characters rely on men for protection and help, they exhibit leadership, intelligence, and bravery in the midst of the problems swirling around them. Mrs. Jorgensen (played by Olive Carey, the veteran silent-film star and wife of western actor Harry Carey) is better educated than Mr. Jorgensen and clearly the head of the household, guiding her family with dignity, fairness, and a sure hand. When her husband complains that "it's this country killed my boy," his wife gently but firmly corrects him. "No, Lars, it just so happens we be Texicans. Texican is nothing but a human man way out on a limb," she explains. "But I don't think it'll be forever. Someday this country's gonna be a fine, good place to be. Maybe it needs our bones in the ground before that time can come." A proud Lars smiles and says, "She used to be a school teacher, you know."

Similarly, the Jorgensen's daughter, Laurie, represents a new generation of independent frontier women. Like her mother, she is well educated and articulate, but Laurie is more aggressive, action oriented, and determined to shape her own life and destiny. She even takes the lead courting Marty. She can't believe it when he says, "You know, Laurie, I was just thinking that maybe it's about time you and me started going steady." Flabbergasted, she replies, "Why, Martin Pawley, you and me been going steady since we was three years old!" "We have?" he responds. She ends the conversation with a declaration: "'Bout time you found out about it."

Even the young Debbie repeatedly demonstrates that she is no shrinking violet. At the beginning of the movie, she is bold enough to ask her Uncle

Ethan for a gold locket like the one he gave her older sister. He smiles and gives her a medal that he had received during the Civil War, foreshadowing her coming bravery. After she is captured by Indians, Debbie does whatever is necessary to survive. Years later, Ethan and Marty catch a glimpse of the girl's intelligence, courage, and initiative when they discover her in Scar's village. At first, the girl pretends she doesn't know them, but later she sneaks out of the camp to warn them that they will be killed if they don't leave immediately. The fifteen-year-old explains poignantly that at first she prayed that they would rescue her, but "you didn't come [and] now, it's too late." Only later does Debbie prove that she never really gave up her dream of returning home. When Marty creeps into Scar's tent to free her from captivity, the girl throws her arms around him, clearly eager to return to family and friends. Overcoming all the trauma, hardships, and terror thrown her way, the young woman finally achieves her goal.

In the film's powerful conclusion, Ethan Edwards and Martin Pawley bring their search full circle. They escort the redeemed Debbie home, ending up at the Jorgensen's place only a few miles from the Edwards's former homestead. Ethan has met his obligations and returned the young woman to her rightful place with a family on the American frontier, but he realizes that he is out of step with the changing times. Instead of entering the cabin with Debbie, Marty, and their new family, Ethan remains outside, both literally and figuratively. The film began with a camera shot taken through a cabin doorway showing John Wayne's character riding up toward the family dwelling. It ends with an almost identical shot, this time framing Ethan still outside, admiring but unable to become part of the new family. The film's haunting theme song plays in the background, summing up not only Ethan's dilemma, but the problems faced by many in postwar America. "A man will search his heart and soul, go searchin' way out there," sing the Sons of the Pioneers, "His peace of mind he knows he'll find, but where, oh Lord, Lord where?" As Ethan turns slowly and heads back toward the wilderness, the song repeats the phrase, "Ride away, ride away, ride away."[6]

New Western Heroes on Changing Frontiers

John Wayne's character in *The Searchers* was only one of many western heroes trying to cope with the changing times. The protagonists in numerous postwar western movies mirrored the anxieties of a nation still reeling from the Great Depression and World War II. The hard times in the thirties and forties marked an end of innocence for many Americans. The

Depression ravaged the economy and scarred the nation, leaving lingering doubts about the American Dream. The ambiguities that came with waging a world war likewise called into question traditional notions of morality, all too often blurring the lines between good and bad behavior.

Even at war's end, there was no turning back to simpler days. Postwar disillusionment, Cold War fears, and rapid social and economic change left Americans wondering who they were and where the nation was headed. The result was a quest for national purpose, as Americans tried to cope with changing times. Anxieties played out in various ways, including paranoia about communism, as well as growing concerns about social ills such as rising divorce rates, increased social alienation, neuroses, and other psychological problems.[7]

One of the ways in which Hollywood responded to the tense times, growing moral ambiguities, and cultural paranoia was with a new realism, which included films noir such as *The Maltese Falcon* (1941) and *The Big Sleep* (1946). An article in *Life* magazine during the summer of 1947 explained the trend: "Whoever went to the movies with any regularity during 1946 was caught in the midst of Hollywood's profound postwar affection for morbid drama. From January through December deep shadows, clutching hands, exploding revolvers, sadistic villains and heroines tormented with deeply rooted diseases of the mind flashed across the screen in a panting display of psychoneurosis, unsublimated sex and murder most foul."[8]

Westerns jumped on board the film noir stage. The clean-cut cowboy heroes who readily triumphed over evil during the Great Depression and World War II did not disappear completely after 1945. More often than not, however, they were joined by darker, more ambiguous heroes shaped by the hard times of the Depression, the gruesome realities of world war, and the psychological anxieties and uncertainties of the new Cold War frontier. Director John Ford pointed the way. Just as his films *The Iron Horse* (1924) and *Stagecoach* (1939) had captured the mood of the nation in earlier decades, his 1946 release, *My Darling Clementine*, demonstrated the continuing relevance of postwar westerns. A good example of a film noir western, *Clementine* features dark characters and plenty of violence. The film, shot in black and white, has a gritty realistic look and uses shadows, a desolate setting, and unusual camera angles to good effect.

The movie offered a fresh take on the gunfight at the OK Corral, which pitted Wyatt Earp, his brothers, and Doc Holliday against the Clanton clan. At first glance, the story seems quite traditional. Wyatt Earp (Henry Fonda) and his three brothers are herding cattle toward California and stop to rest just outside the town of Tombstone, Arizona. When Wyatt and two brothers ride into town for some rest and relaxation, young James stays behind to watch the herd. They return to find their brother shot dead in the back and the herd taken by rustlers. Determined to find the killers, Wyatt accepts a job as town marshal. Soon after, he meets three individuals who will play a major role in his life. Doc Holliday (Victor Mature) is a brooding gambler as quick with his temper as he is with his gun. Chihuahua (Linda Darnell) is a forceful, fiery saloon girl, desperately in love with Doc. And Clementine Carter (Cathy Downs) is a beautiful and virtuous woman who arrives on the stage, looking for her long-lost love, Dr. John Holliday. She soon discovers that John is now just a shell of his former self. The once proud and respected doctor has become the notorious Doc Holliday, debauched by disease, gambling, alcohol, and sex.

When it comes to protagonists and antagonists, Ford's movie seems to stick to the traditional western formula. The Earp brothers are the obvious good guys, while Old Man Clanton (Walter Brennan) and his four sons are evil through and through. Initially, the women also seem like western clichés. The innocent Clementine (a white Anglo-Saxon Protestant) is a paragon of virtue, whereas the lusty Chihuahua (whose parents were Mexican and Indian) is the quintessential bad girl. The only shades of gray can be found in the character of Doc Holliday, who constantly teeters between morality and depravity. The showdown at the OK Corral appears straightforward. When the gun smoke clears, all the Clantons have bit the dust. No wonder many viewers left the theater thinking they had seen a typical western.[9]

As is the case with most John Ford movies, there is far more to *My Darling Clementine* than first meets the eye. In retrospect, the movie is a parable about post–World War II America. It was the first film that Ford made after returning from military service, and it shows. The heroes and villains rang true for audiences in the aftermath of a world war. In many ways, Fonda's Wyatt Earp is a throwback to earlier heroes. A typical good guy, he represents justice and traditional values. The same can be said for Clementine, an honorable lady who symbolizes all that is good about American womanhood. More complicated are the two other protagonists, Doc Holliday and Chihuahua. Both are morally ambiguous and psychologically flawed. Yet, in the end, they overcome their personal problems and do the right thing. These characters provide a bridge from the old, simpler mythic West to a new, more complicated one after World War II. In the wake of world war, morality was still important but no longer as clear-cut.

Postwar audiences had no problems understanding what motivated the villains. Walter Brennan gives an absolutely chilling performance as the evil patriarch of the Clanton clan. He and his four sons are mean, duplicitous, and driven by greed, cruelty, and an utter disregard for humanity. At one point, Old Man Clanton horsewhips his boys for pulling their guns on Wyatt Earp but failing to kill him. Brennan's character—a cold-blooded killer with no socially redeeming qualities whatsoever—shoots two of the Earp brothers in the back and then is shot and killed when he pulls out a concealed weapon to use against Wyatt. American audiences, with memories of Hitler and his Nazi thugs still fresh in their minds, understood the type of pure evil represented by Old Man Clanton and his boys.

Significantly, the good guys defeat the bad guys, but they pay a very steep price. Before it's over, two of Wyatt's three brothers are killed; Doc Holliday is shot dead at the OK Corral; and Chihuahua is murdered by a Clanton. Wyatt's heartfelt remarks said at the gravesite of his younger brother, James, no doubt resonated with Americans at the end of World War II: "[Just] eighteen-years [old]. You didn't get much of a chance did you, James? I wrote to Pa and Cory Sue. They're gonna be all busted up over it. Cory Sue's young, but Pa. I guess he'll never get over it. I'll be comin' out to see you regular, James. So will [brothers] Morg and Virg. . . . Maybe when we leave this country, young kids like you will be able to grow up and live safe." Audiences after World War II and during the Cold War understood the point all too well. Good could win out over evil, but it would never be easy, and there would always be collateral damage.

Even the title of the film—*My Darling Clementine*—can be linked to the mood of the nation after World War II. After all, why would a movie about Wyatt Earp and the famous gunfight at the OK Corral use a title based on a secondary character? (Clementine is played by Cathy Downs, who does not even get top billing.) The answer may lie in what she represents. Arguably, Clementine symbolizes America itself. Not only does she share a name with one of America's most recognizable folk ballads (which is used as the film's theme song), but she stands at a crossroads, just as the United States did in the aftermath of World War II. Clementine came from the civilized East, hoping to keep her life intact by reuniting with her former beau, Dr. John Holliday. External events force her to realize that the old way of life is over; the past is gone forever. Unlike her folk song equivalent, who perished, the cinematic Clementine begins life anew, determined to bring American civilization to the Wild West as a schoolteacher and create a future with a new man (Wyatt Earp), who represents traditional American values. Clementine's rebirth in the mythic West offered hope to a war-weary nation. Despite the many hardships, setbacks, and casualties inflicted by war, America—like Clementine—could begin again and succeed if it retained its values and moved on with life.

My Darling Clementine pointed the way for other westerns with complex heroes who reflected the anxieties and uncertainties of post–World War II America. A good example is Howard Hawks's *Red River*, a 1948 western that starred John Wayne as a troubled hero facing personal and economic problems after the Civil War. When veteran director John Ford first saw Wayne's impressive performance portraying the psychologically damaged character, he joked, "I never knew the big son of a bitch could act!"[10]

In many ways, *Red River* is a very traditional western. The story centers on a cattle drive and includes wagon trains, Indian attacks, cowboys, gunslingers, gamblers, saloon girls, cowboy songs, and other familiar western images. Wayne's character, Tom Dunson, seems to be living the American Dream. The rugged individual starts with nothing and becomes a successful cattle baron in the West. He shares his success with his old friend, Nadine Groot (Walter Brennan), and adopted son, Matt Garth (Montgomery Clift), whom Dunson raised after the boy's family was killed by Indians.

Just when viewers think they're getting an old-fashioned western epic, however, the movie about a cattle drive stampedes in a totally different direction, reflecting the uneasy mood of the nation by the late forties. Bad economic times threaten to wipe out everything that Dunson worked so hard to accomplish, so he decides to risk everything by driving ten thousand Texas longhorns northward to a railhead in Sedalia, Kansas. At first, both the fatherly Groot and the young Matt are determined to help any way they can, but the situation rapidly deteriorates. Stampedes, lack of food and water, and other problems along the trail erode family unity and sap the confidence of all the drovers. As crises mount, Dunson's determination to get the herd to Sedalia veers toward megalomania if not paranoia. Matt reluctantly seizes control of the herd from Dunson, who then vows revenge.

The film's all-too-tidy ending focuses on the showdown between the cattle baron and his adopted son. Dunson tries to provoke Matt into a gunfight, but the kid won't draw. So, Dunson begins to beat him. The young man eventually fights back, and the two wind up punching each other while rolling across the ground. Only the intervention of Matt's strong-willed girlfriend (Joanne Dru) prevents bloodshed. She pulls out a six-shooter and fires a warning shot to get their attention. She then scolds them, pointing out their obvious love for each other. They quickly agree, and all ends well. Dunson forgives Matt, makes him a full partner in the ranch, and offers his blessing so Matt and his girl can live happily ever after.

Very likely, many World War II vets in the audience could identify with both Dunson's economic dilemma and the responses of family, friends, and loved ones. Tom Dunson, Nadine Groot, Matt Garth, and all the drovers comprise a band of brothers on the trail, fighting enemies, hard luck, bad weather, and utter exhaustion. Vets who served under capricious military leaders during the war could empathize with the negative response of the family and cowboys to Dunson's increasingly unreasonable and tyrannical behavior. *Red River* winds its way through other issues facing Americans in the late forties. Dunson after the Civil War and Americans after World War II had to deal with adjustment problems that affected careers, families, personal relationships, and personal worth. In both cases, redemption and success could be found through the family, loved ones, and a willingness to adapt to changing times.

Howard Hawks's epic demonstrates the vitality of westerns after World War II. The new western hero might be more troubled and the plot more complex, but the power of the mythic West was still intact. Just as Wayne's character found a new life and happiness on the old frontier, so could contemporary Americans on new postwar frontiers as long as they adhered to traditional values involving family, community, fairness, and justice.

Of course, not all troubled protagonists in postwar westerns were able to overcome adversity. Anguished cowboy heroes—like some returning World War II vets–were sometimes unable to reenter society. Perhaps the best example can be found in *The Gunfighter* (1950), starring Gregory Peck. Directed by Henry King, the movie tells the story of the fastest gun in the West—Jimmy Ringo (whose last name evokes John Wayne's famous character from *Stagecoach*). Though not a war veteran, Peck's aging gunfighter has been away from home for more than eight years and wants desperately to return to his wife and son. He is sick of life on the run and tired of young guns who call him out and force him to kill in self-defense.

The movie begins with Ringo riding desperately across desolate landscapes. When he finally arrives in a town, the notorious gunslinger heads straight for the saloon, where he is immediately recognized by a punk trying to make a name for himself. As the young man goads the weary gunfighter, Ringo asks: "How come I've got to run into a squirt like you nearly every place I go these days? What are you trying to do? Show off for your friends?" Undeterred, the cocky kid reaches for his gun, but Ringo proves faster on the draw and kills him instantly. Observers agree it was self-defense but urge the gunslinger to flee at once because the boy's three older brothers will seek revenge. So, Ringo rides off, knowing pursuers are not far behind.

Gregory Peck's sad character heads for the town of Cayenne, where his estranged wife, Peggy (Helen Westcott), and his eight-year-old son reside. He's greeted in the local saloon by an old friend, Mark Strett (Millard Mitchell), now the local marshal. Strett wants the gunslinger out of town before there are any gunfights, but Ringo won't go until he talks to Peggy. Mark agrees to contact her on Ringo's behalf but refuses to divulge her whereabouts, explaining that she has taken a new name, started a new life, and hasn't told the boy about Ringo.

As Ringo waits in the saloon for his possible meeting with Peggy, the situation worsens. With every passing minute, the three avengers are getting closer. The community becomes frenzied as news of Ringo's arrival spreads through town. Gentle womenfolk angrily demand that the marshal arrest or kill him. Adult males and youngsters gather outside the saloon, hoping to see a shootout or at least catch a glimpse of the celebrity gunslinger. And Cayenne's number one troublemaker—a vicious and sneaky young delinquent named Hunt Bromley (Skip Homeier)—is eager to test his fast-draw skills on the famous Ringo. Hunt marches into the saloon with spurs jingling and two guns strapped to his hips, itching for a fight, but Ringo has seen his type far too many times before and won't take the bait. As the arrogant youth approaches the gunslinger's table, Ringo dismisses him with disdain, pointing out that he already has his gun out under the table and it's pointed right at Hunt's gut. As the kid is forced to leave the saloon, he says forebodingly, "I'll be seeing you, Mr. Ringo."

All the while, the clock is ticking, with each minute bringing the three avengers ever closer. Not heeding Mark's continued warnings that he has to get out of town before the pursuers arrive, Ringo at last gets a meeting with his estranged wife. He explains he's tired of being a gunslinger and that he's a changed man. All he wants now is a new start, explaining that the two of them and their son can go someplace where nobody knows him. But Peggy isn't buying it. She knows that there will always be young guns eager to find out who is faster on the draw or gunmen seeking justice for previous killings. No, she can't leave with him, she says. She now has a successful career as a schoolmarm and a young son to care for. What kind of life would that be for the boy? Ringo reluctantly agrees to leave but promises to return in one year to try again. After a brief talk with his son, the sad gunman is finally ready to go.

Unfortunately, time has run out. The three men pursuing Ringo arrive and prepare to ambush him as he's exiting through the saloon's back door. Just before they shoot, the marshal's deputy discovers them and forces them to drop their weapons. Ringo breathes a sigh of relief, climbs into the saddle, and turns his horse to leave. Suddenly, Hunt Bromley steps out from the shadows and calls out the gunslinger. As the startled Ringo begins to turn in his saddle to look in that direction, the young punk draws his six-gun and shoots him in the back. An enraged Mark Strett immediately grabs Bromley, but the mortally wounded gunslinger intervenes. Ringo's dying words make it clear that he thinks a beating, hanging, or some other quick death would be too easy. Real justice will take longer. Over time, Hunt Bromley will realize what it's like to be the man who killed Ringo. He'll constantly be on the run, never knowing what gunman is standing in the shadows to take his life. The movie ends as it began with a lone man on horseback riding desperately across a bleak landscape. But this time the figure is Hunt Bromley—whose first name now has added meaning. The hunter has become the hunted.

The Gunfighter influenced the genre in numerous ways. Like other films noir, it was dark and moody and filmed in black and white, which enhanced its intensity and gave it a realistic feel. What distinguishes *The Gunfighter*, though, is its tension and inventiveness. The film was not the first postwar western to feature a complex and tortured hero trying to find redemption in the mythic West, but it did set the standard for a western hero who is unable to overcome adversity. Ringo winds up a sad and tired figure whose tragic tale takes on almost Greek proportions. Not only did the 1950 film establish the aging gunfighter motif that would become a cliché by the end of the decade, but it struck a responsive chord with viewers by reflecting contemporary concerns in the aftermath of World War II. Ringo—like many World War II vets—longs to trade his violent past for a more peaceful future. He wants to start anew with his wife and family and get a piece of the American Dream. The film's glorification of the family, community, and traditional values fit perfectly with the era's Cold War culture.

At the same time, *The Gunfighter* picks up on growing social concerns after World War II. Anticipating the rise of McCarthyism, it warns against self-righteous citizens, such as the pack of women who want to drive Ringo out of town, or the type of vigilante justice symbolized by the three vengeful brothers who are determined to take the law into their own hands. The film also questions the shallowness and conformity of America's postwar society just as social critics, such as David Riesman, Paul Goodman, and

William Whyte, were making their mark with similar critiques. Like many Americans who grew up in a capitalistic and materialistic culture, Ringo initially wanted only fame, fortune, and glory. Only years later did he realize that this path did not bring true happiness. He wound up losing the things that mattered most, including love, family, and friends. And, ironically, after all those years of trying, he still didn't "even have an expensive watch." Furthermore, the praise he sought from society—his *other-directed* behavior (to borrow a phrase from sociologist David Riesman)—contributed to his demise. Society built him up only to destroy him. Not only does this suggest the ephemeral nature of America's postwar consumer culture, but it is a sharp indictment of how capitalism promotes a new product only to discard it when a newer one comes along. Or, to continue the western metaphor, there will always be a faster gun.

The seminal western mirrored postwar America in other ways. Ever since World War II, civic leaders, parents, and other adults had noted with dismay the rise of juvenile delinquency. The film's focus on dangerous punks like Hunt Bromley, who callously break the law and threaten social order, plugged into those concerns. Even the movie's relatively benign portrayal of rowdy boys who skip school, throw snowballs at adults, or run around like wild animals played into modern fears of rebellious youth. Ringo is well aware of the problem. Along with condemning "young squirts" who always want to start trouble, he goes out of his way to rein in his own son. He advises young Jimmy to always be good, not to skip school, to respect his mother, and follow the advice of moral and brave men like Marshal Strett.

King's film provides a fascinating glimpse of changing gender roles. During World War II, many American women got the opportunity to work outside the home. Some even began successful careers. When the war ended, they found themselves at a crossroads. Should they keep working outside the home or quit and become housewives again? Some questioned whether they even wanted their husbands or boyfriends back once the war was over. *The Gunfighter* brought those issues into focus. In Ringo's absence, Peggy has dropped her married name, become an effective single parent, and established a successful teaching career. Confident of her ability, the independent woman realizes that she does not need a man to succeed. Not only is she able to spurn unwanted advances from other men, but she even refuses to take Ringo back. The former Mrs. Ringo, now known as Peggy Walsh, is a perfect model for the era's new woman—an independent, intelligent, strong-willed woman who can make it on her own in both the workplace and her personal life.

The Gunfighter had a lasting impact on viewers and the western genre, influencing numerous subsequent films, including *High Noon* (1952), *Shane* (1953), and *The Fastest Gun Alive* (1956), as well as later popular songs, such as Lorne Green's "Ringo" (1964) and Bob Dylan's "Brownsville Girl" (1986). "There was a movie I seen one time I think I sat through it twice," sings Dylan. "All I remember about it was it starred Gregory Peck, he wore a gun, and he was shot in the back. Seems like a long time ago, long before the stars were torn down."[11]

The Gunfighter was not the only western of the postwar era that left a lasting impression on viewers. As America struggled to reintegrate returning veterans into society, faced growing Communist threats, and experienced rapid social and cultural change, westerns became darker and more complex and included troubled if not psychotic heroes, as well as large doses of cynicism, alienation, and violence. Westerns such as *Badman's Territory* (1946) and *Silver River* (1948) focused on the adjustment problems of returning Civil War veterans. In films like *Al Jennings of Oklahoma* (1951) and *Lone Star* (1952), the alienated veterans were able to adjust to society, but in others, like *The Man from Colorado* (1948) and *Horizons West* (1952), individuals had a rougher time making the transition. Protagonists were alienated in other ways, reflecting an era described by some observers as an "Age of Anxiety" characterized by the growing popularity of psychoanalysis, rising mental illness, and the increased use of tranquilizers. Westerns such as *Duel in the Sun* (1946), *Pursued* (1947), and *Jubal* (1956) depicted flawed heroes with mental health issues that bordered on the pathological.[12]

James Stewart played troubled heroes in four psychological westerns directed by Anthony Mann in the early fifties: *Winchester '73* (1950), *Bend of the River* (1952), *The Naked Spur* (1953), and *The Far Country* (1955). In *The Naked Spur*, Stewart stars as Howard Kemp, a maniacal bounty hunter who has traveled hundreds of miles from Kansas to Colorado to capture Ben Vandergroat, a devious, dishonest, and unscrupulous villain played to perfection by Robert Ryan. Driven to the point of mental breakdown by rage, greed, and revenge, Kemp is brought back from the edge of madness (not to mention the edge of a cliff and a raging river) by Lina Patch, an eccentric young woman played by Janet Leigh. Ultimately, the movie's title refers not only to the spur that enabled Kemp to scale a rocky cliff so he could outflank the bad guy, but also to the girl and love that spurred him on to overcome both external and internal demons. Howard Kemp was only one of many anguished protagonists in post–World War II westerns who were plagued by cynicism, greed, and violent tendencies.[13]

Showdown on the Cold War Frontier

Numerous westerns released after 1945 explored Cold War themes. One of the first and best was *Broken Arrow* (1950), directed by Delmer Daves. As a Cold War allegory, the western brought America's foreign policy into focus, using Indians as a metaphor for foreign enemies. The movie begins with former Union army officer Tom Jeffords (James Stewart) searching for gold on the Arizona frontier. Alerted by buzzards circling overhead, he finds an Apache boy near death. Over the next few days, he treats the boy's shotgun wounds. Just when the grateful boy is about to return to his village, an Apache war party shows up. They allow Jeffords to go free after the boy explains that the white man saved his life. After Tom returns to Tucson, he realizes that he has an opportunity to improve relations between the American settlers and the Indians. He spends the next month studying the Apache language and customs, and then sets out to find the Indians' stronghold, where he hopes to talk to the notorious war chief Cochise (Jeff Chandler).

At first, Jeffords is unsure whether the Indians will allow him to live, but Cochise is impressed by his bravery and integrity and agrees to talk. The two men with different world views soon find areas of agreement. Since Jeffords has taken the first step toward peace by opening the discussion, Cochise agrees to take the next one. He promises to allow the U.S. mail to get through to Tucson. Before leaving, Jeffords meets a beautiful maiden named Sonseeahray (Debra Paget). Cochise says her name means Morning Star, and that a warrior has already asked for her hand in marriage, but Jeffords cannot stop thinking about her and arranges to meet her again before returning home.

The people in Tucson are pleased that the mail is now arriving on time but angry about continued Indian attacks against other targets. Some citizens, suspicious of Jeffords's friendly relations with the Indians, condemn him as an Indian lover and even attempt to lynch him as a traitor, but the commanding officer at the local fort, General Howard, intervenes and escorts Tom to his office. The compassionate Howard—known affectionately to his troops as "the Christian General"—asks Jeffords to help him open peace talks with Cochise, which eventually lead to a comprehensive treaty. At times, the tenuous peace is almost shattered by racists and war hawks on both sides of the cultural divide. Jeffords almost gives up himself when his new bride, Sonseeahray, is murdered in an ambush by white renegades, but the treaty endures due to Jeffords's steady diplomacy, the wise leadership of Cochise and Howard, and the sacrifices and determination of reasonable people in both camps. At the end of the movie, Tom Jeffords

Figure 19. Cochise (Jeff Chandler) and Tom Jeffords (James Stewart) try to negotiate peace in *Broken Arrow* (Twentieth Century Fox Film Corporation, 1950).

realizes that even his wife's death was not in vain, since it helped "put a seal upon the peace."

Broken Arrow was a powerful Cold War parable. Prior to the outbreak of the Korean War in 1950—the same year that Daves's movie was released—foreign policy debates hinged on the issue of containment. On one side were policy hawks, such as President Harry Truman and secretary of state James F. Byrnes, who insisted that a hardline approach was the only thing brutal Communists would understand. Liberal opponents, such as former vice-president Henry A. Wallace, argued for a less belligerent approach. "We are whipping up another holy war against Russia," he warned.[14]

Broken Arrow clearly endorses Wallace's approach to foreign policy as it presents a sustained argument for a negotiated peace with a rational enemy. Rather than demonizing the enemy as many Americans were wont to do in the Cold War era, the movie portrays Indians as rational human beings. When Jeffords first crosses path with a wounded Indian boy, he repeats the common wisdom about the enemy: "His kind was more dangerous than a snake. He was an Apache. For ten years we'd been in a savage war with his people. A bloody, no-give, no-take war." As the story moves forward, Jeffords dispels the stereotype. He repeatedly portrays Indians as rational people. Like white Americans, they pray to their God, admire honesty, cherish marriage, and show pride in their leaders and culture. They mourn the dead, express love for family members, and respect fellow human beings. When General Howard asks Jeffords what the enemy wants, he replies that they desire the same basic thing as Americans—"Equality." Cochise is not an unreasonable expansionist trying to grab as much land as possible. He is a "realist," insists Jeffords, and he simply wants a separate territory "ruled by Apaches."

Jeffords explains that the enemy might look and act differently, but they and their leaders are not stupid. Cochise is a reasonable man who understands that securing peace won't be easy. Jeffords describes the enemy leader with words that could apply just as easily to Communist guerilla leaders or peasant nationalists after World War II. "Cochise can't even read a map, but he and his men know every gulley, every foot of every mountain, every waterhole," he notes. "He can't write his name, but his intelligence service knows when you got to Fort Grant and how many men you got." Jeffords adds, "And for the first time in Indian history, he has all the Apaches from all the tribes fighting under one command."

Even as *Broken Arrow* promotes more reasonable attitudes toward foreign enemies, it warns of growing Communist hysteria in the United States. In the years after World War II, Americans became increasingly concerned about the possibility of Communist spies and sympathizers operating within the United States. The House Un-American Activities Committee even launched an investigation of the film industry in 1947 in an attempt to expose Communists and other leftists at work in Hollywood. The committee took special aim at ten directors and screenwriters who were dubbed "unfriendly witnesses" because they refused to answer questions about their politics. Subsequently, the entertainment industry blacklisted the so-called Hollywood Ten and others accused of being reds or pinkos (i.e., leaning toward red).[15] One of the Hollywood Ten was Albert Maltz, who wrote the script for *Broken Arrow*. Because he was blacklisted, the initial release of the film credited the screenwriter as Michael Blankfort (Maltz's pseudonym). The Communist hysteria no doubt inspired several scenes in the movie. Repeatedly, James Stewart's character is shouted down as a traitor to his own kind merely because he believes the enemy is not evil and can be reasoned with. And false accusations and mob frenzy nearly lead to the hanging death of Tom Jeffords.

The racial attitudes depicted in *Broken Arrow* were intertwined with the Cold War. The treatment of Indians by racist whites eager for war paralleled the hostile attitudes that many Americans harbored against Communists after World War II. Released as the civil rights movement was picking up momentum, the movie voices support for oppressed minorities and misunderstood enemies. Indians are portrayed as human beings who deserve equality. "The Bible I read preaches brotherhood for all of God's children," explains General Howard to Jeffords. "Suppose the skins aren't white," says Jeffords. "Are they still God's children?" Howard replies instantly, "My Bible says nothing about the pigmentation of their skin." The movie condemns racists regardless of which side they are on. Cochise exiles Geronimo and his followers because their hatred prevents them from making peace with the whites. Similarly, a white settler named Ben Slade is arrested when his anti-Indian attitudes lead to killings and interfere with peace.

Broken Arrow even addresses one of the hottest racial issues of the day—miscegenation. Cochise warns Tom and Sonseeahray that married life will not be easy for them. Where will they live? If they live with her people, many Apaches will resent him, even blame him for all acts of violence by whites. If they live with the whites, she will be scorned and ridiculed. Only after they insist on getting married does the chief give his blessings. The script endorses the mixed marriage, providing the couple with a beautiful wedding and a blissful honeymoon. But, in the end, the couple's chance to live happily ever after is destroyed by hate and prejudice. First, Sonseeahray's former Indian suitor tries to murder Jeffords for wanting an Indian woman. Then, an Indian-hating white man shoots and kills Jeffords's wife.

Delmer Daves's path-breaking western was anything but subtle when it came to race and politics. Most moviegoers had no problems understanding what the characters represented. Jeffords came across as a traditional hero who stood for truth, justice, and liberty for all (regardless of race, religion, or political leanings). No pacifist, he was ready and willing to fight for the right cause. Cochise and Howard symbolized wise and reasonable leaders, who wanted what was best for their people. Geronimo and Ben Slade were racist hard-liners undermining the peace process. And Sonseeahray—the Morning Star—symbolized a possible new day for peace, love, and understanding between people of different nationalities, races, and beliefs.

If *Broken Arrow* promoted negotiations with a reasonable enemy, another major western—*High Noon* (1952)—took a harder line, advocating violence against an implacable foe. The differences in approach might be related to the changing Cold War dynamic. *Broken Arrow* was made just prior to the Korean War; *High Noon* was released after war had broken out and America's foreign policy had gotten tougher. Directed by

Fred Zinnemann with a screenplay by Carl Foreman, *High Noon* (1952) won Oscars for Best Actor, Best Original Song, Best Music Score, and Best Film Editing, as well as nominations for Best Picture, Best Director, and Best Screenplay. Shot in black and white, the film captured the bleak look of a dusty and morally deficient town in the Old West. Even the town's name—Hadleyville—evoked Mark Twain's classic tale about greed and human frailty, "The Man That Corrupted Hadleyburg."

The movie begins with three gunmen riding across the desolate landscape as the title song is sung mournfully and ominously by Tex Ritter. The bad guys are coming to Hadleyville to meet a train carrying Frank Miller, the gang's leader, who has just been released from prison. Miller, a cold-blooded killer, seeks revenge on the marshal and town that sent him to prison. Earlier that day, Marshal Will Kane (Gary Cooper) had married the beautiful Amy (Grace Kelly) and resigned his position partly in deference to her pacifist Quaker beliefs. But when he learns of Miller's imminent arrival, he realizes that he can't walk away from trouble. He and the town have to stand up to the bad guys and defend their lives and principles against evil aggression.

Kane soon learns that the townsfolk are not willing to fight for their beliefs. The judge who had helped put Miller behind bars decides to run away, explaining "nothing that happens here is really important." The minister won't get involved, because he doesn't want to tell his congregation "to go out and kill, and maybe get themselves killed." The rest of the town also refuses to stand up to evil. Some people have economic reasons or family obligations. Others are just cowards. Even his new bride urges Will to get out of town while he can and threatens to leave him if he doesn't. "My father and my brother were killed by guns. They were on the right side but that didn't help them any when the shooting started," Amy explains. "That's when I became a Quaker. I don't care who's right or who's wrong. There's got to be some better way for people to live." The only person who might have been willing to stand by Will Kane is his former lover, Helen Ramirez (Katy Jurado), a forceful Mexican woman whose saloon and brothel have made her one of Hadleyville's wealthiest, albeit most disreputable, citizens. Abandoned by Kane, the pragmatic Helen realizes this is not her fight, so she leaves town to avoid Frank Miller, another former lover. As the clock ticks away the minutes until Miller's train arrives, Will Kane is painfully aware that he must face the bad guys on his own, but the proud lawman refuses to compromise his principles, even if it means certain death. When asked why he's doing it, he replies simply, "I've got to, that's the whole thing."

At high noon, the determined lawman strides out into the street for his showdown with destiny. "Then all of the suspense that has been gathering in the town of Hadleyville breaks out in one of the grimmest, deadliest, and realistic gun battles ever recorded on the screen," wrote a reviewer.[16] Kane picks off some of Miller's gang. Just as he's getting outflanked, he receives unexpected help from his peace-loving wife. Rather than abandoning him, Amy decides to stand by her man. She exchanges her pacifist views for a pearl-handled gun and shoots one of the bad guys in the back to prevent him from killing her husband. Will then finishes off Frank Miller. Only then do the good citizens come out of hiding to congratulate their marshal. Disgusted by the cowardice and lack of principles of these sunshine patriots, Will Kane takes off his badge and throws it to the ground. He and his wife then ride off, hoping for a better future elsewhere.

The dark and tense film resonated with Cold War audiences who could relate to the notion that an evil enemy was a threat to individuals, the community, and the American way of life. Not surprisingly, viewers with different political views came away with opposite insights. Some interpreted the movie as a call to action against communism, as well as a robust defense of Senator Joseph McCarthy, who was making headlines in the early fifties with his crusade against internal Communist subversion. McCarthy—like Kane—refused to abandon his fight even though some segments of the community decried his actions and wanted him to back off.[17]

Other observers took the opposite tack, insisting that *High Noon* was an allegory that warned about the excesses of McCarthyism. From their perspective, Hadleyville's abandonment of Will Kane, an honest American standing up for his principles, was akin to contemporary citizens turning their backs on decent Americans who were being persecuted by McCarthy's witch hunt, the House Un-American Activities Community (HUAC), or private groups that tried to blacklist anyone whose loyalty was suspect. Screenwriter Carl Foreman revealed that his script about a principled lawman abandoned by a feckless community was meant to embarrass Hollywood for refusing to aid writers, directors, actors, and others accused of Communist leanings. Not coincidentally, at the time, Foreman was being investigated by HUAC, but few in the movie industry came to his defense. "There must be times these days," suggested a writer in the *Nation*, "when Mr. Foreman feels that he too [like Will Kane] has been deserted."[18]

The movie's director, Fred Zinnemann, downplayed the film's connection to McCarthyism. "To me, the story is about the character and commitment to duty of a man who is under pressure and who triumphs over his own strongest fears—which is true courage. I believe it was the first time that the hero of a Western did not symbolize the myth of a superman, forever victorious, who doesn't know the meaning of fear," wrote Zinnemann years later. "Also, I thought it was a commentary on the human condition: people who can find all kinds of excuses to avoid becoming personally involved in a dangerous crisis. . . . The theme I was interested in had a much broader meaning than a purely political angle would have had."[19]

High Noon reflects 1950s America in other ways. Just as social critics condemned a variety of ills in postwar America, the film explored similar issues involving conformity, materialism, public apathy, gender, and ethnicity, as well as the constant tension between the rights of the individual and the needs of society. The mayor and other citizens of Hadleyville, for example, want Kane to get out of town, because they fear violence will undermine the town's image and hurt the economy. Similarly, citizens do not want to get involved in controversy and are eager to remain part of the crowd. Helen Ramirez's character likewise sheds light on the era's social dynamics. Not only is she looked down upon because she is Hispanic, but her independence, lower-class background, and the questionable source of her economic success provide additional reasons for the town's resentment.[20]

Regardless of how contemporary observers interpreted *High Noon*, the movie reveals much about the times in which it was made. Controversy over the film continued for years. Early on, a newspaper editorial in 1952 decried it as Communist propaganda because it questioned American society at a time of "international crisis." Almost twenty years later, John Wayne was still calling it the "most un-American thing I've ever seen in my whole life." He was particularly offended by the ending: "The last thing in the picture is ole Coop putting the United States marshal's badge under his foot and stepping on it."[21] (Actually, Will Kane never stepped on the badge, although he did throw it into the dirt in disgust.)

Wayne was not the only person in Hollywood upset by the film. Howard Hawks felt so strongly about the "moral cowardice" of *High Noon* that he rebutted it with a film of his own in 1959, which starred none other than John Wayne. "I made *Rio Bravo* because I didn't like *High Noon*. Neither did Duke [John Wayne]," explained Hawks. "I didn't think a good town marshal was going to run around town like a chicken with his head cut off asking everyone to help. And who saves him? His Quaker wife. That isn't my idea of a good Western."[22]

Rio Bravo offered a variation on the *High Noon* plot. Instead of a bad guy coming to town to get revenge against the marshal, Hawks's movie has a villain threatening the sheriff in order to secure the release of his brother arrested for murder. The biggest difference between the two films is how the lawmen react. Where Gary Cooper's character almost begs the town for support, John Wayne's sheriff John T. Chance actually refuses it. The sheriff explains he doesn't need "some well-meaning amateurs, most of them worried about their wives and kids." That would "just be giving them [bad guys] more targets to shoot at." Chance prefers to rely instead on his hand-picked deputies, a dubious group composed of a recovering alcoholic who used to be an excellent deputy (Dean Martin); a cantankerous old coot with a limp (Walter Brennan); and an inexperienced young gun (Ricky Nelson). A beautiful card sharp and saloon girl named Feathers (Angie Dickinson) lends moral and other kinds of support to Wayne's character. The film ends predictably with a showdown featuring the sheriff's motley crew at their best.

Rio Bravo was both entertaining and well done. "To watch *Rio Bravo* is to see a master craftsman [Howard Hawks] at work," said film critic Roger Ebert. "It is uncommonly absorbing, and . . . contains one of John Wayne's best performances." Other writers felt the movie accomplished its goal by demonstrating to Cold War audiences that both individuals and the community were capable of defeating enemies if they adhered to traditional values. "*Rio Bravo* is very much a picture about being (or becoming) a man," suggests film historian Douglas Brode. "Most important of all, nobody throws his star down in the dust at the end."[23]

Westerns released between 1945 and 1963 explored Cold War themes in other ways. Following the lead of *High Noon*, westerns frequently focused on communities threatened by external enemies. In most cases, people banded together in common cause, but sometimes they were reluctant to fight, as evidenced by movies such as *Man with the Gun* (1955) and *Friendly Persuasion* (1956). Even individuals opposed to violence usually wound up joining the cause in Cold War westerns such as *The Command* (1954), *The Fastest Gun Alive* (1956), and *The Horse Soldiers* (1959). In *The Command*, for example, Guy Madison plays a peace-loving doctor who decries violence until he is placed in charge of troops deep in hostile Indian country. The realities of war force him to become more hawkish. At the same time, some westerns warned about the dangers of irrational communities. *The Moonlighter* (1953), *Johnny Guitar* (1954), *Three Hours to Kill* (1954), and *The Quiet Gun* (1957) appeared shortly after America witnessed the excesses of McCarthyism. All four feature mobs disregarding civil rights of individuals or trying to lynch people who later turn out to be innocent.

Overall, though, the basic message of Cold War westerns was that America could defeat evil aggression if individual citizens and communities cooperated. Two films released shortly after the start of the Korean War drove the point home. *The Last Outpost* (1951) features Ronald Reagan and Bruce Bennett as brothers—one a Confederate, the other a Yankee—who put aside political differences to defend settlers against marauding Indians. The characters in *Little Big Horn* (1951) faced similar problems with the opposite result. The plot centers on cavalry troops trying to make it through hostile Indian country to warn Custer that he is about to be ambushed. Personal differences cause the mission to fail as the soldiers get picked off one by one. The message was clear to moviegoers in the Cold War era: united we stand, divided we fall.

Post–World War II westerns portrayed foreign enemies in ways familiar to Cold War audiences. Movies such as *California Conquest* (1952) and *The Alamo* (1960) depicted foreigners as threats to the American way of life. Images of Indians were also linked to the Cold War. *Tomahawk* (1951), *Hondo* (1953), and *Taza, Son of Cochise* (1954) continued the benign approach to Indian-white relations established by *Broken Arrow*. Once the United States and the Soviet Union settled into a period of peaceful coexistence after 1955, even more pro-Indian westerns were released, including *Walk the Proud Land* (1956), *Run of the Arrow* (1957), and *Geronimo* (1962). But westerns that took a hard line toward Indians were also popular with Cold War audiences. McCarthyism, the Korean War, and events such as the Hungarian revolt, the U-2 incident, the Berlin crisis, and the Cuban missile crisis reinforced the notion that the enemy could not be trusted. Savage Indians continued to be used as stand-ins for bloodthirsty Communists in numerous westerns, including *Flaming Feather* (1952), *The Charge at Feather River* (1953), and *Trooper Hook* (1957). The last film opens with weary captured soldiers lined up at the edge of a cliff and shot down mercilessly by cold-blooded Apaches. Following the war crime, Sergeant Hook (Joel McCrea) makes sure that the official record explains that the men were not killed in battle but were brutally "executed."

Along with containing enemies, patriotic Cold War westerns such as *Pony Express* (1953), *The Oregon Trail* (1959), *Cimarron* (1960), and *How the West Was Won* (1963) glorified westward expansion. At the conclusion of the last film, for example, Debbie Reynolds's character, now a senior citizen, rides in a wagon with her nephew and family—the next generation of westerners—across a beautiful western landscape. A voice-over proudly proclaims, "The heritage of a people free to dream, free to act, free to mold their own destiny." In the background, the patriotic theme song adds, "They all pulled together . . . that's how the West was won."

Other westerns praised the nation's military capabilities. While sophisticated armaments helped make the United States the world's number one superpower throughout the forties and fifties, westerns such as *Winchester '73* (1950), *Springfield Rifle* (1952), and *The Gun that Won the West* (1955) made it clear that advanced weaponry had always played a key role in America's success story. Westerns also reminded Cold War audiences about the brave men willing to fight and die for their country. *Only the Valiant* (1951) told the story of a dedicated officer driving his troops forward to recapture an important mountain pass from marauding Indians. *Davy Crockett: King of the Wild Frontier* (1955) spotlighted the legendary hero who fought Indians, Mexican tyrants, and other bad guys who threatened America. And John Wayne's *The Alamo* (1960) celebrated the valor of citizen soldiers who made the ultimate sacrifice for their country.

Some westerns picked up on Cold War strategies and tactics. *The Eagle and the Hawk* (1950), *Springfield Rifle* (1952), and *The Magnificent Seven* (1960) employ undercover agents or special ops teams to contain threats posed by Indians, foreign nations, or other evil enemies. *The Magnificent Seven*, for example, features a select group of brave Americans with the specific skills needed to defeat the enemy. The seven come to the aid of helpless Mexican peasants in a fight for liberty against a tyrannical enemy, just as the United States was launching counter-insurgency forces to defend Third World countries from brutal Communist guerillas. Just before the bandito leader breathes his last breath, he asks the head of the American team, "You came back to a place like this, why? A man like you, why?" The answer was obvious to most Cold War audiences—Americans always defend liberty and freedom against evil enemies.

If westerns taught Americans how to deal with Cold War enemies and fears, they also allowed audiences a respite from contemporary problems. Like all historical fiction, westerns were popular in part because they enabled audiences to visit a different time and place. Viewers could escape real-world problems by transporting themselves, even for just an hour or two, to an idyllic land where justice was dispensed quickly and fairly. "Fewer and fewer persons today are exposed to farm, open land, animals, nature," explained director John Ford. "We bring the land to them. They escape to it through us." Audiences could relate to the western heroes who lived in simpler times. "We all wish to leave behind us the civilized world," said Ford.[24] And what better place to escape to than the exciting and colorful West of yesteryear? Patriotic Americans of the Cold War era could be proud of how their nation was depicted on screen.

John Ford's Cavalry Trilogy and the Cold War

Of all the Cold War westerns, John Ford's cavalry trilogy may offer the most nuanced and patriotic view of America and the military. The three loosely-related movies focus on the U.S. Army's epic wars against enemies in the Old West. *Fort Apache* (1948) tells the tale of a glory-seeking martinet (Henry Fonda) who leads his troops into a Custer-like debacle despite warnings from his most experienced officer (John Wayne). *She Wore a Yellow Ribbon* (1949) has Wayne's character in charge of soldiers fighting Indians. This time his resolve and rational approach allow him to diffuse a major Indian war. And *Rio Grande* (1950) features Wayne's officer near the end of his career, using his grit and determination to defeat the Apaches and to make peace with his estranged wife. The trailer for *Rio Grande* could have been used to describe all three films. It begins with U.S. troops battling Indians, with a scroll that reads: "The thundering romantic triumphs of the United States cavalry. . . . Starring John Wayne at his fighting best!"[25]

The three cavalry pictures are classic John Ford: they feature magnificent scenery, multilayered stories, colorful details, wonderful characters, and powerful drama interspersed with comic relief. Common threads run through the films. Each is based on a short story written by James Warner Bellah for the *Saturday Evening Post*. Many of the same actors and characters appear in each. John Wayne plays Captain Kirby York in the first film, Captain Nathan Brittles in the second, and then reprises an older Kirby Yorke in the last movie (this time he's a Lieutenant Colonel and has added an "e" to his last name). Victor McLaglen is a gruff sergeant in each of the installments: he appears as Sergeant Mulcahy in *Fort Apache* and then as Sergeant Quincannon in the last two. Similarly, other stock players in Ford's stable, such as John Agar, Ben Johnson, Harry Carey Jr., and George O'Brien, appear as different characters in at least two of the movies. The fact that each was filmed in part in the Southwest adds to the common look and feel of the trilogy. Similar soundtracks, which feature rousing renditions of "The Girl I Left Behind Me" and "She Wore a Yellow Ribbon," likewise contribute to the trilogy's unified feel.

Most important, the three cavalry pictures explore the same themes. Reflecting America's Cold War culture, they focus on the fear of external enemies, the celebration of traditional American values, and the glorification of the military. American Indians are the de facto enemy in each case. The opening of *Fort Apache* quickly establishes the potential for confrontation. Patriotic music plays proudly when U.S. troopers are shown, but

Figure 20. The influence of the artist Frederic Remington on director John Ford is evident in this scene from *Fort Apache* (Argosy Pictures/RKO, 1948), which evokes Remington's painting *The Last Stand.*

the music turns ominous as the camera shifts to Indian warriors. The first scene of *She Wore a Yellow Ribbon* also makes it clear that bloodthirsty Indians are a threat to good Americans everywhere. With the 7th Cavalry's bright red guidon fluttering in the wind, a voice-over explains that news of Custer's Last Stand has spread across the land via telegraph, stagecoach, and pony express. As images of fierce warriors in war bonnets flash on the screen, the narrator adds that Indians are now united in total war across the American frontier.

The three films portray Indians as dangerous and brutal enemies. Cochise in *Fort Apache* outmaneuvers Henry Fonda's character, annihilating the officer and his soldiers. Sitting Bull is described in *She Wore a Yellow Ribbon* as a powerful Indian leader who is "preaching a Holy War." A long camera shot of a Sioux village looks remarkably like a Frederic Remington painting. Brightly colored warriors ride triumphantly past tipis while others pound out a menacing drumbeat. A voice-over describes the mounted warriors as the world's greatest light cavalry. Yet, Ford is careful not to demonize the enemy. The movies distinguish between good Indians and bad ones. *She Wore a Yellow Ribbon* depicts an old chief who wants peace but is unable to control younger, more militant warriors. *Rio Grande* is even more obvious. The Apaches are treated as bloodthirsty savages, while the Navajos become scouts for the U.S. military, and one of them is actually awarded a medal for bravery.

Ford suggests that short-sighted policies of U.S. leaders and unconscionable actions of a few citizens have forced the enemy to fight. In *Fort Apache*, for example, John Wayne's Captain York character explains that Cochise and the Apaches wanted to live in peace on the reservation, but corrupt whites gave them whiskey instead of beef, turning the men into "drunken animals," degrading the women, and making the children sick. So Cochise "did the only thing a decent man could do." He left the reservation and took most of his people to Mexico. Unfortunately, York's reasonable approach falls on deaf ears. His commanding officer, Lieutenant Colonel Owen Thursday (Henry Fonda), insults the enemy, deceives them, and dismisses their military capabilities. Even though the commanding officer realizes that the Indians have legitimate complaints, he refuses to negotiate. Instead, he instructs his interpreter to tell the enemy that "they're not talking to me but to the United States government. Tell them that government orders them to return to their reservation. And tell them that if they have not started by dawn, we will attack." Thursday's ill-conceived response results in a horrendous defeat for the U.S. military.

John Ford's cavalry trilogy offered a prototype for what later would be called peaceful coexistence. Its Cold War message was clear: a potentially dangerous enemy should be dealt with respectfully and fairly, but forcibly when necessary. Film historian Ronald L. Davis points out that John Wayne's lead characters in *Fort Apache* and *She Wore a Yellow Ribbon* argued for a peaceful resolution with the Indians. Not until *Rio Grande*, which was released shortly after the beginning of the Korean War, does Wayne's officer opt for a less conciliatory, military solution to destroy the enemy.[26]

The three cavalry pictures picked up on other Cold War attitudes. Ford's celebration of the military mirrored the attitudes of patriotic Americans after World War II. Almost every sight and sound in the movies glorifies the U.S. Cavalry. Ford consciously recreated the romantic images of troopers found in paintings by Frederic Remington. In *She Wore a Yellow Ribbon*—the only one of the three filmed in Technicolor—Ford makes excellent use of the soldiers' blue and gold uniforms, contrasting them against red sunsets and the magnificent earth tones of Monument Valley. Music adds to the effect. The use of orchestral arrangements of songs such as "She Wore a Yellow Ribbon" and "The Girl I Left Behind Me" creates a patriotic mood in all three films, while the smooth harmonies of the Sons of the Pioneers add to the middle-class sentimentality of *Rio Grande*. Not coincidentally, the last name of John Wayne's character in the first and last film evokes Sergeant York, the most decorated American soldier of World War I. In each movie, Wayne's character is heroic, decent, responsible, and respectful toward friends and enemies alike. In *She Wore a Yellow Ribbon*, he even echoes President Truman's "the buck stops here" statement. "Only the man who commands can be blamed," he says to a young woman who tries to apologize for causing his patrol's problems. "It rests on me—mission failure!"

The trilogy portrayed responsible officers and ordinary enlisted men as brave, hardworking Americans who were the backbone of the U.S. military. "Put out of your mind any romantic ideas that [military life is] a way of glory," explains Wayne's character to new recruits in *Rio Grande*. "It's a life of suffering and hardship, an uncompromising devotion to your oath and your duty." Ford's soldiers are more than up to the task. In the first movie, Ward Bond plays a common-man soldier awarded the Congressional Medal of Honor. In the second one, Captain Nathan Brittles (John Wayne) and a sergeant admit they are scared as they ride bravely into a hostile Indian encampment in an attempt to negotiate. When diplomacy fails, Brittles leads his troops in a surprise attack on the Indian village. Although the attack at dawn recalls the U.S. cavalry's slaughter of Indian men, women, and children at the notorious Battle of the Washita (1868), this time the ethical soldiers' only goal is to disperse the Indians' horse herd. Following their success, Brittle says proudly, "No casualties; no Indian war; no court martial." In the final film, Lieutenant Colonel Yorke reminds his son that ordinary Americans always show courage in times of danger: "At Chapultepec [during the Mexican-American War], my father, your grandfather, shot for cowardice the son of a United States Senator."

John Ford's cavalry consisted of citizen-soldiers. Their camaraderie, determination, and courage enabled them to defend the American way of life against all foes. The army community in the cavalry trilogy mirrored America's ethnic diversity. Some of the soldiers were southerners, demonstrating that the frontier army came from all parts of the country. Others were Irish, in keeping with the large numbers of foreign-born soldiers in the Army of the West.

Women and families also played important roles in Ford's cavalry trilogy. All three films have "The Girl I Left Behind Me" playing in the background as troops deploy. Women are shown sending their men off to war and then waiting anxiously for their return. Such images reinforced expected gender roles in the years after World War II. Yet, the women portrayed in these cavalry pictures were not just passive figures. These girlfriends, wives, and mothers added support, determination, and continuity to the military effort. Significantly, they did it in dominant and often aggressive ways. In *Fort Apache*, for example, Emma Collingwood (Anna Lee) takes it upon herself to welcome the new commandant's daughter (Shirley Temple) to the fort. Soon thereafter, Temple's determined character is able to set up and run a household on her own. Olivia Dandridge, the young woman played by Joanne Dru in *She Wore a Yellow Ribbon*, is equally independent. Along with convincing two young officers that the yellow ribbon in her hair is for each of them, she repeatedly demonstrates determination to succeed. Women like Olivia provided continuity from one military generation to the next. Her steadfastness impressed John Wayne's middle-age character so much that one night while visiting his wife's grave, he confides, "[She's a] nice girl . . . reminds me of you."

Military wives could be every bit as brave as their husbands. Abby Allshard (Mildred Natwick), the wife of the fort commander in *She Wore a Yellow Ribbon*, is a perfect example. After a drunken sergeant has beaten up several soldiers for trying to arrest him, she marches into the building and orders the unruly soldier to get to the guardhouse. He complies immediately. Later, Mrs. Allshard helps a doctor treat soldiers severely wounded in an Indian attack. When necessary, these strong-willed women even correct the men. Mrs. Allshard felt it necessary to scold Wayne's character, who was retiring and trying to say good-bye to her. "You'll do no such thing, Nathan Brittles," she declares. "*Good-bye* is a word we don't use in the cavalry. To our next posting. . . ." Similarly, Mrs. Kathleen Yorke (Maureen O'Hara) repeatedly stood up to her husband whenever she thought he was wrong (which was often). The supremely confident wife knew only one thing could challenge her, as evidenced by her toast: "To my only rival, the United States Cavalry."

Although Ford's cavalry pictures glorify the military and common-man soldiers, they are far less complimentary toward civilian and military leaders. Lieutenant Colonel Owen Thursday, Henry Fonda's arrogant character in *Fort Apache*, is the quintessential incompetent officer. Disregarding all practical advice from experienced Indian fighters, he explains that his tactics are based on a paper written years ago by a young Robert E. Lee when he was still at West Point, as well as a maneuver employed by Genghis Khan at the Battle of Ginshan in 1221. Predictably, Thursday and his command are wiped out by the Indians.

Civilian leaders are equally bad. In *Fort Apache*, Captain York describes the politicians and businessmen responsible for inciting the Indian war as "the dirtiest, most corrupt political group in our history." Similarly, an unscrupulous merchant in *She Wore a Yellow Ribbon* sells contraband firearms to the Indians. In *Rio Grande*, John Wayne's character must contend with incompetent bureaucrats who don't provide him with the necessary manpower to fight the Indians, as well as civilian leaders who refuse to allow the soldiers to pursue hostile Indians south of the Rio Grande. Finally, Wayne's superior officer tells him to disregard official government policy. "I want you to cross the Rio Grande, hit the Apache and burn him out," the exasperated general says. "I'm tired of hit-and-run. I'm sick of diplomatic hide-and-seek." Ford's art was clearly imitating life. The film was released just as President Truman was preventing General Douglas MacArthur from launching an all-out fight against Communist forces north of the 38th parallel in Korea. Frustrated by the president's decision to fight a limited war in Korea, John Ford immediately took down the autographed picture the president had given him. More significantly for moviegoers, Ford directed John Wayne and the cavalry to chase the enemy across the border.[27]

Even if the cavalry trilogy criticized the actions of individual civilian or military leaders, the overall effect was still pro-military and pro-America. Just as World War II veterans could condemn military leaders they served under but still be proud of their military service, so could John Ford disparage questionable leaders but still praise the military as an institution. In Ford's capable hands, the military became a microcosm of America. It represented the goodness of the common man, the importance of the family and community, and the courage and industriousness of ordinary Americans. The cavalry trilogy reaffirmed Americans' faith in their past, present, and future. It assured post–World War II Americans that no soldier ever died in vain and promised moviegoers that as long as Americans remained true to basic values, they could defeat all enemies, whether Indians in the Old West or Communists on Cold War frontiers.

Perhaps the ending of *She Wore a Yellow Ribbon* said it best. John Wayne's character is once again leading a group of soldiers out against a dangerous enemy. With flags flying and patriotic music playing, a voice-over says: "So here they are, the dog-faced soldiers, the regulars, the fifty-cents-a-day professionals riding the outposts of a nation. From Fort Reno to Fort Apache, from Sheridan to Starke, they were all the same. Men in dirty-shirt blue and only a cold page in the history books to mark their passing. But, wherever they rode—and whatever they fought for—that place became the United States."

CHAPTER SIX

Shane

Western Heroes and the Culture of the Cold War

Shane was released in 1953. The film starred Alan Ladd as a quiet gunslinger who rides into town and winds up protecting homesteaders from a cattle baron and his hired gun. "There never was a man like SHANE," bragged a movie poster. "There never was a motion picture like SHANE. Acclaimed the greatest story of the West ever filmed—SHANE!" This was one case where the movie almost lived up to the hype. George Stevens's film became a box office hit and did well at Oscar time, earning an academy award for Cinematography as well as nominations for Best Picture, Best Director, and Best Screenplay. It also picked up Best Supporting Actor nominations for Jack Palance and Brandon de Wilde.

Shane arrived in theaters in the midst of the Cold War between the United States and the Soviet Union. In 1953, a Senate subcommittee chaired by Joseph McCarthy began investigating possible Communist spies in the U.S. government. Overseas, the Korean War, a test case in America's determination to contain the spread of communism, was in its third year. Nikita Khrushchev and the Soviet Union seemed bent on worldwide expansion. Adding to American fears, the Russians exploded their first hydrogen bomb that year. By the fifties, fears of communism permeated almost every level of American life and thought. The emergence of a Cold War culture influenced myriad institutions, such as government, religion, marriage, and the family, as well as everyday life and attitudes toward race, ethnicity, and gender.[1] On the surface, the postwar years appeared to be a period of consensus and conformity, a patriotic era marked by fears of communism and praise for traditional values that

Figure 21. This movie poster for *Shane* depicts the hero shooting the bad guy and protecting a youngster (Paramount Pictures, 1953).

supported God, country, and family. But not far below, conflict was already brewing over race, ethnicity, gender, youth, and a variety of issues.

Shane was in step with the culture of the Cold War. Not only did the movie provide audiences with a classic western hero who stood for truth, justice, and the American way of life, but it mirrored the changing times. It dealt with important issues involving the use of violence and notions of right and wrong, and it plugged into contemporary trends involving youth, gender, family, and community. *Shane* was unusual in that it addressed most of the fears and ambiguities found in America's Cold War culture, but it certainly was not the only western that reflected the times.

Westerns produced between 1945 and 1963 captured the anxious mood of the nation. While most relied on time-honored images of the mythic West and conventional heroes and plots to promote consensus behavior and conformity, others set out for new regions of the mythic West to explore the changing times. They featured complex characters and complicated plots that portrayed the West in shades of gray rather than just black and white. Some postwar westerns revealed conflict beneath the surface of America's Cold War culture. They revised images of women, minorities, immigrants, and youths; they reinterpreted the roles played by individuals, families, society, and government in the settlement process; and they investigated the exploitation of the West's native peoples and resources. Significantly, these films anticipated the rise of the New Western History by at least three decades, suggesting that popular culture is often faster on the draw than academia.[2]

Westerns demonstrate that the postwar period was far more complicated than generally thought. Between 1945 and 1963, more was going on in America than just conformity and stereotypical "happy days." The era was characterized by powerful and contradictory forces swirling within the culture of the Cold War. Postwar westerns provide evidence of consensus and conflict, as well as continuity and change.

Shane and 1950s America

Shane begins with Alan Ladd's drifter character riding up to a homestead set in a beautiful valley ringed by towering snowcapped mountains. He is greeted by Joe Starrett (Van Heflin) and his boy, Joey (Brandon de Wilde). Just as Shane is about to move on, local cattle baron Rufus Ryker and his henchmen ride up, trampling a vegetable garden and making it clear that there is no room on the range for sodbusters. When the situation turns menacing, Shane positions himself next to Starrett for support.

Afterwards, the grateful farmer and his wife, Marian (Jean Arthur), invite Shane to stay for supper. Next morning, he signs on as a farmhand. The plot thickens as the drifter draws closer to the entire family, including the lovely Marian. Slowly but surely, he also gets dragged into a budding range war between Ryker and the homesteaders. Eventually, Shane has a showdown with Ryker and his hired gun, Jack Wilson (Jack Palance). Once the bad guys are dead and victory is assured for the homesteaders, the lonely hero rides off into the night.

Shane became one of the year's most successful films not only because of its dramatic story line, compelling characters, and majestic scenery, but also because it tapped into the affluence and anxieties of post–World War II America. The economic and class issues in the movie probably seemed familiar to many moviegoers. Just as powerful cattlemen and ordinary farmers vied for resources on Wyoming's freewheeling frontier, Americans were jockeying for position in the booming postwar economy. Starrett's community organizing would have seemed quite natural to blue collar workers of the fifties, who viewed collective bargaining as the means to check corporate power and greed. The Wyoming frontier, like contemporary America, offered opportunities to expectant capitalists from varied economic and cultural backgrounds. Although not as diverse as 1950s America, Wyoming society did include immigrants from all over the country. One of the characters, an ex-Confederate soldier nicknamed Stonewall Torrey, exemplified the West's acceptance of everyone regardless of background.

The film also picked up on changing attitudes toward sex and gender. As the Motion Picture Production Code eased restrictions after World War II, westerns such as *Shane* could openly address adultery. Throughout the film, Shane and his friend's wife, Marian, share tender moments and knowing glances. The woman's young son even tries to convince Shane not to leave town by saying innocently, "Pa's got things for you to do. And Mother wants you. I know she does!" Significantly, Marian Starrett does not fit the fifties stereotype of the content housewife. Despite her seemingly perfect family and economic success, something is missing in her life. Her restlessness anticipates by a decade or more similar frustrations that were implicit in Betty Friedan's 1963 publication *The Feminine Mystique* and unleashed by the sexual revolution of the late sixties and seventies.

Young Joey Starrett's high profile in the movie was in keeping with the prominence of youth culture in the fifties. The story often spotlights Brandon de Wilde's precocious character. When Shane first rides up to the Starrett homestead, he notices that the boy had been watching him. "You know," he tells the child, "I . . . like a man who watches things go on around. It means he'll make his mark someday." Joey doesn't let Shane down. He even plays a major role in the climactic showdown, preventing Shane from getting bushwhacked by a hidden rifleman.

While *Shane* hints at social change, it endorses the traditional values of postwar America. The homesteaders typify hardworking Americans who believe in freedom, fairness, equal opportunity, religion, and family. Shane is an archetypical western hero who defends liberty and justice for all. He protects the innocent and aids the defenseless against bullies and evil. Before riding off into the sunset, he gives one last piece of advice to his young friend: "You go home to your mother and your father and grow up to be strong and straight." Not surprisingly, Shane's celebration of traditional values appealed to Cold War audiences. The film also resonated because of its focus on evil enemies. Ryker's insatiable hunger for new territory and the ever-present danger posed by the cattle baron and his hired gun were all too familiar to fifties Americans, who lived in constant fear of Soviet expansionism and threats, which hung like dark clouds over Cold War America.

Reflecting the growing ambiguities of postwar American culture, the film's protagonists and antagonists are complex. Shane, for example, appears to be an old-fashioned good guy. The clean-cut, blond-haired hero dresses in buckskins just like Davy Crockett, and he is polite to womenfolk, friendly to youngsters, and modest about his considerable talents with his gun and fists. Yet, he is also a troubled hero with a mysterious past. He longs for society and family ties but knows that his gunslinger ways won't allow it.

Joe Starrett is just as complicated. The broad-shouldered, intense farmer is determined to stand up for his principles, but ultimately he is simply too honest and trusting to deal successfully with wicked opponents such as Ryker or his hired gun. Starrett's stubbornness clouds his judgment. He truly believes he can organize the community and reason with the enemy. His naiveté convinces him he should go to town to negotiate with Ryker, even though Shane tries to tell him it's a deadly trap.

Starrett's wife is equally complex. No doubt, female viewers in the fifties, an era that glorified female domesticity, could relate to Marian, who appears to be the perfect wife and mother. She is attractive, takes care of her son, and is a good cook and supportive wife. Yet, there is a darker side to this model housewife. She evidently has strong feelings for Shane, which suggests inner desires that supposedly were alien to "good girls" of the fifties. When Shane brutally and unfairly knocks her husband unconscious in a vicious brawl, she rushes to Shane's side for an intimate talk rather than tending to her husband, who may have suffered a concussion.

Even the bad guys are complicated. Ryker offers a powerful rationale for his dubious actions. He points out that rugged individuals like him were the pioneers who conquered the wilderness and defeated the savage Indians, thereby opening the wild country to the ungrateful homesteaders now threatening his livelihood. At first, he tries to be fair and offers Starrett good money and even a job in exchange for his claim, but the intransigence of Starrett and the other farmers coupled with Ryker's own greed eventually cause him to hire a killer to resolve the situation once and for all. One of Ryker's henchmen, Chris Calloway (Ben Johnson), heads in exactly the opposite direction. At the beginning of the movie, he constantly harasses the sodbusters. By the end, he concludes that Ryker has gone too far. Calloway quits his job and becomes a whistleblower, warning Shane of Ryker's evil plans to kill Starrett.

The most obvious villain is Jack Palance's gunslinger. Jack Wilson is evil personified. He dresses in black, has a constant cruel sneer on his face, and revels in killing. When he first walks into the saloon, even the dog skulks out of the way. One of the more memorable scenes in the film is when the malevolent gunslinger goads a hot-headed sodbuster into a gunfight. Drawing fast and aiming his six-gun directly at his opponent's heart while the farmer is still trying to clear his holster, Wilson pauses for what seems an eternity and then shoots the man in the chest. The cold-blooded gunslinger smiles maliciously as the sodbuster falls face down into the muddy street. Even in his case, though, some viewers might wonder what dark secrets are responsible for his violent and callous behavior.

Additional tension results from a major question posed by the film: Is violence necessary to defeat a foe? At first, the peace-loving farm community is confident that rational discussion can resolve the impasse between the homesteaders and the greedy cattle baron, but Shane's violent approach wins out in the end. The perceptive cowboy hero understood the tensions inherent in the changing times. Even though civilized communities were rapidly replacing the wild frontier, society still needed courageous individuals who could defeat enemies in times of trouble. But once the crisis was over, there would be no place for vigilantes in a civilized world. Fast guns like Shane—no matter how well intentioned—were a threat to social order. Violence would follow him to his dying day. "There's no living with a killing," admitted Shane. "Right or wrong, it's a brand. . . . There's no going back." The tragic hero was a threat not just to the community but also to family values. The sexual tension between him and Marian was obvious. So far, his better angels had won out, but he knew he had to move on for everyone's good. There could be no redemption for Shane.

Despite his complicated situation, Shane was determined to act quickly and decisively. Appeasement was not an option for this Cold War cowboy. He knew intuitively that it was impossible to negotiate with treacherous bad guys like Ryker and Wilson. Violence was the only thing they understood. "A gun is a tool, Marian; no better or no worse than any other tool," he explained to Starrett's pacifist wife. "A gun is as good or as bad as the man using it." Only hard-liners like Shane, who were willing to use violence to defeat violence and ready to adopt the enemy's unfair tactics, could succeed. Shane's situational ethics not only enabled him to beat Ryker and his hired gunman at their own game, but allowed him to fight dirty against his friend, Joe Starrett. When Shane couldn't defeat the strapping farmer in a fair fistfight, he used his gun as a club to knock out Starrett. Shane knew he hadn't fought fair, but all that mattered was the outcome. He stopped his friend from going into town, where he would have faced almost certain death.

George Stevens's film demonstrates the relevance of the mythic West in fifties America. Audiences could relate to Shane's pragmatic and aggressive style. His quest for justice in the Old West suggested that contemporary Americans could overcome their complex problems and cut through the ambiguities of modern life if they—like Shane—adhered to the values that made the nation great. The cowboy hero's expedient use of unfair and violent tactics for a good cause was understandable in a Cold War era that saw the United States relying on violence and questionable policies to contain the Communist threat. In both cases, the end justified the means.

Of course, once evil was defeated, violent individuals like Shane would no longer be needed. With peace and security assured, families could once again pursue the American Dream. Adult moviegoers after World War II did not need anyone to explain why Shane rode off into the night as Little Joey shouted to no avail, "Shane! Shane! Come back!"

Westerns and the Culture of the Cold War

Most westerns released between 1945 and 1963 fit in perfectly with the era's conformity. Like the nation as a whole, westerns showed support for the Cold War culture by endorsing patriotism, religion, capitalism, family values, and the American way of life in general. Patriotic films such as *Davy Crockett: King of the Wild Frontier* (1955), *The Alamo* (1960), and *How the West Was Won* (1963) praised democracy, while *The Far Horizons* (1955), *Westward Ho the Wagons* (1956), and other films recalled the nation's glorious westward expansion.[3]

Westerns celebrated traditional values linked to America's greatness. Movies such as *Wagon Master* (1950) and *Pillars of the Sky* (1956) demonstrated the important role of religion in the Old West. Westerns also glorified the family. As many Americans turned to marriage and the family for shelter from communism, westerns idealized family life.[4] Despite the common wisdom that cowboy heroes never got the girl, the reality is that western heroes of the fifties and early sixties typically lived happily ever after only because they wound up with the girl, as evidenced by films such as *Hondo* (1953), *The Naked Spur* (1953), and *Jubal* (1956). *Hondo* is a perfect example. At first, John Wayne's character is a loner. He's an accomplished Indian fighter and a successful scout, but there's emptiness in his life. That changes when Hondo arrives at an isolated ranch, where he meets a woman and boy abandoned by the woman's husband. Slowly but surely, he is drawn to the woman and her home. Later, Hondo is captured by Apaches who had befriended the woman's son. When they mistake him for the boy's father, they escort Hondo back to the woman's cabin, where he at last finds happiness carving out a future with the woman and boy. Whenever the hero does not wind up happily married to the woman he loves (e.g., *Shane* or *The Gunfighter*), the results usually aren't too good. Gregory Peck's sad character in *The Gunfighter* winds up dead, while Alan Ladd's tragic gunfighter, Shane, may or may not be better off as he rides off into the sunset with a gun wound and a broken heart.

Like Cold War America in general, westerns subscribed wholeheartedly to capitalism.[5] Movies such as *Red River* (1948), *Fort Worth* (1951), *Texas Lady* (1955), and *Cimarron* (1960) became veritable odes to the American Dream as they showed how ordinary people struck it rich in the West.[6] Westerns also promoted America's burgeoning consumer culture. They helped popularize cowboy images and styles, which resulted in increased sales of western music, cowboy hats, clothes, toys, and other products. They aided western tourism by sparking interest in dude ranches, rodeos, national parks, and restored towns of the Old West, such as Tombstone and Dodge. In addition, westerns promoted popular fads and new technology. There were horror westerns like *The Beast of Hollow Mountain* (1956) and *Curse of the Undead* (1959), as well as numerous 3-D westerns. The most popular was Guy Madison's *The Charge at Feather River* (1953), which featured arrows and spears aimed at the audience, as well as soldiers charging at the audience waving sabers. The film became a cult classic because the sound clip of Private Wilhelm screaming when shot by an arrow—now known affectionately as the Wilhelm Scream—was later used in innumerable films, including *Star Wars* and *Indiana Jones*.

Even as post–World War II westerns endorsed America's Cold War culture, they offered evidence that social change was brewing beneath the surface of the dominant culture. Images of women, minorities, and young people in postwar westerns offer glimpses of the changing times.

Sex, Gender, and Postwar Westerns

Most westerns followed society's prescribed gender roles. While male heroes were typically depicted as active, aggressive, dominant, and rugged individuals who guaranteed the safety and rights of all Americans, women were portrayed as subordinates who were dependent on men for success. Social expectations maintained that females existed to please males; become wives; have babies; keep house; be attractive, nurturing, subservient; and follow a man's lead in all matters. Women were idealized as the upholders of religion, morals, education, virtue, truth, and justice. Cold War Americans believed that the nation would benefit if men and women lived up to their expected gender roles. Men would become the leaders in the fight against communism, while women would provide auxiliary support. "In keeping with the American tradition, it was up to women to achieve successful families," explains historian Elaine Tyler May. "If women fulfilled their domestic roles, as adapted to the atomic age, they would rear children who would avoid juvenile delinquency (and homosexuality), stay in school, and become future scientists and experts to defeat the Russians in the cold war."[7]

Most women in postwar westerns fulfilled gender expectations. They served as loving wives and daughters, nurturing girlfriends, and in other domestic roles. Typically, women were supporting players in the frontier saga, providing love and help in films such as *Shane* (1953), *Hondo* (1953), and *The Virginian* (1946). They watched over hearth and home, cowered in terror when there was violence, and waited passively while aggressive males stood up to evil.

At the same time, westerns often featured bright, capable, and determined women who functioned magnificently within the traditional domestic arena. These take-charge ladies may not have been equal to men in politics or society, but they ruled at home. In *She Wore a Yellow Ribbon* (1949), the head matron, Mrs. Allshard, and the younger Olivia Dandridge were intelligent ladies who took active roles in all matters even remotely related to the domestic sphere. Maureen O'Hara's strong, independent character in *Rio Grande* (1950) repeatedly held her own against her husband, a tough military officer played by John Wayne. Similarly, Mrs. Lowe in *Hondo* (1953) and Mrs. Jorgensen and her daughter in *The Searchers* (1956) were smart and aggressive females who steered men in the direction they wanted their own lives to go.

Some westerns suggested that in emergency situations good wives could do jobs normally reserved for males. Amy Kane, the marshal's bride in *High Noon* (1952), is a perfect example. The well-mannered, educated, and nonviolent religious woman actually picked up a gun and shot a bad guy in the back in order to protect her husband. While such actions were certainly not part of a wife's job description in the Cold War era, the film confirmed that in the right circumstances, traditional wives could act in nontraditional ways. Indeed, if conditions were truly extraordinary, a western woman might even stray from marriage vows and still find redemption. In *The Sea of Grass* (1947), Katharine Hepburn's character is driven to adultery by her cattle baron husband (Spencer Tracy), who neglects her, devotes all his time and energy to his business, and treats homesteaders and other rivals with contempt. Hepburn's character is forgiven only after she is appropriately punished, shows remorse, and makes it clear that she will abide by traditional gender roles in the future. Interestingly, the film came out just after World War II and may have resonated with veterans and spouses trying to rescue troubled marriages.

In most cases, western women who violated society's prescribed gender roles were dismissed as unworthy wives, saloon girls, or other "bad girls" who did not fit in proper society. Jennifer Jones's over-the-top character in *Duel in the Sun* (1946)—the hot-blooded Pearl Chavez—cannot resist evil men or sex, a bad combination that results in her death. Similarly, Linda Darnell's Chihuahua character in *My Darling Clementine* (1946), a fiery saloon girl with loose morals, is shot to death after she beds one man too many. And the adulteress wife in *Jubal* (1956)—played by Valerie French—is beaten to death by a former lover.[8] In every instance, bad girls wind up with a bad hand in the game of life, in keeping with the era's double standard and good girl/bad girl dichotomy.

While most westerns endorsed traditional gender roles, some offered opportunities for moral women to succeed outside normal boundaries. These nontraditional films reflected changing expectations of women in the post–World War II era. By war's end, many women were accustomed to working outside the home, often doing jobs previously reserved for men. Although most wound up returning to domestic roles after the war, they soon reentered the job market. In 1950, they composed just 17 percent of the total workforce; ten years later, it was 30 percent.[9]

After 1945, an increasing number of films featured independent women in the workplace performing jobs or activities traditionally reserved for men.[10] *Westward the Women* (1951), directed by William Wellman, is a good example. It follows a wagon train of women heading west to become wives. When the men hired to escort the wagons abandon their posts, the determined women refuse to turn back. Only a few know how to use guns, ride horses, or drive a wagon, so the misogynist wagon master (Robert Taylor) has to teach them the necessary skills. The resolute women prove to be fast learners and become adept at doing jobs normally reserved for men. Heading west, they fight Indians, stop stampedes, traverse deserts, haul wagons through steep mountain passes, and survive flash floods, downpours, and lightning bolts. Even the sexist wagon master is won over by their bravery and abilities, and he eventually falls in love with one of the women. As soon as the wagon train arrives in California, however, the women revert to traditional gender roles by donning dresses and bows and eagerly pairing off with the men waiting to marry them.

Westward the Women offers a feminist take on the mythic West as it follows ordinary women heading west to an exotic land, where they find success, happiness, and redemption through hard work and adherence to traditional values. Yet, the film reinforces rather than rejects gender attitudes of the day. Wellman's western tale serves as a fascinating metaphor for what happened to women during and after World War II. When American men went off to fight the Axis powers, women on the home front had to step up and do men's jobs extremely well. But, once the crisis was over, they returned to their expected gender roles as wives and mothers. Like the female characters of *Westward the Women*, the independent women found in other post–World War II westerns initially appear to be throwing off the shackles of traditional gender roles, but in the end they usually conform to expectations or are punished if they don't. In most cases, they have to be rescued by men, they follow the male's lead, and ultimately they wind up accepting domestic bliss. By film's end, they typically give up their newfound careers, get married, and presumably live happily ever after in keeping with prescribed gender roles.

Some cultural conservatives in postwar America might have argued that independent women simply needed a real man to straighten them out.[11] *The Moonlighter* (1953) provides a good example. The film stars Fred MacMurray as Wes Anderson, a cattle thief brazen enough to rustle cows only by the light of the moon (hence the title), and Barbara Stanwyck as Rela, his strong-willed ex-girlfriend, now betrothed to his brother. Rela appears to be quite the independent woman. She dresses in jeans and boots and wears a six-gun strapped to her hips. She rides a horse better than most cowboys and shoots as well as any gunslinger. Rela warns Wes that she'll kill him if he ever gets his younger brother involved in criminal activities. Shortly thereafter, Wes and a former partner in crime bring the brother along on a bank job. When the brother is killed, Rela volunteers to become a deputy, and she tracks down her former lover. After shooting and killing Wes's partner, she captures Wes. On the way back to town, Rela slips and falls into a raging river. Wes immediately comes to the rescue. Seeing her in the river, he says, made him realize the truly important things in life. He decides to turn himself in, serve jail time, and then go straight. Rela's love for him is thus rekindled, and she promises to wait for him so they can live happily ever after. In effect, Stanwyck's tough-as-nails female character not only winds up needing to be rescued by a male, but she then jumps at the chance to take the cad back so she can become his loving, nurturing, and forgiving wife. This could have been a western movie version of Marynia Farnham and Ferdinand Lundberg's 1947 best seller, *Modern Woman: The Lost Sex*. As in the book, *The Moonlighter* suggests that women can find true happiness only if they accept their natural roles as wives and homemakers.

While Stanwyck's character falls short of being an independent woman who controls her own destiny, she needs to be judged not by today's standards but by those of her day. Compared to most women in forties and fifties westerns, who operated within the confines of traditional gender roles, the hard-riding and straight-shooting Rela is far more independent and aggressive. Female viewers undoubtedly understood why she ultimately had to defer to a man. "The feminine mystique [of the 1950s] limited male anxieties about changing female sexuality by prescribing the boundaries of change," explains historian Sara M. Evans. "In the 1950s women could—even should—be sexual . . . but they could not be in control." Even though Stanwyck's strong female character was not totally in charge of her destiny, she pointed the way toward greater gender equality. Historian Glenda Riley maintains that Stanwyck helped "feminize" the western. "In Stanwyck's westerns, women were not simply adjuncts or satellites," notes Riley. "They could, and did, express their own wills and take action for themselves. Moreover, a strong woman did not have to choose between the worlds of work and love. She could have a ranch *and* a man." No wonder President Ronald Reagan—who starred with Stanwyck in *Cattle Queen of Montana* (1954)—could praise her in 1981 with these words: "Long before it was fashionable, you were a paradigm of independence and self-direction for women all over the world."[12]

Barbara Stanwyck's heroines were not the only protofeminist characters in postwar westerns. Indeed, some movies went well beyond Stanwyck's moderate approach. Movies such as *Johnny Guitar* (1954), *Gunslinger* (1956), and *Snowfire* (1958) depicted independent females in nontraditional gender roles who succeeded on their own terms with little or no help from males. Perhaps the best example is *Johnny Guitar* (1954), directed by Nicholas Ray. The film stars Joan Crawford as Vienna, a strong-willed woman who owns a gambling parlor and is waiting for the railroad to come through her property to make her rich. Local ranchers, led by John McIvers (Ward Bond) and Emma Small (Mercedes McCambridge) are determined to stop her. Emma does not want the railroad around because it will bring in homesteaders and ruin the cattle frontier, and she hates Vienna for having an affair with the man she loves, the smooth-talking but shady Dancin' Kid (Scott Brady). Anticipating problems, the shrewd Vienna brings to town another of her former lovers, Johnny Guitar (Sterling Hayden), supposedly a performer but actually a notorious gunslinger.

Vienna does not have to wait long for trouble to start. Emma, McIvers, and their allies show up at the casino determined to run her out of town. They accuse Vienna and the Dancin' Kid and his gang of a recent robbery that resulted in the murder of Emma's brother, and they order them to get out of town within twenty-four hours.

Feeling unjustly blamed, the Kid and his gang decide to get even by stealing the town's gold. Afterward, Emma convinces the townspeople that Vienna and the Dancin' Kid (whom she now despises for rejecting her) were behind the gold robbery. Emma and McIvers put together a posse to track down the Kid's gang. At Emma's urging, the posse heads for Vienna's place, where they find her defiant. The situation worsens when the posse discovers that Vienna is hiding a young gang member named Turkey, who had turned to her for help after being wounded while attempting to escape the posse. Emma convinces the vigilantes to hang both Turkey and Vienna immediately. The gang member is the first to die, but just when Emma is about to hang Vienna, Johnny Guitar rides to the rescue. A furious Emma sets fire to Vienna's saloon. As the flames leap in the air, she and the posse pursue the fleeing couple like a pack of hellhounds. Eventually, they track them to the Dancin' Kid's hideout. With bullets whizzing in all directions, the spiteful Emma shoots the Dancin' Kid in the head, setting the stage for a climactic showdown between her and Vienna. By then, McIvers and the rest of the posse back off, because they realize that this is personal between the two women. Emma gets off the first shot and wounds Vienna, but Vienna fires back, killing her wrathful rival. Johnny then rushes to Vienna's side, and the two walk away as the posse watches. On the way out of the hideout, Vienna and Johnny pass under a waterfall, symbolically washing away their sins as the film ends.

Johnny Guitar is a dark western that reflects not just changing gender attitudes but also various fears and anxieties in post–World War II America. In some ways, it is a traditional western. Johnny seems like the usual gunfighter hero who rescues his girl, while Vienna comes across as a familiar heroine: she cares for Turkey when he is wounded; she nurtures her employees like a doting mother; and she refuses to kill posse members unless warranted. The movie also relies on conventional western props and themes, including gunfighters, guitars, and saloon girls with hearts of gold. Even the film's obvious symbolism was drawn from innumerable westerns. When the posse comes for Vienna, she is dressed in white, while they are decked out in black. The railroad is equated with civilization taming the Wild West, and the burning of Vienna's casino recalls William S. Hart's apocalyptic *Hell's Hinges* (1916).

At the same time, *Johnny Guitar* is innovative in the way it deals with gender and other contemporary issues. On one level, the film is a Cold War allegory about the Red Scare of the fifties. Evoking memories of Senator Joseph McCarthy, the film depicts Emma as a frontier demagogue who incites community leaders and citizens to persecute innocent victims. Johnny and Vienna are both aware of the dangers of mobs. "They're men with itchy fingers and a coil of rope around their saddle horns, lookin' for somebody to hang," explains Vienna, "and after riding a few hours they don't care much who they hang." That mob dynamic no doubt resonated with audience members familiar with the Communist hysteria of the fifties.

Nicholas Ray's film explores contemporary gender issues. Both leading female characters in the film are aggressive and powerful women. Emma is able to dominate and direct her male counterparts throughout most of the movie. Vienna is an equally determined, independent, and capable woman accustomed to getting her way. Vienna is smart and tough, and she can use a gun as well as her wits. She understands that women have always had it rougher than men. "A man can lie, steal, and even kill," she tells Johnny, "but as long as he hangs on to his pride, he's still a man. All a woman has to do is slip once, and she's a tramp!" Yet, Vienna never lets gender boundaries stop her. She does what she needs to do to win, even if it means using guns or sex as weapons. For the most part, Vienna makes it on her own. The big exception is when Johnny rescues her from a lynching. Throughout the rest of the movie, Vienna is in total control. She makes her own decisions, solves her problems, and controls her destiny. She—not Johnny or any other man—is the one who kills the chief villain, Emma, in a showdown. Even the end of the movie is ambiguous enough to make audiences wonder whether Vienna will revert to a domestic model and settle down with Johnny or move forward on her own.

Johnny Guitar is generally recognized as one of the more unusual westerns in film history. Described by renowned film maker Martin Scorsese as "one of the great operatic works of the cinema," the movie is now included in the Library of Congress's National Film Registry.[13] A big reason for the film's success is Joan Crawford's tough and self-sufficient character.

Perhaps no better description of Vienna can be found than the one offered by one of her employees: "I never seen a woman who was more a man. She thinks like one, acts like one, and makes me feel like I'm not."

Postwar westerns picked up on changing attitudes toward sex. As the country took notice of the Kinsey reports (1948 and 1953), suggestive songs such as the Dominoes' "Sixty Minute Man" (1951), provocative novels like *Peyton Place* (1956), and steamy movies such as *From Here to Eternity* (1953) and *Butterfield 8* (1960), western movies chimed in with provocative themes and explicit sexual images. The coming of more sexually explicit adult westerns was linked in part to the relaxing of the Motion Picture Production Code after World War II. Adult westerns were also an obvious way for movie studios to distinguish their product from the tamer westerns available on television. *Duel in the Sun* (1946), for example, was commonly referred to as "Lust in the Dust" because of numerous sexually suggestive scenes. *The Indian Fighter* (1955) included the first nude scene ever in a western. In *Yellowstone Kelly* (1959), a beautiful Indian woman, naked under the covers, tells Clint Walker's character, "I owe you my life, and when I am well, I will cook, bear wood and water for you. I will do anything you ask. *Anything*!" Even previously taboo subjects began popping up in western movies. Along with the individual rapes referenced in *Duel in the Sun* (1946), *Jubal* (1956), and *The Searchers* (1956), gang rape was threatened in *Ride the High Country* (1962). Some viewers detected homosexuality in *Johnny Guitar* (1954), *Warlock* (1959), and *The Last Sunset* (1961).[14]

All of these westerns provide evidence of changing attitudes toward sex and gender after World War II. While most westerns released between 1945 and 1963 depicted women in traditional gender roles in keeping with the era's Cold War culture, an increasing number of films featured independent women who crossed traditional sexual boundaries and found success as gunslingers, marshals, business leaders, or in other activities previously reserved for males. Long before the advent of the women's liberation movement or Title IX, protofeminist heroines in western movies were already finding equal opportunities in the mythic West.

Changing Images of Race and Ethnicity

Just as westerns explored changing images of sex and gender, they mirrored Cold War attitudes toward race and ethnicity. From the late forties through the early sixties, the civil rights movement picked up momentum, with a string of successes culminating in the passage of the Civil Rights Act of 1964. Despite such gains, African Americans had a difficult time integrating into movies, TV shows, and other forms of mass media throughout the fifties and early sixties.[15]

Only a handful of postwar westerns included African American actors. *Look-Out Sister* (1949) was a novelty film with an all-black cast led by singer Louis Jordan. *Stars in My Crown* (1950) starred well-known cowboy hero Joel McCrea as a minister who comes to the aid of a black man terrorized by white vigilantes. *The Guns of Fort Petticoat* (1957) featured a black slave as a minor character who was as capable with her wits as she was with a gun. Her expert marksmanship helped her play a major role in turning back an Indian attack. When she is finally mortally wounded, she turns to her less capable white mistress and says, "You're gonna have to do your own hair and shooting from now on." Several westerns featured African American actor Woody Strode, a former football and track star at UCLA. Strode later recalled that director John Ford got into an argument with movie executives at Columbia over whether to cast the black actor as an Indian chief in *Two Rode Together* (1961). "But in costume," explains Strode, "I looked so much like an Indian that the studio bosses couldn't argue."[16]

By far the most important western to address racism against African Americans was *Sergeant Rutledge* (1960), directed by John Ford. The movie centers on the court-martial of a black cavalry sergeant named Braxton Rutledge (Woody Strode), who is charged with the rape and murder of a young white woman. Through a series of flashbacks, the audience learns about the bravery of Rutledge and other Buffalo Soldiers (black cavalrymen) in the U.S. Army, as well as the racism of white soldiers and the prejudice of whites living around the fort. In the end, Rutledge's defense attorney, Lieutenant Cantrell (Jeffrey Hunter), proves Rutledge's innocence by demonstrating that an unscrupulous white man committed the heinous crime.

The powerful film had obvious links to the era's civil rights movement. When Cantrell warns Rutledge not to escape or else he'll be "haunted" by guilt the rest of his life, the black soldier replies sardonically: "You forget, sir. We been haunted a long time. Too much to worry. Yeah, it was all right for Mr. Lincoln to say we was free. But that ain't so. Not yet. Maybe some day, but not yet!" Later on, Rutledge explains to the military tribunal why he decided to return to his unit after deserting. "It was because the Ninth Cavalry was my home, my real freedom, and my self-respect, and the way I was desertin' it, I wasn't nothin' worse than a swamp-runnin' nigger, and I ain't that," he explains. "Do you hear me? I'm a man!"

Figure 22. Woody Strode (center) plays an African American soldier accused of rape and murder in John Ford's *Sergeant Rutledge* (Warner Brothers, 1960).

Sergeant Rutledge was released two years before Gregory Peck starred as Atticus Finch, the country lawyer who defended a black man wrongly accused of rape in *To Kill a Mockingbird*. Yet, Peck's film gained the reputation as the landmark civil rights movie of its day. Two factors probably hurt Ford's movie. Some viewers may have dismissed it because it took place in the Old West and not in twentieth-century America. Others may have thought that the movie went too far. Not only was Strode's character accused of brutally raping and murdering a pretty middle-class white girl, but his cause is championed by another beautiful middle-class white woman (played by blond actress Constance Towers). When Rutledge is vindicated, he proudly returns to duty as a trooper. In effect, the confident black man triumphs over racism and the system. In comparison, *To Kill a Mockingbird* offered a less compelling rape victim and a resolution that was probably more acceptable to most white Americans in the early sixties. In Peck's film, the black defendant is accused of raping a lower-class white woman. Despite his obvious innocence, he is unjustly convicted. Significantly, he never has the opportunity to prove white society wrong, because he is shot and killed in an escape attempt.

Even though *To Kill a Mockingbird* found a more receptive audience in its day than *Sergeant Rutledge*, Ford's film demonstrates the ability of postwar westerns to change with the times. Braxton Rutledge's mythic West was a land of opportunity and justice for all Americans regardless of skin color. That message hit home with many moviegoers in an era of expanding civil rights. "I just saw your movie, *Sergeant Rutledge*," wrote a young black man to Ford, "[It] is, in my opinion, the most significant Negro-theme movie that I have ever seen. If it were up to me, I would have it shown in every classroom in America." Ford no doubt felt gratified by the compliment. "The colored soldier played a great role in our history," explained the director, "and I wanted to tell that story."[17]

Although few westerns featured African Americans, many zeroed in on racial issues, typically using Indians as less controversial stand-ins for blacks.[18] Delmer Daves's *Broken Arrow* (1950) pointed the way for films with benign representations of Indians and other minorities. The poignant western portrayed the fierce Apaches not as bloodthirsty savages, but as rational human beings who fought to defend their families, land, liberty, and way of life. Along with offering an Indian perspective on frontier violence and racial intolerance, the film endorsed miscegenation and depicted Native American culture in positive ways. Not everyone was pleased with *Broken Arrow*'s approach. Movie critic Bosley Crowther called the movie patronizing, while film historian Philip French complained that "liberal, anti-racist" films like *Broken Arrow* merely reshaped Indian stereotypes.[19] While such criticisms were partly true, they tend to overlook the significance of the movie. Given the racist times, the film's message of racial equality was truly revolutionary. *Broken Arrow* became one of the most successful and talked about movies of 1950. It was nominated for three Oscars and won a Golden Globe as Best Film Promoting International Understanding.

The success of Daves's film threw open the floodgates to other westerns that featured benign if not benevolent images of Native Americans.[20] *Chief Crazy Horse* (1955) portrayed the well-known Indian leader as a tragic hero. The prologue immediately establishes the famous Sioux war chief (played by Victor Mature) as an American patriot: "This is a true story, photographed in the Black Hills of the Dakotas, where it actually happened. It is the story of an American, a leader of his people, one of the great generals of all time—Chief Crazy Horse of the Lakota Sioux." Despite its claim to truth, the film is rife with historical inaccuracies. The story plays loose with facts and embellishes the Lakota's life. Even the Indians' costumes reveal more about Hollywood than life on the Great Plains.

Mature's character wears a tailored outfit consisting of a beautiful war bonnet with a matching brown suit that looked like it came straight out of Nudie's of Hollywood. Other Indians wear bright purple headdresses that may have been perfect for Technicolor but were hardly authentic culturally. And just about every Indian man, woman, and child is decked out in brightly colored beads that almost pop off the screen.

Other westerns suggested that innocent Indians were victimized by crooked politicians, corrupt businessmen, racist soldiers, or other unscrupulous whites.[21] *Tomahawk* (1951), which starred Van Heflin as famed scout Jim Bridger, offers a particularly interesting example because it was based on actual events on the Indian frontier. The story line includes the Sand Creek Massacre, the building of the Bozeman Trail, the Fetterman Massacre, the Wagon Box Fight, and the Second Treaty of Fort Laramie. The movie portrays Red Cloud and the Sioux in fairly accurate terms, and unlike most westerns of the day, the film employed real Indians in most of the leading roles. The plot demonstrates how Indians suffered at the hands of racist soldiers and incompetent politicians. An Indian-hating officer who had taken part in the slaughter of Cheyenne men, women, and children at the notorious Sand Creek Massacre convinces another racist soldier, Captain Fetterman, to lead a small detachment of troops against the Sioux with devastating results. Even though the Indians later suffer a setback at the Wagon Box Fight because soldiers have breech-loading rifles, they still manage to win a major victory at the negotiating table, resulting in the Second Treaty of Fort Laramie, which guarantees the Sioux their hunting lands. In accordance with the treaty, the cavalry withdraws from Fort Kearny and abandons the Bozeman Trail. The movie ends triumphantly for the Indians, as Red Cloud and the victorious Sioux celebrate by burning the hated fort to the ground.

Numerous films, including *Taza, Son of Cochise* (1954) and *Trooper Hook* (1957), focused on racism and Indian rights.[22] *Cattle Queen of Montana* (1954) featured a college-educated Indian explaining to Barbara Stanwyck's character that she should not judge all Indians by the actions of a few bad ones. "Because some white men steal and kill, are all white men evil?" he asks. "Is it hard to believe that I'm a human being, too?" Shortly after the Supreme Court rejected public school segregation in *Brown v. Board of Education* (1954), westerns with integrationist themes began popping up in theaters across the country. *Apache* (1954) starred Burt Lancaster as Massai, a proud warrior who ultimately realizes that his people must adopt the white man's way of life to survive. *Walk the Proud Land* (1956) told the story of Indian agent John Clum (Audie Murphy), who taught Apaches how to live as whites. And *Reprisal!* (1956), which starred Guy Madison, dealt with integration, miscegenation, and other racial issues.

Numerous postwar westerns spotlighted miscegenation.[23] Just the suspicion of interracial romance was enough to set tongues wagging. In *Cattle Queen of Montana* (1954), white women condemned Barbara Stanwyck's character merely because she had befriended an Indian man. "There's only one reason why a white woman takes up with an Indian," explains a matron, "and it has a mighty nasty name." In most cases, the racial "problem" was resolved quickly and neatly by either killing off the man (as in *Seminole*) or woman (*Broken Arrow*). A few films allowed an interracial couple to live in the community if there were special circumstances (e.g., in *The Searchers*, Marty Pawley was only one-eighth Cherokee and had been raised as a white man). Otherwise, the interracial couple was allowed to survive only if they moved elsewhere (*White Feather*, *Yellowstone Kelly*, and *The Unforgiven*), an ending that suggests that equality and opportunity might not exist in current society but could be found elsewhere in the mythic West.

The Unforgiven (1960) is a good example. The movie's title refers to an interracial couple—a white man (Burt Lancaster) and an Indian woman (Audrey Hepburn)—who have violated a taboo that neither white nor red society can forgive. The Indian chief refuses to allow his sister (Hepburn) to remain with the whites. Similarly, Lancaster's brother does not want an Indian woman in the family's house. "I'm not stayin'. Not with a red-hide nigger!" he says. In the end, the couple's only chance for happiness is to move elsewhere. As they prepare to leave, they look up at the sky and see a flock of geese flying away. The sight recalls an earlier scene where Hepburn's character had explained that geese are "only human, they just fly a little higher than us folk, that's all." Finally freed from societal restraints, the couple can now soar toward their own higher truth somewhere else in the mythic West.

If westerns such as *The Unforgiven* and *Broken Arrow* suggest that racial attitudes were beginning to change after World War II, others provide evidence that racism and old stereotypes were still very much alive in Cold War America. Indians were depicted as savages and warlike heathens in numerous films, including *Little Big Horn* (1951), *Warpath* (1951), and *Arrow in the Dust* (1954). They were portrayed as buffoons in *The Paleface* (1948) and *Annie Get Your Gun* (1950). Other films were even harsher. The Apache leader in *Arrowhead* (1953), Toriano (played with malice by Jack Palance), is a treacherous, cold-blooded killer. When the film's protagonist (Charlton Heston) kills his Indian mistress, who turned out to be an assassin sent by Toriano, he callously tells the soldier on duty, "There's a dead Apache in here. Get *it* out."[24]

Some of the westerns that took a hard line against Indians were merely substituting savage Indians for bloodthirsty Communists. In *The Command* (1954), Indians are described in ways similar to Communist guerillas. "Injuns fight in two ways," explains a soldier. "When they're runnin' against a little outfit, they will go ring around right away and close in quick for the kill. But if they're runnin' against a big outfit . . . they keep hackin' and choppin' away at your weak spots 'til they wear you down."

While most westerns that dealt with racial issues focused on Indians, some spotlighted other ethnic or racial groups. Films such as *The Eagle and the Hawk* (1950), *The Alamo* (1960), and *The Magnificent Seven* (1960) reinforced traditional racial stereotypes, as well as Cold War fears, by featuring patriotic white Americans fighting heroically against Mexicans or foreign enemies. In keeping with the rising civil rights movement and the era's increasing awareness of cultural diversity, other movies featured sympathetic portrayals of Hispanics or white ethnic groups.[25] *Thunder in the Sun* (1959), for instance, showcased a wagon train of Basques headed west to establish vineyards in California's Napa Valley. The heroic immigrants use their traditional *irrintzi* (a long, high-pitched trilling sound) to communicate, and at the conclusion, they use their mountain-climbing skills to outflank and defeat hostile Indians.

The plight of Asians in the West was the subject of two highly unusual westerns—*Bad Day at Black Rock* (1955) and *Walk Like a Dragon* (1960). The former stars Spencer Tracy as John J. Macreedy, a one-armed World War II veteran who shows up one day in a remote western town on a mysterious mission. The community soon learns that he is looking for Mr. Komoko, an elderly Japanese man who had moved there just before Pearl Harbor. At first, townspeople insist that Komoko moved away to a relocation camp, but Macreedy eventually learns the truth. The old man was shot and killed by Reno Smith (Robert Ryan), the racist town bully, after he and others had gotten "patriotic drunk" and decided to take out their anti-Japanese feelings on Komoko. The cowardly community then conspired to cover it up. After Macreedy reveals that he has come to Black Rock to give Komoko the posthumous medal that Komoko's son received for saving Macreedy's life in combat, he decides to leave town. When Reno tries to ambush him, Macreedy kills him in self-defense. Just as Macreedy is about to leave, the town's doctor, who had helped Macreedy survive his bad day in Black Rock, asks if the town could have the medal to help it heal. Macreedy gives it to him and boards the train. The dark film made it clear that racism and evil existed throughout America. But in the end, the mythic West still offered hope and redemption for Americans willing to fight for what was right.

While *Bad Day at Black Rock* focused on racism toward Asians in modern times, *Walk Like a Dragon* suggested that anti-Asian discrimination had deeper roots. The film stars Jack Lord as Lincoln "Linc" Bartlett. The westerner lives up to his first name when he emancipates Kim Sung (Nobu McCarthy), a Chinese woman who is being sold as a sex slave. He brings her back to his hometown, where he lives with his mother. At first the mother doesn't want the heathen girl living there, but she soon takes a liking to her and teaches her English. Racist townspeople are extremely upset with the girl's arrival and warn Linc not to cross the color barrier. The business community applies pressure by boycotting his freight line and refusing him credit, but Linc refuses to repudiate the pretty young woman, with whom he has fallen in love. Despite society's disapproval, he decides to marry Kim. His mother warns him that society will not accept the couple, but when she realizes that Linc and Kim truly love each other, she reluctantly gives her blessing.

Linc soon learns that residents of Chinatown are equally opposed to the mixed marriage. Cheng, a recent immigrant from China, is also in love with Kim. Unlike his Uncle Wu, who grovels to the whites in order to help his laundry business, Cheng demands respect. He even hires a local gunslinger, nicknamed the Deacon, to teach him how to draw fast and shoot straight. Cheng and Linc eventually have a showdown over the girl. Kim does not want to be the cause of either man's death and understands that society will never approve an interracial marriage between her and Linc. So she chooses to marry Cheng even though she loves Linc. She explains to a broken-hearted Linc that it is better for everyone if she lives with Cheng in Chinatown rather than marry Linc and be the cause of his financial and social ruin.

Walk Like a Dragon is a surprisingly powerful film that paints a sympathetic portrait of Chinese people and culture. The Chinese are depicted as rational individuals, who work hard and value family, love, and honor. Though their God is different, their religion is equal to Christianity. The title of the movie refers not only to Cheng learning how to become a gunfighter and demanding respect from whites, but also to Kim for standing up for her right to choose Cheng and her people over Linc and the white man's world. Broader racial implications are evident throughout the film. At one point a white man refuses to allow Cheng to join in a game of poker and shouts, "I don't sit with blacks, yellows, or red skins!" Later on, Kim explains to Linc that society would never sanction their interracial marriage. "I am that which I am," she says. "As much as I pray, not even my God can change the color of my skin. Or yours."

Kim's decision to follow social dictates rather than individual desires adds tension to the film and ultimately results in a sense of disappointment. Despite the movie's sympathetic portrayal of Chinese culture and condemnation of racism, it winds up siding with society against miscegenation. The film provides a troubling counterpoint to other westerns that resolved interracial romances either tragically by killing off one of the spouses (e.g., *Broken Arrow*) or hopefully by allowing the interracial couple to find happiness elsewhere in the mythic West (*The Unforgiven*). The conclusion of *Walk Like a Dragon* is far more cynical. Not only does it question the potential for personal happiness in the mythic West, but it suggests that the era's civil rights movement would not bring about meaningful social change.

Walk Like a Dragon was written and directed by James Clavell, who later gained fame with the path-breaking civil rights movie *To Sir, With Love* (1967) and the historical novel *Shogun* (1975). Clavell was born and raised in Australia, came of age in England, and didn't move to the United States until 1953, when he was almost thirty. The fact that he was born and raised abroad could explain why the West he depicted in *Walk Like a Dragon* falls short of the mythic land of freedom, opportunity, and redemption familiar to most Americans.

Westerns and Youth Culture

Westerns and youth culture became staunch allies in Cold War America. Realizing that huge profits could be had by tapping into the era's emerging youth market, movie studios cranked out numerous films with youth appeal, including Disney movies like *Davy Crockett: King of the Wild Frontier* (1955) and *Westward Ho the Wagons* (1956).[26]

Western movies developed a profitable symbiotic relationship with rock & roll. Elvis Presley played a young homesteader in *Love Me Tender* (1956) and a cowboy who is half Indian in *Flaming Star* (1960), while Ricky Nelson starred as a gunslinger in *Rio Bravo* (1959). Western imagery became common on the rock charts. The Olympics' 1958 hit, "Western Movies," alluded to colorful characters like Wyatt Earp and Cochise and used gunshots to emphasize the beat. Marty Robbins's "El Paso," a number one hit in 1959, was a rambling ballad about cowboys, gunfights, and posses. Larry Verne's "Mr. Custer" (1960) poked fun at characters commonly found in westerns, while two other hits from the same year, Al Caiola's "The Magnificent Seven" and Johnny Horton's "North to Alaska," rode the coattails of popular films. Other hits, including George Hamilton IV's "Abilene" (1963) and numerous Beach Boy songs about California, were powered by traditional images of the mythic West as a land of happiness and opportunity. Even rock & roll pioneer Bo Diddley got in on the western action. In 1960, he recorded a song and album entitled, *Bo Diddley is a Gunslinger*. The cover featured the rock star dressed in a cowboy outfit with two six-guns strapped to his hips.[27]

Many westerns picked up on the era's fears about juvenile delinquency. *The Gunfighter* (1950) was a prototype for later westerns, such as *The True Story of Jesse James* (1957), *Gun for a Coward* (1957), and *The Left-Handed Gun* (1958), which featured immoral young "squirts" who were fast on the draw and even quicker to break the law. In *The Left-Handed Gun*, Paul Newman portrays Billy the Kid as a frontier delinquent. He first kills a man for insulting his mother. He kills again to avenge the death of a kindly boss. Eventually, he escalates the violence to include anyone who crosses him. A movie poster emphasized the connection between Billy and juvenile delinquency. "This is William Bonney, a juvenile 'tough' from the back-alleys of New York," it explains, "a teenager wanted dead or alive throughout the West. This is the screen's first real story of the strange teen-age desperado known to legend as 'Billy the Kid.'"[28]

The Bravest of Them All

The close connection between westerns and youth culture was evident in 1962 when rock singer Gene Pitney made it all the way to number four on the record charts with "The Man Who Shot Liberty Valance." Although the song did not appear in John Ford's film of the same name, it became a million-seller and helped fuel interest in the western, which starred John Wayne as a rugged cowboy, James Stewart as an aspiring lawyer, and Lee Marvin as a desperado ironically named Liberty. The elegiac western was an early sign that western movies were about to change significantly.

The movie begins with an elderly senator named Ransom Stoddard (James Stewart) and his wife, Hallie (Vera Miles), returning to their hometown of Shinbone for the funeral of old friend Tom Doniphon (John Wayne). When the local newspaper editor demands to know why the famous senator has come to town to attend the funeral of an obscure citizen, Stoddard reluctantly agrees to tell his story. The tale begins decades earlier, when the young eastern lawyer first came west. Just before his stagecoach reaches town, it is held up by desperadoes led by the sadistic Liberty Valance. After the crooks grab the strong box, they order the passengers to turn over wallets and jewelry. When a woman refuses to give up a brooch given to her by her dead husband, Stoddard steps forward to help. The brutal Valance whips him and leaves him for dead.

Doniphon finds Stoddard the next day and brings him to town, where he is nursed back to health by Hallie, the woman Doniphon loves. Doniphon warns Stoddard that his law books are not going to help him against Valance, but the stubborn lawyer refuses to listen. He sets up a law practice in the local newspaper office and begins to teach American history and civics on the side. Stoddard runs into trouble when he organizes the town and local farmers against the cattle barons and their hired gun, Liberty Valance. Marvin's evil villain demands a showdown, and Stoddard reluctantly agrees, even though he barely knows how to fire his pistol. To everyone's surprise, when the smoke clears, Valance is lying dead in the street. When Hallie throws her arms around Stoddard and professes her love, Doniphon is crushed because he knows he has lost the woman he planned to marry.

Stoddard's law skills and reputation as "the man who shot Liberty Valance" soon get him nominated for a high political office, but Stoddard balks because he does not want to succeed based on his reputation as a gunman. Doniphon intervenes and explains to Stoddard what really happened. It turns out that Doniphon was hiding in the shadows that fateful night and fired the deadly bullet to prevent the evil Valance from killing the determined but helpless Stoddard. Doniphon admits it was "cold blooded murder," but adds, "I can live with it [because] Hallie's happy. She wanted you alive." Stoddard replies incredulously, "But you saved my life." Doniphon admits, "I wish I hadn't. Hallie's your girl now. Go back in there and take that nomination. You taught her how to read and write. Now give her something to read and write about." As the stunned Stoddard returns to the cheering assembly hall, the broken Doniphon turns and walks sadly away. Over the next few decades, the lawyer would rise to prominence as the esteemed governor, ambassador, and senator who helped bring civilization to the Wild West, while the rugged gunman Doniphon would wind up a forgotten old man. But the senator and Hallie Stoddard knew the truth. The man who shot Liberty Valance was Tom Doniphon.

John Ford's western is a poignant tribute to the passing of the Old West. Rugged cowboys like Doniphon, who knew how to use their guns, were vital to the taming of the frontier, but once their job was done, they had to be replaced by more civilized types like Stoddard with law books in their hands. The film was a watershed for westerns. Ford understood that both the times and western movies were changing and that the mythic West of old was being reshaped to fit the needs of new postwar audiences. Significantly, as he eases out John Wayne's old-fashioned western hero, Ford spotlights a more inclusive mythic West. His film includes independent women, such as Vera Miles's character, Hallie. It features a proud and capable African American character named Pompey (Woody Strode), who works for Doniphon and is his close friend. Wayne's character goes out of his way to emphasize Pompey's equality. When a bartender refuses to serve a black man, Doniphon intervenes. "Who says he can't [be served]?" he asks, and he tells Pompey to pour himself a drink. Pompey emphatically declines. He knows Doniphon is getting drunk and points out that there's work to be done and somebody has to be responsible enough to do it. Pompey later risks his own life to save Doniphon from a burning building. John Ford also portrays ethnic groups with sensitivity. He depicts a capable Swedish couple who run the town's best restaurant and become proud U.S. citizens. And he portrays Hispanics in a positive way. Although they are segregated in the town, they clearly are part of the community's social fabric. The marshal is married to a Mexican woman, and their children are learning how to read and write in order to become successful Americans.

The Man Who Shot Liberty Valance is an elegy for westerns. Ford understood that old-fashioned westerns were on the way out, but that the mythic West would live on. That is why when Senator Stoddard finishes his historical account of what really happened the night that Liberty Valance died, the newspaper editor is stunned but refuses to print the truth. "This is the West, sir," he explains to the senator. "When the legend becomes fact, print the legend."

John Ford's classic was not the only western that suggested that the Old West was gone. Others included *Two Rode Together* (1961), *The Misfits* (1961), *Ride the High Country* (1962), *Lonely Are the Brave* (1962), and *Hud* (1963). *Ride the High Country* (1962) starred veteran film cowboys Joel McCrea and Randolph Scott as aging gunfighters. Directed by Sam Peckinpah, the film has a nostalgic if not wistful quality. McCrea plays a former lawman now just a shadow of his former self. Wearing worn boots and tattered clothes with no money in the pockets, he accepts a menial job as a security guard responsible for bringing gold down from a mining camp in the mountains. He brings along his old deputy (Randolph Scott), who has fallen on equally hard times. When the two meet by chance, Scott is a carnival pitchman dolled up to look like Buffalo Bill. He ekes out a living pulling off various carnie scams. By film's end, the two down-on-their-luck lawmen regain a modicum of dignity. In a showdown with a violent gang, they protect the gold and save a young woman, but not without paying a heavy price. McCrea's character is shot and killed. Scott's is wounded but at least salvages his pride and manages to limp away with his life. The story about aging gunfighters and the passing of the Old West offered lessons for postwar America. Even though neither of the protagonists finds happiness or success, they do find inner peace by rediscovering basic principles. And that was enough. "All I want is to enter my house justified," explains McCrea's character.

These elegiac films mark the end of an era for postwar westerns. By the early sixties, old-time movie cowboys such as Joel McCrea and Randolph Scott were getting up in years. Veteran directors such as John Ford were nearing the end of the line. Even the old-style mythic West was fading from view. The simpler, black-and-white days of heroes and villains were being replaced by a newer, more complicated mythic West in vivid Technicolor and cinemascope. Though still a land of dreams, it was now more ambiguous and receptive to Americans regardless of race, ethnicity, religion, or gender. But if the old mythic West was almost gone, it would not be forgotten. As in previous decades, the myth would be reshaped to fit the needs of a new generation.

The sophisticated westerns produced in the two decades after World War II pointed the way for later films that were even more revisionist. After 1963, westerns would turn to new themes relevant to modern America. They would address assassinations, Vietnam, race, gender, class, and youth culture, as well as other social, cultural, and political issues. Despite the changes, the mythic West would survive, and westerns would remain potent symbols and effective means for Americans to address concerns and national goals.

In retrospect, John Ford's *The Man Who Shot Liberty Valance* marks the passing of the Old West, as well as the end of an important chapter in the history of western movies. As it said farewell to the wild frontier, *Liberty Valance* served notice that the mythic West still had the power to deal with America's problems. It suggested that western heroes would continue to play an important role in the modern world. No wonder Americans could smile knowingly in 1962 when Gene Pitney sang, "The man who shot Liberty Valance, he was the bravest of them all."[29]

PART THREE

"New Western" Horizons

1964–1999

CHAPTER SEVEN

A Fistful of Dollars

Spaghetti Westerns and Changing Times

A movie poster for Clint Eastwood's *A Fistful of Dollars* depicts a grizzled gunslinger who looks nothing like earlier cowboy heroes. He wears a beard and smokes a cigarillo. Dressed in a Mexican poncho and flat-top cowboy hat, his gun is drawn, and his menacing stare shows he is ready for business. "This is the man with no name," explains the poster. "In his own way he is, perhaps, the most dangerous man who ever lived!" The poster adds, "*A Fistful of Dollars* is the first motion picture of its kind. It won't be the last!" That proved to be no idle boast. Directed by an Italian, Sergio Leone, and filmed in Italy and Spain, *A Fistful of Dollars* ushered in a new chapter in the history of western movies.

Leone's film, inspired by Japanese director Akira Kurosawa's *Yojimbo* (1961), is a dark and violent tale about a mysterious lone cowboy who protects innocent and helpless townspeople from warring outlaws. "The thing that aroused my interest was that Kurosawa had taken the idea from an American book entitled *Red Harvest* by [Dashiell] Hammett," explains Leone, "I thought to myself, 'Why not bring this story back to its homeland through a western? It seems to have all the necessary schemes.'"[1]

A Fistful of Dollars was the first Italian western to become a box office hit worldwide. Released in Europe in 1964 and in the United States in 1967, the film cost two hundred thousand dollars to make and grossed over eleven million dollars in the United States alone. Its phenomenal success pointed the way for other so-called spaghetti westerns and copycat films in the sixties and seventies that offered new images of the mythic West. Gone were the obvious good guys, majestic landscapes, and heroic

Figure 23. This movie poster for *A Fistful of Dollars* was not just bragging. Clint Eastwood's Man with No Name character had a tremendous influence on westerns (Constantin/Jolly/Ocean Film Productions, 1964; U.S. distribution by United Artists, 1967).

western tales of John Wayne's heyday. In their place was a darker West filled with amoral antiheroes, psychopathic villains, unrelenting violence, and bleak landscapes. Bizarre soundtracks added to the dissonance and surrealistic mood.

The desolate spaghetti West depicted on the silver screen hit home with moviegoers in an era marked by a rising tide of violence, cynicism, and despair. These revisionist westerns offered new images and story lines that resonated with audiences in the years following the assassination of President John F. Kennedy. As the nation and world recoiled from assassinations, political corruption, corporate greed, the Vietnam War, campus protests, urban violence, and tumultuous social movements that rippled across America and Europe, these dark films proved a perfect fit for the dark times. Not only did spaghetti westerns reshape the western genre to fit the needs of contemporary audiences, but they revitalized the western film industry as they generated a "fistful of dollars" for producers and studios.

Leone and Eastwood Blaze a New Trail

A *Fistful of Dollars* changed the direction of western movies. Although American directors had been producing revisionist images of the mythic West since the end of World War II, Italian director Sergio Leone blazed a new path that was darker than anything that had come before. The new revisionist trail passed through desolate landscapes and forsaken towns. It was marked by violence and brutality, and littered with corpses and failed dreams. This was not the familiar mythic West of opportunity, hope, and redemption. It was the darker, nightmarish version that had always lurked in the shadows of the American Dream.

Leone's grim western begins with Clint Eastwood's character riding into the border town of San Miguel, not on a magnificent horse but on a small mule. He sees a little boy run up to a shuttered house. A man yells at the child, then kicks him, shoots at his feet, and chases the crying boy across the street. Eastwood's nameless character takes it all in dispassionately and catches a glimpse of a beautiful woman watching sadly from a window. As a church bell tolls, he continues his slow ride into town. He sees a hangman's noose dangling from a lifeless tree, then a horse riding toward him with a dead man in the saddle. Suddenly, a loco bell ringer runs up to him and says gleefully, "Everyone here has become very rich, or else they are dead."

Eastwood continues his slow ride into the hellish town. Turning a corner, he is harassed by gunmen. Keeping his cool, he heads toward the saloon, where he is greeted by the owner, Silvanito. When Eastwood learns that the town is controlled by two corrupt and brutal families—the Baxters (who make money by selling guns) and the Rojos (who profit from the liquor trade)—he quickly realizes that money can be made by playing one side off against the other. "Baxter's over there," he explains to Silvanito, "Rojo's there, me right smack in the middle. Crazy bell-ringer was right. There's money to be made in these parts."

The stranger sets his plan in motion by picking a fight with Baxter's henchmen, who mocked him when he first rode into town on his mule. "My mule don't like people laughin'," he tells them. "He gets the crazy idea you're laughin' at him." When the four gunslingers reach for their guns, Eastwood whips out his six-shooter and shoots them dead. His cold-blooded murder of Baxter's men because they insulted his mule convinces the leader of the Rojo clan to hire him. Once inside the Rojos' operation, Eastwood learns that the beautiful woman he had seen when he first rode into town is named Marisol, and she is being held hostage by Ramon, the cruelest Rojo brother. He also learns that Ramon has stolen gold from the Mexican government. Those revelations convince Eastwood to alter his plan. He still wants to profit by playing the Rojos off against the Baxters, but now he is equally determined to rescue Marisol and retrieve the gold.

Through Eastwood's duplicity, the Rojo-Baxter feud soon turns into a bloody all-out war. Eastwood's scheme begins to unravel when Ramon realizes that the stranger has helped Marisol escape and is probably in cahoots with the Baxters. The furious bandit leader orders his men to torture Eastwood to the point of death. But when his sadistic henchmen pause to allow their victim to regain some strength before applying more torture, the badly beaten Eastwood escapes to an abandoned mine, where Silvanito and the town's coffin maker nurse him back to health. Meanwhile, Ramon, who wrongly suspects that the Baxters were behind Eastwood's escape, turns on the rival family with fury, burning down their home and callously shooting down the clan one by one as each pleads for mercy.

Several weeks later, the coffin maker arrives at the mine to tell a rejuvenated Eastwood that Ramon is torturing Silvanito for helping Eastwood. The coffin maker hands Eastwood his gun, as well as a stick of dynamite stolen from the Rojos. Smiling, he says, "Seems to me, the moment's come for you to light the fuse and send it back to them." A determined Eastwood then sets out to rescue his friend and settle the score with the brutal Rojos.

The climactic showdown begins with an explosion that interrupts Ramon's torture of Silvanito. Out of the smoke walks the Man with No Name, looking more like a grim avenging angel than a moral cowboy hero. Dressed in a Mexican-style poncho, Eastwood walks purposefully toward Ramon and his hired guns. "You shoot to kill," he says tauntingly to Ramon, "you better hit the heart." Livid, the expert rifleman Ramon fires directly at Eastwood's heart. The mysterious stranger falls to the ground but quickly gets up. Ramon fires again and again, but to no avail. Eastwood simply smiles and lifts his poncho to reveal a protective steel plate on his chest. With lightning speed, he whips out his gun and fires a hail of bullets, cutting down Ramon's brother and lackeys. Pausing for a moment, he mocks Ramon one last time, daring him to reload and fire his rifle before Eastwood can do the same with his six-shooter. The Man with No Name proves quicker and shoots Ramon down like a rabid dog. Silvanito helps out by shooting the remaining Rojo brother as he attempts to bushwhack Eastwood.

Afterward, Eastwood tells Silvanito, "Well, I guess your government will be glad to see that gold back." When Silvanito asks him why he doesn't want to be around when the Mexican soldiers arrive, Eastwood smiles and says, "You mean the Mexican government on one side? Maybe the Americans on the other side? Me right smack in the middle? Uh-uh. Too dangerous. So long." The Man with No Name climbs onto his mule and rides off, while the camera zooms out to show the carnage left in his wake. The final scene includes a hanging lantern bringing light to the darkness and counterbalancing the hangman's noose depicted at the beginning of the film.

A Fistful of Dollars offered audiences of the mid-sixties a new, darker vision of the mythic West. Sergio Leone's West was more a postapocalyptic wasteland than a promised land of milk and honey. Grisly images abound as Eastwood rides into the wasted Mexican village. The barren landscape, bleached-white buildings, hangman's noose, corpse riding slowly by on a horse, and old cabinet maker constantly making coffins while sizing up prospective clients all foreshadow the death and violence to come. The soundtrack—featuring dirge-like music, forlorn whistling, and the constant rushing of wind—adds to the macabre surrealism. Toward the end of the film, a lonely trumpet playing a somber "no quarter" tune is used to foreshadow the bloodbath that is about to occur in the climactic showdown.

Leone's movie brought western violence and brutality to new levels. The opening credits evoke the beginning of a James Bond film. Animated figures draw their guns and fire in all directions. Gunshots punctuate the music as bodies pile up on the blood red background. The violence and sadism become even more pronounced when real actors replace the animations. Eastwood's character repeatedly witnesses the brutality and blood lust of Rojo gang members, who are veritable altar boys compared to their vicious employer, Ramon. Early on, Eastwood sees Ramon and his gang massacring soldiers during a gold heist. The bloody scene, which lasts a long two minutes and eleven seconds on the screen, graphically depicts Ramon gunning down the unsuspecting troops. Eastwood later discovers that the Mexican villain has forcibly taken the beautiful Marisol from her husband and child and raped her night after night. Soon thereafter, he experiences Rojo's cruelty firsthand when the sadistic bandit orders his men to beat and torture the gringo gunslinger. The explicit torture scene, replete with blood, gore, and extended suffering, fills the big screen for almost three and half minutes. "Our orders are to make sure he does not die," explains one of the Rojos' henchmen gleefully, "but also to make sure he regrets the day he was born." When Ramon's men return later to resume the torture, Eastwood crushes them by rolling a heavy wine cask on top of them. The brutally beaten and mangled Eastwood then makes his escape by hiding in a casket.

Significantly, Eastwood's antihero turns out to be even more prolific at brutal cold-blooded killing than Ramon. Never in the history of western movies was a cowboy as lightning fast on the draw or a more efficient killing machine. Eastwood lays waste to two gangs of bad guys, single-handedly gunning down almost twenty of them. He dispatches them with as little remorse as one would have torching pesky bedbugs. Before one killing spree, he tells the undertaker to prepare three coffins. "My mistake," he later says callously. "Four coffins." Even the innovative way that the killings were filmed underscored the violence. American movies and TV westerns had always abided by the Hollywood Production Code, which prohibited single scenes from showing a gun being fired and a person being shot. "You had to shoot separately, and then show the person fall. On television we always did it that way," explains Eastwood. "And, you see Sergio [Leone] never knew that."[2]

Eastwood's protagonist is no heroic John Wayne–type character. He is not even the typical good badman in the tradition of William S. Hart. He is a violent and ruthless killer who murders opponents for fun and profit. Behind his cold and stony stare is a cynical mind powered by a dubious morality. Unlike earlier clean-cut cowboy heroes, Eastwood's character constantly smokes a small cigar and hardly ever shaves. He wears a flat-topped hat and Mexican poncho instead of more traditional western garb, like a ten-gallon hat, cowboy shirt, or chaps. And he rides an ugly brown mule instead of a beautiful white horse or spirited stallion. Eastwood's antihero character does not even have a name. He never introduces himself when he meets anyone, and nobody ever asks his name. Only the eccentric coffin maker takes it upon himself to call Eastwood's anonymous character "Joe," a sobriquet that evokes the generic name applied to American GIs during the World War II era.

Yet, despite all the differences, Eastwood's Man with No Name is still part of the pantheon of western heroes. His lack of a formal name is actually a longtime western tradition that can be traced back at least as far as Owen Wister's seminal western hero, known only as the Virginian, if not to James Fenimore Cooper's Natty Bumppo character, more commonly known by generic names such as Deerslayer, Hawkeye, or Leatherstocking. Like Shane and hundreds of other celluloid cowboys before him, Eastwood's character confronts evil and protects the weak and helpless against bad guys. When Eastwood helps Marisol and her family escape from Ramon's clutches, the incredulous woman wonders about his motive.

"Why?" replies Eastwood. "Because I knew someone like you once, but there was no one there to help. Now, get moving." Like earlier cowboy heroes, Eastwood's character rides off into the sunset after he vanquishes the bad guys. Perhaps to underscore the point that Eastwood's dark hero was actually pure of heart, Leone adds some Christian allusions. The coffin maker calls Eastwood's character "Joe," and like Joseph in the Bible, he protects Marisol (the Spanish equivalent of Mary) and her son, whose name in the film is Jesus.

A *Fistful of Dollars* anticipated the anxious mood of America in 1964. The movie's violence and the antihero's ambiguous morality resonated in the dark days following JFK's assassination. Violence seemed all too commonplace in mid-sixties America. TV news programs showcased vicious attacks on civil rights demonstrators; the free speech movement at Berkeley foreshadowed the growing disenchantment of college students; and concerns about Vietnam heightened as Congress approved the Gulf of Tonkin Resolution, which authorized the president to use military force to combat Communist aggression. Republican presidential hopeful Barry Goldwater even suggested using tactical nuclear weapons if necessary.

Leone's film opened a new chapter in the history of western movies. It pointed the way for antiheroes, increased violence, and darker images of a mythic West, where landscapes were bleak instead of majestic, and hope and opportunity were far more elusive. It also put forth ambivalent messages about morality that were more in step with the rapid social and cultural changes engulfing sixties America. Leone's film paved the way for other westerns made outside the United States. The surge in popularity of westerns worldwide suggests how complete America's rise to globalism was in the decades after World War II. But for all the changes, Leone's revisionism was not a complete break with the mythic West. When the gun smoke cleared, liberty and justice for all could still be found at the end of Leone's dark western trail. The enigmatic Man with No Name had great appeal. His cynicism and decisive if brutal methods for vanquishing evil calmed apprehensive viewers, assuring them that good would always win out over the evil that lurked in the shadows of the Old West or of modern America.

Sergio Leone capitalized on his initial success with two additional Clint Eastwood westerns that followed the same formula. Eastwood's antihero blazed a brutal trail as he gunned down bad guys and brought cosmic justice, law, and order to an unforgiving and malevolent Old West in box office hits such as *For a Few Dollars More* (1965) and *The Good, the Bad and the Ugly* (1966). Like A *Fistful of Dollars*, the sequels featured ambiguous morality, plenty of violence, lots of sadism, desolate western landscapes, and macabre soundtracks that added to the anomie and despair. The first title card in *For a Few Dollars More* captures the dark tone of all three films as it explains, "In a land where life had no value, death, sometimes, had its price." Leone's West was not the traditional mythic West of hope and redemption. It was a bleak postapocalyptic land of brute force, where only might makes right.

The Leone-Eastwood westerns eventually came to be known as the Dollar Trilogy. "I think [these movies] changed the style, the approach to Westerns," explains Clint Eastwood. "They made the violence and the shooting aspect a little more larger than life, and they had great music and new types of scores." These films, adds Eastwood, had "stories that hadn't been used in other Westerns. They just had a look and a style that was a little different at the time. . . . They were more fragmented, episodic."[3]

No matter how one explains the popularity of Leone's Dollar Trilogy, one thing is certain. Anxious audiences in the midst of the violence and chaos of the troubled sixties and seventies could not get enough of antiheroes like Eastwood's Man with No Name, whose ends-justifies-the-means approach brought order to chaos. The phenomenal success of the Leone-Eastwood westerns pointed the way for other revisionist westerns—both non-American and American—that would be at least as dark and violent. Among the first to follow Leone's lead were Italian directors and producers, who began cranking out what came to be known as spaghetti westerns.

Good, Bad, and Ugly Spaghetti Westerns

The Italian film industry produced more than five hundred spaghetti westerns between 1964 and the late seventies. Some were very good, others pretty bad, and more than a few were downright ugly. No one knows for certain who coined the term *spaghetti western*, but in an era when many Americans commonly used derogatory terms to describe racial and ethnic groups, it clearly wasn't meant as a compliment. Some Italians found the term downright offensive. "'Italian western' is acceptable because technically that's what it is," explains Italian film director Sergio Sollima. "'Spaghetti western' is another thing. [It] is a term that I find horrendous."[4] Despite such criticisms, the term eventually became a synonym for all Italian westerns.

Spaghetti westerns were usually made on shoestring budgets and featured actors from various countries. Italian producers initially wanted

American stars for leading roles, because European audiences saw westerns as an American phenomenon, but budgetary constraints made that nearly impossible. Sergio Leone, for example, tried to sign a big name American actor for *A Fistful of Dollars*. After Henry Fonda, Lee Marvin, and Charles Bronson rejected his paltry fifteen-thousand-dollar offer, Leone turned to Clint Eastwood, who was known for his role as Rowdy Yates on the TV series *Rawhide* and eager to try feature films. Other Italian producers and directors ran into similar problems and usually wound up with American actors such as Lee Van Cleef and Cameron Mitchell, who were well-known character actors hoping to become leading men, or better known stars like Richard Widmark or Joseph Cotten, whose Hollywood careers were on the downside. If Italian studios were unable to sign Americans, they simply gave Italian or European actors more American-sounding names. Mario Girotti and Carlo Pedersoli, for instance, were billed respectively as Terence Hill and Bud Spencer in the popular Trinity series. In other cases, Italian westerns, which depended on actors and capital from Italy, Germany, Spain, and other European counties, juggled international casts to broaden appeal. Top billing depended upon which country the movie was playing in.[5]

Spaghetti westerns initially followed the formula for success established by Leone's Dollar Trilogy. First and foremost, there had to be plenty of action. Almost like clockwork, these films featured shootings, knifings, fistfights, beatings, shootouts, or other violent action every five to ten minutes. "The issue of morality belongs to the American western," explains Italian director Ferdinando Baldi. "The violence in our movies is more gratuitous than in the American films. There was very little morality because often the protagonist was a bad guy."[6] Not coincidentally, the explicit violence and ambiguous morality found in spaghetti westerns paralleled similar trends associated with tumultuous social movements in 1960s America and Europe. The violent antiheroes of Italian westerns also fit into a folk tradition in southern Italy that honored mafioso and vigilantes who used any means to combat corrupt government or church officials who threatened the peasants of the Mezzogiorno. Arguably, Eastwood's Man with No Name was a prototype for Don Corleone, the violent and morally ambiguous protagonist of Francis Ford Coppola's 1972 movie, *The Godfather*.[7]

Django (1966), in particular, took violence to new levels and became so popular that it spawned numerous sequels made by various directors and starring different actors. The original starred Franco Nero and was directed by Sergio Corbucci. From the get-go, its goal was to be violent.

"We wanted to create this [Django] character, a silent western, almost," explains producer Manolo Bolognini. "This guy shoots at every sound. He's not interested in talking." The violent tone is established immediately. The opening scene has Django walking across a forbidding landscape, dragging a coffin behind him. He comes to a rise and sees a band of Mexicans tying a beautiful woman to a torture rack. The gang's leader rips off the back of her blouse. He smiles wickedly and proceeds to whip her bare back as his grimy friends grin sadistically. Suddenly, the Mexicans are shot dead—not by Django but by five gringos in red masks that evoke the Ku Klux Klan. They remove her from the rack but make it clear that they're now going to burn her on a cross because she had sex with the Mexicans. When Django interrupts the gang's plan, they reach for their guns, but the mysterious stranger is faster on the draw, and he mows them down. One of the fallen Klansmen survives the barrage of bullets, but Django nonchalantly shoots him dead like he was taking a potshot at a fly. Django then resumes his death march into town, dragging the coffin behind him.

Throughout the rest of the film, one violent action scene follows another. One of the most brutal involves vicious banditos cutting an ear off a Bible-toting member of the opposition gang and then force-feeding the bloody pulp into the screaming victim's mouth. Just when it appears that the violence can't get any worse, the movie kicks into high gear. Viewers learn that Django is out for revenge, and his secret weapon is a machine gun hidden in the coffin. Like a western grim reaper, Django proficiently and cold-bloodedly cuts down anyone and anything in his path. The bloody film with its over-the-top violence, ghost-town setting, bizarre characters, and dreamlike sequences often feels more like a horror movie than a western. The graphic violence got *Django* banned in several markets but helped turn the movie into a profitable cult classic.

More than thirty subsequent Django films were produced by various studios with different lead actors, but their titles and grisly tales always reflected the gratuitous violence that became the franchise trademark. Among the bloodiest were *Django Kill . . . If You Live, Shoot!* (1967); *Django, Prepare a Coffin* (1968); and *Django's Cut Price Corpses* (1971). Film historian Phil Hardy describes *Django Kill*, which featured Tomas Milian in the lead role, as "probably the most brutally violent spaghetti western ever made." The plot has Django "overcome bizarre obstacle after bizarre obstacle while around him children are shot, outlaws roasted on a spit, animals disemboweled, and a man is suffocated by molten gold."[8] The explicit violence, rather than repelling viewers, attracted audiences

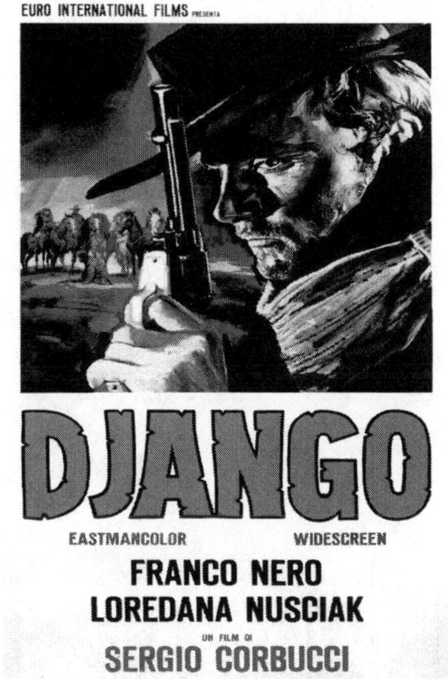

Figure 24. This movie poster for *Django* (B. R. C. Produzione Films, 1966) shows the first actor to play Django, Franco Nero. The character didn't speak much but was one of the most violent antiheroes of the day.

like moths to a movie projector light bulb. Django became a veritable cottage industry, demonstrating the public's insatiable appetite for violence.

Django was just one of many strange protagonists found in spaghetti westerns, which took their cue from Sergio Leone's idiosyncratic heroes and villains, as well as from the weird times. As the sixties and early seventies descended into chaos and despair over the Vietnam War and tumultuous social change, spaghetti westerns commonly featured violent, cynical, and bizarre characters. In *Sabata* (1969), Lee Van Cleef dresses in black and plays a cold-blooded gunslinger who teams up with a drunken ex–Mexican soldier, a weird acrobat, and a duplicitous musician-gunfighter named Banjo. Villains were equally bizarre. *Death Sentence* (1967) features a scoundrel who is an epileptic albino, while *Django* (1966) and *Sabata* (1969) include antagonists who revel in sadomasochism.[9]

Spaghetti westerns copied the look and feel of the Dollar Trilogy. Often filmed on the very locations in Spain used by Leone, these westerns offered desolate landscapes that created dark moods. Their small budgets were at least partly responsible for the austere feel. *Django* producer Manolo Bolognini recalls that he wanted his western to be different, so his director recommended that they use snow in the town. Bolognini replied, "Never! Snow in a western is bad luck! Plus, it's expensive!" So, they hit on a compromise. "We took a truckload of soil and bathed it every day in water," explains the producer, "and this gave us a very unique and gloomy village unlike any other."[10] In effect, necessity was the mother of invention for the uninviting feel and unique look of *Django*. Nero's character dragging that coffin slowly through the brown mud of that grimy town adds to the film's despair and surrealistic appearance.

Spaghetti westerns had other things in common. Reflecting the backgrounds of southern European producers, directors, writers, actors, and audiences, they made extensive use of Catholic iconography, including myriad images of priests, crucifixes, churches, statues, cemeteries, coffins, and angels. Filmed primarily in Spain and Italy, they used local talent with identifiable Mediterranean features. This gave spaghetti westerns an ethnic feel, which American westerns lacked. For practical reasons, spaghetti westerns had very little dialogue. These international movie projects attracted directors, actors, and crews from various countries, so communication wasn't always easy. Sergio Leone and Clint Eastwood, for example, had to use an interpreter. The actors in any given scene of any spaghetti western could easily be from two, three, or four different countries. And since the Italian films had to be dubbed for release in the United States, Germany, Japan, and other foreign markets, the less dialogue the better.

Spaghetti westerns made up for the lack of talking with innovative soundtracks that sounded fresh to American ears. Sergio Leone led the way when he signed Italian composer Ennio Morricone to write the score for *A Fistful of Dollars*. The haunting melodies and exotic-sounding instruments used by Morricone gave the Dollar Trilogy a distinct sound that audiences found irresistible. The phenomenal success of the Dollar soundtracks established Morricone as the maestro of spaghetti western music. He went on to compose soundtracks for numerous Italian westerns, always making sure to tailor the music to the specific project. Spaghetti westerns that did not hire Morricone borrowed freely from his sound and style, giving Italian westerns a distinct sound that was readily identifiable to American audiences. (It is tempting to theorize that Morricone and other Italian composers were bringing a new sound to westerns at the same time that the Beatles and other British artists were introducing a new sound to American rock & roll. Perhaps in the aftermath of President Kennedy's assassination, Americans were looking for new things or unfamiliar diversions.)

Once Upon a Time . . .

By the late sixties, more westerns were being made in Italy than in America. In 1968 alone, Italy released seventy-two westerns compared to Hollywood's twelve.[11] Despite all the imitators, Sergio Leone remained the acknowledged master. In 1968, he released what promised to be his greatest western ever. Unlike his previous efforts, *Once Upon a Time in the West* was a big-budget production bankrolled by Paramount Pictures in Hollywood. Leone spared no expense: he filmed not just in Spain and Italy but also in Monument Valley and other locations made famous by American westerns; he signed big stars like Henry Fonda, Jason Robards, Charles Bronson, and Claudia Cardinale, as well as well-known character actors such as Woody Strode, Jack Elam, and Keenan Wynn. Leone "wanted this to be his last western, and it had to be his best," explains longtime Leone collaborator Sergio Donati. "That was our intention, the end of the West. When the railroad arrives in the West, the adventure is over."[12]

Unfortunately, the film turned out to be as bloated as the budget. The original version released in Italy in December 1968 was 166 minutes long. Worried about its length, Paramount cut it back to 145 minutes for its U.S. release in 1969. Later versions restored the material cut, and some actually added footage, bringing the film up to 175 minutes. Not only were audiences and critics confused by the multiple releases, but many moviegoers came away puzzled by the numerous subplots and underwhelmed by the lack of action and the extended scenes. The opening scene, for example, features three bad guys waiting silently for a train to arrive while a clock ticks away. One of them gets distracted by a fly in a scene that seems to go on forever. Even the climactic showdown between Fonda and Bronson lasts far too long. Calling it a fast-draw contest is a misnomer. Leone stretches the scene out over fifteen minutes through flashbacks and close-ups of the participants squinting, sweating, staring, and spitting.

The long and confusing film flopped at the box office. Vincent Canby's review in the *New York Times* called it the "the biggest, longest, most expensive Leone Western to date, and, in many ways, the most absurd."[13] Leone's convoluted plot often gets sidetracked by subplots and character development scenes. The story revolves around four main characters: Frank (a cold-blooded gunslinger played by Henry Fonda); Cheyenne (an outlaw with a heart of gold played by Jason Robards); Harmonica (a mysterious gunman played by Charles Bronson); and Jill McBain (a beautiful yet tough widow and ex-prostitute played by Claudia Cardinale).

The story line has Jill arriving in town as a mail-order bride only to learn that her new husband and his children from a previous marriage have been gunned down, allegedly by men working for Cheyenne. When a harmonica-playing stranger with no name arrives on the scene, the plot thickens, and it is revealed that Cheyenne did not commit the murders. Instead, they were committed by Frank, a sadistic hired gun acting on behalf of an immoral businessman who needed rights to the dead man's ranch to ensure expansion of his railroad. Cheyenne and Harmonica come to the widow's aid. Eventually, they succeed in stopping the railroad baron and his hired killer, but not without a heavy price. The drama inches forward like a slow-moving train, with its jerking stops and starts set against broader themes of westward expansion (as represented by the coming of the railroad); women's rights (as suggested by Jill's determination to stand her ground); social class divisions (evidenced in the contest for power between the working classes and wealthy individuals); and the passing of the Old West (as represented by the demise of the gunfighters played by Fonda, Robards, and Bronson).

If Leone set out to make a complicated western, he accomplished his goal. *Once Upon a Time in the West* is a multilayered, baffling blend of the old and the new, which casually mixes ingredients from traditional Hollywood westerns with those of revisionist spaghetti westerns. Leone filmed in familiar locations, such as Monument Valley and Moab, Utah. He employed well-known western actors like Fonda, Bronson, and Robards. And he relied heavily on western conventions, including good guys and bad guys; a revenge motive; a whore with a heart of gold; a corrupt businessman; an evil gunslinger; and a climactic showdown. Like many traditional westerns, this one deals with the coming of the railroad, good badmen, and redemption. It even features a good guy riding off into the sunset.

At the same time, Leone injects large doses of revisionism into the mix. In keeping with the spaghetti western formula that he pioneered, *Once Upon a Time in the West* features bleak landscapes, a nameless protagonist, amoral heroes, sadistic and deformed villains, and graphic violence. A macabre soundtrack helps establish the dark tone. Leone uses sound the way impressionist painters used color to create texture and mood. Like the Dollar Trilogy, this film is powered by the eerie music of Ennio Morricone.

Adding to the ambience are foreboding sounds caused by menacing wind, creaking boards, squeaky signs, and the ticking of clocks.

Leone turns the mythic West inside out. Audiences accustomed to seeing Henry Fonda as a good guy and Charles Bronson a villain were stunned when Leone reversed their roles, which added to the film's dissonant, surreal feel. He also tinkers with traditional gender roles. Reflecting the rise of the women's movement, Jill McBain is a strong and independent woman who is willing to do anything to survive, including having sex with the sadistic gunfighter who murdered her husband. Later, when she thinks that another outlaw is about to rape her, she says defiantly: "If you want to, you can lay me over the table and amuse yourself. And even call in your men. Well. No woman ever died from that. When you're finished, all I'll need will be a tub of boiling water, and I'll be exactly what I was before, with just another filthy memory." Ultimately, Jill is the only main character who finds success in the western promised land.

Once Upon a Time in the West demolishes the image of the mythic West as a land where rugged males can find happiness and redemption. By film's end, western archetypes like the good guy, the gunslinger, and the good badman are irrelevant, and the Old West is overtaken by modernity. The only winners are Jill, who represents the civilizing effects of women in the West, and the ordinary Americans who are building railroads and creating new towns. If Jill symbolizes the transition to a new West by carrying water to the railroad workers, the two gunslingers played by Bronson and Fonda represent the end of the Old West. Just before their showdown, Harmonica tells Frank that men like them are "an ancient race," anachronisms facing off against each other. As the movie ends and Bronson's Harmonica character rides off into the sunset, the name of the film—*Once Upon a Time in the West*—swings into place on the screen like the hands of a ticking clock. Time has run out on the mythic West.

Leone's spectacular but plodding western employs the Old West in new ways to subvert the western myth. Its postmodern mix of nostalgic visions of the Old West and revisionist images of a new West reflect the ambiguities of the time in which it was made. The movie was released in 1968, as student protests, social upheaval, urban violence, and anti–Vietnam War demonstrations were spreading throughout America and Europe. By 1968, everything was confused and unclear. Why not the mythic West as well?

Although Leone's complex vision of the West did not do well at the box office when it was first released, the film has garnered accolades ever since. In 2009, the movie was selected for inclusion in the Library of Congress's National Film Registry, and a recent review in the *New York Times* noted, "At its full length, *Once Upon a Time in the West* is Leone's operatic masterwork, worthy of its legend-making title."[14]

From Spaghetti to Fagioli Westerns

By the time Leone's masterpiece reached theaters, the spaghetti western phenomenon was already beginning to ebb due to overproduction and a tired formula. Directors tried everything they could to stand out in a crowded field. Spaghetti westerns with strong political messages became common as student protests escalated against the Vietnam War and the Establishment. *A Bullet for the General* (1966) used the Mexican Revolution to critique U.S. foreign policy; *The Big Gundown* (1966) questioned the morality of politicians and corporate officials; and *The Price of Power* (1969) used a plot to kill President Garfield as a metaphor for the assassination of John F. Kennedy. Others, such as *Face to Face* (1967) and *Duck, You Sucker* (1971), mirrored the era's social movements by emphasizing group rather than individual action.

Some movies relied on gimmicks to attract attention. Films featured strange titles such as *Death Rides a Horse* (1967), *If You Meet Sartana Pray for Your Death* (1968), *Dead Men Don't Make Shadows* (1970), and *Karate, Fists, and Beans* (1973). One reviewer quipped, "There may be a general rule in spaghetti land that the better the title, the worse the movie." Other movies hoped glitzy weapons would lure audiences. The high-tech guns used by Sartana and Sabata would have made James Bond envious, while the protagonist in *Run, Man, Run* (1968) tacks in the opposite direction and uses a low-tech knife to defeat a gunslinger in a fast-draw contest. Producers tried everything to sell tickets. There were spaghetti western musicals (e.g., *Little Rita of the West*, 1967) and comedies (*They Call Me Trinity*, 1970). Other spaghetti westerns tempted audiences with sex. Misogyny was the norm as evidenced by numerous rapes, shootings, and beatings of women. Female victims typically were depicted in ripped clothing that revealed bare legs and bare backs, or they were shown in titillating poses. Films such as *Sabata* (1969) and *Man Called Amen* (1972) picked up on the era's prejudice against gays by suggesting that villains were deviant, sadistic homosexuals. *Django Kill . . . If You Live, Shoot!* (1967) tried a little of everything. Critic Kyle Anderson summed it up thusly: "A gay, gothic, horror spaghetti western . . . Need I say more?"[15]

Spaghetti westerns that mocked the genre proved the most damaging. "Parody is usually a reliable indicator that a genre is tottering towards the end of its lifecycle," suggests writer Daniel Krupa, "since a parody can only really work if the audience is overly-familiar with that genre's conventions."[16] The beginning of the end for spaghetti westerns came with the release of *They Call Me Trinity* in 1970. The comedic western starred Terence Hill (aka Mario Girotti) and Bud Spencer (Carlo Pedersoli) respectively as Trinity and Bambino, two low-life brothers who never did an honest day's work in their lives. The ne'er-do-wells spend most of their time arguing, drinking, carousing, eating, and scheming to make an easy buck. Trinity is perhaps the laziest cowboy hero of all time. He likes to sit around doing nothing and loves to eat, particularly beans, thereby providing a nickname—fagioli (i.e., the Italian word for "beans")—for this spaghetti western subgenre. Yet, the good-natured, handsome, blue-eyed cowboy is not without virtues. In particular, Trinity is as fast with his gun as he is with the ladies.

The film has a simple plot. Trinity arrives in town to find his brother posing as a sheriff. Bambino plans to steal horses from a crooked cattle baron, who in turn is trying to steal land from pacifist Mormons. Trinity complicates the situation when he falls in love with two pretty Mormon girls who let him know that polygamy is allowed in their church. Hoping for his just reward, Trinity helps the Mormons defeat the rancher and his men in a mammoth fistfight. Afterwards, he gives the rancher's horses to the grateful Mormons, who then tell Trinity that he can marry both girls. Trinity's joyous dream of a threesome is short-lived. When he learns that married Mormon men are obligated to work hard, the lazy cowboy jumps on his horse and rides off into the sunset.

The thin plot is merely a setup for lots of sight gags and funny lines. *They Call Me Trinity* lampoons the entire spaghetti western formula. The title emphasizes that this is not a Man with No Name. Terence Hill's happy-go-lucky good-guy character is an obvious counterpoint to the dark antiheroes typically found in spaghetti westerns. Trinity grins rather than frowns; he wears dirtier and more ragged clothes; he loves women and food far more than vengeance and whiskey; and he is so fast on the draw and quick with his fists that he seems more like a mischievous cartoon character than a moody, pathological gunslinger. The film also pokes fun at villains such as the Major (who is effeminate and bumbling) and Mexican banditos (depicted as ineffectual buffoons). Both are far less threatening than the psychopathic killers found in the films of Leone or Corbucci. Even the Mormon victims in *Trinity* exist primarily for comedic purposes. Though real-life Mormons in the West were hardly nonviolent, the Mormons in *Trinity* are depicted in ways more befitting Quakers. The movie describes them as "pacifistic Mormons" merely to use polygamy as a setup for Trinity to get not just one girl but two.

Audiences loved the chemistry between the good-looking Trinity and his disheveled brother, Bambino. The film established Terence Hill as a spaghetti western superstar and became one of the biggest movie hits of 1970, spawning a sequel and numerous copycat fagioli westerns. Many film critics loved the characters played by Hill and Spencer as much as the audiences did. Christopher Frayling called them "the Laurel and Hardy" of spaghetti westerns. But not everyone appreciated the duo's humor or the way they mocked westerns. "Leone really disliked this genre," explained one of his collaborators, scriptwriter Sergio Donati. "He'd say: 'I don't understand it. It doesn't make me laugh.'"[17]

My Name Is Nobody

Sergio Leone responded to the fagioli western fad by producing his own comedy western in 1973. Entitled *My Name Is Nobody*, the humorous film explored the relationship between mythic westerns and comedic parodies in a serious way. The allegorical story employs an aging gunfighter named Jack Beauregard (played by the iconic Henry Fonda) to symbolize the Old West. Representing the fagioli West is a mysterious character named Nobody (played by Terence Hill of Trinity fame). Significantly, this is not a showdown between the old mythic West and the spaghetti west, as many movie critics have suggested. Instead, it is a collaboration between the two that shows continuity not conflict.

Throughout the film, Beauregard (the Old West) and Nobody (the New West) have a symbiotic rather than adversarial relationship. Beauregard helps Nobody establish his reputation, while the latter helps the old gunslinger become a legend by defeating the bad guys who are gunning for him. If the Old West made the New West possible, the New West was now paying tribute to the Old. "For me, the interesting thing about *My Name Is Nobody* was that it confronts a myth with the negation of that myth," says Sergio Leone. "I do not see this as *destructive* at all. On the contrary. The moral of this adventure attempts to show that people never attack a nobody: in the West as in life, the only person who is taken into account is the man who is thought to be unbeatable." In effect, Leone was attempting to reconcile the old mythic West with the more revisionist spaghetti West.[18]

Even though the film was Leone's idea, he decided at the outset not to direct. "I originally went into the role of producer with this principle in mind: 'A Sergio Leone film directed by someone else,'" he explains. That someone turned out to be Leone's friend Tonino Valerii, who had served as assistant director on *A Fistful of Dollars*. Leone, however, left his imprint on the entire production. Along with coming up with the idea and title for the movie, he hired Fonda and Hill for the leads and selected his longtime collaborator Ennio Morricone to compose the music. He also directed a few scenes, provided input for many others, and closely supervised the writing of the script.[19]

The story takes place in the West at the end of the nineteenth century. Aging gunfighter Jack Beauregard wants to hang up his gun and retire to Europe. The arrival of a mysterious gunman called Nobody—an obvious spoof on Eastwood's character in Leone's Dollar Trilogy—complicates the situation. He grew up idolizing Beauregard and wants to guarantee the gunfighter's reputation by having him defeat a gang of 150 gunslingers known as the Wild Bunch (a poke at Sam Peckinpah's film). Even though Beauregard wants no part of the suicidal showdown, Nobody sets it up anyway. Beauregard is forced to fight back and kills most of the gang with help provided by Nobody. Beauregard understands that all the remaining gang members along with every fast gun in the West will now want to test their skills against the man who took on the Wild Bunch, but once again, Nobody comes to the rescue. He stages a gunfight between him and his hero, and Jack is allegedly killed. His epitaph states ironically, "Nobody was faster on the draw." Of course, now the remnants of the Wild Bunch and other gunslingers will take aim at the man who killed Jack Beauregard.

The movie ends with Beauregard on a sailing vessel bound for a retirement home in Europe. He is writing a farewell address to Nobody and reflects on the passing of the Old West, where people thought a fast gun could solve any problem. He explains that life is now far more complicated. Yet, Nobody is continuing the illusion and romance of the mythic West. "I guess looking back, it seems we were all a bunch of romantic fools," says Beauregard.

Leone's production bridges the gap between traditional westerns (represented by Fonda) and spaghetti/fagioli westerns (represented by Hill). It suggests that the two approaches are not in opposition to each other but need each other. Both the old and the new have a place in Leone's spaghetti West. Fonda's tough gunslinger—the symbol of the Old West—blazes the trail for Hill's revisionist character, who is more trickster than antihero. Though lightning fast on the draw, Hill's enigmatic cowboy is not just another knight of the Old West. He is a court jester who pokes fun at the mythic West as he helps protect its legacy. Nobody celebrates the myth through fakery as he transforms the aging western hero Beauregard into a "national monument."

Sergio Leone came to praise westerns not to bury them. Unlike fagioli westerns, which could be outright mean and disrespectful to the western genre, *My Name Is Nobody* gently spoofs both the Old West and the revisionist West. The title mocks the notion of the nameless hero made famous in Leone's previous films. The Leone production jokes about the Wild Bunch and has Peckinpah's name on one of the tombstones in a cemetery. The film pokes fun at almost every imaginable western convention, including fast-draw contests, drinking in saloons, train robberies, cowboy hats, and showdowns. Hill's trickster character even steals fruit from a baby.

My Name Is Nobody deconstructs the western myth as it reshapes it. It is at once an elegiac tribute to traditional westerns and a requiem for spaghetti westerns. The movie is all about endings. It takes place in 1899—at the end of the century. The iconic gunslinger's career is coming to a close, and the Old West is rapidly fading from view, replaced by a more modern America with steamships, trains, and bustling cities. In the final scene, Fonda's aged cowboy, dressed in a navy pea coat and sailor cap, sits on a sailing ship heading East as a huge steamboat in the background heads West. Both the Old West and the spaghetti West have been passed by.

Arrivederci, Spaghetti Westerns

Several spaghetti westerns were released after *My Name Is Nobody*, but none did well at the box office. In 1976, Italian director Enzo Castellari and Franco Nero (who gained fame as the original Django) tried to resuscitate the genre with *Keoma*, which was billed as "a real Western masterpiece." But the movie flopped. One line in the film inadvertently offered a clue about why audiences stayed away in droves. When a witch asks Nero's character why he returned, Nero replies, "The world keeps going around and around. So you always end up in the same place." The same might be said of spaghetti westerns in general. As the world turned and changed, spaghetti westerns remained in place, with hackneyed plots and poor production values.

By the mid-seventies, spaghetti westerns were no longer in step with audiences. America's mood changed considerably as the tumultuous sixties and early seventies ran out of steam. Watergate drove President Nixon from office; the Vietnam War ended; campus protests faded; and urban unrest burned itself out. Americans were sick and tired of violence and despair. They turned to happier thoughts or diversions such as the nation's upcoming bicentennial. And just as sixties rock music fans sought escape in disco or other ephemeral sounds of the seventies, movie audiences sought respite in the seventies through glitzy action films, escapist comedies, or new fantasy genres.

Although spaghetti westerns rode off into the sunset in the mid-seventies, their tracks remained on the cultural landscape. These brooding revisionist westerns reveal a great deal about the times in which they were made. During the sixties and seventies, the United States was staggered by an unpopular war in Vietnam. American society unraveled as the optimism and peaceful tactics initially associated with the civil rights movement, college protests, and the counterculture degenerated into pessimism, polarization, rebellion, and violence. Spaghetti westerns redefined the western genre to fit the tumultuous times. Rather than portraying the traditional mythic West as an exotic and beautiful land of opportunity, hope, and redemption, they depicted a desolate and forsaken West more in keeping with the dark days of the sixties and seventies. In these violent and troubled times, spaghetti westerns, with their antiheroes, ambiguous morals, brutality, and anti-Establishment themes, resonated with audiences. The films' gratuitous violence, surrealistic style, gloomy look, and eerie sound captured the era's melancholy, anomie, and despair.

As American society divided over myriad issues or splintered along political, racial, ethnic, or gender lines, notions of right and wrong became increasingly more complex. Gone were the black-and-white days of yesteryear, with their absolute truths and clear-cut values. In their stead were many shades of gray, which countered absolute morality with situational ethics. Spaghetti westerns thrived in this confused environment. Sergio Leone offered audiences an ambiguous protagonist who was perfect for the anxious times. This new type of antihero—typified by Clint Eastwood's Man with No Name—was often violent, brutal, and amoral. Like earlier cowboy heroes, he was fast on the draw, but his killer instinct was not constrained by traditional morals. He could shoot down a villain in cold blood with no remorse, and he didn't think twice about mass murder as he left dozens if not hundreds of bleeding corpses to rot in the sun. Armed and dangerous, this antihero was a man of action, ready for any cause or problem that came his way. And in the sixties and seventies, there were plenty of each, making the spaghetti western protagonist the perfect man for the desperate times. In an age characterized by rebellion and a growing sense that the individual was oppressed by a corrupt Establishment, audiences could relate to spaghetti western antiheroes who fought back against the powers that be. That anti-Establishment message resonated in a time of great social change, when intellectuals decried the loss of individualism and citizens felt helpless before big business, big government, or a callous military machine determined to draft men to fight a questionable war in the faraway jungles and rice paddies of Vietnam.

Spaghetti westerns exploded nearly every convention of traditional westerns. The films of Sergio Corbucci provide an excellent example. Corbucci's West was not a beautiful and majestic land. It was a desolate world of dust and mud in a movie like *Django* (1966) or a forbidding landscape of snow and ice in *The Great Silence* (1968). Nor were Corbucci's characters like those in earlier Hollywood westerns. Instead of being hopeful and moral, they were dark, brooding, and amoral. For example, the excessively violent antihero Django lacked the moral core of earlier cowboy heroes. Even the prostitutes in *Django* were so strange and surreal that it seemed like they had just stepped out of a Federico Fellini film.

The commercial success of spaghetti westerns led to a globalization of the western genre. Before long, westerns were being produced throughout Europe, in Asia, and in South America. Even America's Cold War rivals got in on the action. Not surprisingly, most "red westerns" made in the Soviet Union, Eastern Europe, or China blasted capitalists and the U.S. military for oppressing Indians and the masses. But some simply followed typical western conventions with gunslingers, saloon girls, and climactic showdowns between good guys and bad guys.[20]

Spaghetti westerns even influenced the American movie industry, which had given birth to the western. Spaghetti westerns created new Hollywood stars like Clint Eastwood and resuscitated the careers of numerous others. They proved to Hollywood that westerns could be profitable if they were updated by revisionist themes, quirky heroes, more violence, and darker images of the mythic West. Spaghetti westerns forced American film makers to rethink the West. The result would be some of the finest westerns ever made. Some, like *The Wild Bunch* (1969), would be revisionist. But others would be neotraditional films, such as *True Grit* (1969), which blended old-fashioned images of the mythic West with revisionist elements and themes. These films would demonstrate continuity as well as conflict in America of the sixties and seventies.

The sheer quantity of spaghetti westerns made them a force to be reckoned with. More than five hundred were produced between the mid-sixties and the late seventies. They ranged from excellent films with unforgettable stars and story lines to horrible B pictures with few stars and even fewer plots. But all of them spotlighted the mythic West and reflected the times. In the end, spaghetti westerns, like old soldiers, never died completely; they just faded away. But, before they exited the stage, they left their mark on audiences and film makers around the world.

CHAPTER EIGHT

The Wild Bunch

American Westerns on a Revisionist Trail

Sam Peckinpah's 1969 film, *The Wild Bunch*, offered moviegoers a new vision of the West that was in sync with the troubled times. By the end of the sixties, America was reeling from ubiquitous violence, growing polarization, and countless assaults on almost every imaginable American institution. Vietnam called into question basic beliefs about war and foreign policy, while the civil rights movement, assassinations, urban unrest, campus protests, the counterculture, and rapid social change sent shock waves across the country. Americans could sense that the past was rapidly falling by the wayside as they struggled to make sense of the present and were uncertain about the future. A movie poster for *The Wild Bunch* focused on Americans of an earlier era who faced similar problems. "Unchanged men in a changing land," it read. "Out of step, out of place, and desperately out of time." Just as the Wild Bunch were out of place in 1913, the mythic West was out of step with America in 1969. Peckinpah's darker vision of the West resonated with both moviegoers and critics.

The Wild Bunch was just one of many American revisionist westerns attracting audiences in the sixties and seventies. These films show that American westerns were just as quick on the draw as spaghetti westerns when it came to unorthodox heroes, violence, moral ambiguity, or cynical visions of the mythic West. Revisionist westerns were a perfect fit for the tumultuous times. Significantly, the new western images that emerged from these films predated by decades the New Western History, which featured similar reinterpretations of the West.[1]

Figure 25. The movie poster for *The Wild Bunch* (Warner Brothers—Seven Arts, 1969) captures the alienation of the film's characters as well as the violence.

Although the mythic West would change considerably on the silver screen after 1963, it would remain a fixture on the cultural landscape. Like the North Star, the ever-present West would point the way for Americans bogged down in the jungles of Vietnam or lost at home in a maze of rapid social and political change involving women, youth, and minorities. American revisionist westerns would be powerful reminders of the nation's hopes, dreams, and fears.

American Westerns and a Revisionist West

Revisionist westerns like *The Wild Bunch* were inspired in part by the success of Sergio Leone and spaghetti westerns, but their roots were firmly planted in American culture. Throughout the twentieth century, westerns had always reinvented themselves to remain relevant in changing times. Post–World War II films such as *Broken Arrow* (1950), *Johnny Guitar* (1954), and *Sergeant Rutledge* (1960) offered new visions of the West that reflected changing roles of women and minorities. American westerns of the late sixties and early seventies continued down that revisionist trail. When basic American beliefs were challenged by the Vietnam War and other divisive issues, numerous films began to question the traditional notion of the West as a land of freedom, opportunity, success, and redemption. Others used familiar western characters and images in new ways to critique the changing times. *The Wild Bunch* did both.

Peckinpah's film went into production in 1968, one of the most violent and chaotic years in American history. The year began with the surprising Tet Offensive in Vietnam. Other traumatic events followed in rapid succession: President Lyndon Johnson decided not to run for reelection; Martin Luther King was assassinated; urban riots erupted across America; Bobby Kennedy was assassinated; millions protested the Vietnam War and questioned the Establishment; and violence exploded at the Democratic National Convention. Ubiquitous media coverage spotlighted the violence, polarization, and despair that wracked the nation during the nightmare year of 1968. The angry mood of the country worsened the following year. As violence escalated in Vietnam and on college campuses and cities throughout America, the new president, Richard Nixon, added to the polarization by pitting various groups against each other.

The Wild Bunch, released in June 1969, reflected the nation's dark mood. The opening scene foreshadows the violence to come. The year is 1913. Pike Bishop (played by William Holden) and his Wild Bunch gang ride into a Texas town disguised as U.S. soldiers. Pike is briefly distracted by gleeful children watching a swarm of ants killing two scorpions. He and his men continue on to the railroad bank office, where they stage a holdup. They soon realize they've ridden into a trap. Across the street on a roof are a railroad detective, bounty hunters, and an ex-member of Bishop's gang, Deke Thornton (Robert Ryan), who agreed to help the railroad company catch the Wild Bunch in order to avoid going to jail. Pike and his men grab the money and rush out into the crowded street, determined to shoot their way out of trouble. Bullets fly in all directions. Some of Pike's men are killed; many railroad men are shot dead; but even more innocent men, women, and children are slaughtered in the crossfire. Undeterred, the railroad detective sends Deke and the bounty hunters on a manhunt to get the Wild Bunch dead or alive.

Pike and the surviving gang members—Dutch Engstrom (Ernest Borgnine), Tector Gorch (Ben Johnson), Lyle Gorch (Warren Oates), and Angel (Jaime Sanchez)—hide out in the home of their retired comrade, Old Freddie Sykes (Edmond O'Brien). Later, the Wild Bunch head to Angel's hometown in Mexico, where they are greeted like returning heroes. Angel had joined Pike to get money to purchase weapons so the villagers could defend themselves against the Mexican dictator Huerta and his army, led by a brutal general named Mapache.

Next day, the gang travels to a nearby town and finds Mapache dining with a German envoy. When Angel's former girlfriend, now the general's mistress, arrives, Angel loses his temper and shoots her. Just as Mapache's soldiers are about to retaliate, the German envoy intervenes and invites the Americans to dinner. That night, he and Mapache offer the American outlaws ten thousand dollars to steal a rifle shipment from a U.S. Army train. Pike accepts the deal. But when Angel balks at helping Mapache, Pike agrees to give him some of the guns to aid the peasants' fight against the corrupt Mexican dictatorship.

The Wild Bunch set off to intercept the train, which, unknown to Pike, is also carrying Deke Thornton and the posse. The robbery goes as planned when the Wild Bunch outmaneuver the inept U.S. soldiers and steal not just rifles but also a modern machine gun. Pike soon realizes that Deke and the bounty hunters are hot on their trail. The Wild Bunch, which now includes Old Sykes, successfully fight off Thornton's men en route to Mexico. Before turning the weapons over to Mapache, Pike gives Angel the promised box of rifles. But when Dutch and Angel are sent to exchange the rest of the stolen weapons for the agreed-on fee, the general seizes Angel for stealing some of the rifles.

Determined not to leave one of his men behind, Pike rounds up his gang. Side by side, the four heavily armed members of the Wild Bunch march through town for a showdown. All the while, slow Mexican music plays in the background, with a steady drumbeat giving it a pronounced military feel. When they arrive at the general's headquarters, the drunken Mexicans look at them with surprise. "Gringos," says the debauched Mapache, "what do you want?" Pike replies, "We want Angel." So, Mapache gives him Angel, but first he slits Angel's throat.

Pike responds instantaneously with a bullet that kills Mapache, while other members of the Wild Bunch shoot the general's officers. For one brief moment, it appears the Wild Bunch will escape, because Mapache's stunned soldiers don't seem to know how to react. But then Pike spies the callous German envoy and shoots him dead. Gunfire immediately erupts in all directions. Soldiers get shot, civilians are killed, women and children gunned down. Tector Gorch seizes control of Mapache's new machine gun and blasts Mexican troops. Dutch grabs a woman to use as a shield but discards her when she becomes a bloody corpse. Pike is wounded by a gunshot to the back. Other members of the Wild Bunch are hit several times by bullets. Yet, they fight on. When Tector is killed, his brother grabs the machine gun and continues the bloodbath. When he falls, Pike takes over the machine gun and mercilessly mows down row after row of Mexican soldiers. Just when Pike looks invincible, he is shot by a little boy who sneaks up behind him. As Dutch comes running up, the two longtime partners are shot numerous times and die together next to the machine gun.

The violent, bloody shootout finally ends. Lasting for what seemed like an eternity, it results in wholesale carnage, including the deaths of the Wild Bunch, the vicious Mapache, and his coterie of corrupt officers and civilian sycophants, as well as hundreds of soldiers. Perched on the walls of the town are numerous vultures ready to swoop down, while mournful women dressed in black move slowly among the dead searching for loved ones. Just then, Deke's posse arrives. The greedy bounty hunters begin picking the carcasses for valuables, just as the vultures had hoped to do. They even chip the gold out of Dutch's teeth. Deke is disgusted by their pillaging as he looks sadly at the fallen bodies of Pike and Dutch. Deke allows the greedy bounty hunters to ride away with the Wild Bunch's dead bodies, which they plan to turn in for a reward, because he realizes they will all be killed by Mexican rebels hiding in the hills. As they ride off, he sits down and watches townsfolk gather their dead. When shots ring out in the distance, Deke knows that the disgusting bounty hunters have finally gotten what they deserve.

In the last scene, Old Sykes, whom the Wild Bunch had given up for dead in an earlier ambush, rides up with rebel fighters from Angel's village. Seeing Deke, he says, "I didn't expect to find you here." "Why not?" asks Thornton. "I sent them back. That's all I said I'd do." "Well," replies Old Sykes, "me and the boys got some work to do. You want to come with us? It ain't like it used to be; but it'll do." Deke agrees to join the revolution, and the camera shows him and Sykes riding off into the sunset with the peasant nationalists. Superimposed on the screen are images from earlier in the film that show the Wild Bunch riding out of Angel's village as Mexican singers and music serenade them.

Peckinpah's revisionist western not only subverts the notion that the mythic West is a land of beauty, opportunity, and regeneration, but it uses traditional western images and characters in new ways to critique modern American society and culture. Reflecting the escalating violence in America related to assassinations, urban riots, civil rights marches, campus protests, and Vietnam, *The Wild Bunch* includes some of the most violent scenes in westerns to date. The gunfight at the beginning of the movie, for example, drags on in gory detail for about four minutes. The scene shows carnage in graphic detail—bullets hitting people's bodies, blood spurting out everywhere, even small children shot down in the street.

The film includes obvious comparisons to Vietnam. Just as some antiwar protesters glorified the Vietcong as peasant nationalists who fought against a corrupt regime and imperialistic power, *The Wild Bunch* idealizes Angel and his fellow peasants as revolutionary guerrillas fighting for freedom against an oppressive dictator backed by a foreign government. Similar to Vietnam, the film depicts innocent people caught in the crossfire between corrupt government forces, rebel insurgents, and outsiders who profit from the fighting. Even the corrupt Mexican soldiers and collaborators who benefited from Mapache's brutal regime evoke contemporary images of South Vietnamese counterparts who profit by cooperating with Ngo Dinh Diem's government. During the shootout at the end of the film, for instance, Pike runs into a room to hide from Mapache's men and discovers a Mexican whore. Thinking she is an innocent victim, he spares her life. Then, when he turns to fire at the soldiers outside, the Mapache sympathizer shoots him in the back. The wounded outlaw whirls around, yells, "Bitch!" and shoots her dead. Later, Pike is killed by a young boy who also supports the evil Mapache.

The Wild Bunch mirrors anti-Establishment attitudes of the sixties. The anti-government film depicts Mexican leaders as corrupt and brutal, the German government as cold and warlike, and the American government as ineffectual at best. The film takes a strong antimilitary stance. The Mexican forces of Huerta and Mapache are evil to the core. The German envoy is a conniving warmonger, who represents a militaristic state that is hostile to America. Even the U.S. Army is depicted in unflattering ways. American soldiers guarding the train are raw recruits who are unprepared for combat duty (perhaps a reference to young draftees being sent to fight in the jungles of Vietnam), while the officers in charge are totally incompetent. The movie likewise shares the anticorporate attitudes held by many Americans in the sixties. The railroad company is ruthless in its quest for profits and dispatches unscrupulous bounty hunters to do its dirty work. The company forces Deke to betray his Wild Bunch friends, and it shows little concern for the deaths of innocent bystanders caught in the middle of the ongoing battle between the corporation and Pike's outlaw gang.

The Wild Bunch provides other glimpses of the times in which it was made. Reflecting changing sexual attitudes, the film includes nudity and several sexually explicit scenes. At one point, whores expose their legs seductively as they dance on a table in front of Mapache and his officers. One soldier pours whiskey on a prostitute's bare leg and then licks it all the way up toward her thigh. *The Wild Bunch* also captures the unsympathetic attitudes that many people in the sixties had toward social activists. At the beginning of the movie, a group of sanctimonious reformers parade through the street accompanied by a temperance union marching band and curious onlookers. Their naiveté becomes abundantly clear as they march blithely toward a bank robbery in progress. The reformers' lack of awareness about the real world results in multiple deaths when a gun battle erupts between the railroad men and the Wild Bunch. The film's message about social reform is clear: real change comes not from duplicitous government officials or out-of-touch social activists, but from clear-headed realists (such as Pike and his friends) or from aggressive community action (such as that taken by Angel and the rebels).

The Wild Bunch demolishes the mythic West. What emerges on screen is not a beautiful land populated by hardworking, rugged individuals in search of opportunity and success. It is a dusty, desolate place filled with evildoers who prey on the weak and quash the dreams of the innocent. Heroic figures with old-fashioned values and morals are nowhere to be found in Peckinpah's West. Instead, the protagonists are antiheroes whose ambiguous values resonated with audiences familiar with the complexities of 1960s America. The film uses familiar western characters in new ways to critique modern society. Everything is turned upside down as government officials, soldiers, and posses become the bad guys, while lawbreakers like the Wild Bunch become the good guys. Pike and his gang might not always obey the law, but they adhere to a basic code that calls for honor among thieves. Pike even makes the ultimate sacrifice to help his country. After killing Mapache, he and the rest of the Wild Bunch might have escaped, but instead Pike shoots the envoy who represents the German threat to America prior to World War I. The selfless act sparks the shootout that kills all the members of the Wild Bunch.

Pike and his men were not the only casualties of the shootout. The Old West also dies in that bloody climactic scene. Even before the aging outlaws breathe their last breaths, they realize that time has passed them by. At one point, Pike, whose old injuries and creaking bones make it difficult for him to climb up on his horse, tells his gang poignantly, "We've got to start thinking beyond our guns. Those days are closin' fast." Peckinpah's film addresses the passing of the Old West in other ways. Pike and his gang are astounded by the first car they see, amazed to learn about airplanes, and fascinated by high-tech machine guns. These old-fashioned outlaws meet their end when they are overwhelmed by twentieth-century international politics and insurgent rebellions. The Wild Bunch's "last stand" against Mapache's troops represents the end of an era not just for the outlaws but for a way of life. The Old West was gone.

Peckinpah's portrayal of the West—like the times in which the film was made—is complex. Its revisionism is balanced by traditional themes and images. The Wild Bunch, whose name alludes to Butch Cassidy's actual gang, exhibit the "band of brothers" camaraderie found in earlier westerns. Pike and his men are an extension of the good badman tradition that dates back at least to Broncho Billy and William S. Hart. They steal from the rich, fight bad guys, and defend the weak and innocent. The film's climax is a classic western showdown. Like Gary Cooper in *High Noon*, the members of the Wild Bunch stride down the street to confront evil, in this case, the Mexican soldiers and their sinister boss, Mapache (whose very name invokes one of the fiercest Indian tribes ever to appear in westerns). The Wild Bunch's "last stand" recalls other famous frontier battles, including Little Big Horn and the Alamo (which was also against a brutal Mexican general and army). To the very end, the Wild Bunch fight to defend honor, liberty, even America. Arguably, their martyrdom was simply a bloodier, more adult version of the iconic end of Fess Parker's character in *Davy Crockett: King of the Wild Frontier* (1955).

Peckinpah's film even suggests eventual redemption—in the next world if not this one. Pike and his gang redeem themselves by their selfless act of helping their comrade Angel. When they proclaim to the evil Mapache, "We want Angel," they are in effect asking for religious salvation. They find political redemption by sacrificing their lives to kill the German envoy, an enemy of the United States, while their comrades, Sykes and Deke, find salvation by joining the peasant nationalists' just war. Significantly, the end of the movie shows the dead gang members laughing as they ride off into eternity. Arguably, this suggests a happy ending, because the Wild Bunch die for their principles and find eternal life in the mythic West.

The Wild Bunch is a powerful reinterpretation of the mythic West. Like all the best pop culture products, this film has diverse messages that can be interpreted in various ways. It is revisionist because it uses old-fashioned western images in new ways to comment about Vietnam, social change, corruption, violence, and other issues facing modern America. Yet, the film is traditional in that it accepts many conventions associated with the mythic West even as it offers a requiem for the passing of the Old West. It is that tension that gives the movie its power. And it is that tension that connects *The Wild Bunch* to the complexities of 1960s America.

The Mythic West Revised

By the late sixties and early seventies, numerous American westerns were questioning the image of the West as a glamorous land of freedom, opportunity, and redemption.[2] A good example is *Monte Walsh* (1970), which offered a devastating critique of the mythic West. Directed by William A. Fraker and based on a novel by Jack Schaefer (who also wrote *Shane*), the story revolves around two aging cowboys, Monte Walsh (played by Lee Marvin) and his friend Chet Rollins (Jack Palance). The longtime pals work on the Slash-Y ranch, which has recently been purchased by a corporation back east. Slowly but surely, the company is downsizing the operation by laying off cowboys, including Monte and Chet's friend Shorty. Despite signs that the cowboy way of life is on the way out, Monte refuses to hang up his spurs. At one point, he says, "As long as there's one cowboy taking care of one cow it ain't dead."

The movie's slow, hypnotic rhythm adds to the melancholy feeling that time is running out for the aging cowboys and all their friends. "Nobody gets to be a cowboy forever," laments Chet as he explains that he's decided to get married, settle down, and work in a hardware store. The love interest in Monte's life, a prostitute named Martine, confides to him that she's getting too old for her profession and has to make money while she can. Her plan is to move to a different town where business is better. Shorty also sets out in a new direction. After losing his job at the Slash-Y, the young man begins hanging out with two shady drifters who get him into trouble rustling cows from the corporation that fired him. Even Monte realizes that time is passing him by. Feeling down after Chet gets married, he rides forty miles to the next town to propose to Martine and promises that he'll find a new job so they can settle down.

Monte soon breaks that promise. Unable to quit the cowboy way of life, he returns to town and rides a bucking bronco. When a stranger witnesses the wild ride, he offers to hire Monte as the star attraction of his Wild West show. But Monte will have to change his name to the more colorful-sounding Texas Jack Butler and wear a fancy buckskin jacket and hat similar to Buffalo Bill Cody's famous outfit. The lucrative offer is tempting, but Monte winds up rejecting it, because he refuses to make a mockery out of his chosen career as a cowboy. "I ain't spittin' on my whole life," he explains.

Soon thereafter, Monte's life spirals downward. When he tells Martine that he has turned down the job as a Wild West performer, she realizes that their marriage will never happen, because Monte won't ever give up being a cowboy. Chet faces more immediate danger. One morning, Shorty and his outlaw friend walk into Chet's hardware store. When Chet refuses to give them money, Shorty's outlaw pal tries to take it by force. Chet kills the outlaw but then is mortally wounded by Shorty.

Monte is heartbroken by the death of his best friend. Just when it appears things cannot get any worse, Monte finds out that he is losing his job as a cowboy because the corporation is closing the Slash-Y. The downtrodden cowboy rides off, determined to track down Shorty and avenge Chet's death. When news reaches him that Martine is deathly ill, he immediately gallops off toward her house, but he arrives too late and finds her dead. One more piece of Monte's heart breaks, as he tenderly cuts off a lock of her hair as a memento.

On the way out the door, Monte is confronted by Shorty. The erstwhile friends shoot it out in the shadows, and then come out into the open for a showdown. When Shorty holsters his gun for the expected fast-draw contest, Monte pulls out a hidden six-shooter and guns down the man who murdered Chet. At best, the gunfight is a pyrrhic victory. By film's end, Monte Walsh has lost everything: his friends and girl are dead; his cowboy life is over; even the West he so desperately loved is rapidly fading from view. In the final scene, an older Monte is all alone, talking to his horse and reminiscing about the good old days.

Watching *Monte Walsh* is akin to reading an obituary for the Old West. The depressing film eviscerates the western myth. There is no happiness, no success, no redemption for anyone or anything. Monte loses everything that ever mattered to him—his friends, his fiancée, his career as a cowboy. Even the Old West falls prey to modernity as ranches are bought by eastern corporations and cowboys are given walking papers.

Significantly, the film uses classic western references to gut the mythic West. The opening credits employ Charles Russell's famous sketches and paintings of cowboys to establish a traditional mood. References to Buffalo Bill's Wild West underscore the inauthenticity of the myth. Equally devastating are the allusions to Owen Wister's seminal western novel, *The Virginian*. In both the novel and the movie, a young cowboy named Shorty is led astray by bad guys. Monte Walsh—like the Virginian—is a proud cowboy with unequaled abilities when it comes to riding, roping, and shooting. But, in keeping with the film's revisionist approach, Monte fails where the Virginian succeeds. The Virginian holds on to his principles, wins the showdown with the bad guy fair and square, and then lives happily ever after with a virtuous schoolmarm. Monte displays more ambiguous values on the way to a sad ending. He uses unfair tactics to kill a former friend in a showdown; he loses his prostitute girlfriend; and he winds up all alone with no discernible future. Monte Walsh's West—unlike the Virginian's—is far darker, filled with failure and despair. Its revisionist view resonated with moviegoers who were being bombarded in 1970 by depressing news stories about Vietnam, America's troubled economy, and Kent State. During these troubled times, audiences undoubtedly understood the irony as rock star Mama Cass Elliot sang the title song to *Monte Walsh*, "The Good Times Are Comin'."

The depressing image of the West in *Monte Walsh* seems almost benign when compared to the dark portrayal of the West in *McCabe & Mrs. Miller* (1971). Robert Altman's western stars Warren Beatty as John McCabe, a drifter and gambler hoping to find a new life out west, and Julie Christie as Constance Miller, an independent woman with entrepreneurial talents and a willingness to do anything to succeed. At the beginning of the movie, McCabe arrives in an isolated mining town, tucked away in the mountains, and sees opportunity for success. His plan is to start up a combination saloon/gambling house/brothel. He partners with the beautiful Mrs. Miller, a prostitute he is attracted to. With his determination to succeed and her business sense, they soon begin to make money. Smelling profits, the greedy mining company attempts to buy McCabe's business, but McCabe refuses because he's convinced that the next offer will be even bigger. When Mrs. Miller finds out what he's done, she tells him he's crazy because the company will kill him. But McCabe firmly believes he can negotiate a better deal.

Shortly thereafter, three hired gunmen arrive in town. A frightened McCabe turns to a lawyer for help. The fast-talking lawyer (William Devane) assures McCabe that justice will prevail. "When a man goes into the wilderness," explains the lawyer in glowing terms that evoke the mythic West, "and with his own bare hands gives birth to a small enterprise . . . no dirty sons-of-bitches will take it away from him." The lawyer, who sees this case as an opportunity to further his own political ambitions, promises McCabe that he will become a symbol of the little man fighting big business. The lawyer assures McCabe that he won't be killed, because the mining company will be afraid to touch him after newspapers turn him into a cause célèbre.

The naïve McCabe returns home convinced that everything will be fine. When he brags to Mrs. Miller that his plan is to stand up to the "trusts and monopolies" on behalf of the "little man," she points out that the company will kill him and begins to cry. McCabe soon realizes that Mrs. Miller is right and that he could get killed at any moment by the mining company's gunslingers. So, in the tradition of the Old West, he grabs his gun and decides to rely on his own rugged individualism. Nothing ends well in this depressing western as McCabe, Mrs. Miller, and the townspeople all sink deeper and deeper into despair and eventual destruction.

Altman's dark film rejects the mythic West as an exotic land of beauty, opportunity, and redemption. The mood is ominous from the moment McCabe arrives in the remote mining town in the gloomy mountains of the Pacific Northwest. It is nighttime, and the weather is rainy and wintry. The streets and buildings are filled with mangy dogs and even mangier people, who are more depressing than the miserable setting. Later action scenes and the climactic showdown are filmed during snowstorms, suggesting that the weather is as dangerous as any varmint or hombre. Adding to the melancholy mood is a soundtrack that features mournful songs by singer-songwriter Leonard Cohen.

McCabe & Mrs. Miller dispenses with western heroes, as well as the myths of success and rugged individualism. Altman's protagonists have numerous faults and questionable values that give them no chance at success. McCabe truly believes that he has what it takes to succeed in the West. He fancies himself a town leader, a shrewd businessman, and a rugged individual, but he fails horribly whenever faced with a challenge. McCabe is unable to negotiate the sale of his business. He is duped by a fast-talking lawyer. He cannot combat the power or corruption of the mining company. And ultimately, he loses his last stand against the gunslingers. When forced to confront the bad guys, he doesn't walk down the street toward them for a classic western showdown. Instead, he hides in a church, behind fences, and in buildings. When the gunmen spread out to search for him, he shoots two of them in the back, and then plays dead to trick the third into coming closer so he can shoot him in the head. But even when he's winning the battle against the gunslingers, he's losing the war. McCabe is mortally wounded in the gunfight and falls into a snowdrift to die—beaten by bad guys and the elements.

Mrs. Miller is every bit as flawed. Though shrewd and independent, the prostitute ultimately fails. By film's end, she has lost the man she loves, her promising business, and her new life as she sinks into an opium-induced depression. Neither McCabe nor Mrs. Miller makes it in the West. They are beaten back by forces beyond their control, including the mining company, the outlaws, and the harsh environment, as well as their own insecurities and frailties.

Even the citizens of the mining town are not the good and decent townspeople typically found in traditional westerns. The sheen quickly falls away from the mythic West as these simple folk are depicted drinking, swearing, gambling, defecating, urinating, farting, and whoring. When one of them does attempt a noble action by defending his mail-order bride from a crowd that is treating her like a whore, he is quickly shot to death. Adding insult to injury, his widow immediately decides to become a whore. Later in the film, the town citizens come together for an altruistic moment to save the church from burning to the ground, but their moral victory is short-lived when their community spirit deteriorates into just one more occasion for debauchery. In the end, these common folk are anything but rugged individuals who evoke the superiority of the common man. Instead, these crude denizens of a frontier town are merely miserable examples of human beings and oblivious to everything happening around them.

Altman's revisionist film uses the Old West as a springboard for social commentary.[3] The movie launches a frontal assault on mainstream values, morals, and social conventions through profanity, crude behavior, and attacks on traditional attitudes toward gender, marriage, and religion. The protagonists have dubious morals and operate a disreputable business based on alcohol, gambling, and illicit sex. The minister is portrayed as ineffectual, and the town's church, the symbol of civilization, is set on fire but saved by a motley group of drunks and whores. The prostitute, Mrs. Miller, is depicted as a bright, independent businesswoman, who is far more perceptive than McCabe and all the other males around her. She understands how society views her profession, but also realizes that her job is market driven and perhaps not that much different from more traditional female occupations. Mrs. Miller maintains that being a prostitute is actually a better job than being a wife and in many ways not that much different since in both cases women trade sex for money, room, and board.

Picking up on other popular attitudes, *McCabe & Mrs. Miller* attacks big business (the mining company); disingenuous politicians (the lawyer); religion (the useless minister); and technology (the negative impact of mining on the environment and society). The film also reflects the counterculture's preoccupation with sex, drugs, and rock & roll. Sex and promiscuity are dealt with openly; drugs and alcohol are prominent; and the soundtrack featuring Leonard Cohen's plaintive music and pointed lyrics echoes the musical tastes of a youth culture that favored introspective singer-songwriters like Bob Dylan. The haunting Cohen songs featured in the movie—"The Stranger Song," "Sisters of Mercy," and "Winter Lady"—add to the film's dark feel and sense of hopelessness.

McCabe & Mrs. Miller offers a pessimistic message not just about the West, but about contemporary America in general. The revisionist western suggests that Americans cannot find happiness or success—in the West or anywhere else. Altman's dark vision maintains that individuals will always be overwhelmed by forces beyond their control, as well as their own stupidity and naiveté. Not surprisingly, Altman's downbeat film struck a responsive chord with moviegoers in the seventies. Like the protagonists in the film, many audience members felt overwhelmed by the political, economic, social, and cultural forces swirling around them.

While some American directors were producing grim revisionist westerns, comedy films such *Cat Ballou* (1965), *The Ballad of Cable Hogue* (1970), and *Blazing Saddles* (1974) were taking potshots at traditional western images and myths.[4] *Blazing Saddles* (1974) became one of the era's biggest hits. Directed by Mel Brooks and nominated for three Oscars, the film stars African American actor Cleavon Little as a sheriff with an attitude and Gene Wilder as a reformed alcoholic gunslinger who is so fast on the draw that it looks like his hand never moves. No clichés are spared. The film lampoons tired western plots about the coming of the railroad, a lone sheriff who has to save the town, and a gunfighter who finds redemption. It also ridicules hackneyed images of good guys, bad guys, gender, and race. Little's African American character is named Bart (as in Black Bart), and he clearly is superior to all the racist whites in the Old West. Gene Wilder's Waco Kid mocks gunslinger characters typically found in westerns. When asked how fast he is on the draw, he replies matter-of-factly, "I must have killed more men than Cecil B. DeMille." Among the film's funniest scenes are a dance hall girl, Lili Von Shtupp (Madeline Kahn), ridiculing Marlene Dietrich's Frenchy character in *Destry Rides Again* (1939) and Alex Karras's fierce Mongo character punching a horse. Even the film's ending—a postmodern mélange of traditional westerns and the modern film industry—mocks traditional westerns, spaghetti westerns, and Hollywood in general. The climax is an overblown fistfight that parodies the brawl at the conclusion of *They Call Me Trinity*. *Blazing Saddles* ends with the two good guys riding off into the sunset—in a Cadillac limousine.

Revisionist Westerns and American Society

Along with rejecting established images of the mythic West, revisionist westerns used familiar western characters in new ways to critique contemporary society and culture. Heroes who represented traditional values and clear-cut distinctions between right and wrong were often replaced by antiheroes whose dubious actions and questionable ethics were more in keeping with the ambiguities of American life in the late sixties and seventies.[5] *Butch Cassidy and the Sundance Kid,* directed by George Roy Hill, is a good example. Along with becoming one of the biggest box office hits of 1969, the movie helped popularize a new type of western protagonist. The new archetype—an amiable antihero who didn't follow the rules and was bad but not evil—was a perfect fit for the rebellious sixties. His ambiguous morality and awareness of the changing times reflected the complexities of modern America, as social change overwhelmed old values.

Based loosely on the exploits of two real-life outlaws, the movie establishes its nostalgic view of the Old West immediately with flickering images on the screen of Butch and Sundance's Wild Bunch gang that recall Edwin S. Porter's 1903 film *The Great Train Robbery*. The first scene has Butch Cassidy (Paul Newman) checking out a bank for a possible robbery. He is surprised to see a thick safe and all sorts of newfangled locks and alarms. "What happened to the old bank?" he asks the guard. "It was beautiful." When the guard explains that people kept robbing it, Butch says matter-of-factly, "Small price to pay for beauty."

The next scene introduces the audience to the equally interesting Sundance Kid (Robert Redford), who is playing cards in a saloon. Butch walks in just as the other player accuses Sundance of cheating. When Butch points out to the fellow that he is about to draw against the fastest gun in the West, the amazed man immediately backs off. "I didn't know you were the Sundance Kid when I said you were cheating," he explains. "If I draw on you, you'll kill me." Sundance replies coolly, "There's that possibility."

From the outset, it is clear that Butch and Sundance are not typical western good guys or bad guys. These roguish antiheroes fall somewhere in between. They make their living as outlaws who don't play by society's rules, but despite their ambiguous morals, they are still likable guys with good dispositions. Butch views himself as the idea man, while Sundance is the man of action. At one point, Butch brags, "Boy, I got vision, and the rest of the world wears bifocals." Sundance is more bemused than impressed by his friend's never-ending schemes.

Unlike typical protagonists in western movies, Butch and Sundance don't feel honor bound to follow traditional values or any code of the West. When the two return to their Hole-in-the-Wall hideout, for example, they find their gang on the verge of rebellion. The ringleader, Harvey Logan, believes they need to change with the times by robbing trains instead of banks, and he challenges Butch to a fight to the death to determine who will be the gang's leader. Butch appears to take the high road, explaining that he doesn't want to fight Harvey, but the unruly gang member refuses to back down and draws his knife. Butch calmly walks over to Sundance and whispers to his buddy, "Listen, I don't mean to be a sore loser, but when it's done, if I'm dead, kill him." Sundance grins back as he says, "Love to." Butch then approaches Logan and says in gentlemanly fashion that before the fight begins, he wants to make sure he understands the rules. The astonished Logan says, "Rules? In a knife fight? No rules!" At which point, Butch in a very ungentlemanly fashion kicks him in the groin. As Logan writhes on the ground in pain, Butch knocks him out with one punch.

Once the fight is over, the whimsical Butch decides that maybe Logan's idea wasn't so bad after all, and he announces that the Wild Bunch will hold up a train. Their first train robbery goes well, but their second attempt is interrupted by the arrival of another train carrying a posse. The gang flees with the determined posse not far behind. Butch and Sundance try every trick they know, but the posse, led by a man wearing a distinctive white straw hat, remains hot on their trail. "Who are these guys?" wonders an incredulous Butch. The outlaws climb higher and higher into the hills until finally they are trapped. Butch assesses the situation and concludes the only way out is to jump off the cliff into a river far below. But Sundance is reluctant. When Butch asks what the problem is, his friend admits sheepishly that he doesn't know how to swim. Butch breaks out laughing and says, "Are you crazy? The fall will probably kill you." As Sundance screams, the two leap off the cliff to the river below.

The outlaws survive the plunge and head for the home of Sundance's girlfriend, Etta Place (Katharine Ross). When they learn that the posse pursuing them has been ordered by the Union Pacific Railroad to stay on the trail until they kill the two outlaws, Butch and Sundance decide that they have to get out of the country fast. Butch knows exactly where they should go—Bolivia! There, he insists, they can find happiness by resuming their careers as bank robbers.

No sooner do Butch, Sundance, and Etta arrive in Bolivia than they realize this new frontier looks even more desolate than the old one. The outlaws agree to make the best of it, but soon discover that they can't even rob banks because of the language barrier. After Etta teaches them the necessary Spanish words, they pull off enough holdups to attract the police's attention. Just when things appear to be going well, the partners in crime spot a man wearing a white straw hat. Butch is convinced it's the same invincible fellow who pursued them relentlessly in America, so he suggests that they lay low by going straight. The erstwhile robbers land jobs as payroll guards, but on their first time out, they are attacked by banditos. They succeed in killing the robbers, but the irony is not lost on either Butch or Sundance. As outlaws, they never killed anyone, but as honest guards they shot dead several bandits at close range. Shortly thereafter, the two resume their outlaw ways, causing Etta to leave them. She reminds them that back in the States, she promised to help them any way she could with one exception: "I won't watch you die."

A few days later, Butch and Sundance hold up a payroll mule train. When they head to a nearby village to eat, they are identified, and law enforcement officials, joined by Bolivian soldiers, quickly go after them. The two outlaws scamper for shelter in a nearby house, but they are low on ammunition and surrounded by hundreds of men. They take some solace in the fact that neither can see the mysterious man in the white straw hat among the hundreds of men surrounding them. "Oh, good," sighs Butch. "For a moment there I thought we were in trouble." Wounded and out of options, Butch Cassidy and the Sundance Kid play their last card. They charge out of the house with their guns blazing as hundreds of soldiers and lawmen open fire. Their images freeze on the screen and slowly fade into an old-fashioned sepia tintype, suggesting that both the outlaws and the Old West have faded into history.

George Roy Hill's revisionist western uses traditional western images and characters in new ways to comment on the Old West as well as America of the late sixties. The two protagonists are antiheroes who are constantly at odds with the Establishment. Butch and Sundance won't settle for middle-class jobs as merchants, farmers, ranchers, or security guards. Their refusal to conform is in sync with the sixties counterculture. The outlaws don't play by society's rules. They don't worry about careers, they like to drink, they are sexual libertines, they form their own communal groups—first with the Wild Bunch and then with Etta Place in Bolivia. Like hippies, they act like eternal children. Butch and Etta, for example, have a wonderful time riding a bicycle while the playful song "Raindrops Keep Falling on My Head" can be heard in the background. Like sixties counterculture activists, Butch and Sundance take stands against the law, the government, banks, railroads, and other symbols of big business, while championing the cause of the common man. And just as many of the era's young men dodged the draft by going north to Canada, Butch and Sundance evade U.S. law by heading south to Bolivia.

As the two antiheroes test the boundaries of society, they call into question the entire notion of the mythic West. In keeping with the myth, they keep searching for a heart of gold. In typical western fashion, they remain optimistic and never give up, no matter what the odds. Even when their future looks hopeless and they are trapped by hundreds of Bolivian soldiers and lawmen, Butch is still convinced that happiness and success await them on the next frontier. Just before he and Sundance rush out to face their fate, he assures his friend that he knows exactly where they should go next. "We get out of here alive, we go to Australia," he tells Sundance. At first, Sundance dismisses the idea, but the optimistic Butch won't be denied, explaining why they'll find success on the next frontier. Not only do they speak English in Australia, but that land has lots of horses, thousands of wide open spaces to hide out in, a great climate, even lots of beaches so Sundance can learn how to swim. Still unconvinced, Sundance asks whether they have banks there. "Very easy," replies Butch. "Easy, ripe, and luscious." When Sundance asks whether his friend is talking about the banks or the women, Butch declares, "Well, once you get one, you get the other." The Sundance Kid is still reluctant, though, and points out that Australia is so far away. "Oh, please!" says Butch, "Everything with you has got to be perfect!" He asks Sundance to at least think about it, and the Sundance Kid agrees. "All right. . . . I'll think about it." The two outlaws, still believing they will eventually find happiness in the mythic West, then rush out the door to meet their destiny in a blaze of glory.

Throughout the film, there are numerous hints that the protagonists and the Old West are being overwhelmed by the forces of modernity. Butch and Sundance are portrayed as anachronistic strangers in a strange land filled with new technologies that make it more difficult to rob banks, relentless posses paid for by big business, and large armies equipped with high-powered rifles. One scene in particular suggests how much the old-fashioned outlaws are out of place in modern America. Butch is intrigued when he sees a salesman roll out a bicycle and say, "Ladies and gentlemen, boys and girls . . . meet . . . the future!" Butch buys the newfangled contraption and takes it for a spin, with Etta sitting on the handlebars. But eventually he crashes and tosses the bike away, saying, "The future's all yours, you lousy bicycle."

Time was rapidly running out for Butch and Sundance as well as the Old West. When the two outlaws ask their old friend Sheriff Ray Bledsoe to help them get a pardon so they can be safe from the relentless posse and the railroad company, he just shakes his head and tells them that the times have changed. "You should have let yourself get killed a long time ago when you had the chance," explains Bledsoe. "It's over, don't you get that?" In the end, Butch Cassidy and the Sundance Kid die still hoping they'll find success on the next frontier. Moviegoers in 1969 grasped the important point that eluded the two antiheroes: the mythic West is simply an empty promise. Opportunity, happiness, success, and redemption were hard to come by, not just in the Old West but in contemporary America.

While Butch and Sundance were loveable rogues, an edgier antihero rode the otherworldly landscapes of Clint Eastwood's *High Plains Drifter* (1973). The movie begins with a man galloping across the plains with heat waves shimmering around him like an ethereal haze. He rides into Lago, a western town made up of brand new buildings on the shore of a crystal- blue lake. He passes silently down a street while everyone stops to stare. Only a man in a wagon cracking a whip on his horses catches his attention. The stranger hitches his horse and walks into a saloon, where three men warn him that drifters aren't welcome in Lago.

The stranger heads across the street to a barbershop for a shave. The hostile men follow and continue to provoke him as he's sitting in the barber chair. When one of them violently spins the chair around, the stranger instantly shoots him between the eyes and then kills the other two as they're reaching for their guns. Afterwards, the stranger is approached by a dwarf named Mordecai (played by Billy Curtis, who starred in *The Terror of Tiny Town* in 1938, and the following year appeared as a Munchkin in *The Wizard of Oz*). The curious Mordecai asks, "What did you say your name was again?" The stranger, evoking Eastwood's Man with No Name persona, replies, "I didn't." The mysterious man then walks down the street, where he literally runs into a pretty blond woman, who turns out to be a prostitute. She insults him and slaps the small cigar out of his mouth, at which point he drags her into a barn and rapes her. Next, the stranger checks into a hotel. As he's dozing off, he dreams about a man getting whipped by three men in a town street, while the rest of the town merely watches.

Next morning, the sheriff pays the nameless gunman a visit and tells him that the town council wants to hire him for protection against three outlaws who are coming back to Lago for vengeance. At first, the stranger refuses, but he changes his mind when town leaders agree to give him anything he wants in return—anything. He soon begins to collect. After a shopkeeper insults some Indian customers, the stranger demands candy for the two Indian children and blankets for the old Indian man. He follows up with presents for himself, including boots and a new saddle. Walking into a bar, he demands free drinks for everyone. Further testing the limits of his power, he names Mordecai, the brunt of everyone's jokes, the town's new mayor and sheriff. The stranger also demands that the hotel be emptied of all guests so he can have privacy.

By this time, members of the town council, including the minister and hotel owner, are beginning to have second thoughts about the demanding stranger. Several conclude that the gunman is more trouble than he is worth and attempt to kill him that night. But when they rush into his hotel room, he tosses a stick of dynamite at them and escapes into the street. Then, as they make their hasty retreat, he shoots them down one by one. Afterwards, when the hotel owner's wife berates him for cruelty and explains that the explosion destroyed all the hotel rooms other than the one used by her and her husband, the stranger drags her off to her bedroom. Her husband watches impotently knowing that she will have sex that night with the gunfighter.

Next morning, the stranger and the remaining town leaders make plans for the outlaws' imminent arrival. By then, the stranger has ordered the men of the town to train as a militia, with Mordecai in charge. He also orders them to paint the entire town red in preparation for the coming of the outlaws. As they begin, the stranger takes a brush with red paint, crosses out the name "Lago" on the welcome-to-town sign, and replaces it with the word "Hell." Meanwhile, the flashbacks continue. Through the mind's eye of Mordecai and others, the scene involving the man being whipped to death becomes clearer. The victim was the previous town marshal, Jim Duncan, and the bad guys cracking the whips were the three outlaws now headed toward town. And the people watching the grisly murder were the citizens of Lago. The townsfolk wanted the marshal dead, because he had discovered that the town mine was on government land. Their subsequent cover-up guaranteed that profits would continue. The hotel owner's wife reveals to the stranger that the marshal wasn't even given a decent burial. "They say the dead don't rest without a marker of some kind," she adds ominously.

The three outlaws soon arrive in Lago determined to get revenge on the people who were complicit in the marshal's death but then remained silent when the outlaws went to jail. When Mordecai alerts the stranger, the mysterious gunman simply climbs on his horse and rides away slowly, leaving the townsfolk to face the bad guys alone. Lago's cowardly citizens collapse under the pressure. The outlaws rampage through the streets, killing several members of the town council, setting the freshly painted red buildings on fire, and rounding up all the survivors in one building. Just then, the mysterious stranger reappears. He uses a whip to kill two of the outlaws, and then, with the burning town as a backdrop, he brutally guns down the remaining gang leader. As the outlaw is dying, he asks with a mixture of fear and wonder, "Who are you?"

With his mission accomplished, the mysterious stranger leaves town the next morning. He stops by the cemetery, where he sees Mordecai putting the finishing touches on a gravestone for the murdered marshal, Jim Duncan. The two outsiders say their good-byes, and the ethereal "high plains drifter" then rides off into the heat from which he came.

Clint Eastwood not only starred in *High Plains Drifter*, but he produced and directed it. The movie borrows heavily from traditional westerns. Riding familiar trails, it tells the story of a gunslinger seeking vengeance and justice for a murdered marshal. The lonesome drifter singlehandedly defeats bad guys, protects the weak and innocent, cleans up the town, and then rides off into the sunset. The movie evokes memories of earlier western classics such as *High Noon* (1952), which also featured outlaws returning for revenge while the town cowered in fear, and *Hell's Hinges* (1916), which—like Eastwood's film—climaxes with a corrupt town named Hell burning as the hero exacts vengeance.

Despite its ties to traditional westerns, *High Plains Drifter* is clearly a revisionist film, because it uses familiar western characters and settings in contrary ways to subvert the mythic West and critique modern America. The mysterious stranger is no ordinary gunfighter. Unlike typical western protagonists, he is an amoral if not immoral antihero. Cruel and coldhearted, he abuses townsfolk, brutally rapes women, and sadistically whips, hangs, or guns down opponents. The sheriff is an incompetent coward. The town council is corrupt. The preacher is a hypocrite. The women are adulteresses and whores. Even the beauty of the Old West is questioned. The town's spanking new buildings set on the shores of a pristine blue lake with majestic mountains in the background stand as a stark counterpoint to the ugliness at the town's core.

The anti-Establishment message of *High Plains Drifter* resonated with audiences in an era marked by violence, divisive social change, and concerns about the misfeasance and malfeasance of those in authority. Almost every person, authority figure, and social institution in Lago was thoroughly corrupt, including government officials, businessmen, the sheriff, the minister, and husbands and wives. Not even the town prostitute had a heart of gold. In the end, the entire town is guilty of covering up the marshal's murder to protect economic interests.

High Plains Drifter included sadistic whippings, brutal killings, violent rapes, and plenty of blood and gore. All of this reflected the ubiquitous violence of sixties and seventies America as well as the influence of spaghetti westerns. Eastwood clearly learned a few tricks making movies with Sergio Leone. Like the Italian director, Eastwood injected large doses of violence and symbolism into his western, using images of coffins, undertakers, churches, and cemeteries backed by an eerie soundtrack. He also continued the grim antihero persona established in Leone's Dollar Trilogy. Eastwood's humorless character was once again a Man with No Name, who smoked small cigars and wore a distinctive flat-topped hat.

High Plains Drifter picked up on changing sexual attitudes of the seventies. Unlike typical westerns, it featured sexually explicit scenes involving rape, adultery, and misogyny. When Eastwood's character rapes a flirtatious woman, she initially struggles but soon begins to enjoy the moment. The next day she tries to shoot him, leading the stranger to ask, "Wonder what took her so long to get mad?" Mordecai replies, "Because maybe you didn't go back for more?" Similarly, the film used explicit language not normally heard in westerns, including contemporary slang like "shit" and "balls."

Given the uncertainties of the seventies, the film's mysticism resonated with many moviegoers. Eastwood's enigmatic protagonist proved particularly compelling at a time when many Americans were following different paths to get them through troubled times. Some sought relief through religion, self-awareness, or alternative communities. The counterculture rejected society's reliance on science and reason and turned instead to drugs and other means of arriving at truth. The mysterious stranger took on allegorical dimensions as he sought justice and retribution. At times, he seemed more like a supernatural gunslinger or an avenging angel sent to earth to mete out punishment than a human being. He orders the town painted red to resemble hell. He smites evildoers. Even his final enigmatic words caught the attention of moviegoers accustomed to deconstructing the symbolism and meaning of the latest Dylan song or Bergman movie. In the last scene, Eastwood's nameless character rides into the cemetery where Mordecai is tending a grave. Mordecai says, "I never did know your name." The mysterious stranger replies chillingly, "Yes, you do." As he rides away, the camera pulls back, revealing the writing on the tombstone—"Marshal Jim Duncan. Rest in peace." As eerie music plays in the background, the mysterious gunslinger rides off and disappears in the shimmering haze.

Lago is the end of the trail for the mythic West. Despite all the beauty and legendary promises, no one finds happiness, success, or redemption in this corrupt land. Viewers expecting a traditional western were not pleased. "That isn't what the West was all about," complained John Wayne. "That isn't the American people who settled this country."[6] Evidently, most moviegoers did not agree, as evidenced by the fact that *High Plains Drifter* left Wayne's *Cahill U.S. Marshal* in the dust at the box office. By 1973, Eastwood's revisionist approach seemed far more relevant to cynical audiences than Wayne's more optimistic vision of the Old West. As the Pentagon Papers revealed that government officials had been lying about Vietnam for years and Americans watched the Watergate scandal unravel, Eastwood's pessimistic film reinforced what seemed to be an obvious truth. Corruption, greed, and injustice permeated all of society and culture. Americans' pursuit of happiness was a futile quest, whether it occurred in contemporary America or in the mythic West.

In addition to offering audiences new types of heroes, revisionist westerns used the Old West as a vehicle to explore contemporary issues involving race and ethnicity. As the civil rights movement blossomed in the sixties and seventies, western movies began featuring African Americans in prominent roles that advanced racial equality. *Duel at Diablo* (1966), for example, stars Sidney Poitier as a heroic ex-cavalry sergeant, whose fists, guns, and brains earn him respect and success in the Old West. In *The Scalphunters* (1968), Ossie Davis plays an educated runaway slave who outsmarts and outfights the racist whites around him. African American actor Louis Gossett Jr. costarred with James Garner in *Skin Game* (1971), a story about two smart con artists who play the race card for fun and profit. Throughout the film, Gossett mocks and outsmarts racist whites, and in the end he proves his mettle by establishing a settlement for free blacks and runaway slaves.[7]

Numerous movies also showcased American Indians, Hispanics, and other minorities.[8] One of the more sophisticated treatments of race and ethnicity can be found in *Cheyenne Autumn*, released the same year that Congress passed the landmark Civil Rights Act of 1964. Directed by John Ford and based on Mari Sandoz's historical novel of the same name, the movie focuses on an actual event. In 1878, approximately three hundred Cheyenne Indians, led by Dull Knife and Little Wolf, escaped from a desolate Oklahoma reservation and embarked on an arduous 1,500 mile journey to their original homelands on the northern plains. The big-budget movie chronicles all the hardships encountered along the way. As the Indians fight off the pursuing cavalry, they have to cope with lack of food and water, punishing rain and windstorms, and deadly blizzards, as well as threats from bureaucrats, cowboys, townsfolk, and even tribal factionalism. On the verge of defeat, the Cheyenne are saved by a sympathetic cavalry officer (Richard Widmark), who secures help from secretary of the interior Carl Schurz (Edward G. Robinson).

Cheyenne Autumn is a flawed but fascinating film. Self-conscious of its civil rights message, the narrative is plodding and depressing. Even the climax, which sees the Indians achieve their goal of a new reservation in the north, winds up a pyrrhic victory. By then, many of the Indians have died, and their heroic leaders go their separate ways after Little Wolf (Ricardo Montalban) kills Dull Knife's son for stealing his wife. Evidently sensing the futility of the tale, Ford tries to lighten it up with the addition of subplots. The result is an episodic film that does not hold together very well. For example, the Dodge City sequence—which features James Stewart as Wyatt Earp living in a veritable Sodom and Gomorrah of a town replete with ineffectual politicians, killer cowboys, and happy hookers—does not even seem like it belongs in the picture. Ford's western does have its moments, though. It features spectacular visual shots, as well as the types of intriguing details that only Ford would think of including, such as smoke coming out of tipis, soldiers roasting a whole steer on a spit, and the ubiquitous dust on soldiers' faces and uniforms. The film explains the basics of the historical flight of the Cheyenne, although the story is embellished with fictional characters and contrived Indian customs. Most important, Ford succeeds in providing the Indians' perspective. "I've long wanted to do a story that tells the truth about them [Indians]," he explained. "There are two sides to every story, but I wanted to show their point of view for a change. Let's face it, we've treated them very badly."[9]

More than just a story about the early frontier, *Cheyenne Autumn* provides fascinating glimpses of racial attitudes in 1960s America. It shows that the roots of racism run deep in America's past. One scene, for instance, depicts a racist cowboy who callously guns down and scalps a starving Indian. Others offer evidence of institutional racism, portraying callous politicians who ignore Indian rights and military officers who blindly obey orders to the detriment of helpless victims. At the same time, *Cheyenne Autumn* captures the optimism of the era's civil rights movement as it underscores the notion that eventually "We shall overcome" racial problems. Widmark's humane military officer is determined to cut through red tape in order to protect Indian rights. The compassionate Quaker missionary (Carroll Baker) evokes the era's resolute civil rights workers and Peace Corps volunteers, who worked side-by-side with those in need. And Robinson's reform-minded secretary of the interior could have stepped out of President Johnson's Great Society. At one point, the secretary gazes at a photograph of Abraham Lincoln hanging in his office and asks, "Old friend, what would you do?"

Cheyenne Autumn picks up on changing attitudes toward ethnicity and gender. It offers sympathetic portrayals of white ethnics, spotlighting principled Irish American and Polish American soldiers who respect Indian rights. It depicts women in positive ways, reflecting the emergence of women in 1960s America. Carroll Baker's missionary character, for example, is determined to advance the cause of Indian rights even if it means choosing career over marriage and personal well-being.

Ford's film offers other insights about contemporary American life and thought. It reveals ambivalent attitudes toward social and cultural change. One scene depicts Indians trying to cross railroad tracks that "contain them like steel bars." The striking juxtaposition of the desperate fugitives sneaking beneath a trestle as a powerful train rumbles overhead suggests that American progress and technology had not benefited everyone. Similarly, a scene in Dodge City underscores modern concerns about the nation's growing consumer culture. The quirky vignette suggests that Wyatt Earp and other Dodge City residents are far more interested in money, gambling, drinking, and hedonistic pleasures than American principles or enemy threats. The national media are also portrayed in a bad light. Greedy and unethical newspaper editors repeatedly lie about the Cheyenne uprising merely to sell more papers.

Cheyenne Autumn is not a great movie, yet even a mediocre Ford western reveals much about the West and contemporary America. The film's innovative approach to history, race, gender, and ethnicity, as well as its attacks on the Establishment for supporting corruption and exploitation, anticipated the nuanced approaches that would be associated decades later with the New Western History. The movie ends with the downtrodden Little Wolf riding off into the sunset. In retrospect, it is the perfect metaphor for the end of John Ford's career. Like the weary Indian chief, the director had accomplished his goal, but it had taken its toll. From the 1920s onward, John Ford had provided some of the most memorable moments in western movie history, as well as telling glimpses of the mythic West. But, the director—like Little Wolf—understood that time had passed him by. Not only was Ford getting up in age, but he realized that changing expectations and contemporary issues made it difficult if not impossible to make traditional western movies. *Cheyenne Autumn* was Ford's last western. "It's just no fun anymore," said the greatest western movie director of all time.[10]

Numerous revisionist westerns reflected the rise of the women's rights movement in the sixties and seventies.[11] One of the more surprising feminist westerns was *The Ballad of Josie* (1967), starring Doris Day. Directed by Andrew McLaglen, the story takes place in a Wyoming town at the turn of the century. It begins with Josie's alcoholic and abusive husband coming home after a night of drinking. When Day's character threatens to fight him off with a pool cue, he accidentally falls down the stairs and dies. Josie is tried for murder but acquitted, no thanks to one of the jurors, a misogynist rancher named Arch Ogden (George Kennedy). Even though Arch admits that Josie's late husband was a wife beater and all-around cad, he insists that she still should be convicted of murder. "You can't fault a man for jostling his woman around a little bit in his own home," he explains. "A woman needs it now and then. There's a principle involved."

Josie is found innocent, but since she has no livelihood, the judge orders her to send her young son to live with his paternal grandfather in Cheyenne. The determined woman decides to remedy the situation by starting up a cattle ranch on the four-hundred-acre spread that she and her husband owned just outside of town. But male ranchers rise up in opposition. The sheriff laughs off the notion that a woman could run a ranch as "nutty" and tells her, "Josie Minick, you remember your place." Refusing to back down, she replies, "What's so wrong about a woman on a cow ranch? I'm strong, and I'm able to do anything." Josie's words fall on deaf ears. Even rancher Jason Meredith (Peter Graves), who is in love with her, tries to convince her that her plan is ridiculous. Josie stands her ground, noting "To you, a woman is a species of idiot to be kept in a back closet somewhere and spoon-fed three times a day." He replies, "I got no prejudice against women, not entirely anyway. There are places where women belong, and places they don't. And one of the places they don't is all alone on a cattle spread with Indians, drunk saddle tramps, con thieves, and round-ups that mean roping and branding and castrating."

Blocked by a solid wall of male resistance, Josie tries a different tack and applies for various jobs normally reserved for males, including working for a newspaper and a bank. Each time, the males in charge suggest that she try more typical women's work. Some even make sexual advances. With her options running out, Josie accepts a job as a waitress only to run into more problems with men. After being humiliated by the boss and sexually harassed by male customers, she quits and heads to Cheyenne to see her son. When she arrives, her father-in-law condescendingly agrees to let her live there if she is willing to work as a domestic servant. When her little boy says he hates living with his grandfather, Josie turns down the job and returns home to come up with a new plan.

As soon as she gets off the stagecoach, she heads to the general store and buys men's jeans and a work shirt. She then changes into the men's clothes and walks out into the street to rent a horse. Both men and women onlookers are stunned to see Josie dressed like a man and not riding sidesaddle. When local ranchers learn that her new plan is to start a sheep ranch in the middle of cattle country, they become outraged. Jason convinces the men that he can sweet talk Josie into changing her plans, but the situation quickly spins out of control when he invites her to meet with the ranchers. As tensions mount, Jason warns her that she's causing a fight and that women are not "put together" to fight or to be ranchers. The irate Josie tells Jason and all the rest of the men to "shut up." Then, she explains her position clearly and sternly: "Forget I'm a woman. I'm a human being, and I can take care of myself and my son without anybody's charity. I can think, and I can work. I'm not going to [a boarding house] and wait for some nice man to come and rescue me. I don't want a man. And I don't need a man. I've got myself and I've got my sheep. . . . and I'm going to double my money. And, nobody—do you hear that—*nobody*, not a *damn* one of you is going to get in my way!"

The cattlemen-versus-sheepherder contest quickly morphs into a battle of the sexes. Having failed to sweet talk the woman of his dreams into backing off the sheep ranch idea, Jason becomes more forceful. He and his cowboys ride to Josie's ranch to physically remove the sheep, but Josie pulls out a gun and threatens to shoot anyone who tries to take her livestock away. Just then, Arch Ogden and his hired hands arrive on the scene, threatening to club the animals to death. When Jason and his men block their advance to protect Josie and her property, a full-scale range war threatens to erupt. Jason convinces Josie to ride to town until the gun smoke clears. She arrives to find a women's rights rally in full swing, with placards demonstrating the ladies' support for Josie and women's rights. Josie takes the stage and explains that blood is about to be spilled on the range. Arch Ogden then physically removes her from the stage and announces that the men of the town won't back down. At that point, Josie runs into the store and returns with enough pool cues to arm the women protesters. When Josie smacks Ogden with her pool stick, the riot is on. Male onlookers prove no match for the determined women, who club, poke, and prod the men into submission. Their success earns them a quick trip to the calaboose, where they are locked up for disturbing the peace. Shortly thereafter, the town prosecutor, an ardent lobbyist for statehood, secures their release.

Next morning, Josie returns to her ranch and tells Jason that for the good of everyone, she needs to abandon her plan to raise sheep, because it is causing trouble throughout the territory. It is interfering with the movement for statehood, and women are even withholding sex from their husbands. Their conversation is interrupted when Ogden and other ranchers ride up with the town prosecutor. Bending to social and political pressure, Arch announces that the cattlemen are willing to give in to Josie's demands if she's willing to compromise. He'll buy all of her sheep at a profit for her, plus he will sell her at cost the finest cattle available if she promises to trade in sheepherding for cattle ranching.

In effect, Josie won a complete victory. Unfortunately, the movie—probably for commercial and political reasons—was not willing to push the point too far. Instead of allowing Doris Day's character her well-earned moment of triumph, the script winds up having Josie cry tears of joy as Jason holds her in his arms and replies for her: "She'll take your proposition, Arch." The next scene shifts to Josie's house, where she has exchanged her jeans and work shirt for a new dress, French bonnet, and expensive corset. There's a knock on the door and in walks Jason. He tells her how beautiful she looks and that they're going to get married. She asks him to wait one moment. She then tosses her work shirt and jeans into the fire and leaps into his arms, saying, "Now I'm ready to marry you." The movie ends with a parade on the town's main street to celebrate Wyoming's statehood. Jason and his new wife, Josie, along with Josie's son are riding happily ever after in a carriage plastered with a campaign sign that reads "Jason Meredith for U.S. Senator." Significantly, the women marching in the parade are all wearing jeans and work shirts, and Wyoming has become the first state to grant women the right to vote.

Few if any movies in 1967 offered as strong a feminist message as *The Ballad of Josie*. Yet, even this revisionist western knew where the boundaries were, as evidenced by the advice Josie gives to her pet skunk at the end of the film. "You don't want to get too independent," she explains. "Some's good. Too much is miserable. It only goes so far." The film was willing to empower Josie; it allowed her to achieve her economic goals; it even helped her win the battle against men. But, in return, she couldn't get "too independent." Josie had to cheerfully accept her "proper" role as a housewife in keeping with the era's dominant attitudes toward gender. Despite that, the feminist western more than lived up to the promise of its opening theme song. "The Ballad of Josie" described the determined and capable western woman as "a pretty girl, a sturdy girl, made of solid timber. She set her sights and fought a fight, for justice was her aim."[12]

Revisionist westerns mirrored the changing times in other ways. In keeping with the era's sexual revolution, numerous films featured nudity and explicit sex, including *A Man Called Gannon* (1968), *Sam Whiskey* (1969), *The Last Picture Show* (1971), and *Pat Garrett & Billy the Kid* (1973). Homosexual themes appeared in *Lonesome Cowboys* (1968), *A Professional Gun* (1968), and *The Missouri Breaks* (1976). Following Watergate, Kirk Douglas's *Posse* (1975) focused on a cynical power-hungry man with presidential ambitions. Other westerns turned the spotlight on the military and by extension the Vietnam War. *Soldier Blue* (1970) used the slaughter of Indians at Sand Creek in 1864 as a thinly veiled metaphor for the My Lai Massacre in 1968, while *Bad Company* (1972) explored another issue related to Vietnam by glorifying draft dodgers and deserters during the Civil War era who headed west to become outlaws.[13]

Revisionist westerns also tapped into the era's counterculture. Stereotypical hippie images of love, peace, drugs, or tribalism are obvious in films such as *A Man Called Gannon* (1968) and *Zachariah* (1971). *The Great Northfield Minnesota Raid* (1972) portrays Jesse James, Cole Younger, and their gang as though they were a band of hippie outlaws. The frontier nonconformists wear beards, long hair, and distinctive clothes as they do drugs, engage in frequent sex, criticize society, and stand up to the Establishment. Jesse (Robert Duvall) sees the gang as revolutionary guerilla fighters opposing the powers that be. At times, the maniacal Jesse seems less like a western outlaw than a Charles Manson–type figure or a member of the Weathermen. A disagreement with Cole Younger evokes the divisions within the New Left by the early seventies. Jesse tells his friend, "We'll make this smug Yankee town weep, or we'll blow it to kingdom come!" The more reasonable Younger replies, "No, we ain't either, Jesse. Only a fool smokes up a town when it ain't necessary."

Soundtracks were often geared toward young audiences. Rock music and other countercultural sounds established the mood of films such as *A Man Called Gannon* (1968), *Monte Walsh* (1970), and *The Great Northfield Minnesota Raid* (1972). Some movies even featured high-profile rock singers. Mick Jagger plays a rebellious antihero in *Ned Kelly* (1970), who fought against the Establishment on the Australian frontier, while Bob Dylan and Kris Kristofferson appear as gunslingers in *Pat Garrett & Billy the Kid* (1973).

One of the best examples of a western with a countercultural feel is *Jeremiah Johnson* (1972). The film begins with a young man (Robert Redford)

Figure 26. This movie poster for *Jeremiah Johnson* (Sanford Productions III/Warner Brothers, 1972) questions the notion that success and happiness can be found in the West.

dressed like a sailor getting off a boat at a small river port out West. The introductory theme song, inspired by folk music of the early seventies, suggests that this will not be a traditional western: "Jeremiah Johnson made his way to the mountains, bettin' on forgettin' all the trouble that he knew," explains the singer. "The story doesn't always go the way you have in mind, and Jeremiah Johnson was that kind."[14] Jeremiah immediately heads toward a general store to buy clothes and supplies so he can begin life anew as a mountain man. As he's leaving, he asks the storeowner where he can find animals to trap. The reply is short and sweet: "Ride due west as the sun sets. Turn left at the Rocky Mountains."

At first, the greenhorn knows nothing about being a mountain man. As fall turns to winter, he finds himself desperate for warmth and food. When he tries to catch a fish with his bare hands, he tumbles off a snow-covered bank into the icy mountain stream. As he's thrashing around after the fish, he looks up and sees a mounted warrior holding a rifle staring down at him. Jeremiah's rifle is too far away for protection, and for a long moment the two simply gaze at each other. The Indian then turns his horse around and rides off.

Over the next few days and weeks, Johnson's bad situation gets worse. He is freezing and starving, but the snow keeps falling, and his hunting skills are negligible. Just when failure seems imminent, Jeremiah runs into a veteran mountain man named Bear Claw (Will Geer). The grizzled old-timer takes pity on the greenhorn he calls Pilgrim, and he offers to teach him how to shoot straight, stalk game, trap furs, live off the land, and understand the potential hazards and dangers lurking in the mountains. At times, the old codger gets exasperated with his pupil's lack of knowledge. As they're stalking an elk, Bear Claw suggests that Johnson walk behind his horse to get close enough to shoot. "What if he sees our feet?" asks the naïve Jeremiah. The incredulous Bear Claw shakes his head and says, "Elk don't know how many feet a horse has!"

Fortunately, Johnson proves to be a fast learner, and he absorbs lesson after lesson about mountain man skills and survival. One day, as the mentor and student are riding through the woods, an arrow whizzes by them and hits a nearby tree. Bear Claw determines it's a Crow arrow, and the red markings suggest it belongs to their chief, Paints His Shirt Red. The mountain man is proved right when Paints His Shirt Red and the Crows ride up. Jeremiah quickly realizes that the Crow chief is the same Indian who had watched him fish in the icy stream. For a brief moment, the Indians consider taking the mountain men's horses, but instead they accept some furs offered by Johnson and then ride off. Not long after, Jeremiah decides the time has come to strike out on his own. Bear Claw tells him that he's learned his lessons well and cautions him to protect his scalp. Johnson rides off into the Rockies, alone again but no longer a greenhorn.

As Jeremiah is making his way through the mountains, he comes across a homesteader's cabin. A deranged woman in the front yard is talking to a scalped corpse that appears to be her daughter. Nearby is the body of a scalped young boy. After Johnson helps the woman bury her children, he goes into the cabin and finds a young boy hiding in the corner. The boy, in shock from the atrocities he witnessed, refuses to speak. When Johnson tries to get the woman and child to leave with him, she refuses to abandon the graves of her two children but insists that he take the boy away.

Jeremiah then rides off with the young boy, who refuses to talk. Not knowing the boy's name, Johnson decides to call him Caleb. After traveling a while, they come upon a bizarre sight—a man is buried with only his bald head sticking out above ground. When Jeremiah asks if he's okay, the man jokes, "Sure, sure, I got a fine horse under me!" The unlucky fellow explains that he's a mountain man named Del Gue. Just recently a band of Blackfeet Indians had stolen his horse, gun, and pelts. Jeremiah digs him out and promises to help him track down the Indians. They locate the camp by nightfall and sneak in to steal back Del's property. Suddenly, Del shoots one of the sleeping Indians. The others jump up and try to fight, causing Del and Jeremiah to kill them as well. Johnson is furious, but Del insists that the Indians had it coming. When the disgusted Johnson refuses to share in the scalps, Gue keeps them all to sell later.

The next morning, Jeremiah, Caleb, and Del are riding along when they hear some suspicious sounds. Del covertly hangs the scalps on the saddle of Johnson's pack mule. Luckily, the Indians who ride up turn out to be Flatheads, who are friendly toward whites but enemies of the Blackfeet. When the warriors find the Blackfeet scalps dangling on the saddle of Johnson's mule, they are overjoyed and take the three whites back to their village to celebrate.

Upon their arrival, Johnson and Gue are introduced to the Flathead chief, who looks at the scalps with envy. Jeremiah, wanting to get rid of the scalps, offers them to the chief as a present. The amazed Gue tells Johnson that he has just committed a faux pas because the chief will feel insulted unless he can think of an even better present to give Jeremiah in return. Both men are stunned when the chief's present turns out to be his daughter, Swan. When Johnson indicates that he doesn't want the girl, Del points out, "You turn down this gift, and they'll slit you, me, Caleb and the horses from crotch to eyeball with a dull deer antler!" So Jeremiah reluctantly marries Swan. After Del bids them good-bye, Johnson sets off into the mountains the next morning, accompanied by his new bride and the boy. Slowly but surely, the three individuals from disparate backgrounds come together as a family unit: they work together to build a cabin; they have fun as a group; Jeremiah and Caleb hunt and trap together; and Jeremiah and Swan become not just a man and woman living together but a loving husband and wife.

One winter day, a detachment of the 3rd Cavalry arrives at Johnson's cabin with a request that will forever alter the mountain man's life. Lieutenant Mulvey explains that three wagons loaded with settlers are stranded on the other side of the mountains. He asks Jeremiah to guide them through the mountain passes before the settlers die from starvation, blizzards, or an Indian attack. When Johnson hesitates, a reverend accompanying the troops reminds him that these settlers are Christians in desperate need of help. Jeremiah reluctantly agrees, and they set out immediately on a wintry trek through the mountains.

The rescue party makes steady progress through rugged terrain, deep snow, and occasional blizzards, but Jeremiah brings them to a sudden halt when they come upon a Crow Indian burial ground blocking their path. He balks at taking them any farther, because they will be violating Crow taboos if they pass through the cemetery. Jeremiah suggests a different route, but the lieutenant and the reverend are reluctant to take the alternate trail, which is twenty miles out of the way. The reverend insists that the lives of good Christians must be weighed against the Indians' pagan beliefs. When the lieutenant asks what the Crows will do if the troops go through the burial ground, the apprehensive Jeremiah replies, "I just don't know. I just don't know." Lieutenant Mulvey then makes his decision. He concludes that he and his men have to take the quickest route or else the settlers are doomed. Against his better judgment, Jeremiah agrees to guide them on the trail through the burial ground.

As soon as Johnson and the troops reach the settlers, Johnson immediately heads home. As he rides once again through the burial ground, a morbid thought flashes through his mind—the Crows might seek retribution for Johnson's transgression by killing Swan and Caleb. With a look of terror on his face, he spurs his horse onward. But he arrives home too late. Inside the cabin, he finds the bloody bodies of his wife and boy. An arrow with distinctive Crow Indian markings is sticking in the front door. The despondent Jeremiah collapses onto the floor next to his murdered loved ones and stares blankly at the cabin walls.

Next morning, Jeremiah places the bodies of Swan and Caleb on a bed, tenderly covers them with fur blankets, and sets fire to the cabin. He then sets off to track the war party responsible for the attack. When he finds them, he kills them one by one. The last surviving Crow goes running off into the deep snow. When Johnson charges after him, the terrified Indian stumbles and falls into a snow drift. Realizing the end is near, the warrior begins to sing his death song. The solemnity of the moment gives Jeremiah pause. Instead of killing the man, Johnson simply walks away, having had enough of revenge killing.

From that day on, Jeremiah Johnson is a living ghost—dead to the world around him but still a target for Crow Indians seeking retribution. One by one, Crow warriors track Jeremiah. And one by one, he kills them. When Jeremiah runs into Del Gue, he asks his old acquaintance where he's headed. "Same place you are, Jeremiah," is the reply. "Hell, in the end." Del is present when a Crow warrior tries to ambush Jeremiah. "Is it always like this?" he asks. "One at a time?" When Johnson says yes, Del replies, "Lucky they were Crow. Apache would have sent fifty at once." But Del understands the seriousness of the situation. "Amongst Injuns," he says, "a tribe's greatness is figured on how mighty its enemies be."

After Jeremiah and Del part company, Johnson continues to roam through the mountains, vanquishing every Crow who comes after him. One winter day Johnson encounters his mountain man mentor, Bear Claw. The friends share a meal as they recall all that's transpired. "You've come a long way, Pilgrim," says the old man. "Was it worth the trouble?" The disheartened Jeremiah replies ironically, "Ha. What trouble?" When they're done eating, Bear Claw gets up quietly and climbs on his horse. He looks sadly at his protégé and says with fatherly pride, "You've done so well to keep so much hair, when so many's after it." Jeremiah says nothing in reply and simply watches his old mentor ride away.

The final scene shows Jeremiah Johnson once again riding through deep snow in the rugged mountains. He comes up over a rise and sees a mounted Indian not far away. Instinctively, he reaches for his rifle, but then he notices that it is Paints His Shirt Red. The two simply gaze at each other as the Indian's powerful painted pony paws at the ground and whinnies. Then the Crow, no longer wearing war paint, raises his hand in salute to the brave white man who had experienced so much since that winter morning so long ago when the two had first met. Johnson likewise raises his hand in salute to his respected adversary. As the camera fades from a close-up of the mountain man to a view of the forbidding snow-covered Rockies, the poignant theme song is reprised: "Jeremiah Johnson made his way into the mountains. He was bettin' on forgettin' all the troubles that he knew."[15]

Sydney Pollack's *Jeremiah Johnson* offered seventies audiences a perspective on the mythic West in keeping with the era's youth culture and liberal attitudes. Jeremiah had much in common with hippies. When he dropped out of society in search of happiness and spiritual rejuvenation in the idyllic mountains of the West, he just as easily could have been following the contemporary advice of countercultural hero Timothy Leary, who advised young people to "turn on, tune in, drop out." And any member of the audience familiar with countercultural music of the late sixties and early seventies probably found it impossible to watch Jeremiah heading off into the Colorado mountains without thinking about John Denver's hit song, "Rocky Mountain High," released in 1972, the same year as Pollack's movie, or Johnny River's earlier hit, "Summer Rain" (1968), which included the lines, "She wants to live in the Rockies. She says that's where we'll find peace."[16] Robert Redford's character even looked like a hippie. He let his hair grow long, wore a beard, and dressed in surplus military pants, just as many members of the sixties youth culture wore Vietnam-era army jackets and battle fatigues.

Like modern-day hippies and antiwar activists, Jeremiah had no love for the Establishment and disdained politics, the military, and organized religion. Johnson simply ignored Bear Claw when the old mountain man looked at his striped military trousers and said, "Missed another war down there, hmm?" A later conversation between Jeremiah and Del Gue no doubt resonated with many American youths of the early seventies who were dodging the draft to stay out of Vietnam. When Del asks Johnson where he might go to avoid trouble, Jeremiah quickly replies, "Canada, maybe." The film portrays the U.S. military as the cause of Jeremiah's problems. Just as U.S. foreign policy and military actions in the post–World War II era often disregarded indigenous cultures in Southeast Asia and throughout the Third World, the cavalry troops callously violate the burial ground and cultural traditions of the Native Americans, thereby setting off a chain of events that destroy Johnson's life. And the movie's ending, which shows that Jeremiah and Paints His Shirt Red have gained mutual respect for each other and found a nonviolent resolution to their conflict, suggests that the movie supported "peaceful coexistence" rather than a military solution to Cold War hot spots such as Vietnam.

Organized religion is likewise portrayed in negative ways. Johnson repeatedly expresses disapproval whenever Swan tries to pray. He shows disdain for the condescending army reverend who is dismissive of Indians and their non-Christian beliefs. Del Gue likewise doesn't miss an opportunity to take a shot at organized religion. As he rides off into the magnificent Rockies, he offers a soliloquy in praise of the mountains and the freedom they provide: "These here [mountains] is God's finest sculpturings! And there ain't no laws for the brave ones. . . . And there ain't no churches, except for this right here! And there ain't no priests excepting the birds."

Pollack's film endorsed countercultural attitudes toward racial equality. Right from the outset, moviegoers learn that the Old West was as prejudiced as the rest of America. When Jeremiah first arrives in the river port, he sees a sign over the door of the general store that reads, "We got what you want. White Men Only." The rest of the film makes a strong case for the racial and cultural equality of Native Americans. Indian life is portrayed accurately and sympathetically. Indian practices, including religion, the use of the calumet, death songs, and the importance of gift giving, are showcased.

The movie makes it clear that not all Native Americans were alike. They spoke different languages, resided in different types of dwellings, produced different arrows, wore different hairstyles, and reacted in different ways to the coming of whites. The Indians in the film are not demonized but portrayed as fallible human beings, who laugh, love, and mourn like anyone else. And while their specific life-styles and belief systems may have been different from those of white Americans, they were nonetheless worthy of respect. Demonstrating the equality of the two races, Jeremiah Johnson, in defiance of both nineteenth- and twentieth-century proscriptions against miscegenation, even falls in love with an Indian woman.

In keeping with revisionist trends of the sixties and seventies, *Jeremiah Johnson* rejects the notion of the mythic West. Ironically, the film hoists the mythic West on its own petard of purple mountain majesties, capturing the cathedral-like beauty of the Rocky Mountains magnificently in Technicolor and Panavision. "Ain't this somethin'?" points out Del Gue, as he marvels at the mountains' natural beauty. "The Rocky Mountains is the marrow of the world." Moviegoers soon realize, however, that nothing good will come from this apparent western paradise. Director Sydney Pollack uses that very beauty to undermine the western myth. Scene after scene of breathtaking peaks, valleys, rivers, woods, snow drifts, and other natural wonders create a dissonant setting for all the violence that occurs. The myth of the West as a land of opportunity, redemption, happiness, and success is perhaps the biggest casualty in the movie. Jeremiah lives up to his part of the bargain. Seizing opportunity, he heads west in search of the American Dream. The rugged individual learns survival skills, falls in love, begins a family, and even builds a cabin in the tradition of settlers on every frontier. He fights off Indians, wolves, grizzlies, and blizzards. Yet, despite his skills, determination, hard work, basic goodness, and morality, Jeremiah still fails. The American frontiersman comes up empty-handed, because the mythic West reneges on its promise of success. No wonder Johnson's downbeat story resonated with moviegoers in 1972. Given their pessimistic outlook about Vietnam and their own future, Americans understood that happiness and success were eluding them in the contemporary world, just as they had eluded Jeremiah Johnson in the Old West.

Along with reflecting American attitudes and social change of the sixties and seventies, revisionist westerns reinterpreted American history. By the end of the sixties, many Americans were questioning whether the nation was living up to its principles and reputation as the home of the brave and land of the free. Arthur Penn's *Little Big Man* (1970) explored these contemporary doubts within the familiar context of the Old West. Based on Thomas Berger's historical novel from 1964, the film became the cinematic equivalent of Dee Brown's best-selling revisionist history of the Indian wars, *Bury My Heart at Wounded Knee*, published in 1970.

The movie begins in an old folks' home in 1970, with a young scholar interviewing a 121-year-old man named Jack Crabb (Dustin Hoffman). When the ancient-looking fellow puffing on a cigarette insists that he is the only white man to survive Custer's Last Stand, the orthodox researcher condescendingly dismisses his remark as just a tall tale. Furious, Jack demands that the scholar turn on his tape recorder so he can set the record straight. Jack then tells his life story, which refutes the common wisdom found in history books. The old man's determination to stand his ground against the erudite representative of the academic Establishment resonated with moviegoers in an era known for its skepticism and mistrust of authority figures.

Crabb's story begins more than a century earlier when Indians attack his family's wagon as it heads west. The young boy is rescued by a friendly Cheyenne, who takes him back to an Indian village, where he is adopted by Old Lodge Skins (Chief Dan George). Jack learns how to live and think like a Cheyenne. After he saves another Indian youth from a Pawnee attack, the small but brave Jack is rewarded with a new name, Little Big Man.

Throughout the picaresque film, Hoffman's character moves from one misadventure to another, sometimes in the role of the Indian, Little Big Man, and other times the white man, Jack Crabb. His travels lead to Indian villages, western towns, and military encampments and involve gunslingers, preachers, prostitutes, snake oil salesmen, soldiers, and Indians. The result is a sweeping revisionist history of the Old West. Replete with panoramic views of majestic western landscapes, Jack's escapades bring him into direct contact with legendary westerners like George Armstrong Custer, Wild Bill Hickok, and Buffalo Bill Cody. They also place him at seminal events, such as the Battle of the Washita and Custer's Last Stand. The tale rejects established stories about Custer, Indians, and white westerners as it exposes the mythic West as a fraud. White westerners are portrayed as religious hypocrites, greedy capitalists, killers, cutthroats, con men, and fools. For example, the Reverend Pendrake, who takes Jack in after he leaves the Cheyenne village, is a cruel, self-righteous prig. His beautiful wife (Faye Dunaway) is just as hypocritical. After welcoming Jack to their family, she bathes, caresses, and kisses the naked young man, all the while reading him scripture. Fleeing the "religious" couple, Jack hooks up with a greedy snake oil salesman (Martin Balsam), who is more than willing to sacrifice his own body parts to turn a profit. Jack's next stop is with his long-lost sister, who teaches him how to be a gunslinger but turns out to be stupid and shallow. Jack then becomes a shopkeeper, who suffers from a bossy immigrant wife and a dishonest partner. Next, he finds employment as a mule skinner with Custer's 7th Cavalry. After every unsuccessful foray into the white man's world, Jack always returns to the Indian way of life, where he succeeds as Little Big Man.

Jack's tale makes it clear that the true heroes of the Old West were Indians not whites. He values the Native Americans' sense of honesty, fairness, compassion, and respect for the environment. In the Indian world as Little Big Man, Jack finds happiness. There, he has a caring grandfather, four loving wives, a beautiful baby, and accepting friends. Even the one Indian enemy he makes—Younger Bear—treats him as a respected foe and saves Jack's life at the Battle of the Little Big Horn. Jack comes to appreciate the name the Cheyenne had for themselves—the "human beings." As Old Lodge Skins explains pointedly, "There is an endless supply of white men. There has always been a limited number of human beings."

Along with revising western history, the film reflects attitudes of 1970s America. Its skeptical tone fit the cynical mood of contemporary audiences familiar with government lies, hypocritical leaders, and a society plagued by conformity, corruption, and greed. The film lampoons some of the mythic West's most sacred cows. Gunslingers like Wild Bill Hickok are depicted as neurotic killers; famed Indian fighters such as Custer are vainglorious brutes; white settlers are exposed as simple-minded, gun-toting loudmouths who take the law into their own hands; frontier ministers are hypocritical buffoons; and businessmen come across as dishonest, incompetent, or conniving.

Little Big Man takes its cue from the era's civil rights movement as it advances Indians as a minority and condemns prejudiced whites. After witnessing a brutal attack by U.S. soldiers against an Indian village, Little Big Man says to Old Lodge Skins, "Do you hate them? Do you hate the white man now?" The wise old man holds up a portion of a white man's scalp as he replies, "Do you see this fine thing? Do you admire the humanity of it? Because the human beings [the Cheyenne], my son, they believe everything is alive. Not only man and animals. But also water, earth, stone. And also the things from them . . . like that hair. . . . But the white man, they believe everything is dead. Stone, earth, animals. And people! Even their own people! If things keep trying to live, white man will rub them out. That is the difference."

The movie mirrors the seventies in other ways. In keeping with the antiwar movement, the film condemns the U.S. military for butchering innocent Indian women and children, while the quintessential general, George Armstrong Custer, is depicted as an incompetent but dangerous megalomaniac. Just as the antiwar movement adopted John Lennon's "Give Peace a Chance" as an anthem, Jack Crabb decries violence. Even though he was fast on the draw and an expert shot, Jack hangs up his gun because he doesn't want to kill anyone. His sister is furious when he sells his snazzy all-black gunfighter outfit and matching gun. "There's ain't nothin' in this world more useless than a gunfighter who can't shoot people," she declares as she disowns him. The movie also picks up on the era's sexual revolution. Reverend Pendrake's wife is portrayed as a lusty woman with insatiable sexual needs. Not only is young Jack tempted by her seductive behavior, but he accidentally sees her having adulterous sex with a local merchant. "She was calling him a devil and moaning for help," says Jack knowingly, "but I didn't get no idea she wanted to be rescued." Sex within the Indian culture is treated far more openly and naturally. Little Big Man has sex one night with three of his wife's sisters. At first, he tries to avoid the women lying naked beneath the blankets. "I was determined to stay out of them buffalo robes," he explains. "Three young and healthy women with no man for who knows how long. The very idea kinda shrunk me like a spider on a hot stove." But he soon succumbs to their charms, fulfilling a vision foretold by his grandfather, who saw it all happen in a dream. "Yes, there were three or four, it was hard to tell," said Old Lodge Skins. "It was very dark in your tipi and they were under buffalo rugs as you crawled among them. Anyway, it was a great copulation."

Little Big Man shared the counterculture's belief that Native Americans were honest, authentic, and innocent children of nature unspoiled by the greed and corruption of western civilization.[17] The movie portrays Indians sympathetically and offers one of the most accurate portrayals of Indian culture ever found in western movies. Cheyenne material culture is meticulously recreated through historically accurate clothes, tipis, and travois. The film offers correct representations of other aspects of Cheyenne culture, such as the importance of buffalo, visions, music, marriage and birthing practices, mourning wars, counting coup, scalping, and smoking the calumet. It accurately depicts the honored places of "contraries" and homosexuals in Plains Indian culture. Unlike most Hollywood westerns, it even featured a real Native American in a major role. Chief Dan George, a Salish Indian, earned an Oscar nomination for Best Supporting Actor for his poignant portrayal of Old Lodge Skins.

One of the last scenes in *Little Big Man* best captures the majesty yet practicality of Native American culture as it sums up a universal truth about life. Old Lodge Skins, now blind and very old, has decided the time has come for him to die. He asks his adopted grandson, Little Big Man, to take him to the top of the mountain so he can enter the Spirit World. Upon reaching the summit, Grandfather, who throughout the movie has demonstrated the power and accuracy of his visions and dreams, begins to dance and chant. He prays to the Great Spirit, acknowledging that this is a "good day to die." Then, he lies down on the ground ready for his imminent death. Little Big Man watches in amazement as the clouds grow dark and a soft rain begins to fall on the cheeks of the old man, who appears to have passed away. After a few moments, Old Lodge Skins opens his eyes. "Am I still in this world?" he asks. "Yes, Grandfather," says Little Big Man, to which Old Lodge Skins replies, "I was afraid of that. Well, sometimes the magic works. Sometimes, it doesn't."

While the magic might have failed Old Lodge Skins on that day, it clearly was working throughout Arthur Penn's film. *Little Big Man* remains not just an excellent example of a revisionist western, but one of the best western movies of all time.

CHAPTER NINE

True Grit

Traditional Westerns Ride Again!

Henry Hathaway's *True Grit* (1969) is a traditional western that stars veteran film cowboy John Wayne, as well as a revisionist tale that features newcomer Kim Darby. A movie poster captures the tension. In the center is a close-up of Wayne's grizzled character sporting a big grin and eye patch that makes him look more like a roguish pirate than a cowboy. Behind him is Glen Campbell's secondary character wearing a coat and cowboy hat. In the foreground slightly to Wayne's left and the only figure shown in its entirety is Darby's character, ready for action in a boyish haircut and a split-riding skirt, holding an oversized revolver. The caption reads: "The strangest trio ever to track a killer. A fearless one-eyed U.S. marshal who never knew a dry day in his life . . . a Texas Ranger thirsty for bounty money . . . and a girl still wet behind the ears who didn't care what they were or who they were as long as they had true grit."

The movie won a Golden Globe as Best Picture of the Year and earned Wayne his first and only Oscar as Best Actor. *True Grit* arrived in movie theaters the same year as Sam Peckinpah's *The Wild Bunch*. Both were big-budget productions with major stars; both were huge successes at the box office; and both earned two Oscar nominations. But that's where the similarities ended. While *The Wild Bunch* revised the mythic West in numerous ways and reflected conflict in America, *True Grit* reinforced the traditional myth of the Old West, demonstrating continuity in American life and thought.

The phenomenal success of the two movies suggests that Hollywood westerns remained relevant because they changed with the times.

Figure 27. John Wayne won an Oscar for his portrayal of Rooster Cogburn in *True Grit* (Hal Wallis Productions/Paramount Pictures, 1969).

American westerns played off the political, social, and cultural changes that transformed the United States in the years after John F. Kennedy's assassination. The result was a new duality in portrayals of the West. Although revisionist westerns dominated throughout the sixties and into the seventies in terms of numbers and box office receipts, old-fashioned westerns were not far behind. Encouraged by the success of *True Grit*, a new wave of neotraditional westerns arrived on the scene, including *The Outlaw Josey Wales* (1976) and *The Electric Horseman* (1979). These movies often blended traditional images of the mythic West with revisionist themes and elements, but in keeping with old-fashioned westerns, they glorified the mythic West as an exotic land where one could find freedom, opportunity, and redemption. They told familiar tales about cowboys, Indians, gunslingers, and other colorful western characters. And they continued to serve as morality plays, with good guys representing justice, fair play, and other basic virtues.

The potent combination of neotraditional and revisionist westerns resulted in some of the finest western movies ever made. The contrasting western images found in these films reflected social and cultural change of the sixties and seventies, as well as the growing polarization of American society. If revisionist westerns were more in step with the anxious mood of the country during the sixties, then the growing popularity of neotraditional westerns by the late seventies signaled the end of that tumultuous period and anticipated the rise of Ronald Reagan. As the nation struggled to retain its identity in the dark years after President Kennedy's assassination, neotraditional westerns assured audiences that Americans would eventually triumph because they had "true grit."

Old Hero in a New West

True Grit tells the story of an independent young woman named Mattie Ross, who brings her father's killer to justice with the assistance of Rooster Cogburn, a grizzled, drunken, one-eyed lawman. The movie begins with Mattie's father preparing for a trip to Fort Smith to buy horses for the family ranch. Mattie, a mature teenager who helps run the family business, gives her father last-minute advice and travel money for the 140-mile round trip. When Mr. Ross takes his Civil War revolver off the shelf, Mattie makes fun of the large old-fashioned gun and urges him to buy a new one. The two then go outside, where they are joined by Mrs. Ross and two younger siblings. Mr. Ross says his good-byes and sets out on horseback, accompanied by his hired hand, Tom Chaney. The trip ends tragically. One evening the two travelers are in a Fort Smith saloon, and the drunken Chaney is losing at poker. Ross escorts him out into the street, where the angry Chaney turns on his employer, shoots him dead, and steals his money.

Not long after, Mattie and a trusted ranch hand, an African American named Yarnell, arrive in Fort Smith to claim the body. Determined to bring Chaney to justice, young Mattie orders the elderly Yarnell to accompany the casket back home while she attempts to hire U.S. marshal Rooster Cogburn to track down the killer. She tells the marshal, "Mr. Cogburn, they tell me you're a man with true grit." But the tough, ornery, hard-drinking old coot wants no part of the young girl or Tom Chaney, who has escaped to Indian Territory. He changes his mind when he learns that Mattie will pay him a hundred dollars cash to capture Chaney, who is traveling with a gang led by Ned Pepper, an outlaw Rooster has been after for years. The deal almost falls apart when a Texas Ranger named La Boeuf (Glen Campbell) shows up. La Boeuf is after Chaney for a murder committed in Texas and suggests that he and Rooster join forces and split the hefty reward money they'll receive for bringing Chaney to justice in Texas. An angry Mattie demands that Rooster honor his contract with her, because she wants Chaney to hang for her father's death in Arkansas, not for the murder down in Texas. Rooster, however, thinks she's just splitting hairs, so he agrees to throw in with the Texas Ranger.

Next morning the two lawmen ride off alone, but Mattie is determined to join the search for the man who killed her father. Spurring on her pony, Little Blackie, Mattie catches up to Rooster and La Boeuf, who reluctantly agree to let the feisty young girl join the search. Not only is this not a traditional western posse, but the three don't even get along. Rooster and La Boeuf constantly snipe at each other, while Mattie refuses to take any grief from either. Rooster talks down to her, calling her Baby Sister, but the plucky girl won't give an inch. She routinely insults her companions and makes it clear that she won't follow anybody's orders.

One morning when Mattie has gone off alone to wash in a nearby creek, she looks up and is startled to see Tom Chaney watering his horse not far away. She calmly pulls out her father's hefty revolver and says, "I'm here to take you back to Fort Smith and hang you." Chaney looks at the teenager and replies, "And I think I will not go, now how do you like that?" As he moves toward her, she pulls the trigger. Only slightly wounded, Chaney continues coming toward her. She tries firing again, but the gun jams, and he grabs her. Hearing the commotion, Rooster and La Boeuf rush toward the creek, but Ned Pepper and another gang member get there first. Pepper orders Chaney to take the girl away, while he and the other outlaw fire a few shots at the good guys. Ned warns Rooster to leave immediately or else the girl will be killed.

After the lawmen ride off, Pepper questions the girl about why she's there. "Tom Chaney shot my father to death in Fort Smith. I was told that Rooster Cogburn has grit. I hired him to go after the murderer," she explains. "I found him myself and I shot him. If I killed him I would not be in this fix. My revolver misfired." Ned Pepper laughs and says that guns do misfire, adding, "Most girls like little play pretties, but you like guns, don't you?" Refusing to back down, Mattie replies, "If I did, I'd have one that worked." Once Ned is convinced that Rooster is no longer a threat, he decides to escape with three of his gang members. Since they're one horse short, he orders Chaney to stay behind with the girl but promises to come back for him later.

Not long after the outlaws leave camp, Mattie tries to escape, but Chaney tackles her. Just then, La Boeuf shows up. Ordering Chaney off to the side, the Texas Ranger motions Mattie to move closer to the cliff so they can watch Rooster battling Ned Pepper's gang down below in the valley. While the Texas Ranger is distracted, Tom Chaney plots his escape. He grabs a rock and smashes La Boeuf in the head. Mattie immediately pulls out her revolver and once again shoots but only wounds Chaney. The recoil from the bulky Colt Dragoon pistol sends her flying backward into a pit filled with rattlesnakes. Chaney peers down at her from atop the pit, laughing at her broken arm and desperate situation.

Before he can do any further damage, Chaney is shot and killed by Rooster Cogburn, who has returned from his battle with Pepper's gang. Rooster then moves quickly to help Mattie. As he lowers himself into the pit, Mattie screams when a rattler bites her arm. Rooster shoots it instantly and then tries to haul the wounded Mattie upward. Finding the going rough, Rooster muses, "Damn that Texan. When you need him, he's dead." Surprising everyone, La Boeuf appears at the top of the pit and says sarcastically, "I ain't dead yet, you bushwhacker. Hang on." LaBoeuf then ties the rope to his saddle and pulls Rooster and Mattie up from the snake pit. He collapses just as they reach the top. Both go rushing to his side, but he's dead. Rooster looks down at him and says affectionately, "Texican saved my neck twice. Once after he was dead." Rooster knows he doesn't have time to bury LaBoeuf. If he doesn't get Mattie medical treatment fast, she'll die from the snakebite. So, he rushes her to the nearest town, where an Indian doctor patches her up.

The next scene shows Rooster back home playing cards with his Chinese friend. Suddenly, in walks Mattie's lawyer, J. Noble Daggett. He pays Cogburn the money Mattie owes him for bringing Chaney to justice, as well as a two-hundred-dollar bonus for saving the girl's life. When Daggett confides that young Mattie is still gravely ill, Rooster says not to worry because he knows she is tough enough to pull through. Sure enough, Mattie recovers, and Rooster then escorts her back to the family ranch. The aging lawman and Baby Sister part as friends, knowing that someday they'll meet again, in the next world if not this one.

True Grit was an instant hit with both moviegoers and film critics. The movie worked in large part because of a great story line powered by Wayne's Oscar-winning performance as the hard-drinking, unwashed, tough old marshal. But the film resonated with audiences in 1969 for other reasons as well. The independent and determined young woman played by Kim Darby suggested the new role of women in 1960s America. On the one hand, Mattie was a sensitive young lady, who could cry when reminded about her late father. But on the other, she was a shrewd businesswoman who kept the family's financial accounts and held her own against adults. She outmaneuvered a wily horse trader; she argued repeatedly with the arrogant Texas Ranger and refused to accept his terms for Tom Chaney's arrest; she negotiated a better rental price from the woman who owned the boarding house; she bravely joined the manhunt for her father's killer; she even stood up to the outlaws who captured her, saying exactly what was on her mind and never displaying fear. She was at her best when dealing with Rooster Cogburn. She always demanded respect and equality from the crusty old lawman. When necessary, she insulted him and pushed him to be a better man. Impressed by the young girl's determination and spunk, Rooster declares proudly, "By God, she reminds me of me."

Yet, for all of Mattie's intelligence, independence, and courage, she still has to be saved by men in keeping with established gender roles. La Boeuf comes to her rescue twice: first he stops Tom Chaney from killing her, and then he helps pull her out of the snake pit. Rooster Cogburn, however, is her ultimate champion: he defeats Ned Pepper's gang, kills Tom Chaney, saves her from the snake pit, and then carries her on a heroic race to town so she can be treated for the snakebite. Even the movie's theme song underscores that Mattie cannot make it on her own alone. "The pain of it will ease a bit," sings Glen Campbell, "when you find a man with true grit."[1] Despite the gender limitations of the day, Mattie still emerges as one of the brightest, toughest, and bravest female protagonists ever featured in a western.

Henry Hathaway's movie tapped into other social trends of the sixties. At a time when hippies, college protesters, and youth culture were fixtures in mass media, *True Grit* showcased a teenage protagonist who not only was on the young side of the generation gap but could go toe-to-toe with any adult. The link to youth culture was reinforced by the choice of Glen Campbell, who had earned numerous hits on the rock charts, to costar and sing the movie's theme song. Similarly, the film gave a nod to the rising civil rights movement. The African American ranch hand, Yarnell, is treated as a respected part of the Ross family who can be trusted to chaperone the teenage girl on a 140-mile round trip and assume responsibility for accompanying Mr. Ross's body on the journey back home. The articulate and educated bailiff in the court is also a black man. The medical practitioner who treats Mattie's snakebite is an Indian. And a Chinese shop owner is Rooster's landlord and close friend, who always teases him and beats him at cards.

Even though *True Grit* mirrors social and cultural change of the sixties, the movie is first and foremost a traditional western that upholds the mythic West. Hathaway's film depicts the West as a beautiful region of green valleys, sparkling creeks, lush meadows, and majestic snowcapped mountains. The exotic land is populated by traditional western characters: gunfighters, outlaws, homesteaders, Texas Rangers, and, of course, a U.S. marshal who is as rugged an individual as one would hope to find. Rooster Cogburn is a flawed hero, in keeping with the era's skepticism and fondness for realism. But significantly, he is no antihero like Clint Eastwood's Man with No Name or William Holden's leader of the Wild Bunch. Rooster might drink and smoke too much and not wash enough, and he might be ornery and cut corners when it comes to tracking down bad guys, but beneath his craggy and rugged exterior beats a heart of pure western gold. He is tough, courageous, and shows no mercy to evil opponents as he fights for justice and helps those in need, such as the young Mattie.

Indeed, Rooster provides audiences with one of the greatest showdowns in western movie history. As Ned Pepper and his gang are trying to escape, they ride into a mountain clearing. Suddenly, Marshal Cogburn emerges on horseback from the woods across the field. John Wayne's entrance is his most dramatic since *Stagecoach* back in 1939. The camera zooms in as Rooster twirls his rifle to cock it, just as Wayne did in that memorable moment thirty years earlier when the Ringo Kid stopped the stage in the John Ford classic. The camera then draws back for a long shot, showing the rugged mountains and beautiful forests, with splashes of bright yellow and light green foliage slicing through the dark green pines. At the center of the screen are the opponents lined up on either side of the grassy battlefield. The four bad guys are to the left, the good guy to the right. Rooster slowly rides closer to the villains and yells out, "Where's the girl, Ned?" The gang leader tells Cogburn to step aside so they can pass. The determined Rooster warns the three other gang members to back off, because his quarrel is only with Ned Pepper. When all four outlaws hold their ground, Rooster shouts out, "I mean to kill you in one minute, Ned. Or see you hanged in Fort Smith at Judge Parker's convenience. Which will it be?" Pepper merely laughs, and says mockingly, "I call that bold talk for a one-eyed fat man."

A clearly insulted Cogburn does a double-take and wrinkles his face, glaring at Pepper with his one eye. Rooster then bellows indignantly—"Fill your hands, you son of a bitch!"—as he spurs his horse and charges the four outlaws. A close-up shows Cogburn in all his frenzied glory, reins in his mouth, six-gun blazing in one hand, and rifle twirling and firing in the other. The opponents sweep back and forth toward each other like knights in a jousting match. The marshal kills them one by one, until only he and Ned are left. The outlaw shoots Rooster's horse from under him, trapping the lawman's leg under the weight of the fallen mount. Just as Pepper is about to finish off the defenseless Cogburn, a gunshot rings out, and Pepper falls dead from his horse. The camera angle changes to show La Boeuf high up on a cliff, lowering his long-range rifle. The Texas Ranger's deadly aim saved Cogburn's life and made a prophet out of Rooster, who joked earlier in the movie, "Any man who packs a big-bore Sharps carbine could come in mighty handy, if we're attacked by buffalo, or elephants."

No sooner does Rooster vanquish Ned Pepper's gang than he has to face another heroic test. Realizing that Mattie will die from the snakebite unless he gets her to a town quickly for medical treatment, Rooster begins the ride of both their lives. He carries her on her horse, Little Blackie, on a frantic quest to reach the town before the venom takes its toll. He drives the horse ever onward, until it drops dead of exhaustion. He then sweeps her into his arms and carries her over the wide open spaces. At gunpoint, he "borrows" a buckboard from three strangers for the final stretch. They arrive in town just in time to save her life.

In the end, not only does Rooster Cogburn succeed in defeating evil and protecting the innocent Mattie, but he finds personal redemption in the mythic West. The final scene of the movie takes place in the cold of winter at the Ross homestead. With snow-covered mountains and fields as a backdrop, Mattie takes Rooster up a hill to the family cemetery. Her broken arm is still in a sling, and he has just returned from Texas, where he buried La Boeuf and collected a bounty for Tom Chaney's body. She points to her father's grave, as well as all the other spots where the family will be buried in the future. And then she assures the old lawman that he will always have a burial plot right next to her in the family cemetery. He is clearly touched and says jokingly that he won't be claiming it too soon. The always contentious Mattie then warns the lawman that he needs to be careful riding his new horse because he's getting old and fat. The grizzled cowboy hero grins and climbs on his horse. Waving his hat he says, "Come see a fat old man sometime!" He then spurs his horse, jumps over a fence, and rides away as Mattie smiles. No cowboy in western movie history ever rode off into the sunset with a more grandiose gesture.

True Grit was a traditional western with heroic characters and a happy ending. But it also freshened up the old western formula by including a liberated female protagonist and allusions to social issues of the sixties. Equally important, the movie offered a positive message at a time when

Americans desperately needed reassurances. "The night I saw a sneak preview, the audience laughed and even applauded," noted Roger Ebert.[2] As the nation tried desperately to cope with the ongoing Vietnam War and tumultuous social change, audiences filed out of the dark movie theater knowing that there was hope after all. Contemporary Americans—like heroes of the Old West—could succeed as long as they had "true grit."

Still Tall in the Saddle

The phenomenal success of *True Grit* was proof that old-fashioned westerns were still riding tall in the saddle as far as many Americans were concerned. John Wayne alone starred in a flurry of neotraditional westerns, including *The Sons of Katie Elder* (1965) and *Rio Lobo* (1970), which showcased typical western heroes and themes. Other westerns of the late sixties also relied on traditional images that glorified the majestic western landscape or featured familiar characters such as cowboys, Indians, or legendary lawmen. Neotraditional westerns perpetuated the notion that the mythic West was a land of opportunity, success, and redemption.[3]

Comes a Horseman (1978), directed by Alan J. Pakula, was one of the era's most successful neotraditional westerns. The film begins just as World War II has ended. Two ex-GIs are trying to start life anew as partners on a small ranch. As they herd cattle, they notice a burial ceremony not far away on a hill. The son of cattle baron J. W. Ewing (Jason Robards) is being laid to rest with full military honors. At the end of the funeral, Ewing eyes rancher Ella Connors (Jane Fonda), who has come to pay respect. He warns her that he is taking over the valley and that she and the two vets who recently bought their ranch from her will not be able to hold out much longer. With greed in his eyes and lust in his heart, he suggests she marry him to avoid imminent ruin, but Ella clearly hates him and refuses outright.

Meanwhile, one of Ewing's men stalks the two vets as they work on their new ranch. He shoots and kills one of them and attempts to kill the other, Frank Athearn (James Caan). Frank is wounded but manages to kill his assailant. The seriously injured Frank is nursed back to health by Ella, along with her mentor, an old cowboy named Dodger (Richard Farnsworth). Frank returns the favor by volunteering to help Ella get her cows to market so she can stay in business for another year. Out of necessity, she eventually takes Frank on as a partner.

As Ella and Frank are struggling to survive financially, J. W. Ewing is facing his own problems. J. W. is deep in debt to an oil company for loans that enabled the Ewing cattle empire to expand throughout the valley. The company's executive is now calling in the debt, determined to take over the ranch in order to drill for oil. But the ruthless Ewing refuses to be pushed around. He arranges to have the oil executive die in a plane crash, and then he kills the local banker, the only other person with knowledge about the oil executive's plan.

When news reaches Ewing that Ella and her new partner, Frank, have sold enough cattle to pay off her mortgage, he and two of his henchmen pay her a visit. Willing to do anything to gain control of her land, he ties up Ella and hides her in a closet. Ewing then knocks out Frank and throws him into the closet as well. The crooks set fire to the house and head outside to watch from a distance. When Frank and Ella escape the burning home, Ewing and his men ride back to finish them off. But Frank and Ella have other plans. Frank quickly kills one of the henchmen, while Ella blasts the other with a shotgun. Frank then shoots and wounds Ewing. As the villain tumbles from his saddle, he gets his foot caught in the stirrup. Frank and Ella then watch the greedy cattle baron's gruesome death play out as the spooked horse drags Ewing to death over the land he coveted. The final scene shows a happy Frank and Ella rebuilding their home as they begin a new life together in the American West.

Comes a Horseman is a very traditional western. In keeping with the tried-and-true western formula, the film features clear-cut good guys and bad guys. The familiar protagonists include Frank, a determined young cowboy with solid values, expert riding and roping skills, and proficiency with his guns and fists, and Dodger, an old cowboy who serves as a mentor and matchmaker for both Frank and Ella. The movie updates the old formula with a less traditional protagonist. Unlike most female characters in westerns, Ella knows how to ride, rope, and shoot, and she can stand up to any man. She's equally liberated when it comes to sex. Earlier in her youth, she had a brief affair with J. W. Ewing, and she later gets involved with Frank. In keeping with acceptable gender attitudes of the seventies, however, the movie does not push her independence too far. Not only does she feel remorse for her youthful indiscretion with Ewing, but ultimately Ella has to be rescued by Frank. He helps her run her ranch, aids her escape from a burning building, and plays a major role in defeating Ewing and his henchmen. At the same time, Ella is not subordinate to Frank or any other man. Frank and Ella achieve success by working as equal partners. They defy the odds by stopping stampedes, weathering storms, and driving their cattle to market to save the ranch. Both contribute in the final shootout: each kills one man; and, after Frank wounds Ewing, both watch the cattle baron's horse drag him to death.

The bad guys in *Comes a Horseman* are pure evil. J. W. Ewing is the quintessential western villain. The powerful rancher is willing to lie, cheat, steal, and even murder to drive smaller ranchers out of business so he can gain a monopoly over all the land in the region. Nothing will stop him from achieving his goals. He even tries to kill Ella, the woman he loves, when she refuses to sell her land. (Perhaps not coincidentally, the name of the conniving rancher played by Larry Hagman in the 1980s TV soap opera *Dallas* is J. R. Ewing.) Just as *Comes a Horseman* updated the protagonists in keeping with contemporary gender expectations, it also freshened up the antagonists. The megalomaniac cattle baron, the corrupt banker, and the oil man who devised a devious scheme to ruin the environment through large-scale drilling undoubtedly seemed familiar to audiences accustomed to news stories about power-hungry politicians, corporate corruption, and greedy oil companies. Similarly, the high level of violence in the movie was a gratuitous nod to modern times.

Yet despite these updates, *Comes a Horseman* remains true to the western formula. The American West is pictured as a beautiful and exotic land. Shot in Panavision and Technicolor, the movie offers panoramic views of the Front Range of the Rocky Mountains. Breathtaking shots of rugged mountains, vast wide open spaces, and enormous thunderheads and lightning strikes add to the film's mood as they reinforce the immense power, mystery, and magnificence of the mythic West. The courageous westerners found in this setting are archetypes of the American Dream. Frank and Ella are guided by a moral compass and aided by all the characteristics typically associated with America's westward movement. These brave, hardworking, innovative, determined, and skilled individuals work together to defeat evil in the fight for truth and justice.

Like protagonists in earlier traditional westerns, this heroic man and equally heroic woman find success in the mythic West. In the climactic scene, Frank and Ella emerge from a burning house—like the legendary Phoenix rising from flames—to defeat the villain and rebuild their home from the ashes. By film's end, they have at last found happiness and redemption. The message was clear to moviegoers. Just as these two courageous westerners held fast to their values and triumphed in the mythic West, so could contemporary Americans rebound from all the social and political turmoil facing the United States in the late seventies.

While following the old-fashioned western formula for success, neotraditional westerns did their best to remain relevant in modern times. Reflecting changing gender attitudes, movies such as *Welcome to Hard Times* (1967) and *Firecreek* (1968) featured independent women and dealt openly with sex and rape. The rise of the civil rights movement resulted in numerous westerns that included positive images of African Americans, Hispanics, Indians, and other minorities. In *The Master Gunfighter* (1975), for example, a slick African American gambler (Lincoln Kilpatrick) turns out to be an undercover federal agent who helps defeat the dastardly villain. "It's a dirty job," he jokes, "but it beats the hell out of pickin' cotton."[4] Significantly, the positive images of minorities and women found in these movies do not qualify as revisionist, because the characters do not undermine traditional western myths. Nor are they used to critique contemporary society. Indeed, by the time most of these films were made, minority characters and liberated women were no longer cinematic breakthroughs. What was revolutionary or revisionist back in the mid-sixties had become commonplace by the late sixties and seventies.

Neotraditional westerns also picked up on the era's rising youth culture.[5] *Rancho Deluxe* (1975), which stars Jeff Bridges and Sam Waterston as antiheroes, is a good example. Directed by Frank Perry, the film pits modern themes involving youth, gender, and race against traditional western motifs. Ultimately, the mythic West wins. The contemporary western takes place in Montana and focuses on two young ne'er-do-wells, Jack McKee (Jeff Bridges) and Cecil Colson (Sam Waterston). Jack rebels from his rich family by drinking lots of beer, smoking dope, whoring around, and rustling cattle from a local cattle baron. Cecil, who is part Indian, is happy to join his close friend in a life of crime and debauchery. The two disrespect elders, the community, and anything else around. They even make fun of old western movies. When Jack and Cecil see an abandoned drive-in movie screen, Cecil asks Jack if he's ever seen *Cheyenne Autumn*. "Well, in another twenty years," he jokes, "they're gonna make *Aluminum Autumn*."

The amoral duo start off rustling one cow at a time from the town's richest rancher, John Brown (Clifton James), a former owner of a Schenectady, New York, hair salon, who has come West in search of freedom and opportunity. His sexy wife, Cora (Elizabeth Ashley), has less lofty interests. While trying to seduce a ranch hand one day, she says aggressively, "Come on, goddamn it! I want gothic ranch action around here! I want some desire under the elms!" At first, the lazy Jack and Cecil don't take rustling seriously. They use an old-fashioned Sharps buffalo rifle to shoot long range, not just at Brown's cows, but also at cars and other targets. But they get increasingly greedy. They shoot more and more cows, steal Brown's prize bull, demand a ransom, and eventually stumble on an even bolder plan to make money. In cahoots with two of Brown's ranch hands, Jack and Cecil decide to load up a huge tractor trailer truck with Brown's cattle and transport them for sale at a faraway feed lot.

John Brown is livid about the escalating assaults on his property. "I won't have a West that's not free," he declares. To solve the problem, he brings in a hired gun, Henry Beige (played by western movie veteran Slim Pickens), who appears to be as lackluster as his name. The old codger can't even walk without help from his pious and pretty young niece, Laura (Charlene Dallas). When Beige picks a bullet out of a dead cow, he tells the ranch owner, "If I wasn't so dad-blamed old, I wouldn't know what this is." Explaining that it's a 50-caliber bullet from a Sharps buffalo rifle, Beige grins nostalgically and says, "This is getting downright romantic."

The rich rancher soon discovers that the old cowboy and his Christian niece should not be underestimated. Laura seduces one of Brown's ranch hands and learns that he is part of Jack and Cecil's scheme. She tips off Henry, who immediately springs into action. He calls in the police and invites the entire town to come out to form a blockade that will prevent the tractor trailer from getting through with its load of stolen cattle. Then, as the huge truck driven by Jack and Cecil approaches, Beige throws away his walking stick, jumps on a white horse, and gallops out to greet the truck. With six-gun in hand, the wily old cowboy forces the young antiheroes to surrender. Rather than being an old fool with a religious niece, Henry Beige turns out to be cagey western hero, aided by his beautiful mistress, Laura.

The movie ends with inmates Jack and Cecil riding off to round up horses in a western prison compound, which they name Rancho Deluxe, while Slim Pickens's traditional cowboy rides off into the sunset with a beautiful girl. Before exiting, Beige makes it clear that he's not in it for the money. "Here's my bill. You can pay it, or use it to wipe the pablum off your chin," he tells rancher Brown. "Don't make me no never mind. I'm just in this for the sport." The film is a clear victory for the mythic West over the revisionist West. Set in Big Sky country, with majestic snow-capped mountains as a backdrop, *Rancho Deluxe* showcases an old cowboy on a white horse who outsmarts the young antiheroes and everyone else in the modern western town. The old-fashioned hero and by extension the mythic West defeat young antihero rustlers (Jack and Cecil); the eastern Establishment (rancher John Brown, who made his money back east); and modernity (represented by a huge tractor-trailer truck and modern police who watch passively as Beige wins the showdown with rustlers). In the end, the Old West triumphs over the new.

If *Rancho Deluxe* put the seventies youth culture in its place, another neotraditional western, *Billy Jack* (1971), placed the counterculture on a pedestal. By the time the contemporary western was released, images of long-haired hippies advocating love, peace, drugs, and alternative religions were common in the media. *Billy Jack*, directed by and starring Tom Laughlin, became a cult classic by siding with the under-thirty crowd in the generation gap. Set out west in the early seventies, Laughlin's good-guy character—a part-Indian ex–Green Beret trained in karate—is a law enforcement officer on an Indian reservation. Billy Jack comes to the aid of the reservation's pacifist teacher, Jean Roberts, and her Freedom School of multicultural hippies, who are discriminated against and abused by the racist, corrupt, and brutal whites living in a nearby town. Young audiences loved the film's glorification of hippies, use of rock music, and plot that featured kids winning out over parents and evil adults. The movie's theme song, "One Tin Soldier" by Coven, even became a hit on the rock music charts.

Not a great western or even a good one, *Billy Jack* is a curious period piece, which highlights images of the counterculture that were already trite by the time the film was released. The hippies at the Freedom School constitute a "gathering" of a multiracial tribe of Native American, Hispanic, black, and white students. Taught by progressive teachers, they believe in goodness, pacifism, human rights, and universal brotherhood. They spread their message of peace, love, and understanding through rock and folk music, poetry, improvisational skits, and street theater. "We're a rainbow made of children, we're an army just singin' our song," sings a young hippie girl at one point in the movie. "There's no weapons that can stop us, rainbow love is much too strong."[6] (Interestingly, their notion of a "rainbow" coalition predated by thirteen years the similarly named organization of the Reverend Jesse Jackson.)

The film reflects other trends of the sixties and early seventies. Basing scenes on well-known events from the civil rights movement, the movie depicts de jure and de facto segregation, as well as racist whites insulting and beating people of color and harassing riders on a Freedom School bus. The film also picks up on changing attitudes toward sex. It preaches to young people that there is a marked difference between sexual relations within a loving relationship and having sex because of peer pressure or for mere recreational purposes. Like many films of the day, it includes gratuitous nudity and rape scenes. Laughlin's film also reflects the era's growing violence and polarization over race, gender, youth, and politics. In keeping with the film's liberal perspective, many of the town's white citizens, both young and old, are portrayed as bigots. They humiliate people of color, they beat and kill Indians, and they harass innocent hippies. When a Freedom School bus pulls into town carrying hippie students singing and giving the peace sign, hostile town citizens merely glare back at them. "When are you gonna do something about those long-haired weirdoes?" one disgruntled man asks Sheriff Cole. "Before or after they start burnin' their draft cards?"

The insults escalate into violence when white youths led by Bernard Posner, the mean son of the town's richest man, humiliate and beat Indian youths trying to buy ice cream cones in a whites-only store. Billy Jack steps in to save the day. Disgusted by Bernard's actions, Billy explains that he tries to follow the nonviolent example of the Freedom School, but when he sees this kind of brutality, he just goes "berserk," at which point he uses karate against Bernard and his buddies, sending the biggest one crashing through the front window. Shortly thereafter, Bernard's father and eleven other men bent on revenge surround the Indian law man. Mr. Posner orders his men to "kill that Indian son of a bitch," whereupon the gang begins beating Billy to a bloody pulp. The Indian is saved only when Sheriff Cole intervenes.

The situation soon worsens. When Mr. Posner and a corrupt deputy sheriff learn that the deputy's pregnant runaway daughter is hiding on the reservation, they are determined to find her and close down the Freedom School once and for all. Their actions set off a flurry of racial hatred and violence. Bernard makes the bad situation even worse when he forces a teenage Indian girl to disrobe at knifepoint; rapes the pacifist schoolteacher; kills an Indian boy; and then has sex with a thirteen-year-old Indian girl. Billy Jack strikes back with a vengeance. After killing Bernard and the deputy, Billy flees with the deputy's daughter to an old church. Surrounded by local and state law enforcement officers, Billy and the girl initially refuse to give up. But finally Jean, Sheriff Cole, and a compassionate doctor convince Billy to surrender in return for government promises to help the girl, the Freedom School, and all the Indians.

At first glance, *Billy Jack* appears to be a revisionist take on the West that supports rebellious youth and minorities against the Establishment. Yet, despite the superficial story line about an Indian karate expert helping hippies and Indians defeat racist and corrupt whites, *Billy Jack* is no revisionist western. Instead, it equates countercultural beliefs with old-fashioned

American values by placing them in the context of the mythic West. The result is a very traditional western. *Billy Jack* endorses the deep-rooted notion that the mythic West is an exotic land that offers hope, opportunity, and redemption. The movie's ties to the western myth are established at the outset when an extended opening scene shows Posner and his men rounding up wild horses on magnificent mesas overlooking rivers and mountains. The villains finally corral the mustangs and are ready to shoot them at close range to sell for dog food, but Billy rides up on his palomino and stops them by pointing out that they have illegally entered the Indian reservation. In effect, the virgin land offers sanctuary for the mustangs, protecting them from the evils of civilization. Breathtaking views of snow-capped mountains and the western wilderness reinforce the bucolic image of the West throughout the rest of the film. Not coincidentally, the Indian reservation and other rural areas are depicted as idyllic, whereas the town is portrayed as a corrupt place filled with racist troublemakers.

The primeval West offers success and redemption for those who are worthy. Jean and all the children at the Freedom School are saved when the courageous Billy Jack defeats Posner and his evil henchmen. In the process, the Indian hero is redeemed from his own violent tendencies by sacrificing his own self-interests for the good of the children. Jean's pacifism shows him the way to redemption. "So easy for you to die dramatically," she tells him. "It's a hell of a lot tougher for those of us who have to keep on trying!" Convinced, Billy Jack surrenders to the authorities in return for assurances of a better future for Jean and the Freedom School. His sacrifice to save others is obvious in the scene where Billy gives up to the police. A crucifix looms overhead as Billy walks out of his hiding place in the old church. When the police take him away, the children salute their savior, transforming Billy Jack into a martyr for truth, justice, and the American Way.

Despite his minority background and fondness for karate kicks and rifles instead of fists and six-guns, Billy Jack is a traditional western hero. He protects the innocent, defeats the bad guys, and upholds American values. Billy's violent actions, unlike those of revisionist antiheroes, are justified and limited. He shoots the deputy in self-defense and karate chops Bernard to death only after the evil teenager has raped Jean, killed an Indian boy, forced an Indian girl to disrobe, and committed statuary rape on a young Indian girl. Arguably, Tom Laughlin's countercultural western is not even an anti-Establishment film. The hippie teachers and students at the Freedom School are not rebelling against mainstream American beliefs; they are trying to defend them. While their appearance and rhetoric might have looked or sounded revolutionary to conservatives in Nixon's America, their progressive goals and values were decidedly traditional. They speak passionately about American rights, including liberty and justice for all.

Significantly, Laughlin's movie does not portray all Establishment figures in negative ways. Billy Jack identifies with mainstream political leaders who dedicated their lives to improving America. His beliefs are made clear in an exchange with the pacifist Jean. When she suggests that Billy needs to abide by the rules of law, he replies, "When that set of laws is applied to everyone, then I'll turn the other cheek too." He reminds her that Martin Luther King Jr. and the two Kennedys were all murdered because people "wouldn't even put the same controls on their guns as they do on their dogs, their bicycles, their cats, and their automobiles." Sheriff Cole, the town's doctor, and some members of the town council are depicted as compassionate and reasonable people who seek justice for everyone in the community. Even state and federal government officials are viewed in positive ways. In the end, they provide a solution to the problems of Billy Jack and the Freedom School, just as the federal government had advanced the civil rights movement throughout the fifties and sixties.

Billy Jack follows the neotraditional path blazed by *True Grit* back in 1969. While *True Grit* employed an independent woman character to keep pace with the changing times, *Billy Jack* modernized the western formula with numerous allusions to the era's youth culture. But in the end, Laughlin's movie—like John Wayne's—was still a traditional western. The final scene underscores the movie's close ties to traditional heroes and the mythic West. Like Shane and countless other western heroes who came before him, Billy Jack rides off into the sunset after defeating the bad guys. Exchanging his freedom for the good of the community, he is escorted away by the police while throngs of young supporters line the streets. As he passes, the grateful students stand up and thrust closed fists upward in a power-to-the-people salute to show respect and solidarity. The camera pulls back for a long shot, showing the motorcade and students stretching for miles, set against a beautiful western backdrop of mountains and exotic landscapes. The emotional impact of the mythic West becomes even more evident as the movie's theme song is reprised. "Go ahead and hate your neighbor, go ahead and cheat a friend," sings the rock group Coven. "[But] there won't be any trumpets blowing, come the judgment day. On the bloody morning after, one tin soldier rides away."[7]

Billy Jack was not the only neotraditional western that reflected the violence and tensions of America in the sixties and seventies. Other examples include *Return of the Seven* (1966), *Welcome to Hard Times* (1967), *Hang 'Em High* (1968), and *Firecreek* (1968).[8] *Firecreek*, directed by Vincent McEveety, was especially brutal. The movie begins when Bob Larkin (Henry Fonda) and his gang ride into the small town of Firecreek. No one or thing is safe as the sociopaths drink heavily, break windows, intimidate and beat people, molest and rape women, and kill anyone who stands in their way. The town is too scared to stop them, and the part-time sheriff, Johnny Cobb (James Stewart) is reluctant to get involved because he is a full-time farmer with a pregnant wife and two sons.

The gang came to town so Larkin could recuperate from a gunshot wound. He checks into a boarding house, where he meets Evelyn (Inger Stevens), who tends his wound and soon realizes that Larkin doesn't approve of his men's sadistic actions. She asks him why he won't stop them and give up his outlaw ways. "Then I'll be like all the rest," he replies. "Today I'm one of the few. I lead. That's important to me." Despite their differences, the two grow closer and even wind up in bed together.

While Larkin is spending time with Evelyn, his men terrorize the town. They molest women, trash the saloon, and bully residents. After the gang hangs a mentally challenged young man who accidentally killed a gang member while trying to stop him from raping a young Indian girl, the part-time sheriff realizes he has to take a stand and arrest the lawbreakers. Cobb admits that he has been fooling himself by thinking he could avoid life's problems by finding sanctuary in a small town. "What I didn't see was the day a man decides not to face the world is the day he better step out of it," he explains.

In typical western fashion, Cobb straps on a six-gun for a showdown with the evil gang. The courageous part-time sheriff soon realizes that the fight for justice won't be easy. He is shot in the arm, the leg, and more. But the determined westerner refuses to quit. He kills the outlaws one by one. Finally, only Johnny Cobb and Bob Larkin are left standing. Just when Larkin is about to kill the wounded sheriff, a shot rings out from a nearby window. Evelyn, rifle in hand, has shot Larkin dead.

Firecreek follows the traditional western formula. The good guy overcomes adversity, defeats the bad guys, and everyone finds happiness and redemption in the Old West. The movie owes much to *High Noon* (1952), which also features a lawman facing off against outlaws while a cowardly town refuses to get involved. Of course, *Firecreek* updated the western formula in several ways. Featuring sadistic outlaws, rapes, murders, and bloody gunfights, the movie reflected the anxious mood of the country in the late sixties. Such terror seemed all too plausible to moviegoers at a time when many Americans felt surrounded by evil and brutality. Released in 1968, one of the most violent years in American history, *Firecreek* offered catharsis to audiences battered by the assassinations of Martin Luther King and Bobby Kennedy, escalating violence in Vietnam, and urban riots and campus protests at home.

Firecreek gave a nod to other contemporary trends. The heroic sheriff succeeds only because he receives help from young people and a liberated woman. First, his sons warn him that a bad guy is sneaking up on him. Then, he is rescued by Evelyn Pittman. Along with being an excellent shot, Evelyn is courageous and independent. Initially, she uses the gang leader for companionship, emotional comfort, even sexual gratification, but she then turns on him and shoots him down like a rabid dog (much to Larkin's surprise). While some women in the late sixties no doubt applauded Evelyn's decisive actions and rejection of an evil male, Inger Stevens's feminist character was not a total departure from earlier westerns. Arguably, Evelyn was just following the lead of Grace Kelly's character in *High Noon*, who saved her husband's life by shooting one of the outlaws. Despite the updates involving gender and violence, *Firecreek* offered audiences a traditional western with an upbeat ending. Just as Cobb and Evelyn found success and redemption in the Old West, moviegoers could rest assured that they, too, might succeed as long as they showed courage and remained true to traditional American values.

Westerns and the End of the Sixties

By the early seventies, the United States was reeling from Vietnam, urban riots, college protests, a stagnant economy, Watergate, and growing polarization over innumerable issues. Almost every social, cultural, and political institution was under attack, and weary Americans questioned their past, present, and even future.

But by 1976, the mood of the country had begun to shift. A collective sigh of relief swept across America following President Nixon's resignation in 1974 and the end of the Vietnam War in 1975. Slowly but surely, the nation began to recover. The Bicentennial in 1976 offered reason and opportunities to celebrate. Coast to coast, Americans cheered on the tall ships, rediscovered their national heritage, and shared hope that the future would be better. If the preponderance of revisionist westerns in the sixties and early seventies reflected the nation's concerns and conflict, the comeback of neotraditional westerns in the late seventies suggested consensus and confidence that America was getting back in the saddle after its prolonged time of troubles.

Two neotraditional westerns released in 1976—*The Outlaw Josey Wales* and *The Shootist*—captured the changing mood of the country. *The Outlaw Josey Wales*, directed by and starring Clint Eastwood, used the post–Civil War West as a metaphor to explore American attitudes in the aftermath of the Vietnam War. The film begins with Josey (Clint Eastwood) and his young son plowing land on their farm. Josey's wife calls the boy to wash up for dinner. Just then, a gang of Redlegs (antislavery Kansas Jayhawkers who indiscriminately raided settlers) swoop down on the homestead, burn the house, and murder Josey's family. Josey is knocked unconscious and left for dead. Shortly thereafter, a group of pro-Rebel Missouri guerilla fighters arrive on the scene. Surveying the situation, their leader tells Wales that it appears the killers were Redlegs. "You'll find them up in Kansas. They're with the Union. And we're goin' up there and set things right," he explains. Wales replies, "I'll be comin' with you."

As the Civil War winds down, one of the leaders of the Missouri guerilla fighters, Fletcher, convinces his men to surrender their weapons to the Union forces. It turns out to be a trap, and almost everyone is killed by the Redlegs fighting on the side of the Union army. The only survivors are Fletcher (who accepted a bribe to convince his men to give up their guns), Josey Wales, and a young guerilla fighter named Jamie.

Throughout the rest of the film, Fletcher and the Redlegs attempt to hunt down and kill Josey and Jamie. Not long afterward, Jamie is shot and killed, but Josey continues to elude his pursuers as he picks up new followers. First, Wales befriends an old Indian named Lone Watie (Chief Dan George). Next, he adds an Indian woman, who had been raped by two bounty hunters searching for him. Then he rescues two supporters of the Kansas Jayhawkers, Laura Lee (Sondra Locke) and her grandmother, from a gang of cutthroats. Wales guides them to a desolate town near a ranch that Granny had just inherited from her son. Josey, Granny, and Laura invite other down-on-their luck people to start life anew on Granny's place just outside of town.

The new community is soon threatened by a Comanche war party that hates all Americans. Josey orders his motley group to barricade themselves in the ranch house (the adobe structure has shutters shaped like religious crosses, foreshadowing the redemption that will later occur), while he heads out to negotiate. He points out to the chief that neither he nor the Indians like the U.S. government, emphasizing that "governments don't live together; people live together." He suggests that the Comanches and the people at Granny's ranch can coexist peacefully. Impressed by the white man's words, the chief agrees to peace. When Josey brings the good news back to the ranch house, Laura is overjoyed that he made it back safely. The two clearly are in love and wind up going to bed together. But Josey is still tormented by the memory of his dead wife and family, so he decides to leave the next morning.

As Josey is preparing to ride off, a gang of Redlegs arrives. They are about to kill him, but suddenly rifles appear in the peepholes shaped like crosses, proving that Josey Wales is no longer alone. Most of the Redlegs are killed in the ensuing shootout, although the leader responsible for killing the Wales family escapes. Josey catches up with him in town and uses the man's own sword to kill him. Wales then walks into the saloon, where he comes face-to-face with Fletcher and two Texas Rangers who have been on his trail. Wales's friends in the saloon quickly introduce him as Mr. Wilson, and they assure the strangers that the man they are looking for is dead. Convinced, the two lawmen leave town, while Fletcher, who knows the truth, remains behind to talk to his former comrade. The two men come to an uneasy agreement that their animosity, like the Civil War, is over. Fletcher then rides south toward Mexico, while Josey heads toward a new life with Laura on Granny's ranch.

The Outlaw Josey Wales upholds the mythic West as it comments on contemporary America. Josie is a traditional western hero. He seeks and achieves justice against those who killed his family and fellow guerilla fighters. He stands up to evil and protects the innocent and downtrodden. And, unlike the antihero Eastwood played in spaghetti westerns, Josey Wales adheres to traditional values and resorts to violence only when necessary. In keeping with the mythic West, Josey and other major characters find success and redemption. Josey rebuilds his life and even makes peace with the Jayhawkers by literally uniting with Laura Lee, a Kansan whose late father was a Redleg and grandmother is a proud Jayhawker. Josey and Laura fall in love and presumably live happily ever after, as do all the downtrodden folk of the desolate town who are helped by Josey. Even Fletcher, who had betrayed the Missouri guerilla fighters, finds redemption by allowing Josey Wales to go free.

The neotraditional western reflects the times in which it was made. The movie picks up on the anti-Establishment mood of the country in the seventies. While civilian and military leaders are portrayed as untrustworthy, Josey comes across as an apolitical figure who opposes injustice, hypocrisy, and immorality. In keeping with the era's civil rights movement, the movie emphasizes just treatment of the West's Indian minority. Josey befriends Indians, saves an Indian woman from rape, and treats the Comanches fairly.

The Outlaw Josey Wales expresses an antiwar message that no doubt resonated with audiences shaped by the Vietnam experience. Along with arguing for peaceful coexistence with enemies, the movie depicts the horrendous impact that war has not only on soldiers but also on innocent men, women, and children. Josey, like moviegoers familiar with Vietnam, is scarred by war. Indeed, by the end of the film, the Civil War has become a metaphor for Vietnam. When Fletcher stays behind to talk to "Mr. Wilson" (i.e., Josey Wales), he explains he's headed to Mexico to find Josey. When Eastwood's character asks him what he'll do when he finds him, Fletcher replies, "He's got the first move, I owe him that. I think I'll try to tell him the war is over." Fletcher adds, "What do you say, Mr. Wilson?" Eastwood's character pauses for a moment and then replies, "I reckon [the war's over]. I guess we all died a little in that damn war." That pointed message was not lost on moviegoers in the late seventies. No matter what position Americans took regarding Vietnam, everyone came away a loser. Yet, the war—whether it was the Civil War for Josey or Vietnam for contemporary audiences—was over at long last. Just as Josey Wales rode off into the sunrise to start life anew at the end of this traditional western, so could Americans in 1976 get a fresh start by putting Vietnam and the sixties behind them. In effect, *The Outlaw Josey Wales* made it clear that the Vietnam War and, by extension, the tumultuous decade known as the sixties were both finally over.

Another western released the same year as *The Outlaw Josey Wales* also focused on the passing of an era. *The Shootist*, directed by Don Siegel, starred John Wayne as an aging gunslinger named John Bernard Books. The movie begins with Wayne's character riding along a trail when suddenly a man tries to hold him up. But the outlaw learns that he's messing with the wrong guy when Books shoots him in the gut.

J. B. Books then rides his horse into Carson City, Nevada. Looking out of place in the turn-of-the-century town bustling with cars, trolleys, and lots of modern activity, the graying cowboy heads directly to the house of Doc Hostetler (James Stewart). After Books explains his pain, the Doc examines him and delivers the bad news. Books has terminal cancer and won't last more than two months. The Doc warns that the end will be extremely painful and recommends suicide. "There's just, uh . . . very little I can do," says Doc. "Uh, if . . . when the pain gets too bad, I can give you something." All the tough old gunfighter can say in return is, "Damn."

Doc gives Books a bottle of whiskey laced with opium to control the pain and recommends he rent a room down the street in a boarding house run by Bond Rogers (Lauren Bacall), a widow who lives there with her son, Gillom (Ron Howard). Hoping to die in peace, Books checks into Rogers's home under an alias, William Hickok. The widow asks, "Where are you from, Mr. Hickok?" When he says Abilene, she asks what he did there. "United States marshal," he replies. "That's nice," says Mrs. Rogers. "No it isn't," responds Books.

Any hope for peace and quiet comes to a sudden end when news leaks out about Mr. Hickok's true identity. The teenage Gillom is impressed that the famed gunslinger is staying with him and his mother, but the local marshal, Walter Thibido (Harry Morgan), has a different take. He just wants Books out of town before any trouble erupts. When Books explains that he's not going anywhere, because he's dying, the marshal replies joyfully, "Hot damn! You know, Books, that's the best news I've had all day."

The news travels fast all over town, and people begin lining up to profit from the gunfighter's demise. Some, like gambler Jack Pulford and an aspiring gunfighter named Cobb, want to enhance their reputations by killing Books in a gunfight. Mike Sweeney (Richard Boone) shows up to avenge his brother, who was killed by Books in a gunfight years earlier. Others see Books's impending death as an opportunity to make money. A local newspaperman volunteers to write a book about the famous gunfighter, but Books calls him a vulture and throws him out. One of Books's former lovers arrives and asks to marry the dying gunman, who declines when he realizes that her only motive is to make money by selling her story as a grieving widow. Even the undertaker hopes to profit from the legendary gunfighter's death. After he offers Books an all-expenses-paid funeral, including two mourners thrown in for free, the gunman glares at him. "You son-of-a-bitch. You aim to do to me what they did with John Wesley Hardin," exclaims Books. "Lay me out and parade every damn fool in the state past me at a dollar a head, half price for children, and then stuff me in a gunny sack and shovel me under."

Only the widow and her son care about the dying man. Books and Mrs. Rogers develop a friendship that in other circumstances might have blossomed into serious romance, while Books becomes a mentor to young Gillom, teaching him how to shoot straight, as well as encouraging him to walk a straight and narrow path in life.

As Books is growing ever closer to Mrs. Rogers and her son, he devises a plan to end life on his own terms. He listened carefully when old Doc Hostetler said, "You know, Books . . . if I were you and had lived my entire life the way you have, I don't think that the death I just described to you is the one I would choose." In keeping with Doc's advice, Books figures out a way to die with dignity while simultaneously ridding the town of three of its biggest troublemakers. The terminally ill gunfighter invites Pulford, Cobb, and Sweeney to meet him for a showdown at the local saloon. He schedules the event for his birthday. Before heading off for his final battle, Books has his Sunday suit cleaned and pressed, gives his horse to Gillom, and gets his affairs in order.

On the appointed day, Books walks into the saloon to face his three possible executioners. Shortly thereafter, the bullets begin to fly, and the aging gunfighter successfully picks off his opponents one by one. Just when it appears that Books has won, the bartender suddenly opens fire. The sneak attack recalled Books's earlier statement to Gillom that it took more than just bravery and proficiency with a gun to win a gunfight. "[Watch out] for that dumbass amateur," he advised. "There's always some six-fingered bastard that couldn't hit a cow in the tit with a tin cup. That's the one who usually does you in."

Witnessing the fatal shooting, Gillom picks up Books's six-gun and kills the treacherous barkeep. The dying Books looks up with a grateful expression on his face. Gillom, appalled that he just took a man's life, throws the gun away, at which point a pleased John Bernard Books smiles and then dies. The young man places his jacket over his fallen mentor's body and then walks out into the street, where his mother meets him. The two walk home silently.

The Shootist is an elegiac tribute not only to the mythic West, but also to the actor who best personified the western myth—John Wayne. The film establishes its ties to the old myths at the outset with flashback images taken from earlier John Wayne westerns. Wayne's character, J. B. Books, is a traditional western hero who wins a moral if not actual victory by defeating bad guys in a classic showdown. Throughout his career, the rugged lawman had always stood for justice and helped the innocent. He never went looking for trouble, but he always stood tall against the bad guys. Books represents the best of the West. With death rapidly approaching, he evokes the mythic West by taking as an alias the name of the legendary Wild Bill Hickok, and he clings to his values. He goes out of his way to mentor young Gillom, imploring him not to drink, swear, or hang out with ne'er-do-wells. In the end, he gives his life teaching the teenage boy, who was fascinated by guns and gunfighters, that there is nothing glorious about bloodshed or killing a man. John Bernard "wins" his last gunfight by sacrificing himself for a greater good.

The Shootist offered audiences a fascinating tale about the passing of the Old West. The prominence of cars, telephones, and trolleys in Carson City showed that modernity was replacing the Old West, while Books's death in 1901 suggested that old western heroes no longer fit in the new century. What made the film particularly poignant was the fact that in real life John Wayne—like his character, John Bernard Books—was dying of cancer. *The Shootist* would be Wayne's last film. He died in 1979, only three years after the release of the neotraditional western.

The Shootist made it clear that even though J. B. Books and the Old West had passed from the scene, their values and significance were still relevant in the twentieth century. When Wayne's character defended his actions, he just as easily could have been speaking for an entire generation battered by Vietnam, civil unrest, college protests, and tumultuous social change. "I won't be wronged. I won't be insulted. I won't be laid a hand on," explains John Bernard. "I don't do these things to other people, and I require the same from them." That message of freedom and fair play was not lost on moviegoers in 1976. Though the Old West and even the old cowboy hero might be gone, the mythic West was still alive and well in modern America.

The Shootist opened the floodgates to a wave of old-fashioned westerns.[9] One of the most successful was Sydney Pollack's *The Electric Horseman* (1979). The contemporary western shows where westerns were headed as the decade drew to a close. It focuses on a former rodeo star, Sonny Steele (Robert Redford), who has sold out and become a pitchman for a cereal company. Dressed in a gaudy sequined outfit designed by Nudie's of Hollywood, replete with electric piping that lights up his shirt, hat, pants, boots, and saddle like a Christmas tree, Sonny's electric cowboy would have made Gene Autry or other rhinestone cowboys envious.

Sonny's dazzling visage proved that not everything that glitters is gold. Debauched by too much alcohol and partying, the former rodeo star is just a shell of his former self. In a scene that evokes a notorious incident involving Gene Autry at a rodeo, the drunken Sonny even falls off his horse during a performance. The dissipated cowboy discovers his own moment of truth in Las Vegas—the capital of crass materialism. Sonny is supposed to appear with a champion racehorse, but the one-time magnificent horse turns out to be as drugged, electrified, and debauched as the former rodeo star. Redford's character, in a moment of clarity, is repulsed by the corporate greed that reduced the splendid stallion to a side show attraction. He decides to bolt with the animal. His plan is not thought out, but his goal is clear: he wants to free the abused horse.

When the electric horseman rides out of the convention center onto the Vegas strip on his equally electric steed, the race is on. Like a western version of David versus Goliath, the erstwhile rodeo star and former racehorse are up against a corporate giant backed by high-tech law enforcement. Somehow, the man on horseback manages to elude police cars, motorcycles, even helicopters. Enter Hallie Martin, a hard-nosed TV newswoman played by Jane Fonda. Eager for a scoop on a story that has captured the public's attention, Hallie zeroes in on Sonny's location. The frustrated cowboy just wants to be left alone. But the no-nonsense Hallie points out, "You ride off with somebody else's twelve-million-dollar horse, did you think we wouldn't notice?" She convinces him that she can help him garner public support for the mistreated animal through her exclusive TV reports. The two of them—with the car before the horse—set out on a journey into the unspoiled wilderness. At one point, they even sing "God Bless America."

Ultimately, the travelers find success and redemption at the end of their western odyssey. Sonny redeems himself through his honest, unselfish act of setting the horse free and is born again as a cowboy and a man, finally free from corporate greed and debauchery. Hallie is transformed from a callous career woman into a caring human being. She becomes an honest advocate instead of just a media celebrity intent on high ratings. Surprised that she finally met an honorable man, she even has a love affair with the cowboy en route to the hidden valley where Sonny plans to set the horse free. Three days later, they are all resurrected, including the horse, who is set loose in a beautiful valley and gallops off with a herd of mustangs. When all the media attention turns Sonny and the horse into pop culture heroes, the greedy corporation drops the charges against the cowboy to avoid a public relations disaster.

In keeping with the traditional western formula, the good guys—or, in this case, the good guy, good gal, and good horse—win big in *The Electric Horseman*. They find success, redemption, and happiness in the beautiful mythic West. The rhinestone cowboy and hard-nosed reporter find peace through their simple unselfish act of giving a beautiful animal his freedom. The moment of redemption becomes evident on the silver screen as the magnificent horse gallops off into the untamed wilderness. By journey's end, Sonny and Hallie have likewise found freedom by discarding superficial values and returning to the basics. Rejecting anything phony, they even decide to call themselves by their real names—Norman and Alice.

As the couple's odyssey into the mythic West unfolds, they defeat enemies that include greedy corporate bosses, the ubiquitous media in search of higher ratings, and high-tech police forces. In effect, Sonny and Hallie fight back against the oppressive forces of modernity. Personifying individualism and the Old West, the two reject the corrupting influences of capitalism and win the race against modern technology, including cars, trucks, motorcycles, helicopters, and electronic communications. All the while, the common people rise up in support. Nationwide, the public cheers them on as their flight to freedom becomes a media event. A farmer (Wilford Brimley) aids their escape. When Sonny tries to thank him for forgoing the fifty-thousand-dollar cash reward that the corporation was offering for their capture, the honest and decent farmer (who represents the goodness of everyday Americans) just smiles and replies, "You'd better get up over the mountain before it comes to me what I'm passing up."

Sydney Pollack's contemporary western resonated with contemporary audiences for other reasons. In keeping with popular attitudes of the seventies, it took a stand against greedy corporations and the phoniness of society and culture. It featured an independent career woman who could be just as rugged, heroic, and sexually active as the accomplished cowboy. It showcased environmental issues and better treatment of animals. And it plugged into the era's growing fondness for country music. Not only did country superstar Willie Nelson play a role in the film as Sonny's friend, but two of Willie's songs were featured prominently in the soundtrack. "Mamas, Don't Let Your Babies Grow Up to Be Cowboys" plays in the beginning over images of a drunken Sonny Steele, while "My Heroes Have Always Been Cowboys" plays in the background as a rejuvenated Sonny leads the horse to safety.

The Electric Horseman showed audiences that the mythic West was still relevant in modern America. Just as Sonny and Hallie found success and redemption by adhering to traditional values, so could contemporary Americans. The good life represented by the mythic West could be had by rejecting unrestrained capitalism, media hype, and the corruption and phoniness of contemporary society and culture. That message comes through loud and clear at the end of the movie when Sonny explains his plans for the future. "I'm gonna get movin' on," he says. "Find me something simple. Hard maybe, but plain and quiet." The notion of getting back to the basics made good sense to many moviegoers as the tumultuous seventies came to a close.

* * *

By the end of the seventies, neotraditional westerns like *The Electric Horseman* (1979) were surging in popularity while revisionist westerns faded from the scene. The reemergence of neotraditional westerns, which reflected continuity and reaffirmed traditional beliefs, suggested that the tumult of the sixties and early seventies was finally over. Americans once again were turning to the mythic West for hope and solutions. Their return to traditional values and myths was symptomatic of larger forces at play in America of the late seventies. Just as western movie fans turned increasingly to old-fashioned heroes and themes, many Americans looked to conservative values and solutions as a respite from the sixties era. Coincidental or not, the political leader who would play a major role in the nation's renewal got his start as an actor in old-fashioned western movies. The growing popularity of neotraditional westerns after 1975 anticipated the rise of Ronald Reagan and his "New Morning in America."

CHAPTER TEN

Silverado

The Mythic West at Century's End

Silverado. The very name of the 1985 movie evokes the mythic West. The exotic-sounding yet unspecified western locale implies potential for immense wealth and opportunity. Maybe even a new life in an exciting land.

A movie poster suggests the adventure to be found on the road to Silverado. "A dangerous place in a lawless time," reads the tagline at the top, "Til four friends risked all to make things right." At the center are four young cowboys. Headshots of two of them are on the top. The one on the right has a determined look on his square-jawed face and is wearing a white cowboy hat; the guy on the left is an amiable-looking bearded cowboy wearing a black hat with a fancy headband. Their friends, poised for action, are directly below. A black cowboy holds a cocked rifle on his shoulder, ready for trouble. Slightly below is the last member of the cowboy team. He's a handsome young man with dark wavy hair and the only one without a cowboy hat. Wearing a fringed buckskin shirt with a red bandanna, he's holding two six-guns pointed ominously at bad guys. Below are assorted western images, including the four cowboys galloping on horses and a wagon train riding off in the distance. Two striking western women grace the poster's center-bottom position. The background is lit up by heavenly clouds with glorious golden rays of sunshine spotlighting the heroes. At the bottom in large western-style font is the name of the movie—*Silverado*. And directly below is a caption that beckons prospective viewers: "Ride with them to the adventure of your life!"

Westerns made during the eighties and nineties rode various trails to their own Silverado. Traditional westerns, such as *Pale Rider* (1985) and

Figure 28. The clouds part as the sun spotlights four western heroes in this poster for *Silverado* (Delphi III Productions/Columbia Pictures, 1985).

Tombstone (1993), that followed well-traveled roads toward the mythic West surged in popularity after 1980. Movies that took revisionist paths also found success. Films such as *Dances with Wolves* (1990) and *Unforgiven* (1992) used the western myth as a jumping-off-point to comment on society and the times. In both cases, these traditional and revisionist westerns showed that the mythic West was still a potent force in American life as the country headed toward a new millennium.

Dueling Visions of the Mythic West

In 1980, two major westerns were released. *Urban Cowboy* was a phenomenal box office hit; *Heaven's Gate* became the quintessential Hollywood bomb. Their contrasting approaches epitomize the two types of westerns that would be produced during the last two decades of the twentieth century. The upbeat *Urban Cowboy* followed a traditional western formula and reinforced the notion of the mythic West. The bleak *Heaven's Gate* took a revisionist approach that attacked the western myth. The public's reaction to the two films in 1980 anticipated the results of that year's presidential election. Just as moviegoers voiced their support for the traditional western at the box office, American voters would select the conservative westerner, Ronald Reagan, in the voting booth. After decades of turmoil and tremendous social and political change, Americans once again were turning to traditional values and familiar myths to save the day.

The movie poster for *Urban Cowboy* made it clear that this was going to be a traditional western with a conservative outlook. The caption on top reads: "Hard hat days and honky-tonk nights." In the center stands the tall, dark, and handsome star of the movie, John Travolta. Dressed like a cowboy, he leans against a bar with a bottle of beer in his hand and looks ready for anybody or anything that comes his way. The star's name and the title of the film are directly below. Both are underscored by the Houston skyline and a prominent set of Texas Longhorns.[1]

The contemporary western begins with Travolta's character, Bud, leaving his family's ranch in rural Texas and driving his pickup to the big city, where he hopes to land a high-paying job at one of Houston's booming oil refineries. Upon his arrival, he goes to stay with his Uncle Bob's family. That night, Bob and his wife, Corene, take Bud to Gilley's, a huge dance hall/saloon that Bob describes as "three acres of concrete pasture." All the men are dressed in tight jeans, western shirts, cowboy boots, and cowboy hats, while the ladies are prettied up as cowgirls in revealing halter tops, fringed blouses, tight jeans, boots, and cowboy hats.

Bud's new life soon takes shape. During the day, he works as a laborer at the same refinery as his uncle; at night he heads to Gilley's to drink, dance, and flirt with pretty cowgirls. Unknown to him, a young woman named Sissy (Debra Winger) has had her eye on him since his first night there. One evening she sees Travolta's handsome cowboy character leaning against the bar. His appearance recalls John Wayne's magnificent entrance in John Ford's western *Stagecoach* (1939). There stands Travolta in a tapered western shirt, tight jeans, cowboy boots, and a striking cowboy hat, ready for any action that comes his way. Sissy sashays up to him and starts a conversation. "You a real cowboy?" she asks. "Well," he replies, "that depends on what you think a real cowboy is." After a pause, she asks him if he knows how to dance the Texas two-step. When he says "You bet," she replies, "Wanna prove it?" The two head for the dance floor and meld together as one. It's love at first dance, and the two become inseparable. Shortly thereafter, Bud and Sissy get married. They continue going to Gilley's, where they socialize with friends, dance, drink beer, and try out all the latest games. When the honky-tonk installs a new mechanical bull, Sissy wants to give it a ride. But Bud insists it's not for girls.

With the issue of the mechanical bull unresolved, the couple continues frequenting Gilley's. One evening an ex-con named Wes (Scott Glenn) shows up and begins flirting with Sissy. One thing leads to another, and Wes and Bud have it out in the parking lot, where Bud winds up on the losing end. Next morning, the beaten and bruised Bud goes to work, while Sissy secretly heads to Gilley's, where Wes (who now works at the saloon) teaches her how to ride the bull. That afternoon, Bud almost gets killed at work when he slips on a scaffold two hundred feet off the ground. Distraught, he comes home early, but his wife is nowhere to be found. Aunt Corene shows up to see if he's okay and is appalled when she sees all the dirty dishes and condition of the trailer, exclaiming, "Damn Bud, ya'll live like pigs!"

When Sissy finally comes home, she is surprised to learn about Bud's accident and lies about where she's been. When the couple goes to Gilley's that night, Bud learns that Sissy has defied him by riding the bull and is furious. He angrily challenges her to do it again. When her ride is over, he hops on and rides it at a higher speed. The operator, Wes, cranks it up even higher and Bud is thrown off. As he is getting up, Wes whips the mechanical beast around, hitting Bud and breaking his forearm.

Bud and Sissy go home and argue. The furious Bud throws her out of the trailer. Next time they meet is at Gilley's. Each has gone there separately; neither is willing to make up. When Bud hooks up with a beautiful woman, the competitive Sissy pairs off with Wes. Their marriage deteriorates rapidly. Bud continues seeing the woman, Pam, the daughter of a rich oilman. Meanwhile, Sissy moves into Wes's dilapidated trailer. Sissy finally realizes that her marriage will fail unless one of them compromises, so she goes home, cleans up the mess in the trailer, and leaves a note telling Bud she misses him and wants him to meet her at Gilley's. Bud never gets her message because Pam destroys the note and takes credit for all the cleaning.

As the couple's marriage continues its downward spiral, Bud learns that Gilley's is going to stage a mechanical bull rodeo with a five-thousand-dollar prize. Winning the contest, Bud realizes, could enable him to win back Sissy and provide the money to buy a ranch out in the country. So

Bud asks his Uncle Bob, who used to be a rodeo performer, to help him improve his riding skills and style. During the weeks that he's practicing, both Bud and Sissy are living a lie. Though they still love each other, neither is willing to take the first step toward reconciliation. As Bud gets more deeply involved in his loveless liaison with Pam, Sissy sinks deeper into an abusive relationship with Wes. All the while, Uncle Bob advises Bud to go after the woman he loves. "You know, Bud, sometimes even a cowboy's gotta swallow his pride to hold on to somebody he loves."

Shortly before the rodeo contest is scheduled to take place, Bud and his uncle are working at the refinery on a stormy night. Just as Uncle Bob climbs up on a scaffold, a bolt of lightning hits, killing him and causing a fire. At the funeral, the distraught Bud tells his aunt that he won't be taking part in the rodeo, but the widowed Corene won't have any of that. She gives Bud a silver rodeo buckle that his uncle wanted him to have for good luck and tells him that he has to compete for both his and Bob's sake. Convinced, Bud shows up for the mechanical bull contest with a determined look on his face and the beautiful Pam on his arm. His main competition is the veteran rider Wes, accompanied by Sissy. When Bud defeats Wes in the final round, the angry ex-con decides to rob Gilley's box office and flee to Mexico with Sissy. When Sissy refuses to leave town, he punches her in the face and forces her to pack. He then orders her to wait in the car, while he goes into the building with a gun.

Meanwhile, as Bud picks up his award on Gilley's stage, Pam realizes that his practicing and winning were motivated by his love for Sissy. "I have to tell you something," she says to Bud. "Remember when you came home . . . and the trailer was all clean and flowers around? I didn't do that. Sissy did it. She was there. She left you a note asking you to phone her. I tore it up, 'cause . . . I wanted to keep my cowboy." Bud immediately charges out to find his true love.

Bud finds Sissy in the getaway car. He declares his love and apologizes for all his previous actions. As she jumps out of the car and rushes into his arms, he notices her bruised face. "What happened to your face?" he asks. "Got hit," she replies meekly. The furious Bud then goes after Wes for a showdown. He finds him coming out of the box office, hits him in the face, and follows up with several ferocious punches. As Wes collapses to the floor, both the gun and the stolen loot fly out of his jacket. Wes is arrested, and Bud and Sissy head off to live happily ever after on the Texas ranch Bud plans to buy with his award money.

Although set in modern America, *Urban Cowboy* is an old-fashioned western. Directed by James Bridges, the movie follows the traditional western formula every step of the way. It takes place in the wide open spaces of Texas and features a rugged cowboy hero who is an updated version of Owen Wister's *The Virginian*. He's tall, dark, and handsome, and excels at every athletic activity he tries, including dancing, fighting, and riding a mechanical bull. A natural man, he's not overly educated but is street smart. Bud's story is a reaffirmation of old-fashioned white Anglo-Saxon Protestant culture. He adheres to Christian beliefs and traditional middle-class values, and his ultimate goal is nothing short of the American Dream. For him, success is settling down with his wife and raising a family on a small ranch they can call their own. Like the Ringo Kid, Shane, and other traditional western heroes, Bud defeats his evil nemesis in a classic showdown, albeit in a modern Houston honky-tonk rather than a dusty saloon in the Old West. And, of course, Travolta's hero finds opportunity, success, and redemption in his postmodern mythic West.

Following the lead of other neotraditional westerns, *Urban Cowboy* updates the mythic West. Pickup trucks replace horses; mechanical bulls take the place of bucking Brahmans; oil refineries substitute for ranches; a modern honky-tonk stands in for the old saloon; and dancing replaces horseback riding as a way for cowboys to show off. In addition, old cowboy clothes are traded for trendy eighties versions of fancy cowboy hats, boots, and tailored shirts for the guys, and for the girls, equally fashionable and sexy western cowgirl outfits replete with cowboy hats.

Urban Cowboy features a modern western heroine who reflects the independent woman of the eighties. Debra Winger's character wears a cowboy hat and boots and holds her own against men. Throughout most of the film, the competitive Sissy wants to do all the things that Bud does. When he scores big on a new electronic punching bag that measures the strength of each punch, she takes a swing at it, bruising her knuckles. When Gilley's installs a mechanical bull, Bud immediately gives it a ride. After he is thrown, she wants to try, too, but Bud insists it's not for girls. "Now, you gotta learn something," he explains. "There are just certain things a girl can't do." Sissy snaps back, "Name one." Her later behavior shows that she refuses to give an inch to males. Sissy flirts with the opposite sex when Bud does, and when he goes off to have an affair with Pam, she matches him by having an affair with Wes.

Even though the movie endorses the era's new liberated women, it cautions that women should not push the boundaries too far. Sissy's insistence on total equality results in the near breakup of her marriage and a dangerous situation where Bud, in the tradition of the Old West, has to rescue her from the evil Wes. Ultimately, there is a message for both sexes: Sissy and Bud have to compromise if their marriage is to succeed. He apologizes for his earlier misogynistic behavior and says she can ride the mechanical bull, while she promises to be a good wife, cook, and clean house. For good measure, she adds that she doesn't want to ride the bull anymore.

Urban Cowboy proved that the mythic West was still relevant in modern times. People across the country raved about the movie. Soon, all of America seemed caught up in Urban Cowboy mania. Cowboy hats, boots, and other western clothes became the new fashion trend. Honky-tonk dance halls patterned after Gilley's—complete with mechanical bulls—popped up everywhere. Before long, the Texas two-step had replaced the hustle and other disco dances, as songs from *Urban Cowboy*'s soundtrack became top pop hits.

The movie showed Americans that they could succeed by getting back to the basics as represented by old-fashioned cowboys, country music, and life's simple pleasures, including love and family values. Even one of the film's most popular songs—Johnny Lee's "Lookin' for Love (In All the Wrong Places)"—seemed to suggest that throughout the tumultuous sixties and seventies, people were seeking happiness in all the wrong ways. The conservative message of *Urban Cowboy* resonated with Americans on the eve of a presidential election. The film's phenomenal impact at the box office, as well as on American culture, offers evidence that the mood of the nation was changing by 1980. Traditional values and the mythic West were making a comeback, riding the same conservative wave that would bring to the White House a traditional westerner and former movie cowboy, Ronald Reagan.

* * *

If *Urban Cowboy* pumped high octane into the mythic West, another film from 1980—Michael Cimino's highly anticipated *Heaven's Gate*—almost slammed the brakes on the West's momentum. Fresh off his success with *The Deer Hunter* (1978), a Vietnam War film that won five Oscars including Best Picture and Best Director, Cimino was determined to make an epic about the West that would juxtapose the beauty and promise of that mythic land against the reality of social class warfare. Costing more than 40 million dollars to make, the movie grossed less than 3.5 million.

Heaven's Gate was released in November 1980 and ran into immediate problems. Viewers found the 219-minute-long movie bloated, pretentious, and tiresome. "The ridiculous scenes are endless," wrote Roger Ebert. "This movie is [money] thrown to the winds. It is the most scandalous cinematic waste I have ever seen, and remember, I've seen *Paint Your Wagon*."[2] The studio immediately withdrew the film from circulation and ordered the director to cut it back to a more reasonable 149 minutes. But the eviscerated re-release did equally bad at the box office, driving the parent studio United Artists out of business. To this day, *Heaven's Gate* is synonymous with Hollywood bomb. In retrospect, though, Cimino's western is not as bad as common wisdom suggests, and it reveals a great deal about the times in which it was made.

The original version begins with a graduation ceremony at Harvard University in 1870. James Averill (Kris Kristofferson) and Billy Irvine (John Hurt), two of the student leaders of the Class of '70, are at the forefront of the pomp and circumstance. As the male students run around campus in joyous celebration, their girlfriends, including Kristofferson's beautiful young lady friend, watch in admiration. Cimino's point—which could have been made in two or three minutes rather than the twenty-plus minutes it takes to complete the scene—is abundantly clear: these frivolous college boys are members of an elite class.

Fast-forward twenty years. Jim Averill is now a sheriff out west in Wyoming. European immigrants are flooding into the area, and Wyomingites are not pleased. The wealthy ranchers, businessmen, and town leaders who comprise the Wyoming Stock Growers Association meet in their elegant wood-paneled club to discuss the crisis. Their leader, Frank Canton (Sam Waterston), is convinced that the foreigners are cattle thieves and anarchists who are ruining the American way of life. He proposes a plan of action, which he says has the support of the governor, state legislature, and even the president. Canton wants to recruit an army of ranchers and hired gunmen to march against the rustlers and anarchists. He even has a list of 125 individuals who will be targeted and killed. Only one member of the organization, Jim's old college friend, Billy Irvine, questions the proposal's legality, but he is quickly voted down.

When Billy reveals the plan to Averill, the sheriff attempts to stop the plot. But the association is unmoved by his arguments on behalf of immigrants. Canton dismisses Averill as a traitor to his class and points out that the sheriff has no jurisdiction in this case since the plan has been approved by the state government. Realizing he can't stop the imminent attack, Averill rides out to the immigrants' town to warn them about the danger. He explains the situation to the town's mayor (Paul Koslo) and local businessman John L. Bridges (Jeff Bridges), who is a close friend. He encourages his immigrant lover, a prostitute named Ella Watson (Isabelle Huppert), to leave Johnson County before it's too late. And he rebukes local resident Nate Champion (Christopher Walken), because Nate was hired by the Stock Growers Association to stop immigrants from rustling cattle. Not surprisingly, the defenseless immigrants are terrified. But, still, they refuse to believe that such a brutal attack could occur in the Land of the Free.

The situation worsens once Canton and his hired guns arrive on the scene and begin murdering innocent people. Several of Canton's men even show up at Ella's brothel and begin to gang rape the woman, who supposedly has been accepting stolen cattle in return for sexual favors. Jim arrives in the midst of the violent act and kills the perpetrators. Again he encourages Ella to leave town, but she refuses to abandon her friends and home. When Nate Champion, who also loves Ella, learns about the rape, he immediately rides out to Canton's camp and shoots the man responsible. After Champion tells Canton that he had better have warrants for all the immigrants being targeted, Canton reminds him, "My grandfather was the secretary of war to Harrison. His brother was the governor of the state of New York. My brother-in-law is secretary of state. And to you, I represent the full authority of the government of the United States and the president." Canton warns Champion not to get in the way, and to prove his point, he cold-bloodedly shoots an immigrant prisoner in the head.

The Wyoming frontier erupts in violence. Canton's men butcher defenseless civilians and even target Nate Champion. They set fire to his cabin, kill two of his friends, and then pump numerous rounds of bullets into him as he charges from the cabin with guns blazing in a futile attempt to take as many of the attackers with him as possible. The enraged immigrants try to fight back. With more determination than skill, the ragtag collection of poorly armed men and women charge forward on horses, in buggies, and on work wagons. The ensuing battle is a virtual slaughter, and the immigrants are forced to retreat. One of the few casualties among Canton's men is Billy Irvine, ironically the only rancher sympathetic to the immigrants' plight. The immigrants soon regroup. John Bridges shows them how to use logs to construct siege wagons similar to those used centuries before by Roman soldiers. Averill arrives and joins the immigrants as they push the siege wagons toward the entrenched invaders. Just when it appears that the immigrants might win, the cavalry rides to the rescue of the invaders. Averill is furious and tries to arrest Canton and his men for murder, but the military officer intervenes. He points out that Canton's force was operating under legal orders from the government, and Averill will be shot for insurrection if he tries to prevent the soldiers from escorting Canton and his men to safety.

The next scene takes place shortly thereafter. Averill is in Ella's cabin waiting for her to finish dressing. At last, she is leaving the area. As she and Jim walk outside, they are met by John Bridges. Suddenly, gunshots ring out, and Ella and John fall to the ground dead. Jim looks up and sees Frank Canton and two others at the top of the hill, and he quickly fires back, killing the evil Canton. He then falls to his knees and weeps as he hugs Ella's bloody corpse.

Fast-forward to 1903. Jim Averill, clean shaven and dressed in his finest clothes, is standing on the deck of his yacht off the coast of Newport. He goes below into an elegant room, where he is greeted by his wife, who decades before was the beautiful young lady who danced with and admired young Jim at his Harvard graduation. The two have little to say to each other, and Jim seems preoccupied with thoughts about his lost love and lost innocence on the frontier. The movie began with a young James Averill graduating from Harvard and looking toward a hopeful future. It ends with an older, more pessimistic Jim. After failing to protect the poor and innocent, he has returned to a life of leisure as a member of the upper class.

Heaven's Gate is an excellent example of a revisionist western. It drives home the point that the mythic West—despite its promises of success, opportunity, and redemption—offered only false hope and devastation for common people. Cimino's film was a visual and audio feast that transported viewers back in time. Featuring the stunning cinematography of Vilmos Zsigmond, the film serves up breathtaking images of the Rocky Mountain West, which provide a stark counterpoint to the movie's dark plot, violence, and brutality. The musical score adds to the dreamlike feel. Together, the visuals and sounds create memorable scenes that alone are worth the price of admission. The Harvard graduation scene includes elegant couples whirling around in circles on the campus green as they waltz to the Blue Danube, while a later scene of lower-class musicians and immigrants dancing and swirling around on roller skates in a crowded arena depicts an equally celebratory if more modest event. At the same time, bloody and graphic images of rape, brutality, and violence capture the darker side of the western experience. The film's powerful visual message is clear: the West—despite its extraordinary beauty—was anything but a land of freedom and opportunity for the lower classes.

Heaven's Gate undercuts the mythic West in other ways. There is no victory or success for hardworking ordinary people in Cimino's West. Instead, only broken dreams and depressing outcomes await innocent victims on this brutal frontier. The film turns the established notion of westerns as morality plays inside out as the bad guys readily defeat the good guys. The rugged westerners who pulled themselves up by their own cowboy boot straps to become successful ranchers and businessmen wind up the villains of this western drama. These high-profile westerners don't even wear cowboy hats (indeed, cowboy hats—the quintessential symbol of the Old West—are nowhere to be found in this film). Instead, the western cattlemen are outfitted in business suits and hats more suitable for city life back east. These cattle barons become corrupt examples of modernity rather than representatives of the Old West. Even the common people are not typical westerners. They are dressed like the European immigrants they are. Instead of Conestoga wagons drawn by horses or oxen, they push two-wheeled hand carts on their journey west. And when they arrive at their Wyoming destination, the crowded street looks more like an immigrant scene from New York City's Hester Street than one in a western town.

Heaven's Gate lays out a revisionist interpretation of American history. The plot revolves around an actual historical incident, the Johnson County War, which pitted large cattle ranchers in Wyoming against a loose coalition of smaller ranchers, homesteaders, and rustlers. But Cimino's film distorts the event. Instead of dealing with the actual issue of cattle rustling and class tensions among American-born settlers on the Wyoming frontier, Cimino transforms the event into social class warfare between wealthy Americans and impoverished European immigrants who had come west in search of the American Dream. Cimino plays loose with known facts about some of the real-life figures featured in the movie. Jim Averill and Ella Watson, for example, were in love as suggested in the film, but in real life the two lived on a farm together and were hanged at the outset of the fighting. Unlike the movie character, the real-life Averill was a homesteader, while Ella was known as Cattle Kate because she allegedly built her herd by bartering sexual services in exchange for stolen cattle. The historical Nate Champion was a trail boss and small-time rancher who was killed for rustling cattle. And, although he was indeed shot by the invaders while fleeing from his burning cabin, the standoff lasted twelve hours rather than just the few minutes depicted in the movie.[3]

Heaven's Gate actually reveals more about the times in which it was made than it does about the history of the Johnson County War. Reflecting trends of the seventies, the movie includes full-frontal nudity, explicit sex, graphic rape, and plenty of violence. Picking up on Watergate and cynical attitudes toward the Establishment, Cimino's film depicts Wyoming's governor, state legislature, businessmen, and even the country's president and U.S. Army officers as corrupt or callous officials who disregard the Constitution and run roughshod over the rights of the people.

The movie mirrors the polarization in the seventies between liberals and conservatives. Like liberals who protested Vietnam or stood up for civil rights, the sympathetic liberal in the movie, Jim Averill, fails to end the "war" and can't protect innocent lower-class people from the Establishment. Defeated, he forgoes activism and returns to his comfortable upper-class lifestyle. One military man, sounding very much like a seventies' conservative blasting the alleged hypocrisy of liberals, tells Averill: "Do you know what I really dislike about you, Jim? You're a rich man with a good name. You only pretend to be poor."

In retrospect, *Heaven's Gate* does not deserve its reputation as a horrible movie. Granted, it was in desperate need of good editing and was not historically accurate, but the plot was adequate and a lot better than many westerns. More important, the cinematography is nothing short of magnificent, and the stunning images capture the beauty and feel of the mythic West. The movie also accomplished Cimino's revisionist goal. It used the mythic West in a new way to critique contemporary American society and politics. Unfortunately, the film was released the same month that Ronald Reagan was elected president. Clearly, the film's message was out of sync with the mood of the nation. While Cimino was focusing on the brutality and injustice in America's past and blasting the mythic West with his film's ironic title, *Heaven's Gate*, the United States was turning to a more optimistic westerner who represented traditional myths. During Reagan's campaign for the presidency, the former governor from a western state and veteran good guy in numerous westerns told voters, "Let's make America great again." Four years later, President Reagan declared that the nation had returned to glory and greatness, explaining, "It's morning again in America." Little wonder that Cimino's dark vision of America failed. By the early eighties, moviegoers wanted upbeat westerns to reflect America's optimism and traditional myths. Hollywood was more than happy to comply.

On the Road to Silverado

Neotraditional westerns surged in popularity after 1980. The tagline for Lawrence Kasdan's *Silverado* (1985) was downright retro in its approach: "Four strangers became friends. Four friends became heroes. On the road to . . . Silverado." Kasdan's cowboys ride into the town of Silverado and join forces to defeat assorted bad guys, including a greedy cattle baron, corrupt sheriff, and sleazy gambler. The movie captured the spirit of old-fashioned westerns. While its bombastic soundtrack evoked sounds of the mythic West, the cinematography portrayed the Old West as a magnificent land of majestic mountains and wide open spaces. The familiar setting included all the expected props, including saloons, six-guns, cowboy hats, and lively horses.

In keeping with the western formula, *Silverado* featured peerless good guys and pure evil bad guys. The cowboy heroes include Emmett (Scott Glenn), Jake (Kevin Costner), Paden (Kevin Kline), and Mal (Danny Glover). The taciturn Emmett rode a white horse, was a crack shot, and had been in jail for five years for killing a corrupt cattle baron who was about to shoot his brother in the back. The handsome Jake was Emmett's hot-headed young brother. He rode a pinto and was fast on the draw with his two ivory-handled six-guns. The sensitive Paden was a skilled gunman and reformed gambler and outlaw, who identified with underdogs, helped those in need, and loved his bay horse and stray dogs. And the proud Mal was a black cowboy who rode a brown horse, was expert with a rifle, and stood his ground against racism. Opposing the good guys was a gang of bad guys led by three villains. McKendrick (Ray Baker) was a power-hungry cattle baron who would stop at nothing to drive homesteaders off their lands; Cobb (Brian Dennehy) was a corrupt sheriff who was getting rich from bribes and extortion; and Slick (Jeff Goldblum) was a sleazy gambler, who cheated at cards and abused his prostitute girlfriend.

The movie begins with a camera shot of cowboy boots and a six-gun in a holster, immediately evoking the mythic West. Emmett is asleep in a cabin. Suddenly, bad guys burst in and try to kill him, but he's faster on the draw and guns down his assailants. Emmett climbs on his horse and rides off, eventually teaming up with the three other cowboys. Together, they defeat the forces of evil in the town of Silverado. Emmett and Jake protect their sister and her family from McKendrick's machinations; Mal avenges the murder of his parents and saves his sister from the bad guys; and Paden protects defenseless women and innocent bystanders. The good guys' resounding victory results in new opportunities and redemption for the heroes. The two brothers ride off into the sunset, bound for a new life in California; Mal rescues his sister from a life of prostitution, and together they begin life anew; and Paden becomes the sheriff of Silverado to ensure that the town will have lasting peace and justice.

At the same time, *Silverado* tweaks the western formula to fit the times. Some of the updates are just cosmetic, such as cowboys wearing the long drover coats that were popular in westerns of the late sixties and seventies. But other changes are more substantive. Women characters, such as the successful businesswoman Stella (Linda Hunt) and the independent homesteader Hannah (Rosanna Arquette), are portrayed as smart, tough, and liberated, in keeping with the higher profile of women in eighties America. The movie also features a black cowboy hero, Mal, who displays courage and determination and proves that he is the equal of any man when it comes to using his wits, fists, or guns. Even though the movie reflects social change, it is influenced by conservative politics of the eighties. In keeping with Ronald Reagan's mantra that the government was the problem not the solution, the film targets a corrupt sheriff, sleazy politicians, and evil ranchers, gamblers, and other businessmen.

Silverado evoked the spirit of the Old West. Like many westerns released after 1980, it depicts the West as a legendary place where cowboys and other colorful characters can find opportunity, success, and redemption. These neotraditional westerns offer solid evidence that the mythic West was alive and well in the mid-eighties.[4]

Veteran movie cowboys and new western stars both jumped on the neotraditional bandwagon. Clint Eastwood, who had achieved movie stardom with a string of revisionist westerns in the sixties and seventies, continued his box office success in 1985 by directing and starring in a neotraditional western, *Pale Rider*. The film was clearly influenced by Eastwood's revisionist roots. Like *High Plains Drifter* (1973), it features an early shot of Eastwood's enigmatic character riding into town. The ending likewise evokes the earlier film, as Eastwood's mysterious character rides away, fading into a blizzard just as the high plains drifter disappeared in shimmering waves of heat. Sergio Leone's influences are evident throughout. Eastwood plays the same type of inscrutable Man with No Name character introduced in *A Fistful of Dollars* (1964). Director Eastwood, like his mentor, uses eerie music as well as sounds such as thundering hooves and a creaking lantern to create certain moods.

Despite the revisionist trappings, *Pale Rider* is a traditional western that features a moral good guy and a classic struggle between good and evil. In the opening scene, a malicious gang rides through a peaceful village made up of small-time miners and their families. The marauders set fire to homes, kill livestock, beat men, and terrify women and children. A fifteen-year-old girl named Megan Wheeler (Sydney Penny) is horrified when the raiders brutally gun down her dog. Later, as she buries the pet, she prays for a miracle to help her community. Her mother, Sarah (Carrie Snodgress), her mother's fiancé, Hull Barret (Michael Moriarty), and the other miners are being driven out by Coy LaHood (Richard Dysart), the unscrupulous owner of the area's largest mining company. Just as Megan's prayer ends, the camera shows Eastwood's character riding a pale horse through the mountains toward town.

Next day, Hull rides his buckboard into town to replenish supplies destroyed in the raid. As he is loading goods onto his wagon, several of LaHood's men begin beating him with hickory clubs. Suddenly, Eastwood's character appears out of nowhere. Grabbing a club, he knocks out LaHood's men. The grateful miner invites his savior back to the mining village. As Hull and the stranger ride into the camp, Megan is reading the Bible to her mother: "And when he had opened the fourth seal, I heard the fourth beast say: 'Come and see.' And I looked, and beheld a pale horse. And his name that sat on him was Death. And Hell followed with him." At that precise moment, her mother looks out the window and sees Eastwood riding up on a pale gray Appaloosa. The eerie coincidence causes Sarah to ask Hull to send Eastwood away. She backs off when the stranger arrives for dinner dressed in a clergyman's outfit. The "Preacher" then says grace before sharing a meal with Hull, Sarah, and Megan.

Meanwhile, LaHood is also concerned about the mystery man who used a hickory club to outfight his best men. Initially, he tries to bribe the Preacher, simultaneously warning him that he plans to hire the infamous gunman Stockburn (John Russell) to drive out the miners. The Preacher refuses the money and points out that it will cost LaHood far less to simply buy out the miners. When LaHood agrees, the Preacher takes the offer to the miners. But Hull and his friends refuse to go along with the deal. They are determined to hold onto their dreams for success in the West even if it means fighting for their rights. LaHood then hires Stockburn and his six gunmen to get rid of the Preacher and the miners once and for all. When LaHood describes the Preacher, the gunslinger says he sounds just like a man he once knew. But it couldn't be, adds Stockburn, because that man is dead.

The situation rapidly deteriorates. When LaHood's vicious son, Josh, tries to rape Megan, the Preacher comes to her rescue. When Josh goes for his gun, the Preacher shoots a bullet through his gun hand. Meanwhile, one of the miners discovers a huge gold nugget in the creek near the village. When he and his son go to town to celebrate, the miner is shot dead by Stockburn and his gunmen. As the boy takes his father's body away, Stockburn tells him to tell the Preacher to come to town tomorrow morning for a showdown.

Back in the miners' village that evening, Sarah goes to see the Preacher and confesses that she loves him. Knowing that he will soon leave town, she explains that she will marry Hull as planned. When she opens the cabin door to leave, the Preacher hears a voice somewhere out in the wilderness calling his name (presumably for his showdown with evil). He asks Sarah to close the door, and they have sex.

Next morning, the Preacher heads to town for the showdown with Stockburn and his men. Hull volunteers to go along, and the two first stop by LaHood's hydraulic mining camp, which they destroy with dynamite. After the Preacher chases Hull's horse away to prevent his friend from taking part in the showdown, he rides into town alone. When several of LaHood's men try to ambush him, he callously shoots them down. Next, Stockburn and his six men come after him, but the Preacher picks them off one by one. Finally, the only two left standing are Stockburn and the Preacher. As Eastwood's dark character approaches him, Stockburn realizes to his horror that the Preacher is . . . the dead man. The desperate Stockburn goes for his gun, but the Preacher is too fast and shoots him several times, leaving the same circle of bullet holes in Stockburn's chest that the Preacher had on his own back. The Preacher's final shot hits Stockburn right between the eyes, just as the evil gunman had killed the miner the day before.

LaHood had watched the gunfight from the safety of his office. As he raises his shotgun to bushwhack the Preacher, Hull suddenly charges in and shoots LaHood dead. When the gun smoke clears, the Preacher says good-bye to Hull and rides off. Just then, Megan comes rushing into town on a buckboard. When she learns that the Preacher has left for good, she looks out at the trail and shouts out that she loves him. The camera then shifts to the Preacher riding off into the mountains from which he came. As eerie music plays, the mysterious stranger is enveloped by a blizzard and the screen fades to white.

Pale Rider supports the mythic West on numerous levels. The cinematography highlights the beauty of the wilderness with its rugged mountains, crystal blue creeks, and pure white snow. The plot focuses on a good guy who comes to town to kill the bad guys and help ordinary people realize their dreams of finding success in the West. In traditional western fashion, the movie is a morality play. The allegory features a moralistic "Preacher" who defends the weak and innocent against the unscrupulous businessman LaHood; his brutal son, Josh; and the evil gunslinger Stockburn and his gang of six. As the Preacher stamps out evil and avenges past injustices, he brings redemption to those he rescues. He saves young Megan from being raped by Josh LaHood; he gently refuses her willingness to have sex with him as he teaches her the meaning of true love; he resolves his relationship with Sarah, allowing her to enter into a happy marriage with Hull; and he inspires Hull to stand up to evil and become a better man.

Like other neotraditional westerns, *Pale Rider* alters the western formula to appeal to modern audiences. Following the lead of contemporary movies, it includes plenty of sex and violence. Eastwood's character even does some fancy stick fighting that would have made the era's martial artists proud. The movie also reflects religious trends of the day. As the Reverend Jerry Falwell's Moral Majority and other evangelical or fundamentalist groups gained a higher profile in America during the early eighties, *Pale Rider* alluded to the Book of Revelation and featured a protagonist who was an avenging angel unleashing retribution and smiting evil.

Eastwood's movie picked up on other trends in Reagan's America. The president said in his State of the Union Address in 1985, "Anything is possible in America if we have the faith, the will, and the heart."[5] *Pale Rider* offered Americans a similar message, suggesting that good will always win out over evil and that ordinary people can succeed if they hold onto their dreams. If Eastwood's movie endorsed Reagan's optimism, it questioned the administration's economic and environmental policies. The greedy LaHood showed no ethical qualms about using questionable tactics to crush economic rivals and exploit the working classes. His unscrupulous character probably seemed familiar to viewers in an era of free market economics that witnessed a growing disparity of wealth in America. Similarly, LaHood's willingness to destroy the environment through hydraulic mining did not go unnoticed by audience members concerned about President Reagan's questionable environmental record.[6]

Despite the updates, *Pale Rider* is still a traditional western that portrays the mythic West as a land of opportunity, success, and redemption. The film unabashedly pays homage to classic westerns. Its climactic showdown evokes *High Noon* (1952), while the ending is straight out of *Shane* (1953). Just as young Joey runs after Shane and shouts, "Shane! Come back," the fifteen-year-old Megan runs out to the trail and calls out to Eastwood's departing character. With her voice echoing through the mountains just as Joey's did, the slightly older and more accepting teenager shouts, "Preacher! Preacher! We all love you, Preacher. I love you! Thank you! Good-bye!" In both cases, the good guy defeated evil and then rode off into the mythic West.

Along with featuring veteran stars like Clint Eastwood, neotraditional westerns showcased a new generation of movie cowboys. *Young Guns* (1988), directed by Christopher Cain and written by John Fusco, is a good example. "SIX REASONS WHY THE WEST WAS WILD," reads one movie poster. Below is a

Figure 29. A new generation of hotshot western heroes debuted in *Young Guns* (Morgan Creek Productions/Twentieth Century Fox Film Corporation, 1988).

group portrait of the young costars: Emilio Estevez, Kiefer Sutherland, Charlie Sheen, Lou Diamond Phillips, Dermot Mulroney, and Casey Siemaszko. The handsome young men are staring straight at the camera with determined looks on their faces. Each is wearing a lawman's badge as well as cowboy garb and six-guns. But none is wearing a cowboy hat. They look more like an eighties boy band than rugged western heroes. Yet, their striking appearance suggests that these six neatly dressed, well-coiffed men may be young and may look different from most cowboys, but they mean business.

Young Guns offers an action-packed retelling of the Billy the Kid story. This time around, the colorful gunslinger (Emilio Estevez) is joined by five buddies, who help him fight bad guys and corruption in the Old West. The movie begins with Billy being invited to live and work at the ranch of John Tunstall, a transplanted English gentleman who mentors troubled youths. Billy grows quite close to the other young men at the ranch, as

Tunstall teaches them how to be cowboys, as well as how to read, write, and follow good etiquette. Their lives change dramatically when Tunstall is murdered by a gang led by Lawrence Murphy (Jack Palance), a greedy rancher who is trying to control all the land in the region. The six "young guns" are determined to avenge the death of their mentor but discover that the governor, sheriff, and other officials are too corrupt to bring Murphy and his men to justice.

After a lawyer friend, Alex McSween, gets the six cowboys deputized and secures warrants for the arrests of the murderers, the young guns set off on their mission. Along with punishing those responsible for Tunstall's death, they want to attract the attention of President Rutherford B. Hayes in the hope that he will take action against the corrupt governor, army officers, and businessmen who are putting the squeeze on working-class ranchers and farmers. The young guns call themselves Regulators and track down the murderers one by one, with Billy often shooting rather than arresting them. Despite the attempts by fellow Regulator Dick Brewer (Charlie Sheen) and lawyer McSween to stop Billy from meting out vigilante justice, Billy clearly wants revenge. He's even pleased when newspapers refer to him as Billy the Kid and suggest he's the leader of the gang.

Every victory adds to the Regulators' reputation among the local citizenry, who view them as champions against the corrupt Establishment. But the young guns' bloody actions only make the villainous Murphy and his cronies that much more determined to stop them. When Billy and the boys are tipped off that Murphy's men are going to kill McSween and his wife, they rush to the lawyer's house, where they are surrounded by the rancher and his gang. When numerous soldiers arrive as reinforcements, Doc Scurlock (Kiefer Sutherland) says, "Billy, we're good, but this is getting ridiculous." The arrogant Billy laughs off the concern, saying, "I like these odds." Soon thereafter, the young guns charge out of the house with guns blazing. Billy and the gang kill numerous attackers, while Chavez (Lou Diamond Phillips) brings up the horses. Then, with bullets flying all around, the young guns make a break for it. Billy, Chavez, and Doc (along with Doc's Chinese girlfriend) get away, but the others, including McSween, are shot to death. Before leaving, Billy turns around and fires a long shot at Murphy, killing him instantly with a bullet to the head. The surviving young guns then split up: Chavez goes to California; Doc Scurlock and his girlfriend head to New York City to get married; while Billy the Kid remains in New Mexico to continue his fight against the Establishment.

The huge success of *Young Guns* guaranteed a sequel. John Fusco returned as the scriptwriter of *Young Guns II* (1990), while Geoff Murphy replaced Christopher Cain as director. Reprising their roles from the first film were actors Emilio Estevez (Billy the Kid), Kiefer Sutherland (Doc Scurlock), and Lou Diamond Phillips (Chavez). The sequel completed the tale of Billy the Kid, suggesting that he was not killed by Pat Garrett as common wisdom has it but instead lived to be an old man.

At first glance, both movies seem to be revisionist westerns because they spotlight "young gun" antiheroes, but a closer look reveals that the two films are actually quite traditional in their approach to the mythic West. Unlike revisionist westerns that either demolished the western myth or used familiar western characters in new ways to critique the myth or society, the *Young Guns* movies build on traditional myths as they glorify the Old West as an exciting and exotic land filled with colorful characters. Estevez's Billy the Kid is an old-fashioned western good badman rather than a dark revisionist antihero like Eastwood's Man with No Name. Billy and his friends always fight for a just cause. In the first movie, the young guns are trying to avenge the murder of their mentor and want to save common folk from a corrupt governor, army officers, and businessmen. That legitimate fight against a corrupt Establishment continues in the second movie.

The two *Young Guns* films follow the traditional western formula in other ways. Like previous Robin Hoods of the Old West, Billy and his band of merry men form a bond with each other, as well as with local citizenry who view them as defenders of the weak and innocent. People cheer when they ride into town, and newspapers describe Billy and the gang as heroes in a battle against oppression and corruption. Like good badmen of earlier westerns, the young guns are rugged individuals who are fast on the draw and quick on their feet. They outsmart, outshoot, and outrun corrupt officials and posses until the very end. Even their tragic deaths are in keeping with the code of the Old West. Having lived by the gun, these good badmen die by the gun, paying the ultimate price for their legal and moral transgressions.

Both *Young Guns* films, like other neotraditional westerns, freshened up the mythic West to fit modern times. Obviously, both movies were geared to young audiences. Billy and the gang are youthful, rebellious, carefree, and hedonistic. Like many young people of the 1980s and 1990s, the members of this outlaw fraternity dress in flashy clothes, drink alcohol, do drugs, and engage in sex. No wonder the term "young guns" became a catchphrase to describe the era's rebellious youth. The movies pick up on other social trends. Reflecting the era's multiculturalism and social behavior, Billy's gang features a Native American (Chavez) who practices the traditional vision quest and uses peyote as a hallucinogen. Another gang member, Doc, falls in love with a Chinese woman. The gratuitous violence and sex found in both movies also reflects the times. Even Billy's belief that the ends justify the means is a perfect fit for the "neocon" approach to international affairs that was popular among many conservatives during the eighties and early nineties.

Although the *Young Guns* westerns feature young heroes, they clearly endorse old myths. They demonstrate that the mythic West was alive and well in Reagan's America. The West remained a colorful land of adventure, excitement, and opportunity, where rugged individuals could succeed in the fight for truth, justice, and the American Way. Not only do both films perpetuate western myths, but even the supposedly revisionist premise of *Young Guns II*—that Billy the Kid was not killed by Pat Garrett but survived as Brushy Bill Roberts—is just a rehash of an old legend.[7] The soundtrack for *Young Guns II* underscores the traditional nature of both movies. The mythic West comes through loud and clear as rock star Jon Bon Jovi sings "Blaze of Glory" and other songs that spotlight familiar gunslingers and the Old West. "I'm going out in a blaze of glory," sings Bon Jovi at film's end, "Lord, I never drew first, but I drew first blood. I'm no one's son, call me young gun."[8]

Young Guns I and *II* paved the way for another traditional western that focused on a band of brothers, *Tombstone* (1993). This time, though, they were old-fashioned heroes and actual brothers—Wyatt Earp (Kurt Russell), Virgil Earp (Sam Elliott), and Morgan Earp (Bill Paxton). They were joined in their fight against evil by the infamous Doc Holliday (Val Kilmer). Directed by George P. Cosmatos, the movie begins with flickering clips from earlier westerns, including *The Great Train Robbery*. A narrator (Robert Mitchum) sets the stage with a voice-over that owes more to legend than fact: "1879. The Civil War is over, and the resulting economic explosion spurs the great migration west. Farmers, ranchers, prospectors, killers, and thieves seek their fortune. Cattle growers turn cow towns into armed camps, with murder rates higher than those of modern-day New York or Los Angeles. Out of this chaos comes legendary lawman Wyatt Earp, retiring his badge and gun to start a peaceful life for his family. Earp's friend, John 'Doc' Holliday, a southern gentleman turned gunman and gambler, also travels west, hoping the dry climate would relieve his tuberculosis. Silver is discovered in Arizona. Tombstone becomes queen of the boom towns, where the latest Paris fashions are sold from the backs of wagons. Attracted to this atmosphere of greed, over one hundred exiled Texas outlaws band together to form the ruthless gang recognized by the red sashes they wear. They emerge as the earliest example of organized crime in America. They call themselves "The Cowboys."

Tombstone includes all the familiar myths about Wyatt and his brothers, the tubercular Holliday, and the Gunfight at the O. K. Corral, as well as new details about Wyatt's drug-addicted wife, Mattie; his romance with a free-spirited actress named Josephine Marcus; and the close friendship between Wyatt and Doc. Yet, this is no revisionist take. *Tombstone* is a typical western morality tale that pits Wyatt Earp and other good guys against Ike Clanton's evil gang. Along the way, there is plenty of violence, culminating in Wyatt's glorious shootout with the Clanton gang. At film's end, the narrator underscores Wyatt Earp's place in the pantheon of western heroes: "The Red Sash Cowboy Gang was broken forever. . . . Wyatt and Josephine embarked on a series of adventures. Up or down, thin or flush, in forty-seven years they never left each other's side. Wyatt Earp died in Los Angeles in 1929. Among the pallbearers at his funeral were early western stars William S. Hart and Tom Mix. Tom Mix wept."

Other neotraditional westerns offered new takes on traditional images and themes. *The Mask of Zorro* (1998) put a new spin on the familiar tale by adding Catherine Zeta-Jones to the mix as a brave swashbuckling heroine who outsmarts villains and holds her own in swordfights against men. "Ms. Zeta-Jones makes her first major film role one to remember," wrote Janet Maslin in the *New York Times*. "Her bold, alluring Elena is one of numerous strong movie heroines . . . on screen this summer." Other movies, such as *Three Amigos* (1986), *City Slickers* (1991), *Maverick* (1994), and *Wild, Wild West* (1999), blended comedy with traditional images of the mythic West.[9] Arguably, the most successful was *City Slickers*, which won Jack Palance an Oscar for Best Supporting Actor. The plot revolves around three New York City yuppies whose lives are falling apart. Accustomed to seeking weekend thrills by running with the bulls, skydiving, or some other exciting activity, they sign on for two weeks at a working ranch out west. After a crash course in riding and roping, they and several other participants face real danger on a cattle drive from New Mexico to Colorado. By the end of the trail, the three city slickers more than earn their spurs. They beat back threats from bad guys, stampedes, river crossings, even death, and find happiness and rejuvenation in the mythic West.

Every step of the way, *City Slickers* is powered by the mythic West. Like easterners in days of old, Mitch (Billy Crystal), Phil (Daniel Stern), and Ed (Bruno Kirby) head west to find themselves. Out west, the New Yorkers find a wild and exotic land of majestic snowcapped mountains, green valleys, raging rivers, and wide open spaces. Their experiences are straight out of the annals of the Old West. They dress up in cowboy garb, learn how to ride and rope, and take part in a real cattle drive. They bond with other tourists taking part in the adventure. And they meet authentic western cowboys. The owner of the ranch, Clay Stone, promises they will learn how to be real working cowboys as they escort his herd from New Mexico to Colorado. The crusty old cook in charge of the chuck wagon makes it clear that even the food will be authentic. "You ain't gonna get any nouveau, amandine, thin crust, bottled water, sautéed city food," he explains. "Food's brown, hot, and plenty of it." The trail boss, Curly (Jack Palance), impresses the city slickers the most. They learn quickly not to mess with the surly old cowboy, who has a reputation for killing people with his knife. "That is the toughest man I've ever seen in my life!" declares an incredulous Mitch when he first sees Curly in action. "Did you see how leathery he was? He was like a saddlebag with eyes!"

The city slickers run into bad guys, too. When two drunken cowboys harass Bonnie, one of the tourists on the cattle drive, Mitch intervenes. His wisecracks might have been able to defuse the situation back east, but they only make the rugged cowboys mad. Curly comes to the rescue when he ropes one of the cowboys around the neck and throws a knife close to his crotch. The city slickers had never seen anything like it. "This guy, Curly, is a true cowboy. One of the last real men," notes Ed. "It'll do us good to be in his world for a while." Mitch, not realizing that Curly was walking up behind him, replies, "Do us good? Didn't you guys see? The man was hanging the hired help! And did you notice his eyes? He has crazy eyes. He's a lunatic!" When Mitch notices that his friends suddenly look scared, he says, "He's behind me, isn't he?" Mitch apologizes, but the cowboy dismisses him with a profane insult.

City Slickers, like other neotraditional westerns, spruces up the western myth to make it relevant to nineties America. The three protagonists are typical nineties yuppies, and they are joined by other readily identifiable nineties types. The Shalowitz brothers, Barry and Ira, operate an ice cream chain similar to Ben & Jerry's. And in keeping with the politically correct times, the amateur cowboy crew is rounded out by a beautiful and independent woman, Bonnie, and two people of color—Ben Jessup and his son, Steve, both dentists from Baltimore.

Despite the updates, *City Slickers* remains true to the mythic West. The city slicker heroes find all they are looking for and more out west. The key to their success turns out to be the cowboy archetype, Curly. Even though Curly and Mitch get off on the wrong foot, the two eventually become friends, in part because the feisty Mitch refuses to be intimidated. Before long, Mitch realizes that Curly is a true western good guy. The tough cowboy becomes his mentor and teaches him how to ride, rope, and understand not just the West but also himself. Mitch and Curly become friends as they ride the range together, share stories around the campfire, and sing the iconic "Tumbling Tumbleweeds." The old cowboy even shares some western wisdom. Holding up one finger, he asks the young city slicker, "Do you know what the secret of life is?" The puzzled Mitch replies, "Your finger?" Curly shakes his head and says, "One thing. Just one thing." Mitch now looks even more confused and asks, "But what is the one thing?" Curly smiles and replies, "That's what *you* have to find out."

Mitch and his friends learn the answer to Curly's puzzle as they continue their odyssey through the mythic West. They face the ultimate test when Curly dies along the trail, forcing them to face the dangers and challenges of the Wild West on their own. Well trained by their cowboy mentor, the three city slickers stand up to bad guys, brave the elements, and overcome other dangers as they escort the herd safely to Colorado. Along with success, they find redemption in the mythic West. Each man discovers the "one thing" that matters most. Mitch confronts internal and external demons en route to the realization that the most important thing to him is his family. For Phil, the important thing is becoming a man. Previously bullied by his ex-wife and her father, Phil finally emerges as his own man. He uses a six-gun to chase off the rowdy cowboys who threatened them, and in the process improves his self-esteem, wins Bonnie's admiration, and carves out a new life for himself. Ed finds rebirth on the trail when he learns that he is dependable in a crisis. That important insight allows him to return home to his young wife and start a family, confident that he will never let them down.

By the end of the movie, these nineties yuppies have found truth and traded their frivolous concerns for basic values. Their success and rebirth is all because of their experience in the mythic West. "When the three of you first got here you were as worthless as hen shit on a pump handle," says Clay Stone after they safely deliver the herd to his Colorado ranch. "Now look at you. You're cowboys."

The comeback of traditional westerns resulted in a flurry of gimmicky films in the eighties and nineties, including 3-D westerns, science fiction westerns, animated westerns, even musical westerns. Television chimed in with numerous made-for-TV westerns, the most successful of which was *Lonesome Dove* (1989), an award-winning miniseries based on Larry McMurtry's epic novel about two retired Texas Rangers on one last glorious cattle drive.[10] Despite the differences among all these westerns, they shared a common approach: they glorified the mythic West.

The Revisionist Trail

Although the eighties were dominated by traditional westerns that were in sync with Reagan's America, revisionist westerns refused to go away. They actually made a big comeback in the nineties, suggesting that the mood of the country once again was shifting. The continuing existence of revisionist westerns that either debunked the mythic West or used familiar western characters in new ways to critique western myths or comment on contemporary society demonstrates that the social activism, revisionist trends, and anti-Establishment views prevalent in the sixties and seventies survived throughout the rest of the century. These films reveal conflict and culture wars in post-1980 America, as well as an ongoing interest in issues involving race, ethnicity, class, and gender.

Many revisionist westerns, including *The Long Riders* (1980), *Harry Tracy* (1982), *The Grey Fox* (1982), and *Billy the Kid* (1989), showcased antiheroes who subverted the notion of the mythic West. *Harry Tracy*, for instance, starred Bruce Dern as the last surviving member of Butch Cassidy's Hole-in-the-Wall Gang. The film takes place at the turn of the century and focuses on Harry's final crime spree against banks, trains, and other big businesses. In the midst of his Robin Hood–like exploits, Harry realizes that the outlaw tradition is on the way out. When a friend, David Merrill, wants to join up with him, Harry asks, "You know what year it is?" Puzzled by the question, Dave replies, "1900." Harry looks at him and says, "There's no more outlaws left, Dave, it's over." Harry adds poignantly, "That actually means that there's not going to be any more Americans left." Tracy's subsequent death symbolizes the passing of the Old West, if not the old America. He meets his end in an unspectacular way. Instead of going out in a blaze of glory in a fast-draw shootout or some other classic showdown, Harry gets shot up by a posse while he's hiding in a cornfield. As a photographer takes a picture of his corpse, surrounded by smiling posse members and disrespectful gawkers, Harry's girlfriend trudges off through the mud. No glorious images of the mythic West here. Antiheroes like Harry Tracy who rode the trails in revisionist westerns not only debunked western myths, but they often served as reminders that the anti-Establishment countercultural attitudes of the sixties and seventies were still around during the last two decades of the twentieth century.

Figure 30. Kevin Costner's revisionist *Dances with Wolves* (TIG Productions/Majestic Films International/Orion Pictures, 1990) became only the second western in history to win an Oscar for Best Picture.

Revisionist westerns suggested new ways to view the Old West.[11] The best example is *Dances with Wolves*, directed by and starring Kevin Costner. The movie offered audiences a fresh approach to Native Americans, as well as a revisionist interpretation of American history. The epic western is over three hours long. Yet, at its core is a simple story line. A decorated U.S. Cavalry officer, Lieutenant John Dunbar (Costner), is transferred out west during the Civil War. When he reports to Fort Hays in Kansas, the commanding officer immediately dispatches him to Fort Sedgwick, on the edge of the frontier, deep in Indian country. When Dunbar arrives at the tiny outpost, he finds it abandoned. He immediately goes to work making repairs, while keeping a detailed journal that includes sketches of the frontier setting. As days turn into weeks, the lone soldier is befriended by a scrawny wolf that hangs around for food scraps.

One morning when Dunbar is bathing in a nearby pond, he is surprised to see an Indian outside his cabin. The warrior, a Sioux named Kicking Bird (Graham Greene), heads toward the corral where Dunbar's horse, Cisco, is kept. After the wet and naked Dunbar scares him off, Kicking Bird returns to his village and spreads the word about the strange soldier and beautiful horse. A few days later, a Sioux raiding party, led by an aggressive young warrior named Wind in His Hair (Rodney A. Grant), attempts to steal Cisco, but the smart horse escapes.

Frustrated by the raid, Dunbar decides to confront his unfriendly neighbors. He dresses up in full military garb, grabs the post's guidon, and rides out to locate the Indian encampment. En route, he comes across a wounded Indian woman and escorts her to her village, which leads to improved relations between the soldier and the Sioux. Over the next few weeks, Kicking Bird and other Indians visit Dunbar at the lonely outpost.

Eventually, Kicking Bird becomes the white man's mentor, teaching him about the Sioux way of life. Dunbar begins visiting the Sioux regularly and comes to admire the Indians' integrity, traditions, and life-styles, as well as their ability to live in harmony with nature. The Indians are as impressed with Dunbar as he is with them. When they see the white man playing with the mangy wolf who follows him around, they even give him a Sioux name, Dances with Wolves. Within a short time, Dunbar becomes good friends not only with Kicking Bird, but also with the tribe's main chief, Ten Bears (Floyd Westerman), and even the previously hostile Wind in His Hair. Dunbar also develops a close friendship with the Indian woman he rescued, Stands with a Fist, who turns out to be a white woman captured when she was young. As she teaches him about the Sioux culture and language, the two fall in love.

One day when most of the warriors are away on a raid, Dunbar and others in the Sioux village learn that a Pawnee war party is approaching. Dunbar rushes back to Fort Sedgwick and returns with rifles to help the villagers withstand the Pawnee attack. When Kicking Bird and the other Sioux warriors return, they are grateful for the white man's help. Dunbar's relationship with the tribe becomes even closer when he marries Stands with a Fist. Over the next several weeks, Dances with Wolves begins spending more time with the tribe to the point where he seldom returns to his post at the fort.

As Dunbar draws closer to the Indians, he reveals to Kicking Bird that it's just a matter of time before whites as numerous as "the stars" arrive in Sioux country. The two explain the situation to Ten Bears, who makes it clear that the Sioux will fight for their land if necessary. For safety, the old chief orders his tribe to pack up and head farther into the interior. Dunbar wants to go with them but realizes he first has to return to the deserted Fort Sedgwick to pick up his journal, before soldiers find it and use the information to track down the Sioux.

Upon his arrival, Dunbar is surprised to find that U.S. Cavalry have already taken possession of the outpost. As he approaches dressed in Indian clothes and wearing feathers in his long hair, the soldiers mistake him for a Sioux and open fire, killing his prized horse Cisco. The troops take him back to the fort, where officers are surprised to learn his true identity. A sergeant looks at the way he's dressed, and cracks, "Turned Injun, didn't yeh?" When Dunbar refuses to help the military locate and attack the Sioux, he is charged with treason. Soon thereafter, a small detachment escorts Dunbar toward Fort Hays for a court-martial hearing. But the Sioux surprise the detachment, kill all the soldiers, and rescue Dances with Wolves.

Dunbar realizes that he can never be truly free. The U.S. Army will now be determined to hunt him down as a traitor and punish the Indians for aiding and abetting his escape. "I think it would be wise to move the village to another location right now," he tells Ten Bears. "As for me . . . I will be leaving with my wife Stands with a Fist as soon as possible. I must go and try to talk to those that will listen." Though the Indians try to dissuade him, Dunbar is determined to go. The day the couple leaves the Sioux is a sad one for them and the Indians.

At that very moment not far away, Pawnee scouts are helping a large force of U.S. troops track Dunbar and the Sioux. What would have happened next is unclear. As the camera shows Dances with Wolves and Stands with a Fist traveling down a snowy path through the mountains, the following writing comes up on the screen: "Thirteen years later, their homes destroyed, their buffalo gone, the last band of free Sioux submitted to white authority at Fort Robinson, Nebraska. The great horse culture of the plains was gone and the American frontier was soon to pass into history."

No doubt many moviegoers came away thinking that three hours and one minute was a long time to spend watching a movie without an ending. Still, *Dances with Wolves* was in many ways a remarkable western. Shot in glorious color and Panavision, the movie featured panoramic views of the Great Plains and spectacular mountain vistas. Yet, as magnificent as the scenery was, this was not the mythic West familiar to most Americans. The movie suggested an alternate myth—the Indians' West. It was the cinematic opposite of John Gast's famous painting *American Progress* (1872). While Gast's nationalistic representation of westward movement depicts white Americans proudly heading west as Indians are pushed to the periphery, Costner's movie places the Indians at center stage.

Not only does *Dances with Wolves* portray the beauty of the West through Indian rather than white eyes, but it turns the traditional notion of good guys and bad guys inside out. The Sioux emerge as the heroes of this new version of the Old West, while white men in general and the U.S. Cavalry in particular become the villains. To the extent that Dunbar does find success and redemption in the West, it is only because he rejects his own culture and walks the Native American path. Perhaps more than any previous western, *Dances with Wolves* humanizes Native Americans. It shows the Sioux laughing, crying, making love, and interacting with families and each other in ways no different from whites. "Nothing I have been told about these people is correct," explains Dunbar. "They are not thieves or beggars. They are not the bogeymen they are made out to be. On the contrary, they are polite guests and I enjoy their humor."

The movie offers fairly accurate depictions of Indian life. The Sioux are pictured as expert horsemen who hunt buffalo, scalp and wage war against enemies, live in tipis, smoke calumets, and use travois to travel. Sioux men wear authentic war paraphernalia, including war bonnets, feathers in their hair, medicine bundles, and bone breast plates. They even paint their faces and horses in realistic ways. Other details are accurate down to the types of clothes and hairstyles being worn, the language spoken, and other activities, such as dancing backed by authentic music and drums. The sophisticated film makes it clear that not all Indians looked or acted the same. It shows that various tribes wore different types of clothing, had distinct hairstyles, spoke different languages, and followed different policies, not just toward whites but toward other Indians as well.

Unfortunately, the movie all too often veers away from historical accuracy toward romantic stereotypes of "New Age Indians" and political correctness. In many ways, the Sioux idealized in *Dances with Wolves* do not resemble at all the historical Sioux who rode the Great Plains in the 1800s, waged ferocious war against Indian and white enemies, and sometimes contributed to the destruction of the Great Plains environment through overkill of animals, the setting of prairie fires to aid hunts, or economically motivated hunts that thinned the buffalo herds.[12] Dunbar's Sioux were too perfect to be real. They were a peaceful and innocent people who always lived as one with nature. When, for example, they come upon buffalo slaughtered by greedy whites for tongues and hides, the sensitive Sioux look like they're about to cry. On other occasions, the innocent Indians are portrayed as nonviolent people who fight only when attacked. After Dunbar helps the Sioux fight off a Pawnee war party, he says naïvely: "It was hard to know how to feel. I had never been in a battle like this one. This had not been a fight for territory or riches or to make men free. This battle had no ego. It had been fought to preserve the food stores that would see us through winter, to protect the lives of women and children and loved ones only a few feet away. I felt a pride I had never felt before." While Dunbar's Sioux may have been more admirable than Indians portrayed in earlier westerns, they nonetheless were just as one-dimensional. "They were a people so eager to laugh, so devoted to family, so dedicated to each other," he explains. "The only word that comes to mind is harmony." No doubt, the enemies of the real Sioux could have thought of numerous other adjectives, for example, the word *Sioux* is derived from a derogatory Algonquian word that meant "enemy" or "snake."

If the movie idealizes the Sioux as good Indians who can do no wrong, it portrays the Pawnees as despicable creatures who can't do anything right. Time after time, the hateful Pawnees are shown killing innocent whites and Indians. Toward the end of the film, the duplicitous Pawnees even sell their services to the white men and guide U.S. troops for an assault on an unsuspecting Sioux village. By film's end, one can't help but think that the poor Pawnees would have had a great legal case against Kevin Costner for defamation of character.

Dances with Wolves serves up other new stereotypes about the West. Costner's character glorifies the Indian West as much as protagonists in traditional westerns idealized the old mythic West of white Anglo-Saxon Protestants. On one occasion, the awestruck Dunbar says, "It seems every day ends with a miracle here. And whatever God may be, I thank God for this day." Dunbar's friend and mentor, Kicking Bird, shares his attitudes about the beauty and true meaning of life. "I was just thinking that of all the trails in this life, there is one that matters most," explains the Indian to his white friend. "It is the trail of a true human being. I think you are on this trail, and it is good to see." By the end of the film, Dunbar has crossed the cultural divide and found redemption in this revised myth of the West. "I had never really known who John Dunbar was," he says. "Perhaps because the name itself had no meaning. But as I heard my Sioux name [Dances with Wolves] being called over and over, I knew for the first time who I really was."

Dances with Wolves resonated with contemporary audiences in part because it was in step with the times in which it was made. Along with offering positive images of Native Americans in keeping with the era's growing acceptance of minorities, the movie endorsed modern gender attitudes. Audiences could relate to strong female characters such as the opinionated Black Shawl (Tantoo Cardinal) and the fiercely independent

Stands with a Fist (Mary McDonnell), who repeatedly displayed her intelligence and determination to survive, first as a young white girl captured by the Indians and then later as an adopted Indian woman who picked up a rifle to shoot marauding Pawnee warriors.

The movie plugged into other aspects of life in modern America. It included plenty of violence and sex, reflecting similar trends in contemporary media. Its negative images of the U.S. military mirrored the growing feeling of many Americans that the nation was on the wrong path by the late eighties. Moviegoers familiar with American adventurism in Granada and Nicaragua or the renewal of the Cold War with the Soviets found it easy to relate to the Indians' mistrust of the U.S. Army and government. In addition, the movie picked up on growing environmental concerns. With stories about Three Mile Island (1979) and the Exxon Valdez oil spill (1989) fresh in people's minds, audiences could appreciate the Indians' relationship to nature. Even the beautiful scenery resonated with environmentally aware audiences.[13] *Dances with Wolves* tapped into the changing mood of the country in one other way. Just as neotraditional westerns like *Urban Cowboy* (1980) presaged the rising tide of conservatism that resulted in Ronald Reagan's election, Costner's revisionist film anticipated the resurgence of liberal attitudes that would contribute to Bill Clinton's victory in 1992.

Dances with Wolves rode the perfect wave to enormous popularity in 1990 and became one of the most successful and honored westerns of all time. The box office hit won seven Oscars, including Best Picture and Best Director, as well as numerous other national and international awards. In 2007, the film was chosen for inclusion in the Library of Congress's National Film Registry. Costner's revisionist take on the mythic West struck a responsive chord with audiences everywhere. The new myth—like the old—offered opportunity, success, and redemption. Yet, the new western vision, like modern America, was more inclusive and accepting of minorities, women, and all those willing to cast aside old prejudices and fears. Ultimately, *Dances with Wolves* showed that hope and success came not from some mythic land or external place, but from within the individual. As one movie poster explained it, "Lt. John Dunbar is about to discover the frontier . . . within himself."[14]

* * *

Dances with Wolves was just one of many westerns that reinterpreted race, ethnicity, or gender. Other revisionist films about Native Americans included *Windwalker* (1980), *Thunderheart* (1992), *Geronimo: An*

American Legend (1993), *Tecumseh: The Last Warrior* (1995), and *Crazy Horse* (1996). African Americans were spotlighted in films such as *Posse* (1993) and *Buffalo Soldiers* (1997). Hispanics were prominently featured in *The Ballad of Gregorio Cortez* (1982), *The Milagro Beanfield War* (1988), and *Lone Star* (1996). And the plight of Asian Americans was the subject of *Thousand Pieces of Gold* (1991).

Numerous films showcased strong and independent women. For example, feminist gunslingers roamed the revisionist West in movies such as *Bad Girls* (1994) and *The Quick and the Dead* (1995). Not all were successful. *The Quick and the Dead*, which stars Sharon Stone as a gunslinger, had a particularly hard time connecting with audiences. "Stone, for all her moxie, spends much of the movie looking as if she's on the verge of tears," complained film critic Owen Gleiberman. "A *sensitive* existential tough-girl gunslinger? Sorry, it's ludicrous." Roger Ebert also poked fun at Sharon Stone's gunfighter character, concluding "She's sexy in leather pants and a trim outfit (and later manages to find a ballroom gown in her saddlebags)."[15]

Perhaps the most intriguing female character in a revisionist western can be found in *Silent Tongue* (1993), written and directed by Sam Shepard. *New York Times* movie critic Caryn James used words such as "eerie," "inventive," and "poetic" to describe the film, explaining "Mr. Shepard's imagistic style is daringly different from anything Hollywood might offer." The plot revolves around a white man (River Phoenix) who is overcome with grief after the death of his Kiowa wife, Awbonnie (Sheila Tousey). Because he refuses to burn her body, the woman's spirit cannot be set free. "So Awbonnie appears as a tortured, vengeful ghost," explains James. "She roams through the film and becomes its strongest character. One side of her face is already shriveling, with a milky-blue eye; the other half is still human, one brown eye lucid." Although her makeup looks fake, says James, "Ms. Tousey makes her character believable as both ghost and woman."[16] Shepard's nuanced portrayal of Awbonnie and other female characters in the film combine with dark western imagery, bleak landscapes, and a complex tale of racial interaction to make *Silent Tongue* one of the more interesting revisionist films of the day.

Revisionist westerns picked up on other social and cultural trends of the eighties and nineties. Reflecting the era's changing sexual attitudes, westerns such as *Heaven's Gate* (1980), *The Long Riders* (1980), *Posse* (1993), and *Hard Bounty* (1995) contain nudity and implicit if not explicit sex. Other westerns capitalized on the higher profile of gays and lesbians. *Zorro: The Gay Blade* (1981) introduces a homosexual version of the famous swordsman, while *Even Cowgirls Get the Blues* (1993) explores lesbian relationships out west.

Throughout the eighties and early nineties, people grew increasingly concerned about violence in America as the number of shootings increased annually. A front page headline in the *New York Times* on July 18, 1990, declared, "Number of Killings Soars in Big Cities Across U.S." Westerns reflected the era's ubiquitous violence. While violent video games like *Streetfighter* and *Double Dragon* surged in popularity, martial arts westerns such as *Samurai Cowboy* (1994) and *East Meets West* (1995) arrived on the scene. The sudden spike in western horror movies such as *Near Dark* (1987), *Grim Prairie Tales* (1990), and *Ravenous* (1999) might also be linked to the nation's preoccupation with violence, as well as possible anxieties about a renewed Cold War abroad. Even high-profile revisionist westerns such as *Heaven's Gate* (1980) and *The Long Riders* (1980) featured graphic violence. In the latter film, director Walter Hill depicts cold-blooded killings and shootouts with lots of spurting blood and slow motion shots to emphasize bullets smashing into body parts.[17]

Comedy westerns also picked up on revisionist trends. A good example is *Wagons East!* (1994), which starred John Candy as a bumbling scout named Harlow and Richard Lewis as Phil, the leader of the wagon train. The movie tells the story of a group of unsuccessful and unhappy pioneers who live in a small western town ironically named Prosperity. They decide to call it quits and return to the East. When a man in a saloon points out that they can't do that because it would violate the "Code of the West," they reply that they have no problem with "giving up." When their wagon train pulls out, Harlow initially leads them in the wrong direction, assuming everyone always wants to go west. When he learns that they want to go east, he just shakes his head and says, "It hardly seems right."

Not only does *Wagons East!* reject the image of the West as a land of opportunity, but it lampoons almost every western cliché and character type imaginable. For example, when the incompetent scout leads the anti-pioneers directly into a hostile Indian encampment, the warriors cannot believe that these settlers are heading east. Rather than killing them, the chief decides to give them an escort to guarantee their safety and success. "Think about it," he explains to his warriors, "White men going east. This is a good trend. If this catches on, we can have our world back." Later, when the cavalry arrives, it is not to save the wagon train, as is usually the case in westerns, but to destroy it before the anti-pioneers start a movement. The officer in charge orders the wagon train "to turn back or face the consequences." When Phil asks what the "consequences" are, the officer replies, "You know, your standard U.S. Cavalry massacre." When Phil and the others decide to continue their eastward journey, one of their Indian guides suggests a new strategy for survival. Instead of circling the wagons, why not position the wagons in a square instead, which will make it more difficult for the soldiers to ride around them? Intrigued, Phil shouts out to his fellow travelers, "Square the wagons!"

In the end, the quitters are the only winners. This group of western misfits includes revisionist characters such as independent women, smart Indians, a gay gunslinger, and other nonconformists who don't buy into the western myth. The tagline for *Wagons East!* sums up its revisionist take on western pioneers: "They came. They saw. They changed their minds."[18]

Westerns at Century's End

By the end of the twentieth century, both traditional westerns and revisionist westerns were going strong. But as the nineties progressed, revisionist films gained momentum. In 1990, *Dances with Wolves* won seven Academy Awards, including Best Picture and Best Director. Just two years later, *Unforgiven* picked up nine Oscar nominations, winning Best Picture, Best Director, Best Actor in a Supporting Role, and Best Film Editing. To place those achievements in proper context, only one other western—*Cimarron* (1931)—had ever won an Oscar for Best Picture.

Clint Eastwood directed and starred in *Unforgiven* (1992). It begins with the silhouette of a man set against a blood red sun, digging a grave near a lone tree and small cabin. A title card appears on the screen. "She was a comely young woman and not without prospects," it reads. "Therefore it was heartbreaking to her mother that she would enter into marriage with William Munny, a known thief and murderer, a man of notoriously vicious and intemperate disposition. When she died, it was not at his hands as her mother might have suspected, but of smallpox. That was 1878."

The scene then shifts to a rainy night in a small Wyoming town, Big Whiskey, two years later. A man is having sex with a prostitute. When he hears a commotion in the next room, he jumps up and rushes out the door. There he finds his friend angrily beating another whore. The irate man pulls out a knife, tells his friend to hold her down, and then slashes his victim several times across the face. He stops only when the owner of the brothel rushes in with a gun.

Within minutes, Sheriff Little Bill Daggett (Gene Hackman) arrives on the scene. He learns that the cowboy attacked the prostitute because she

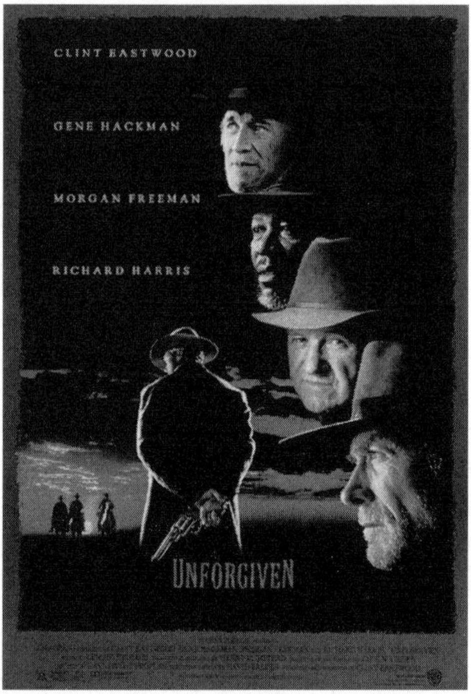

Figure 31. Clint Eastwood's Oscar-winning *Unforgiven* (Malpaso Productions/Warner Brothers, 1992) used the Old West to explore the troubled mood of America at the end of the century.

laughed at his tiny "pecker." When the madam of the brothel, Strawberry Alice, demands that the assailant be hanged for mutilating the prostitute, Little Bill explains that a good whipping will suffice, because the two cowboys were basically good boys and things simply got out of hand. Then Skinny Dubois, the owner of the saloon and brothel, complains that his "property" (i.e., the prostitute) was permanently damaged by the slashing, so Little Bill decides to fine the cowboys instead of beating them. He orders the slasher to give Skinny five ponies, while his accomplice has to hand over two ponies.

Alice is furious and heads back upstairs to care for the wounded prostitute. "Just because we let them smelly fools ride us like horses don't mean we gotta let 'em brand us like horses," she explains to the other girls.

Determined to obtain justice, Alice convinces the women to pool their earnings so they can offer a one-thousand-dollar reward to anyone who kills the two cowboys.

The scene then shifts hundreds of miles away to Clint Eastwood's run-down homestead in Kansas. His middle-aged character is deep in the mud of a pigpen, trying to sort out sick hogs with the help of his young son and daughter. Suddenly, a young gunman calling himself the Schofield Kid (Jaimz Woolvett) rides up and wants to know if the pig farmer is the notorious gunslinger Will Munny. When the two men go to the cabin to talk, the Kid explains to Will about the woman who was disfigured by the two cowboys up in Wyoming. He asks Will to help him kill the two cowboys in return for half the reward money. Will refuses, saying that he gave up being a gunman long ago when he was reformed by his late wife. Before riding off, the Kid tells Will that if he changes his mind, he can join him on the Western Trail bound for Wyoming. With the young gunslinger still visible in the distance, Will glances at the muddy pigpen and his two ragamuffin kids and quickly changes his mind. He realizes that he can earn enough money to improve his and his children's lives if he straps on his gun one last time to kill the two cowboys who cut up a woman. So, the middle-aged Will Munny, who has not been in a gunfight for eleven years, locates his weapons, saddles his horse (which hasn't been ridden in a while), and rides off. He tells his kids he'll be back in a few weeks and that if they run into trouble, they should go see the neighbor woman, Sally Two Trees.

Will's first stop is at Sally's homestead. He explains his plan to her husband, Ned Logan (Morgan Freeman), who used to ride with Munny in the old days. When Will asks if he wants to join him, Ned declines. "Hell, Will. We ain't bad men no more," he says. "We're farmers." But, after Ned hears about the reward money and how the cowboys had cut the woman with a knife, he—like Will—changes his mind. Still a crack shot with his Spencer rifle, Ned agrees to go along on this last gunfighter job. The two old friends then hit the trail, finding the going much harder than it was in their youth. They complain about sleeping on hard ground and not having roofs over their heads. The aged Will repeatedly has difficulty climbing onto his horse. All the while, Will keeps assuring Ned that he's no longer the cold-blooded killer that he used to be. "I ain't like that no more. I ain't the same," he says. "Claudia, she straightened me up, cleared me of drinkin' whiskey and all. Just 'cause we're goin' on this killing, that don't mean I'm gonna go back to bein' the way I was. I just need the money, get a new start for them youngsters." No sooner do Will and Ned catch up to the Schofield Kid than they realize that the Kid is nearsighted and can't hit targets far away. They are also put off by his boasts that he has killed five men in gunfights. But the three continue their ride toward Wyoming to kill the two cowboys for the reward.

It soon becomes evident that Will and his partners are not the only ones hoping to claim the reward. A stagecoach carrying a notorious gunslinger named English Bob (Richard Harris) and his biographer, a dime novelist named W. W. Beauchamp (Saul Rubinek), pulls into the town of Big Whiskey. When English Bob refuses to check his six-gun in compliance with a town ordinance, he is surrounded by Sheriff Little Bill Daggett and his deputies. After Little Bill disarms the gunslinger, he punches the Englishman for insulting America. He proceeds to kick and beat English Bob to a bloody pulp, insisting he is doing it as a lesson to other would-be assassins looking to claim the "whore's gold." Next day, the sheriff runs the bloodied Englishman out of town. The erstwhile biographer, Beauchamp, decides to stick around to write a book about the tough lawman who easily defeated the English gunman.

Not long afterward, Will Munny and his partners arrive in Big Whiskey and head directly to Skinny's saloon to meet Alice. While the Kid goes upstairs to find her, Will and Ned sit down at a table for a drink. The last couple of days had been particularly hard on Will. It was pouring rain every day and night, and while Ned and the Kid drank whiskey to ward off the chill, the teetotaler Will refused to partake. Now, Will is almost delirious with a fever. After a while, Ned heads upstairs to see what's taking the Kid so long.

No sooner does Ned leave than in walks Little Bill and his deputies. They surround Will and demand that he comply with the ordinance by handing over his gun. When Will insists that neither he nor his friends upstairs carry guns, Little Bill's mood suddenly changes. He seizes Will's hidden gun by force and then beats him to a bloody pulp. The sadistic sheriff tells his men to open the door so the victim can crawl outside into the pouring rain. Meanwhile, when the whores upstairs tell Ned and the Kid about what happened to their friend, the two make a hasty exit through a window. They find the badly beaten Will outside in the mud, and the three gallop off into the night to find sanctuary far from town. Over the next few days, Ned tends to Will's wounds. Some of the prostitutes arrive to help. While two of them offer their services to Ned and the Kid, the one scarred by the knifing, Delilah, nurses Will back to health. After his fever breaks, she even offers him sex, but he declines because he wants to be faithful to his late wife.

When Will regains his strength, he sets out with Ned and the Kid to locate the two cowboys. They find them in a canyon looking for strays. Ned takes the first shot with his long-range Spencer rifle, hitting the horse of one of the targets. When Ned balks at finishing off the cowboy, Will grabs the rifle and makes the kill. The three assassins then ride off, planning to circle back later to shoot the other cowboy. Suddenly, Ned announces he is done with killing. He just can't do it anymore. So he bids his partners good-bye and rides off toward home.

Will and the Kid then set off to finish the job. They track the remaining cowboy to a nearby ranch and wait until he goes to the outhouse. Then Will dispatches the nearsighted Kid to finish him off at close range, while he stands guard to make sure no one else comes out of the bunkhouse. The Kid creeps up to the outhouse, throws the door open, pauses for a moment, and then shoots his victim three times in the chest. At the sound of shots, the other cowboys come rushing out of the cabin as the two assassins flee. Afterward, the clearly shaken Kid admits that this was actually the first man he ever killed. He vows never again to take another man's life. As Will and the Kid discuss the situation, Will sees one of the prostitutes riding toward them. She gives them the reward money and explains that Ned is dead. Will is stunned, because he assumed his old friend was safely en route back to Kansas. His amazement turns to anger when he learns the details. Ned was apprehended by cowboys who then turned him over to Little Bill. The sadistic lawman repeatedly whipped him in an attempt to learn the whereabouts of Will and the Kid. Eventually, Little Bill beat Ned to death and then put the body on public display to send the message that this is what happens to assassins in the town of Big Whiskey.

The furious Will gets a wild look in his eyes and gulps down some whiskey, reverting literally and symbolically back to the man he used to be. After instructing the Kid to take the reward money back to Kansas and split it between his kids and Ned's widow, Will rides into the town of Big Whiskey—another obvious metaphor for his return to his old ways—for his showdown with the evil Little Bill. His fury grows as he rides slowly past Ned's body in the coffin. Walking into Skinny's place, pointing his shotgun straight ahead, Will finds the Sheriff bragging to his deputies, Beauchamp, and numerous onlookers. Silence falls over the startled crowd. Will asks if the owner of the saloon is present. When Skinny identifies himself, Will blows him away with a shotgun blast. When the incredulous Little Bill calls him a "cowardly son of a bitch" for shooting an unarmed man, Will replies coldly, "Well, he should have armed himself if he's going to decorate his saloon with my friend." Will then points the shotgun directly at the sheriff and pulls the trigger. When the gun misfires, Little Bill and his deputies reach for their six-guns as Will instinctively throws the shotgun at the sheriff, who flinches. In that split second, Will pulls out his pistol and shoots Little Bill in the chest. He then guns down the other deputies as they reach for their guns.

Will then walks casually over to the bar and drinks more whiskey. Seeing the fallen Little Bill trying to raise his weapon, Will callously steps on his hand until the gun drops out. Looking Little Bill straight in the eye, Will points the shotgun directly at his head. "I don't deserve this," says the terrified Little Bill, "to die like this. I was building a house." Will replies coldly, "Deserve's got nothin' to do with it." Realizing his end is near, Little Bill says defiantly, "I'll see you in hell, William Munny." Will says, "Yeah," and pulls the trigger.

Will turns to head out the door, sees a wounded deputy, and callously shoots him in the chest as he walks past him. "All right, I'm coming out," he shouts to anyone lurking outside waiting to ambush him. "Any man I see out there, I'm gonna shoot him. Any son-of-a-bitch takes a shot at me, I'm not only gonna kill him, but I'm gonna kill his wife, all his friends, and burn his damn house down." He then walks slowly out the door, climbs onto his horse, and warns the people hiding in the shadows that they had better bury his friend, Ned, properly and not mistreat the prostitutes or else he will come back to settle the score.

The final scene—reprising the film's beginning—once again shows a silhouette of Will Munny standing next to his wife's grave set against the blood red sun. A final title card appears on the screen. "Some years later, Mrs. Ansonia Feathers made the arduous journey to Hodgeman County to visit the last resting place of her only daughter," it reads. "William Munny had long since disappeared with the children. . . . some said to San Francisco where it was rumored he prospered in dry goods. And there was nothing on the marker to explain to Mrs. Feathers why her only daughter had married a known thief and murderer, a man of notoriously vicious and intemperate disposition."

Unforgiven is Clint Eastwood's revisionist western masterpiece. At first glance, the film's magnificent scenery underscores the traditional image of the mythic West as a beautiful, exotic land. The majestic mountains, lush forests, pristine rivers, and wide open spaces create a tranquil, almost sacred, setting. But the spectacular views are just an illusion. This seemingly beautiful land turns out to be an "unforgiving" place, where individuals pay a heavy price for their sins, mistakes, and past transgressions. The movie's title, which signifies the rejection of the mythic West as a land of opportunity, success, and redemption, provides an early clue that all is not well in Eastwood's West.

The plot provides a dark counterpoint to the peaceful landscape. There are no heroes in this tale, only antiheroes depicted in various shades of evil. The story ends badly for everyone. Will Munny is the main protagonist and a man with an evil past. He realizes he was a bad man who was mean, drank too much, and slaughtered innocent men, women, and children. After he meets his wife, Claudia, he promises to reform. He gives up alcohol and killing, and settles down as a family man for the next eleven years. But his attempt at redemption ultimately fails. His twenty-nine-year-old wife dies, and he winds up a poor pig farmer, mired in the mud, trying to raise two kids on his own. Despite his repeated insistence that "I ain't like that anymore," Will slowly but surely backslides. He accepts blood money, reverts to whiskey, and once again becomes a cold-blooded killer. Even the final scene of the movie questions whether Will can ever find happiness or a new life in the West. All the final title card can do is rehash the hackneyed notion that opportunity, success, and redemption can be found out West. It suggests that Will and his children wound up going even farther West to California, where "it was rumored he prospered in dry goods." But, significantly, no one knows Will's fate for certain. And the only record left behind—his wife's tombstone—contains no clue.

All the other main characters share fates that are anything but heroic. After Ned realizes he can no longer kill a man, he attempts to go home to resume his life as a husband and farmer, but he is captured and brutally whipped to death by the sadistic sheriff. The Schofield Kid is a wannabe gunslinger who is unable to cope with reality when he finally kills a man. The Kid drinks whiskey to forget his crime and gives away his gun to Will. "I'm never gonna use it again," he says. "I ain't like you, Will." Sheriff Little Bill Daggett is the worst of the bunch. When he's not proudly building his house, the strange and cruel lawman finds pleasure in beating and killing his victims. Little Bill is vainglorious enough to want a dime novelist to tell his story, but not smart enough to defeat Will Munny, whom he dismisses as just a "killer of women and children." Little Bill pays a steep price for his actions when Will blasts his head with a shotgun.

The women characters fare no better. Sally Two Trees, whom Will trusts to look after his children, can only watch helplessly as her husband, Ned, rides off with Will on a dangerous venture to make money. Her marriage and happy life end tragically when Ned is killed. The prostitutes of Big Whiskey have even less hope for happiness. Delilah, whose face was scarred by the knife attack, develops a relationship with Will. Maybe in a traditional western, she and Will could have lived happily ever after in wedded bliss. But not in this film. Instead, Delilah and Will part company. In the end, even though Delilah, Strawberry Alice, and the other prostitutes stood up for their rights as women, their futures are uncertain at best, because the town blames them for all the turmoil, and their employer has been murdered by Will.

Unforgiven captured the shifting mood of America in the nineties. The same forces that caused Ronald Reagan's sunny optimism and pronouncements about "a new morning in America" to fade from view and Bill Clinton's star to rise in the political firmament powered the return of revisionist westerns such as *Unforgiven*. The movie's dark message and rejection of myths about success and redemption resonated with nineties audiences. As the nation careened toward a new millennium, Americans were increasingly uncertain about the validity of the American Dream—whether it was in the Old West or in modern times.

Contemporary audiences could relate to the movie's violent themes. The number of shootings in the United States was on the rise in the late eighties and early nineties, peaking in 1993 at 7 firearm homicide deaths per 100,000 people.[19] Eastwood's 1992 movie, released when violent crime was almost at its high mark, features numerous scenes that depict extreme violence, including shootings, knifings, sadistic beatings, and Will Munny's cold-blooded killings of cowboys, lawmen, and anyone else who got in his way. Yet, even as the movie spotlights violence, it condemns it. After the Kid kills his first man, he says regretfully, "It don't seem real, how he ain't gonna never breathe again, ever. . . . All on account of pulling a trigger." Will agrees. "It's a hell of a thing, killing a man," he explains. "Take away all he's got and all he's ever gonna have." Trying to justify the murders of the two cowboys, the Kid says, "Yeah, well, I guess they had it coming." But Will's not buying it and adds, "We all got it coming, Kid."

Eastwood later noted that many of his films were quite violent, but the violence in *Unforgiven* was different because every killing had repercussions. "It really tears people up when they are violent, and I felt it was time for that kind of thing in the world," he explains. "And it became more contemporary during the last year with law enforcement events [i.e., the Rodney King beating and subsequent violent riots] here in Los Angeles. An incident will trigger decisions, maybe the wrong decisions or the wrong reactions by people, and then there's really no way to stop things. It's a time in my life and maybe it's a time in history when violence should not be such a humorous thing and maybe there are consequences."[20]

Unforgiven reflected the mood of 1990s America in other ways. Audiences familiar with movies such as *Wall Street* (1987), contemporary headlines about Leona Helmsley's mistreatment of her hotel employees, or the Rodney King beating would have had no problem understanding the morally deficient characters in *Unforgiven*. If Eastwood's movie condemned the Establishment, it sympathized with minorities and working classes. Ned, an African American, is Will's only friend and ultimately one of the few decent people in the story. Ned's wife is a trustworthy Native American. Chinese Americans are depicted as innocent victims who are discriminated against, abused, and even shot. And the women prostitutes are portrayed as victims, who struggle for a living and courageously stand up for their rights as human beings.

Even though *Unforgiven* rejected the mythic West and offered only dark images of America, it demonstrated that individuals had at least some control over their lives. Like Will Munny, they could take a stand against evil or fight back against the powers that be. Eastwood later suggested that one of the reasons for the resiliency of the western is because it allows individuals control over their lives in simpler times. "Now everything's so complicated, so mired down in bureaucracy that people can't fathom a way of sorting it out," he explained. "In the West, even though you could get killed, it seems more manageable, like a lone individual might be able to work things out some way. In our society today, the idea of one person making a difference one way or the other is remote."[21]

In 2004, *Unforgiven* was chosen by the Library of Congress for inclusion in the National Film Registry. "For someone with Eastwood's background and reputation, *Unforgiven* was a daring statement. The film ran counter to almost everything the genre promised, and did so with an authority and conviction that was impossible to argue with," wrote Daniel Eagan in *America's Film Legacy: The Authoritative Guide to the Landmark Movies in the National Film Registry*. Eagan added, "*Unforgiven* has influenced every subsequent western, and its moral standing and filmmaking expertise place Eastwood among the best directors working in the industry."[22]

EPILOGUE

Django Unchained

Quentin Tarantino's *Django Unchained* was released on Christmas Day 2012. A movie poster spotlighted the star, Jamie Foxx, standing front and center. Staring straight ahead with determination, he's dressed in black and wearing a cowboy hat with a silver studded band. Ready for action, he holds a six-gun. Slightly behind him to the right stands costar Christoph Waltz, guarding his back with revolver in hand. On the far left is Leonardo DiCaprio's smarmy villain, holding a pipe and glaring menacingly. The tagline at the top—"LIFE, LIBERTY AND THE PURSUIT OF VENGEANCE"—no doubt resonated with many Americans in an age of terrorism and violence.

Django Unchained tells the story of an ex-slave who comes out of the American West to seek retribution for past injustices and rescue his wife from a brutal plantation owner in Mississippi. "I wanted to do an exciting western tale," explains Tarantino, "an almost odyssey voyage that Django goes on, a journey to free his wife from the clutches of an evil empire but use antebellum South slavery as a backdrop for that adventure."[1]

Tarantino's movie is a fascinating western hybrid. On the one hand, it is a throwback to revisionist westerns of another era. It pays homage to *Django* (1966) and other spaghetti westerns of the late sixties and early seventies. It features the same excessive violence and dark characters found in those earlier films. It includes music by the spaghetti western maestro Ennio Morricone. It even offers a cameo appearance by Franco Nero, who starred as the original Django. Tarantino has Nero saunter up to Jamie Foxx and ask, "What's your name?" Foxx coolly replies, "Django." Nero

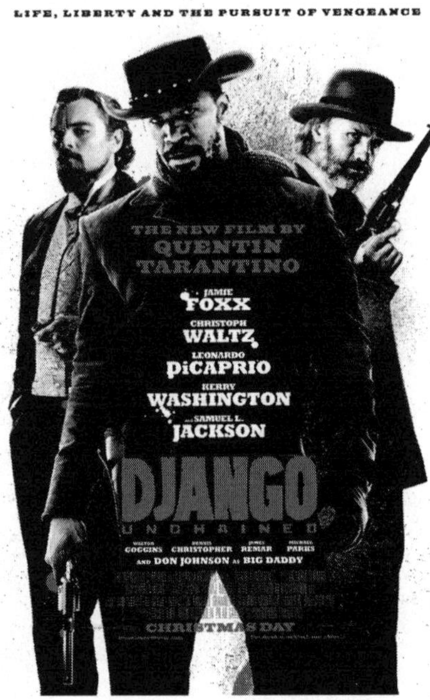

Figure 32. Quentin Tarantino's *Django Unchained* (A Band Apart Productions/Columbia Pictures/Weinstein Company, 2012) transformed the old spaghetti western antihero into a more ambiguous African American gunslinger fighting for just causes.

says, "Can you spell it?" Foxx looks at him and says, "D-J-A-N-G-O. The 'D' is silent." Nero looks at him and replies, "I know."

Like earlier revisionist westerns, Tarantino's film uses western themes and images to comment on both the past and the present. Issues involving race and violence are highlighted throughout. The brutality of slavery in the film and Django's extremely violent reaction to it not only condemn the "peculiar institution," but they reflect ubiquitous violence in modern America. The very fact that Tarantino's Django character is African American indicates the multiculturalism of modern America.

At the same time, *Django Unchained* is a very traditional western. It depicts the majestic beauty of the American West and offers a familiar western morality tale about vengeance and redemption. The movie features a rugged hero who is fast on the draw and determined to succeed. Django rides in from the West to clean up the decadent and corrupt

South. By film's end, he saves his wife and dispenses justice to evil doers. The redeemed couple then ride off into the sunset to live happily ever after in the mythic West.

Django Unchained demonstrates the continuing power of the mythic West. Just as it did in earlier days, the myth in the twenty-first century offers viewers escape to a fantasy world while it simultaneously serves up lessons about the real world around them. "One of the things that's interesting about westerns in particular is there's no other genre that reflects the decade that they were made and the morals and the feelings of Americans during that decade [more] than westerns," explains Quentin Tarantino. "Westerns are always a magnifying glass as far as that's concerned."[2]

Django Unchained became one of the biggest box office hits of 2012 and went on to earn two Oscars and a nomination for Best Picture. The phenomenal success of Tarantino's film was proof of the mythic West's relevance in a new century. Like Django "unchained," westerns would be unleashed to deal with changing times in the new millennium.

Westerns in Troubled Times

Americans began the twenty-first century wondering what new frontiers lay ahead. Some were apprehensive about Y2K and other perceived threats. Others had more realistic problems to worry about in a new age marked by 9/11 and growing polarization over myriad political, social, and cultural issues. These concerns would find their way into numerous westerns—both neotraditional and revisionist—that were released in the early years of the new century.[3]

Neotraditional westerns relied on familiar images of the mythic West to assure viewers that any problem could be solved as long as Americans adhered to the traditional values that had won the West. For example, *Open Range* (2003) starred Kevin Costner and Robert Duvall as old-fashioned cowboys who defend freedom, family, and honor against a greedy cattle baron. Other neotraditional westerns featured heroines or multicultural heroes, which given the changing times was no longer an innovation. Regardless of approach, neotraditional westerns remained true to the notion that good always triumphs over evil. *The Missing* (2003), directed by Ron Howard, is a perfect example. The plot recalls John Wayne's 1956 classic, *The Searchers*, but this time around, one of the protagonists is a strong, determined woman. Maggie Gilkeson (Cate Blanchett) learns that her daughter, Lilly, has been captured by Apache raiders. She teams up with her estranged father (Tommy Lee Jones), whom she hates because he abandoned his family decades before. Along with her younger daughter, Dot, they set out to track down the Indians and rescue Lilly. "*The Missing* features great characters, flawed men and women, who demonstrate enormous courage when they are confronted by an unspeakable horror," explains Howard. "It's a story of healing and reconciliation that also has the twists and turns of a thriller. I wasn't looking to merely exercise an old genre, but rather to tell a story that was relatable on a human level and exciting and suspenseful—but that still treated the period in an authentic way."[4]

Whether intentional or not, Howard's tale of "healing and reconciliation" picked up on American anxieties after September 11. *The Missing* mirrored new fears in a new century just as *The Searchers* reflected the 1950s Cold War culture. The hostile Indians in Ron Howard's western come across as terrorists who attack innocent men, women, and children on the American frontier. Their messianic leader, a brujo (witch) named Pesh-Chidin, is evil incarnate. The similarities to Osama Bin Laden are striking. He uses religious beliefs as a weapon, hates Americans, and dispassionately brutalizes his enemies. Even the name of the movie recalls the phenomenon that occurred in New York City in the days and weeks after 9/11, when posters of missing loved ones were taped to store windows, lamp posts, and anywhere else they might be noticed. "They were a humble catalogue of the missing, on view for months, intense visual windows onto internal disruption and cosmic pain," wrote Jerry Saltz in *New York Magazine*. Bruce Springsteen noticed it, too, and wrote a song called "You're Missing" for his Grammy Award–winning album, *The Rising*, inspired by the horrors of 9/11.[5]

Maggie and her father prove just as relentless as John Wayne's character in *The Searchers*. Ultimately, they brave the elements, defeat the enemy, and rescue Lilly and other captives. En route to success, they also find redemption. Tommy Lee Jones's character redeems himself by sacrificing his life to kill the brujo who is about to shoot his daughter, and Maggie finds redemption by forgiving her father posthumously. She brings his body home for a decent Christian burial, leaving behind her hatred for the man who had abandoned her years before. Like other neotraditional westerns, *The Missing* emphasizes the role of individuals in the fight against evil. When both the town sheriff and the U.S. military refuse to get involved, Maggie and her father take it upon themselves to set things right. Ron Howard's film also highlights women and minorities. Maggie and her daughters are strong, independent, and fearless. Maggie also proves to be an excellent shot as she guns down numerous Indian enemies. But the film is careful not to dismiss all Indians as evil. Just as President George W. Bush reminded Americans after 9/11 that not all Arabs were terrorists, Ron Howard's film distinguishes between evil Apache militants and "good" Apaches. It offers a sympathetic portrayal of the Apaches who help Maggie and her family. The Indians are treated as courageous allies and caring human beings. They speak an Apache dialect, wear historically accurate clothing and hairstyles, and practice traditional religious beliefs.

A neotraditional western released one year after *The Missing* was an even more obvious attempt to connect to the post-9/11 mood of America. *Hidalgo* (2004), which starred Viggo Mortensen as a part-Indian American cowboy and Omar Sharif as an Arab sheikh, told a traditional tale about a cowboy and his horse. This time, though, the story takes place in the Middle East. It focuses on an endurance race between the quintessential westerner and his Arab rivals. The cowboy—and by extension America—triumphs, defeating evil Arabs and winning over moderate Arabs who come to understand that the "infidel" is a good man who can be trusted. *Cowboys and Aliens* (2011) was another neotraditional western that dealt with the threat posed by terrorists from afar. The big-budget film, which featured a traditional cowboy hero and an alien cowgirl using laser ray guns to fight flying saucers that were threatening the planet, showed just how bizarre westerns could get in the new millennium.

Neotraditional westerns frequently picked up on social change. Although heroes in these films were often updated to keep pace with the gains made by women and minorities in modern society, they still defeated evil and found success in the mythic West. Following *The Missing*, other westerns such as *True Grit* (2010), *6 Guns* (2010), and *Sweetwater* (2013) showcased independent heroines with the wherewithal to defeat male villains. *Shanghai Noon* (2000) featured a Chinese martial arts expert as a good guy in the Old West. And African American heroes could be found in westerns such as *Texas Rangers* (2001), *Gallowwalkers* (2013), and, of course, *Django Unchained*.

Revisionist westerns were equally successful in the new millennium. In keeping with the pattern established back in the late sixties, these films rejected the notion of the mythic West completely and/or used familiar western types in new ways to comment on the times. *Brokeback Mountain* (2005) won three Oscars for its innovative portrayal of romantic love between two cowboys. Other films, such as *The Proposition* (2005), *The Assassination of Jesse James by the Coward Robert Ford* (2007), and *There Will Be Blood* (2007), featured antiheroes with dubious morals. The revisionist approach even spilled over to television with the success of HBO's award-winning western series *Deadwood* (2004–2006), which spotlighted antiheroes with ambiguous values who reveled in sex, alcohol, violence, and profanity.

No revisionist western was more successful than *No Country for Old Men* (2007), which won four Oscars, including Best Picture. Directed by Ethan and Joel Coen, the dark film captured the depressed mood of America in the first decade of the twenty-first century. The movie is set in the modern West. A psychopathic killer (reminiscent of the unstoppable villain in the 1978 horror movie *Halloween*) is terrorizing the Texas countryside. A local sheriff (Tommy Lee Jones) sets out to track him down, but the killer (Javier Bardem) just keeps coming as he brutally murders or eliminates all those in his path. Innocent people are shot mercilessly in the head; those who try to stand up to him are hunted down and killed; even the good sheriff feels helpless in the face of omnipotent evil and gives up, opting for early retirement.

Although the Coens' thriller often feels more like a horror movie than a western, it clearly shares attributes of a western movie. Set in the wide open spaces of the West, it features a sheriff who wears a cowboy hat and rides a horse. It also follows a familiar western trail, setting forth what appears to be a classic morality play that pits a good and decent cowboy hero against a thoroughly evil villain. This time, though, evil wins. Bardem's malevolent character personifies the senseless and ubiquitous violence that surrounded Americans in the new century. Audiences that recalled 9/11 and were fearful of new terrorist attacks, anxious about school shootings like Columbine, or troubled by ongoing wars in Afghanistan and Iraq, could relate to the unrelenting horror represented by Bardem's menacing character.

No Country for Old Men drove home the point that not even the mythic West could guarantee happiness and safety. The western landscapes in the Coen brothers' movie are bleak and as depressing as most of the characters. Success and redemption are nowhere to be found. Instead, there is only gloom, failure, and death, which reflected the despair of audiences caught up in bad economic times and fearful of senseless violence from terrorists, drug lords, and deranged murderers. The result was a sense of helplessness and hopelessness, whether it was in the mythic West or the real world. No wonder viewers could relate to the sheriff when he explains to a friend that it seems like the entire world is crumbling around him, yet he feels helpless to stop it. They also understood the friend's reply: "What you got ain't nothin new. This country's hard on people. You can't stop what's coming. It ain't all waiting on you. That's vanity."

If *No Country for Old Men* captured the depressed mood of the country in 2007, the Coen brothers' next western, *True Grit* (2010), showed that the optimism associated with the mythic West was still a force to be reckoned with. The Coens' remake of the John Wayne classic followed the same basic plot as the original, but the new version was more realistic. Even the taglines used to promote the two movies suggest the contrast. Where the first *True Grit* glorified "the strangest trio ever to track a killer," the tagline for the remake states fatalistically, "Punishment comes one way or another."

Despite its somber tone, the Coen brothers' rendition of *True Grit* is very much a traditional western. Like the heroes in the original, the protagonists in the remake defeat the bad guys and demonstrate courage, determination, and, of course, true grit. *True Grit* redux shows that the mythic West was alive and well in 2010, albeit in changed form. The film reflects the anxious mood of a nation reeling from 9/11, mired in two wars in Iraq and Afghanistan, and staggered by a Great Recession. But it also mirrors a new sense of optimism in the country. Its assurance that good will triumph in the end made it a western movie equivalent of Barack Obama's message of hope and change. The Coen brothers' movie brought the mythic West back full circle by showing that individuals could achieve equality and justice as long as they held fast to the values and resolve that had won the Old West.

The 2010 version of *True Grit* was a traditional western morality play with obvious heroes that contrasted sharply with the pessimistic outlook and absence of heroes in *No Country for Old Men* (2007). Despite totally different approaches, the two movies received rave reviews from audiences and critics. Their phenomenal success offered proof that both revisionist westerns and neotraditional westerns resonated with audiences in the new millennium.

Still Riding the Sagebrush Trail

Ever since the late 1890s, westerns have evolved in response to shifts in American history and culture. The changing images of the West in these films offer evidence about ordinary people and everyday life that historians might otherwise miss. Westerns reveal how Americans reacted to political and social movements such as Progressivism, the New Deal, and civil rights. They express attitudes about war, including World War I and II, the Korean War, the Cold War, and Vietnam. And they mirror social change involving race, gender, ethnicity, youth, and class. Westerns became a virtual public forum that allowed Americans to consider a variety of issues, events, beliefs, and actions. They capture ongoing discussions about Americans' hopes, dreams, and fears.

Along with providing new information about the past, westerns suggest fresh historical interpretations. These movies call into question the common wisdom that the years 1945 to 1963 were dominated by conformity and consensus behavior. Westerns released during those years actually reveal considerable conflict and changing attitudes toward race, gender, and youth. Similarly, westerns of the late sixties and seventies require a rethinking of the era known as the sixties. They provide ample evidence of continuity as well as conflict in America during that tumultuous time. Traditional images of the mythic West that supported established values and beliefs coexisted with revisionist images that mirrored polarization over the Vietnam War, race, gender, youth culture, and other issues. Later movies force us to reconsider the Reagan era. Post-1980 westerns suggest that the political, social, and cultural forces that divided sixties America continued to churn throughout the rest of the century and beyond. In addition, western movies provide proof that the New Western History associated with revisionist historians in the last two decades of the twentieth century was actually not that new or different. Long before New Western Historians arrived on the scene, western movies of the fifties and sixties were reinterpreting race, class, gender, the environment, and the role of government in the West.

The men and women found in westerns are—like Hector St. John de Crevecoeur's "new man"—products of a distinctly American way of life. These cinematic westerners take Frederick Jackson Turner's frontier thesis to new heights. They believe in freedom and opportunity. They are independent, self-sufficient, innovative, hardworking, moral, and fair. Though proud of their country, they are suspicious of government bureaucrats, incompetent military leaders, corrupt businessmen, and other special interests. When necessary, these cowboys and their cohorts know how to use guns in the name of justice. But once they clean up Dodge, they ride off into the sunset, making the West safe for democracy. Ever since western movies began, they have remained true to the belief that every American has a responsibility to defend the nation's goals and ideals. If government or society is unable or unwilling to solve a problem, then individuals need to do the job. Westerns have always understood that there is a time and place for everything in the mythic West. For practical Americans, the end always justified the means.

* * *

The twentieth century opened with Edwin S. Porter's ground-breaking western *The Great Train Robbery* (1903). It was only fitting that it closed with an equally important benchmark in the history of western movies—Clint Eastwood's *Unforgiven* (1992).

In the decades that separated those two movies, westerns continued to attract large audiences. Fans plunked down hard-earned cash to see traditional westerns, neotraditional westerns, revisionist westerns, B-Westerns, musical westerns, comedy westerns, space westerns, and other westerns in various shapes and forms. Maybe the draw was the magnificent western scenery. Perhaps audiences loved the gunslingers, cowboys, Indians, and other colorful characters. Or, it could have been the lure of cowboy hats, guns, boots, or spurs that jingled, or the attraction to rugged individuals riding horses. Audiences might have gone for the action, adventure, and excitement. Perhaps they were drawn in by western stories and myths that offered a common heritage, promoted American values, and provided a guide to success—for both the nation and the individual. Or maybe some viewers loved westerns because they provided escape to simpler and more exciting times.

Regardless of the reasons audiences were attracted to westerns, the continuing popularity of these movies throughout the twentieth century demonstrates the power and continuity of the mythic West. Every generation has used that shared memory to define itself and to cope with issues and problems. Like inkblots in a Rorschach test, the mythic West has appeared in various forms in different eras, yet it remains an indelible mark on the American psyche. Movies show that the main elements of the western myth have remained remarkably consistent for over a century. The mythic West has remained a land of enchantment, a place filled with adventure and romance. Predicated on American exceptionalism, it is a fabled land of freedom, liberty, opportunity, and redemption. It not only suggests continuity in American life and thought since the late 1800s, but underscores the nation's self-identity and adds to a better understanding of the American character.

The mythic West epitomized the American Dream that hardworking individuals, regardless of their background or heritage, could strike it rich if they had the skills and determination to succeed. The mythic West helped Americans find their way through times of war and peace, affluence and anxiety, crises and calm. During good times and bad, the mythic West reflected—and possibly helped shape—American life and thought.

All the while, it never failed to remind Americans where they've been, who they are, or where they're bound.

More than one hundred years have passed since Edwin S. Porter amazed audiences with *The Great Train Robbery*. Yet, westerns are still around in the twenty-first century and thriving, albeit in changed forms. Contemporary westerns now ride a variety of western trails, mixing old, new, and postmodern approaches. But in basic ways they remain the same. Westerns continue to explore the mythic West through exciting stories, colorful characters, and exotic landscapes. They rely on the same props, symbols, and artifacts as earlier films. And they continue to blur fact and fiction in legendary tales about cowboys, Indians, and other heroes and villains of the Old West. Equally important, they still provide comfort and escape if not solutions during times of great change or danger. Not surprisingly, westerns grew in popularity during the 1990s as an uncertain nation headed toward a new century. They would spike again in popularity after the trauma of September 11, perhaps because, like an old friend, they provided comfort in a time of sorrow and assurance that America could succeed in the future just as it always had on earlier frontiers.

Since the early 1900s, western movies have enabled viewers to ride alongside all the good guys, bad guys, and other characters who blazed an unforgettable path through the mythic West. This cinematic "sagebrush trail" comprises a valuable cultural history not only of westerns but also of America. To this day, whenever or wherever cowboys, cowgirls, gunslingers, Indians, pioneers, or other westerners saddle up and ride across the silver screen, they are adding one more chapter to America's longest-running cultural attraction—the Sagebrush Trail.

Notes

Prologue

1. Loren Baritz, "The Idea of the West," *American Historical Review* 66 (1961): 619–21; Frank Bergon and Zeese Papanikolas, eds., *Looking Far West: The Search for the American West in History, Myth, and Literature* (New York: Mentor Books, 1978), 59–78.
2. George Catlin, *Letters and Notes on the Manners, Customs, and Condition of the North American Indians* (New York: Wiley and Putnam, 1841), 1:62.
3. Frederick Jackson Turner, "The Significance of the Frontier in American History," *American Historical Association Annual Report for the Year 1893* (Washington, DC, 1894), 199–227; Walter Nugent, "Where is the American West? Report on a Survey," *Montana: The Magazine of Western History* 42, no. 3 (Summer 1992): 2–23; Bergon and Papanikolas, *Looking Far West*, 2.
4. Robert G. Athearn, *The Mythic West in Twentieth-Century America* (Lawrence: University Press of Kansas, 1986), 222, 274, 275. See also Henry Nash Smith, *Virgin Land: The American West as Symbol and Myth* (Cambridge, MA: Harvard University Press, 1950).
5. Edward Buscombe, ed., *The BFI Companion to the Western* (New York: Atheneum, 1988), 426–28; Les Adams and Buck Rainey, *Shoot-Em-Ups: The Complete Reference Guide to Westerns of the Sound Era* (New Rochelle, NY: Arlington House, 1978); Phil Hardy, *The Encyclopedia of Western Movies* (Minneapolis, MN: Woodbury Press, 1984); and "The Western Film . . . by the numbers!" *The Old Corral*, b-westerns.com, accessed July 12, 2012, http://www.b-westerns.com/graphs.htm.

Chapter 1

1. Frederick Jackson Turner, "The Significance of the Frontier in American History," in *The Frontier Thesis: Valid Interpretation of American History*, ed. Ray Allen Billington (New York: Holt, Rinehart, and Winston, 1966), 9–20.

2. Louis S. Warren, *Buffalo Bill's America: William Cody and the Wild West Show* (New York: Knopf, 2005), 419.

3. Charles Musser, *The Emergence of Cinema: The American Screen to 1907* (Berkeley: University of California Press, 1990), 360.

4. Edison Film, *The Great Train Robbery*, no. 201 (Edison Manufacturing Company, 1903), Rutgers University Community Repository, accessed September 10, 2014, http://hdl.rutgers.edu/1782.2/rucore00000001079.Book.16865. See also Filmsite Movie Review, "The Great Train Robbery (1903)," American Movie Classics, accessed September 10, 2014, http://www.filmsite.org/grea.html; and "The Great Train Robbery (1903 silent film)," Internet Archive, accessed September 10, 2014, http://www.archive.org/details/TheGreatTrainRobbery1903SilentFilm.

5. Robert V. Hine and John Mack Faragher, *The American West: A New Interpretive History* (New Haven, CT: Yale University Press, 2000), 503; Holly George-Warren, *Cowboy: How Hollywood Invented the Wild West* (Pleasantville, NY: Reader's Digest, 2002), 44, 46.

6. Hine and Faragher, *American West*, 503.

7. George N. Fenin and William K. Everson, *The Western: from Silents to Cinerama* (New York: Orion Press, 1962), 56; Warren, *Buffalo Bill's America*, 352; Andrew Brodie Smith, *Shooting Cowboys and Indians: Silent Western Films, American Culture, and the Birth of Hollywood* (Boulder: University Press of Colorado, 2003), 53, 54.

8. Smith, *Shooting Cowboys and Indians*, 21, 22, 43–45; Fenin and Everson, *The Western*, 56; Robert Sklar, *Movie-Made America: A Cultural History of American Movies* (New York: Vintage Books, 1976), 5.

9. Foster Rhea Dulles, *A History of Recreation: America Learns to Play* (Englewood Cliffs, NJ: Prentice-Hall, 1965), 289–91; Gerald Mast, *A Short History of the Movies* (Indianapolis: Bobbs-Merrill, 1981), 41, 42; Warren, *Buffalo Bill's America*, 279–81; Smith, *Shooting Cowboys and Indians*, 58–63; Michael Wallis, *The Real Wild West: The 101 Ranch and the Creation of the American West* (New York: St. Martin's Press, 1999), 341–44.

10. Fenin and Everson, *The Western*, 56–58; Smith, *Shooting Cowboys and Indians*, 59–64; George-Warren, *Cowboy*, 46; Wallis, *Real Wild West*, 341–44.

11. Richard W. Etulain, "Broncho Billy, William S. Hart, and Tom Mix: The Rise of the Hollywood Western," in *The Hollywood West: Lives of Film Legends Who Shaped It*, ed. Richard W. Etulain and Glenda Riley (Golden, CO: Fulcrum, 2001), 1–7. The Broncho Billy quotation comes from a 1957 interview conducted by Paul Killiam and William K. Everson, cited at "Broncho Billy Anderson Interview," Wild West Web, accessed June 17, 2014, http://www.wildwestweb.net/broncho.html.

12. Lane Roth and Tom W. Hoffer, "G. M. 'Broncho Billy' Anderson: The Screen Cowboy Hero Who Meant Business," *Journal of the University Film Association* 30, no. 1 (Winter 1978): 5–13; Smith, *Shooting Cowboys and Indians*, 26, 27.

13. William A. Settle Jr., *Jesse James Was His Name: Or, Fact and Fiction Concerning the Careers of the Notorious James Brothers of Missouri* (Columbia: University of Missouri Press, 1966), 3; Smith, *Shooting Cowboys and Indians*, 42, 138, 139; Richard White, *"It's Your Misfortune and None of My Own": A History of the American West* (Norman: University of Oklahoma Press, 1991), 335–37, 623.

14. *Motion Picture World*, November 11, 1909; Smith, *Shooting Cowboys and Indians*, 38, 39, 50, 56, 57; *Views and Films Index*, October 2, 1909, 9.

15. Jon Tuska, "The American Western Cinema, 1903–Present," in *Focus on the Western*, ed. Jack Nachbar (Englewood Cliffs, NJ: Prentice-Hall, 1974), 28; Smith, *Shooting Cowboys and Indians*, 135; Roth and Hoffer, "G. M. 'Broncho Billy' Anderson," 6; *New York Times*, January, 21, 1971, 38.

16. *Bioscope*, July 23, 1914, 401.

17. Quoted in Smith, *Shooting Cowboys and Indians*, 134, 144–50, 133.

18. Roth and Hoffer, "G. M. 'Broncho Billy' Anderson," 10.

19. Fred J. Balshofer and Arthur C. Miller, *One Reel a Week* (Berkeley: University of California Press, 1967), 41.

20. Young Deer got his start working for the circus and as a Wild West performer. By 1908, he and Red Wing were married and acting in westerns. In 1909, Vitagraph hired him to direct and costar with Red Wing in *Red Wing's Gratitude*. But critics doubted Young Deer's claim that he was an Indian. They insisted his real name was J. Younger Johnston; he was born not on the Winnebago reservation, but just north of it in Dakota City, Nebraska; the Bureau of Indian Affairs tribal records did not list anyone by the name of Young Deer (or Johnston); and his marriage license from the 1920s described his race as "white." Balshofer continued to insist that Young Deer was indeed an Indian. See Balshofer and Miller, *One Reel a Week*, 41; Smith, *Shooting Cowboys and Indians*, 72, 74, 75, 76, 79, 80, 81, 92; Daniel Eagan, *America's Film Legacy: The Authoritative Guide to the Landmark Movies in the National Film Registry* (New York: Continuum, 2010), 21; Matthew Sweet, "The First Native American Director. Or Was He?" *Guardian*, Film and Music section, September 24, 2010, 5.

21. Young Deer's sympathetic portrayals of Indians can be found in *The Red Girl and the Child* (1910) and *Red Eagle, the Lawyer* (1912). *Young Deer's Return* (1910) confronted racism and the notion that Indians had to assimilate into the mainstream culture. See Scott Simmon, *The Invention of the Western Film: A Cultural History of the Genre's First Half-Century* (New York: Cambridge University Press, 2003), 30, 31; Eagan, *America's Film Legacy*, 21, 22.

22. In 1913, Young Deer was charged with prostitution and statutory rape. Insisting he was the innocent victim of white racism, he fled to England and made documentaries during World War I. By the early 1920s, he and Red Wing had divorced, and Young Deer was attempting a comeback. In 1922, he appeared as an Indian named Aquila (which actually was the Latin word for "eagle") in a western entitled *Man of Courage*. Two years later, he directed his last film, *Lieutenant Daring RN and the Water Rats*. See Simmon, *Invention of the Western Film*, 31; Eagan, *America's Film Legacy*, 21, 22; Sweet, "First Native American Director," 5.

Chapter 2

1. Fenin and Everson, *The Western*, 61; advertisement in *New York Dramatic Mirror*, December 6, 1911; Louis Reeves Harrison, "The Bison 101 Headliners," *Moving Picture World*, April 27, 1912, 320–22, reprinted in Richard Abel, *Americanizing the*

Movies and "Movie-Mad" Audiences, 1910–1914 (Berkeley: University of California Press, 2006), 79–82.

2. "The Passing of the Western Subject," *Nickelodeon*, February 18, 1911, 181; A. L. Barrnett, "Will Moving Pictures Always Be Popular?" *Motion Picture News*, August 12, 1911, 12.

3. Roxy opened the Roxy Theater in 1927 and Radio City Music Hall in 1932, which featured the "Roxyette" dancers, aka the Rockettes. See Mast, *Short History of the Movies*, 101; Sklar, *Movie-Made America*, 45, 46, quotation on 46, citing Edward Bernard Kinsila, *Modern Theater Construction* (1917), 98.

4. *Motography*, July 31, 1915, 200; Sklar, *Movie-Made America*, 34–37.

5. Smith, *Shooting Cowboys and Indians*, 110.

6. Mast, *Short History of the Movies*, 45–47; Sklar, *Movie-Made America*, 50–54.

7. Quoted in Mast, *Short History of the Movies*, 48, 49.

8. Quoted in Eagan, *America's Film Legacy*, 43.

9. Thomas Cripps, *Hollywood's High Noon: Moviemaking and Society Before Television* (Baltimore: Johns Hopkins University Press, 1997), 28, 29; Sklar, *Movie-Made America*, 55, 56; Eagan, *America's Film Legacy*, 43; Melinda Corey and George Ochoa, eds., *The American Film Institute Desk Reference* (New York: DK, 2002), 32, 385.

10. Wallis, *Real Wild West*, 368, 369; Sklar, *Movie-Made America*, 40; Simmon, *Invention of the Western Film*, 56; Fenin and Everson, *The Western*, 67; Smith, *Shooting Cowboys and Indians*, 107, 109, 110, 112.

11. Balshofer and Miller, *One Reel a Week*, 76.

12. "Bison 101 Feature Pictures," *Motion Picture World*, January 27, 1912, 298; Smith, *Shooting Cowboys and Indians*, 113.

13. Wallis, *Real Wild West*, 370, 371; William H. Goetzmann and William N. Goetzmann, *The West of the Imagination* (New York: Norton, 1986), 307, 309; Fenin and Everson, *The Western*, 72, 77; Smith, *Shooting Cowboys and Indians*, 115, 116, 119.

14. *Moving Picture World*, January 27, 1912, 298; *New York Dramatic Mirror*, April 17, 1912, 25; *Motion Picture News*, April 20, 1912, 252; Smith, *Shooting Cowboys and Indians*, 125–27; Simmon, *Invention of the Western Film*, 62.

15. Buck Rainey, "The 'Reel' Cowboy," in *The Cowboy: Six-Shooters, Songs, and Sex*, ed. Charles W. Harris and Buck Rainey (Norman: University of Oklahoma Press, 1976), 25, 26; *Bioscope*, April 4, 1912, 63–65; Simmon, *Invention of the Western Film*, 67; Fenin and Everson, *The Western*, 72; Smith, *Shooting Cowboys and Indians*, 122, 125.

16. Mast, *Short History of the Movies*, 105; *New York Dramatic Mirror*, December 24, 1913, 34.

17. Sklar, *Movie-Made America*, 71; Fenin and Everson, *The Western*, 67, 68, 72; Mast, *Short History of the Movies*, 105, 106; Simmon, *Invention of the Western Film*, 57, 80; Wallis, *Real Wild West*, 395, 438, 439.

18. Joy S. Kasson, *Buffalo Bill's Wild West: Celebrity, Memory, and Popular History* (New York: Hill and Wang, 2000), 255, 256; Simmon, *Invention of the Western Film*, 62; George-Warren, *Cowboy*, 45.

19. Joseph G. Rosa and Robin May, *Buffalo Bill and His Wild West: A Pictorial Biography* (Lawrence: University Press of Kansas, 1989), 203–6; Warren, *Buffalo Bill's America*, 537–40; Kasson, *Buffalo Bill's Wild West*, 257–63; Don Russell, *The Lives and Legends of Buffalo Bill* (Norman: University of Oklahoma Press, 1960), 456–58.

20. Miles was adamant that scenes should be filmed at actual locations in the Badlands, using the same number of soldiers, eleven thousand, that had been originally deployed. Cody tried to change Miles's mind, insisting that his Wild West show background gave him a better understanding of logistical problems and production costs. Finally, they compromised. They made the fifty-mile trek to the Badlands, but instead of hiring additional troops, Cody simply had Miles march his much smaller force repeatedly in front of the camera to make it appear larger. See Rosa and May, *Buffalo Bill and His Wild West*, 206; Warren, *Buffalo Bill's America*, 538.

21. Russell, *Lives and Legends of Buffalo Bill*, 457; Warren, *Buffalo Bill's America*, 538; Kasson, *Buffalo Bill's Wild West*, 260.

22. Warren, *Buffalo Bill's America*, 538–40; Kasson, *Buffalo Bill's Wild West*, 260, 261; Goetzmann and Goetzmann, *West of the Imagination*, 298.

23. Kasson, *Buffalo Bill's Wild West*, 261, 262.

24. Howard R. Lamar, ed., *The New Encyclopedia of the American West* (New Haven, CT: Yale University Press, 1998), 278; Musser, *Emergence of Cinema*, 447; Eagan, *America's Film Legacy*, 38. See also Barbara A. Davis, *Edward S. Curtis: The Life and Times of a Shadow Catcher* (San Francisco: Chronicle Books, 1985), and Mick Gidley, *Edward S. Curtis and the North American Indian, Incorporated* (Cambridge: Cambridge University Press, 1998).

25. Eagan, *America's Film Legacy*, 38; Lamar, *New Encyclopedia of the American West*, 278. Photographs from Curtis's *The North American Indian* are available online through the Library of Congress American Memory exhibit, *Edward S. Curtis's The North American Indian*, accessed September 10, 2014, http://memory.loc.gov/ammem/award98/ienhtml/curthome.html; see also the University of Virginia American Studies website created by Valerie Daniels, *Edward Curtis: Selling the North American Indian*, accessed September 10, 2014, http://xroads.virginia.edu/~MA02/daniels/curtis/firstpage.html.

26. Musser, *Emergence of Cinema*, 447; quotation from Eagan, *America's Film Legacy*, 38.

27. *In the Land of the Head Hunters* was restored in the 1970s and reissued as *In the Land of the War Canoes* (Image Entertainment, 2000), DVD. See "Edward Curtis Meets the Kwakwa̲ka̲'wakw: 'In the Land of the Head Hunters,'" Rutgers School of Arts and Sciences, accessed September 10, 2014, http://www.curtisfilm.rutgers.edu.

28. Eagan, *America's Film Legacy*, 37, 38; movie review in the *New York Times*, December 8, 1914. The poster can be viewed in "Film Synopsis," part of the "Edward Curtis Meets the Kwakwaka'wakw" project, http://www.curtisfilm.rutgers.edu/film/film-synopsis-mainmenu-33.

29. Buscombe, *BFI Companion*, 300, 301; Sklar, *Movie-Made America*, 42, 44, 68.

30. Pop culture includes many stories about interracial romance. Usually, the plot focuses on white men and nonwhite women, which was more acceptable to the dominant white culture. Occasionally the tables were turned, e.g., James Fenimore Cooper's *The Last of the Mohicans* (1826) or western movies like *Red Eagle's Love Affair* (1910) and *Strongheart* (1914). No matter what the pairing, the result was never good for the Indian partner.

31. Sklar, *Movie-Made America*, 40; Mast, *Short History of the Movies*, 94, 95.

32. For information about Hart's career, see Etulain, "Broncho Billy, William S. Hart, and Tom Mix," 7–13; Diane Kaiser Koszarkski, *The Complete Films of William S. Hart:*

A Pictorial Record (New York: Dover Publications, 1980); and Ronald L. Davis, *William S. Hart: Projecting the American West* (Norman: University of Oklahoma Press, 2003).

33. Davis, *William S. Hart*, 59; Eagan, *America's Film Legacy*, 49, 50; George-Warren, *Cowboy*, 57, 58; Fenin and Everson, *The Western*, 77, 78.

34. Smith, *Shooting Cowboys and Indians*, 165–72 (Hart quotation on 165).

35. *Photoplay*, July 1920; Davis, *William S. Hart*, 137–39; quotations from Smith, *Shooting Cowboys and Indians*, 170.

36. Fenin and Everson, *The Western*, 131; Buscombe, *BFI Companion*, 426; Harding's quote is in the souvenir program, *Jesse L. Lasky Presents . . . "THE COVERED WAGON"—A JAMES CRUZE Production* (New York: Famous Players—Lasky Corporation, 1923), *Silent Film Still Archive*, accessed September 10, 2014, http://www.silentfilmstillarchive.com/covered_wagon.htm, cited hereafter as souvenir program.

37. Robert E. Sherwood, "The Covered Wagon," in *The Best Moving Pictures of 1922–23*, ed. Robert E. Sherwood (Boston: Small, Maynard, 1923), 71–77.

38. James Cruze quoted in Frederick James Smith, "How *The Covered Wagon* Was Made," *Photoplay*, June 1923, 38, 39, 106, 107.

39. Ibid., 38, 39, 106, 107; souvenir program.

40. Souvenir program; Smith, "How *The Covered Wagon* Was Made," 38, 39, 106, 107.

41. James Cruze, "Making *The Covered Wagon*," *Film Yearbook 1924*, 19, 21 (found in the Silent Film Still Archive, http://www.cinemaweb.com/silentfilm/bookshelf/11_loc_4.htm; see also http://www.silentfilmstillarchive.com/covered_wagon.htm, accessed September 26, 2014); souvenir program.

42. Frederick James Smith, "What Happens to Your Movie Money?" *Photoplay*, March 1927, 45, 130, 131; Rainey, "'Reel' Cowboy," 37; Corey and Ochoa, *American Film Institute Desk Reference*, 40; Sherwood, "The Covered Wagon," 71–77; Smith, "How *The Covered Wagon* Was Made," 38, 39, 106, 107; souvenir program.

43. Souvenir program.

44. The movie reviews can be found in the souvenir program.

45. Buscombe, *BFI Companion*, 272.

46. Other film versions of Zane Grey novels include *The Lone Star Ranger* (1923), *Riders of the Purple Sage* (1925), *The Light of the Western Stars* (1925), *The Mysterious Rider* (1927), and *The Last Trail* (1927).

47. Quoted in Rainey, "'Reel' Cowboy," 18.

48. For information about Mix, see Etulain, "Broncho Billy, William S. Hart, and Tom Mix," 13–19; Wallis, *Real Wild West*, 343, 344; Fenin and Everson, *The Western*, 108–21; Tuska, "American Western Cinema," 34, 35.

49. Rainey, "'Reel' Cowboy," 41, 42.

50. Less popular movie cowboys included Jack Hoxie, Tom Tyler, Art Acord, Neal Hart, Yakima Canutt, Pete Morrison, Eddie Polo, and Leo D. Maloney. Some used monikers that took advantage of famous westerners—Bob Custer, Buffalo Bill Jr., Pawnee Bill Jr., and Art Mix and Bill Mix, both of whom claimed to be Tom Mix's brothers (the former was a distant cousin; the latter no relation at all).

51. Fenin and Everson, *The Western*, 159–60.

52. Buscombe, *BFI Companion*, 426; Fenin and Everson, *The Western*, 115, 131; Rainey, "'Reel' Cowboy," 37; Smith, *Shooting Cowboys and Indians*, 187, 190, 202, 204; Corey and Ochoa, *American Film Institute Desk Reference*, 41.

53. For the argument that moviegoers were primarily young males, see Smith, *Shooting Cowboys and Indians*, 189, 193–96. Peter Stanfield maintains that low-budget westerns targeted not young boys but working-class adult audiences; Stanfield, *Horse Opera: The Strange History of the 1930s Singing Cowboy* (Urbana: University of Illinois Press, 2002), 4, 27, 34, 36, 43–45.

54. Tom Mix quoted in Fenin and Everson, *The Western*, 117.

55. Kathryn C. Esselman, "From Camelot to Monument Valley: Dramatic Origins of the Western Film," in Nachbar, *Focus on the Western*, 12, 15.

56. Quoted in Smith, *Shooting Cowboys and Indians*, 203.

57. The comment from *Variety*, January 25, 1928, appears in Robert S. Birchard, *King Cowboy: Tom Mix and the Movies* (Burbank, CA: Riverwood Press, 1993), 212.

Chapter 3

1. Eagan, *America's Film Legacy*, 171–73.

2. Mast, *Short History of the Movies*, 187–89; Cripps, *Hollywood's High Noon*, 100–112; Wendy Ide, "From Silent Films to Talkies," *London Times* (*Sunday Times On-Line Edition*), April 25, 2008; David Bordwell, "The Introduction of Sound," in *The Classical Hollywood Cinema: Film Style and Mode of Production to 1960*, ed. David Bordwell, Janet Staiger, and Kristin Thompson (New York: Columbia University Press, 1985), 300–302.

3. O. Henry, "The Caballero's Way," in *Classic Cowboy Stories: Eighteen Extraordinary Tales of the Old West*, ed. Michael McCoy (Guilford, CT: Lyons Press, 2004), 273–92.

4. Sklar, *Movie-Made America*, 161, 162.

5. Ibid., 175; Steven Mintz, "Hollywood and the Great Depression," *Digital History*, University of Houston, accessed March 22, 2011, http://www.digitalhistory.uh.edu/historyonline/hollywood_great_depression.cfm.

6. Russel Nye, *The Unembarrassed Muse: The Popular Arts in America* (New York: Dial Press, 1970), 302–4 (quotation on 302).

7. Other films celebrated the winning of the West, e.g., *The Trail of the Lonesome Pine* (1936), *Sutter's Gold* (1936), *The Texas Rangers* (1936), *Wells Fargo* (1937), *Badlands of Dakota* (1941), *Brigham Young* (1940), *Western Union* (1941), and *American Empire* (1942).

8. Turner, "Significance of the Frontier" (1977), 10.

9. Buffalo Bill, Wild Bill Hickok, and Calamity Jane are characters in *The Plainsman* (1936). Wyatt Earp and Doc Holliday appear in *Law and Order* (1932) and *Tombstone* (1942). Custer is featured in *Badlands of Dakota* (1940) and *They Died with Their Boots On* (1941). Other films focused on *Annie Oakley* (1935) and *Kit Carson* (1940).

10. Outlaws were featured in *Billy the Kid* (1930), *Jesse James* (1939), and *Bad Men of Missouri* (1941). Pancho Villa became a hero in *Viva Villa!* (1934). A woman desperado was featured in *Belle Starr* (1941). Fictional outlaws were spotlighted in *Three Godfathers* (1936), *The Oklahoma Kid* (1939), and *The Mark of Zorro* (1940), as well as in Cisco Kid films, e.g., *The Cisco Kid* (1931); *The Return of the Cisco Kid* (1939); and *The Cisco Kid and the Lady* (1939).

11. Joseph I. Breen to Howard Hughes, December 1940, quoted in the entry for *The Outlaw*, *American Film Institute (AFI) Catalog of Feature Films*, accessed April 2, 2011, http://www.afi.com/members/catalog/DetailView.aspx?s=&Movie=603.

12. The movie poster is reprinted in Corey and Ochoa, *American Film Institute Desk Reference*, 65. See also Julian Brown, ed., *The Chronicle of the Movies: A Year-by-Year History from the Jazz Singer to Today* (New York: Crescent Books, 1991), 104; Paul Simpson, *The Rough Guide to Westerns* (London: Rough Guides, 2006), 28; and the entry for *The Outlaw* in the *Internet Movie Database*, accessed April 2, 2011, http://www.imdb.com/title/tt0036241.

13. The review can be found in the entry for *The Outlaw*, *AFI Catalog*.

14. John H. Lenihan, "Westbound: Feature Films and the American West," in *Wanted Dead or Alive: The American West in Popular Culture*, ed. Richard Aquila (Urbana: University of Illinois Press, 1996), 118. For a comparison of western outlaws and movie gangsters, see Stanley J. Solomon, *Beyond Formula: American Film Genres* (New York: Harcourt, Brace, Jovanovich, 1976), 26–29.

15. Glenda Riley, "Barbara Stanwyck: Feminizing the Western Film," in Etulain and Riley, *Hollywood West*, 135.

16. R. Philip Loy, *Westerns and American Culture, 1930–1955* (Jefferson, NC: McFarland, 2001), 196.

17. "Movie of the Week: *The Ox-Bow Incident*—It Is an Antilynching Plea," *Life*, March 24, 1943, 41; Alan Gevinson, ed., *American Film Institute Catalog of Motion Pictures Produced in the United States—Within Our Gates: Ethnicity in American Feature Films, 1911–1960* (Berkeley: University of California Press, 1997), 756, 757.

Chapter 4

1. Ray White, "The Good Guys Wore White Hats: The B Western in American Culture," in Aquila, *Wanted Dead or Alive*, 135.

2. Ibid., 145, 146; Smith, *Shooting Cowboys and Indians*, 193, 194, 195, 213; Rainey, "'Reel' Cowboy," 35, 44; Stanfield, *Horse Opera*, 1; Packy Smith and Ed Hulse, eds., *Don Miller's Hollywood Corral: A Comprehensive B-Western Roundup* (Burbank, CA: Riverwood Press, 1993), 508, 509.

3. Fenin and Everson, *The Western*, 301–4; White, "Good Guys," 145; Ray White, e-mail interview with the author, July 10, 2012.

4. Hardy, *Encyclopedia of Western Movies*, 18, 19. Other silent stars who made the transition to sound movies included Tim McCoy, Hoot Gibson, George O'Brien, Harry Carey, Fred Thomson, Tom Tyler, Bob Custer, Jack Perrin, Pete Morrison, Rex Bell, Jack Holt, and Buffalo Bill Jr.

5. George-Warren, *Cowboy*, 116, 117; Tony Thomas, *The West That Never Was: Hollywood's Vision of the Cowboys and Gunfighters* (New York: Citadel Press, 1989), 16; Fenin and Everson, *The Western*, 116, 184.

6. Fenin and Everson, *The Western*, 120; Don Miller, "The Big Guns Speak: Gibson, Maynard, Mix," in Smith and Hulse, *Don Miller's Hollywood Corral*, 27.

7. Tom Mix was fifty years old when talking western pictures became common in 1930. In comparison, Buck Jones and Tim McCoy were thirty-nine; Hoot Gibson was thirty-eight; Ken Maynard was thirty-five; and Bob Steele was only twenty-three.

8. Thomas, *West That Never Was*, 35; Jon Tuska, "From the 100 Finest Westerns: Men Without Law," *Views and Reviews* 3, no. 1 (Summer 1971): 31; Rainey, "'Reel' Cowboy," 34, 35.

9. Wallis, *Real Wild West*, 445; *Pittsburgh Press*, December 1, 1942, 16; Rainey, "'Reel' Cowboy," 35.

10. Miller, "Gibson, Maynard, Mix," 24; Douglas B. Green, *Singing Cowboys* (Layton, UT: Gibbs Smith, 2006), 93, 94; Thomas, *West That Never Was*, 41.

11. Mary Gilmore, "Ken Maynard at RKO Temple," *Rochester Evening Journal*, March 11, 1935, 9; Stanfield, *Horse Opera*, 85; Thomas, *West That Never Was*, 42, 43; Green, *Singing Cowboys*, 94.

12. Buscombe, *BFI Companion*, 363, 364; Don Miller, "The Big Guns Speak: Jones, McCoy," in Smith and Hulse, *Don Miller's Hollywood Corral*, 37–41; Richard W. Bann, "Best of the West: Top Tens and Fan Favorites," in Smith and Hulse, *Don Miller's Hollywood Corral*, 508.

13. Tim McCoy interview in Darryl Ponicsan, "High Eagle: The Many Lives of Colonel Tim McCoy," *American Heritage* 28, no. 4 (June 1977): 52–62; Thomas, *West That Never Was*, 22.

14. McCoy interview in Ponicsan, "High Eagle."

15. The trailer for *Hop-Along Cassidy* (1935) is available on YouTube, accessed May 12, 2011, http://www.youtube.com/watch?v=F37VQnMhssg.

16. Don Miller, "Hoppy," in Smith and Hulse, *Don Miller's Hollywood Corral*, 113–15; "A 'Hoppy' Holiday! Gift Round-Up for Boys and Girls," *Life*, December 4, 1950, 163.

17. Green, *Singing Cowboys*, 13; the less sympathetic quote appears in the *London Daily Telegraph*, October 5, 1998, 23.

18. Paul Kingsbury, *The Grand Ole Opry History of Country Music: 70 Years of the Songs, the Stars, and the Stories* (New York: Villard, 1995), 43, 44; Ray Merlock and Jack Nachbar, "Gene Autry: Songs, Sidekicks, and Machines," in Etulain and Riley, *Hollywood West*, 44–62; Holly George-Warren, "Gene Autry: The Centennial of America's Favorite Cowboy," *American Cowboy* (July/August 2007), 44–50. For a full-length biography, see Holly George-Warren, *Public Cowboy No. 1: The Life and Times of Gene Autry* (New York: Oxford University Press, 2007).

19. George-Warren, "Gene Autry," 49; Kingsbury, *Grand Ole Opry*, 45. Nat Levine insisted that Autry initiated the contact; see Merlock and Nachbar, "Gene Autry," 44–62, as well as Paul Kingsbury and Alanna Nash, eds., *Will the Circle Be Unbroken: Country Music in America* (New York: DK, 2006), 107; Stanfield, *Horse Opera*, 85; Don Miller, "The Men from Music Mountain: Autry and Rogers," in Smith and Hulse, *Don Miller's Hollywood Corral*, 117–19; Simpson, *Rough Guide*, 27.

20. Hardy, *Encyclopedia of Western Movies*, xv; Fenin and Everson, *The Western*, 210–16.

21. Bann, "Best of the West," 508; Stanfield, *Horse Opera*, 150, 151, 152.

22. Richard W. Slatta, *The Cowboy Encyclopedia* (New York: Norton, 1994), 21; Merlock and Nachbar, "Gene Autry," 54; Kingsbury, *Grand Ole Opry*, 44, 45; Autry's Cowboy Code decreed: "(1) The Cowboy must never shoot first, hit a smaller man, or take unfair advantage. (2) He must never go back on his word, or a trust confided in him. (3) He must always tell the truth. (4) He must be gentle with children, the elderly, and animals. (5) He must not advocate or possess racially or religiously intolerant ideas.

(6) He must help people in distress. (7) He must be a good worker. (8) He must keep himself clean in thought, speech, action, and personal habits. (9) He must respect women, parents, and his nation's laws. (10) The Cowboy is a patriot." Publicity releases and Gene's movies and radio show promoted the code throughout the 1940s. The code is online at GeneAutry.com, accessed May 23, 2011, http://www.geneautry.com/geneautry/geneautry_cowboycode.html.

23. Gene Autry quoted in Stanfield, *Horse Opera*, 75.

24. The editorial from the April 1929 issue of *Photoplay* is reprinted in Fenin and Everson, *The Western*, 174; Kingsbury, *Grand Ole Opry*, 45.

25. Simmon, *Invention of the Western Film*, 188; Merlock and Nachbar, "Gene Autry," 45.

26. Merlock and Nachbar, "Gene Autry," 59; Gene Autry with Mickey Herskowitz, *Back in the Saddle Again* (Garden City, NY: Doubleday, 1978), 66.

27. Gene Autry, foreword to Smith and Hulse, *Don Miller's Hollywood Corral*, xi; Autry, *Back in the Saddle*, 53; Kingsbury, *Grand Ole Opry*, 44; Autry quote comes from Slatta, *Cowboy Encyclopedia*, 22.

28. Buttram quoted in Gary H. Grossman, *Saturday Morning TV* (New York: Arlington House, 1987), 183; Merlock and Nachbar, "Gene Autry," 61.

29. Examples include Rex Allen, Bob Baker, Smith Ballew, Eddie Dean, Dick Foran, Tex Fletcher, Kirby Grant, Monte Hale, Tex Harding, Herb Jeffries, John King, Jack Randall, Jimmy Wakely, Ray Whitley, and Tex Williams, to name just a few. Singing cowgirls included Dale Evans, Jane Frazee, Dorothy Page, and Penny Singleton.

30. Thomas, *West That Never Was*, 50, 51; Green, *Singing Cowboys*, 110–13; Don Cusic, *Cowboys and the Wild West: An A–Z Guide from the Chisholm Trail to the Silver Screen* (New York: Facts on File, 1994), 239, 240; and Don Miller, "Have Songs Will Warble," in Smith and Hulse, *Don Miller's Hollywood Corral*, 140–45.

31. Tex Ritter, "I Dreamed of a Hillbilly Heaven," composed by Hal Southern, *Hillbilly Heaven* (Capitol Records, 1961).

32. Bill C. Malone, *Country Music, U.S.A.: A Fifty-Year History* (Austin: American Folklore Society and University of Texas Press, 1968), 148, 149; Raymond E. White, *King of the Cowboys, Queen of the West: Roy Rogers and Dale Evans* (Madison: University of Wisconsin Press, 2005), 6; Cusic, *Cowboys and the Wild West*, 245–48.

33. Green, *Singing Cowboys*, 116; White, *King of the Cowboys, Queen of the West*, 8, 9; Laurence Zwisohn, "Roy Rogers," in *The Encyclopedia of Country Music*, ed. Paul Kingsbury (New York: Oxford University Press, 1998), 456.

34. *Schenectady Gazette*, May 19, 1938, 9; Hardy, *Encyclopedia of Western Movies*, 88; Stanfield, *Horse Opera*, 95–97; Green, *Singing Cowboys*, 118; *Exhibitor*, November 29, 1939, 34.

35. Within a year of Roy Rogers's debut, he shot up to number three on the *Motion Picture Herald*'s annual ranking of the top ten movie cowboys, behind only Autry and William Boyd. He rose to number one in 1943, the year after Autry went into the armed forces. See Bann, "Best of the West," 508, 509.

36. *New York Times*, November 4, 1945; Bann, "Best of the West," 508, 509; White, *King of the Cowboys, Queen of the West*, 175, 176, 70–72; *Montreal Gazette*, September 24, 1945, 2; Laurence Zwisohn, "Happy Trails: The Life of Roy Rogers," article on the official Roy Rogers website: URL: http://www.royrogers.com/roy_rogers_bio.html (retrieved June 22, 2011).

37. Laurence Zwisohn, "Happy Trails: The Life of Roy Rogers," *Official Roy Rogers Website*, accessed June 22, 2011, http://www.royrogers.com/roy_rogers_bio.html; White, *King of the Cowboys, Queen of the West*, 113.

38. Roy Rogers, afterword to Smith and Hulse, *Don Miller's Hollywood Corral*, 521, 522; Roy Rogers and Dale Evans, "Happy Trails," composed by Dale Evans (RCA Victor, 1952).

39. Bann, "Best of the West," 513, 514.

40. Arthur F. McClure and Ken D. Jones, *Heroes, Heavies and Sagebrush: A Pictorial History of the "B" Western Players* (South Brunswick, NJ: Barnes, 1972), 11.

41. White, "Good Guys," 144, 146, 148.

42. Other B-Westerns with World War II themes include *Death Rides the Range* (1939), *King of the Mounties* (1942), *Texas to Bataan* (1942), *The Night Riders* (1939), *Raiders of Sunset Pass* (1943), *Cowboy Commandos* (1943), and *Wild Horse Rustlers* (1943).

43. Hans J. Wollstein, "Dorothy Page Biography," *Moviefone*, accessed July 14, 2011, http://www.moviefone.com/celebrity/dorothy-page/1820584/biography; White, "Good Guys," 149; Green, *Singing Cowboys*, 102. B-Westerns that featured heroines with guns include *The Crimson Trail* (1935), *The Trusted Outlaw* (1937), *New Frontier* (1939), *The Man from Sundown* (1939), *Spoilers of the Range* (1939), *Sonora Stagecoach* (1944), *Thunder Mountain* (1947), *Alias Billy the Kid* (1946), *Trail Guide* (1952), and *Two-Gun Lady* (1955). Linda Stirling starred as a female Zorro in Republic Picture's serial *Zorro's Black Whip* (1944).

44. Autry, foreword, xii; White, "Good Guys," 150. Dale Evans became a role model for young girls. Evidence of her popularity can be found in the success of the twenty-eight films that she made with Roy Rogers and the commercial success of Dale Evans products, including cowgirl outfits, guns, comic books, records, and play sets.

45. The *Outlaw Women* poster is available at Wrong Side of the Art, accessed September 7, 2013, http://wrongsideoftheart.com/2010/09/outlaw-women-1952-usa. The poster for *Jesse James' Women* can be viewed at Movie Poster Shop, accessed September 7, 2013, http://www.moviepostershop.com/jesse-james-women-movie-poster-1954.

46. *The Pittsburgh Press*, July 3, 1938, 24.

47. For an overview of African Americans in B-Westerns, see Loy, *Westerns and American Culture*, chapter 8.

48. The movie poster can be viewed at Movie Goods, accessed September 7, 2013, http://www.moviegoods.com/movie_poster/harlem_rides_the_range_1939.htm.

49. Stereotypical Chinese cooks can be found in numerous films, including Dick Foran's *Moonlight on the Prairie* (1935) and the Three Mesquiteers' *Saddle Mountain Roundup* (1941).

50. Mexican bandits appear in numerous B-Westerns, including *Man from Death Valley* (1931), *Mexicali Rose* (1939), and *The Gay Desperado* (1936). Mexican spitfires are featured in films such as *Man from Monterey* (1933) and *Ride on Vaquero* (1941). More refined Hispanic women can be found in *The Hard Hombre* (1931), *Song of the Gringo* (1936), and *The Cowboy and the Senorita* (1944). Hispanic characters sometimes played dashing characters and saddle pals, e.g., Ricardo Cortez starred as a Zorro-like character in *The Californian* (1937); Mexican pop star Tito Guizar teamed with Roy Rogers to defeat bad guys in *On the Old Spanish Trail* (1947) and then appeared as a rakish kissing bandit in *The Llano Kid* (1939); Richard Martin played

Tim Holt's charming sidekick, Chito Jose Gonzalez Bustamente Rafferty, in a series of westerns in the early 1950s. Comedic Hispanic sidekicks all too often were named Pancho. Julian Rivero played a jokester named Pancho in *Death Rides the Range* (1939); Martin Garralaga starred as the original Pancho Gonzales opposite Duncan Renaldo in early Cisco Kid films, such as *The Cisco Kid Returns* (1945); Leo Carrillo made the Pancho character famous in Duncan Renaldo's later Cisco Kid movies and TV programs.

51. Hardy, *Encyclopedia of Western Movies*, 35, 36; Ted Sennett, *Great Hollywood Westerns* (New York: Abrams, 1990), 180.

52. *Dubuque Telegraph-Herald and Times Journal*, February 11, 1934, 10.

53. The poster for *White Eagle* can be viewed at IMP Awards, accessed September 7, 2013, http://www.impawards.com/1932/white_eagle_xlg.html.

54. The opening of *The Lone Ranger* TV show is available on YouTube, accessed August 1, 2011, http://www.youtube.com/watch?v=Td4RHvyAFsM. Perhaps the closest any B-Western Indian came to equality with white characters is when Chief Thundercloud starred in films such as *Silver Stallion* (1941) and *King of the Stallions* (1942), or when he appeared as a member of Monogram Pictures' trigger trio, the Trail Blazers, costarring in *Outlaw Trail* and *Sonora Stagecoach* (both in 1944). But even then, Chief Thundercloud ultimately played a secondary role to white characters; he received third billing in the Trail Blazer trio pictures.

55. Rainey, "'Reel' Cowboy," 54, 55.

Chapter 5

1. John Ford quoted in Ronald L. Davis, *John Ford: Hollywood's Old Master* (Norman: University of Oklahoma Press, 1995), 205.

2. Jim Kitses, *Horizons West: Directing the Western from John Ford to Clint Eastwood*, new ed. (London: BFI, 2004; repr., London: Palgrave Macmillan, 2009), 96.

3. Stephen J. Whitfield, *The Culture of the Cold War* (Baltimore: Johns Hopkins University Press, 1991), 53.

4. Douglas Brode, *The Films of the Fifties*, reprint ed. (Secaucus, NJ: Citadel Press, 1992), 181.

5. The Warner Brothers press kit is reproduced in *John Wayne Limited Edition Boxed Gift Set: The Ultimate Collector's Edition* (Warner Home Video, 2006). The information about "That'll Be the Day" comes from the author's interview with Jerry Allison of the Crickets (January 5, 1999).

6. Sons of the Pioneers, "The Searchers," composed by Stan Jones, *The Searchers Original Film Soundtrack* (Él Records, 1956).

7. William E. Leuchtenburg, *A Troubled Feast: American Society since 1945* (Boston: Little, Brown, 1983), 104–18. See also William H. Chafe, *The Unfinished Journey: America since World War II* (New York: Oxford University Press, 1986), chapter 5.

8. Donald Marshman, "Mister Siodmak," *Life*, August 25, 1947, 100–101.

9. Bosley Crowther, "*Darling Clementine*, with Henry Fonda as Marshal of Tombstone, a Stirring Film of the West," *New York Times*, December 4, 1946.

10. John Ford quoted in Simpson, *Rough Guide*, 111.

11. Bob Dylan, "Brownsville Girl," composed by Bob Dylan and Sam Shepard, *Knocked Out Loaded* (Columbia, 1986). I want to thank Dan Sawers, an expert on Bob Dylan's music, for calling that song to my attention.

12. Leuchtenburg, *Troubled Feast*, 104; *Duel in the Sun* (1946) featured Gregory Peck and Joseph Cotten as western equivalents of Cain and Abel. The brothers fight over Pearl Chavez (Jennifer Jones), who is torn between retaining her morals and succumbing to temptation. Emotionally scarred characters can also be found in *Along the Great Divide* (1951), *The Man from Laramie* (1955), *The Fastest Gun Alive* (1956), *The Halliday Brand* (1957), *3:10 to Yuma* (1957), and *Man of the West* (1958).

13. Anguished protagonists plagued by cynicism, greed, and violent tendencies can be found in popular films such as *The Treasure of the Sierra Madre* (1948), *Lust for Gold* (1949), *The Furies* (1950), *These Thousand Hills* (1959), *Ride the High Country* (1962), and *Hud* (1963).

14. David F. Trask, "The Imperial Republic," in *The Unfinished Century: America since 1900*, ed. William E. Leuchtenburg (Boston: Little, Brown, 1973), 587; Walter LaFeber, Richard Polenberg, and Nancy Woloch, *The American Century: A History of the United States since the 1890s* (New York: Knopf, 1986), 355.

15. Leuchtenburg, *Troubled Feast*, 29–31; William L. O'Neill, *American High: The Years of Confidence, 1945–1960* (New York: Free Press, 1986), 142–51.

16. Henry Ward, "*High Noon* Classed Tops Among Westerns," *Pittsburgh Press*, July 28, 1952, 6.

17. Stanley Corkin, *Cowboys as Cold Warriors: The Western and U.S. History* (Philadelphia: Temple University Press, 2004), 127–63; Matthew J. Costello, "Rewriting *High Noon*: Transformations in American Popular Political Culture during the Cold War, 1952–1968," in *Hollywood's West: The American Frontier in Film, Television, and History*, ed. Peter C. Rollins and John E. O'Connor (Lexington: University Press of Kentucky, 2005), 175; Buscombe, BFI *Companion*, 269.

18. J. M. Caparros-Lera and Sergio Alegre, "Cinematic Contextual History of *High Noon*," in *Film-Historia* 6, no. 1 (1996): 37–61, accessed June 12, 2012,http://www.publicacions.ub.es/bibliotecadigital/cinema/filmhistoria/Art.HighNoon.pdf; the quote from the *Nation* can be found in John H. Lenihan, *Showdown: Confronting Modern America in Western Film* (Urbana: University of Illinois Press, 1980), 120.

19. Fred Zinnemann to Dr. J. M. Caparros-Lera, September 2, 1988, printed in its entirety in Caparros-Lera and Alegre, "Cinematic Contextual History of *High Noon*," 42.

20. Numerous writers have analyzed the social implications of *High Noon*. See Pauline Kael, *Kiss Kiss Bang Bang* (New York: Bantam Books, 1969); Costello, "Rewriting *High Noon*," 178–80; and Lenihan, *Showdown*, 119, as well as Lenihan's essay, "Westbound," 122, 123.

21. Lenihan, *Showdown*, 119; John Wayne interview, *Playboy Interview* (May 1971), 17, 18.

22. The Howard Hawks quote comes from an online interview, accessed June 12, 2012, http://www.tumblr.com/tagged/carl-foreman. See also Scott Breivold, ed., *Howard Hawks: Interviews* (Jackson: University Press of Mississippi, 2006), 61.

23. Roger Ebert, Great Movie review, "Rio Bravo," *Chicago Sun Times*, July 15, 2009, accessed June 13, 2012,http://rogerebert.suntimes.com/apps/pbcs.dll

/article?AID=/20090715/REVIEWS08/907159989/1023; Brode, *Films of the Fifties*, 279.

24. John Ford quoted in Davis, *John Ford*, 203, 204.

25. Trailer for *Rio Grande*, YouTube, accessed June 15, 2012, http://www.youtube.com/watch?v=007CHY544HY.

26. Davis, *John Ford*, 214, 243.

27. Davis, *John Ford*, 243.

Chapter 6

1. Whitfield, *Culture of the Cold War*; Elaine Tyler May, *Homeward Bound: American Families in the Cold War Era* (New York: Basic Books, 1988); Douglas T. Miller and Marion Nowak, *The Fifties: The Way We Really Were* (New York: Doubleday, 1977).

2. For information about the New Western History, see Patricia Nelson Limerick, Clyde A. Milner II, and Charles E. Rankin, eds., *Trails: Toward a New Western History* (Lawrence: University Press of Kansas, 1991); William Cronon, George Miles, and Jay Gitlin, eds., *Under an Open Sky: Rethinking America's Western Past* (New York: Norton, 1992).

3. Numerous movies featured traditional heroes and values or patriotic themes: *The Virginian* (1946), *Unconquered* (1947), *Seven Brides for Seven Brothers* (1954), *Oklahoma!* (1955), *Gunfight at the O.K. Corral* (1957), *The Sheriff of Fractured Jaw* (1959), and *Cimarron* (1960).

4. Other westerns that highlighted religion include *The Twinkle in God's Eye* (1955), *The Peacemaker* (1956), *The Parson and the Outlaw* (1957), *The Persuader* (1957), *The Miracle of the Hills* (1959), and *The Singer Not the Song* (1962). For how religion, marriage, and the family were linked to the Cold War, see Miller and Nowak, *The Fifties*, 90, 91; May, *Homeward Bound*, 3.

5. Many Americans equated capitalism with American democracy. See Godfrey Hodgson, *America in Our Time* (New York: Doubleday, 1976), 67–98.

6. *Red River* (1948) told the rags-to-riches tale of a man in the Texas cattle business. *Cimarron* (1960) focused on town building and newspaper publishing, while films such as *Fort Worth* (1951) and *Texas Lady* (1955) explained how ordinary Americans succeeded despite the opposition of powerful rivals or corrupt businessmen.

7. The Cold War model for female behavior was spelled out in Ferdinand Lundberg and Marynia F. Farnham's *Modern Woman: The Lost Sex* (New York: Harper, 1947), which encouraged women to accept their natural roles in life by becoming wives and homemakers; Miller and Nowak, *The Fifties*, 150–55; May, *Homeward Bound*, 109.

8. Unhappy fates awaited aggressive females in westerns such as *Ramrod* (1947), *Raton Pass* (1951), and *Rancho Notorious* (1952).

9. Harvey Green, *The Uncertainty of Everyday Life, 1915–1945* (New York: Harper Collins, 1992), 152; Sara M. Evans, *Born for Liberty: A History of Women in America* (New York: Free Press, 1989), 252.

10. Career women are featured in *Take Me to Town* (1953), *Cattle Queen of Montana* (1954), *Texas Lady* (1955), *Strange Lady in Town* (1955), and *The Second Time Around* (1961). They become gunfighters in *Bandit Queen* (1950), *Cattle Queen*

(1951), and *The Oklahoma Woman* (1956). They are sharpshooters in *The Paleface* (1948), *The Beautiful Blonde from Bashful Bend* (1949), and *Calamity Jane* (1953); cardsharps in *Red River* (1948) and *Rio Bravo* (1959); a spy in *The Redhead and the Cowboy* (1951); law women in *The Moonlighter* (1953) and *Gunslinger* (1956); and outlaws in *Montana Belle* (1952) and *The Maverick Queen* (1956). They also defend a base against Indians in *The Guns of Fort Petticoat* (1957).

11. I wish to thank Valerie Aquila, a doctoral student in communications at Indiana University, for her insight into how conservatives might have viewed these films.

12. Evans, *Born for Liberty*, 248; Riley, "Barbara Stanwyck," 121, 122, 140. The Reagan quotation is on page 140 of Riley.

13. Martin Scorcese quoted in Eagan, *America's Film Legacy*, 486.

14. For information about changing sexual attitudes, see Michael Barson and Steven Heller, *Teenage Confidential: An Illustrated History of the American Teen* (New York: Sterling, 2005), 93, 102; Miller and Nowak, *The Fifties*, 154, 155; and James T. Patterson, *Grand Expectations: The United States, 1945–1974* (New York: Oxford University Press, 1996), 355–58. Adultery was addressed in *The Sea of Grass* (1947), *Pillars of the Sky* (1956), and *Jubal* (1956). Sex and promiscuity powered many postwar westerns, e.g., *Duel in the Sun* (1946), *My Darling Clementine* (1946), *Man Without a Star* (1955), *Jubal* (1956), *Rio Bravo* (1959), *Yellowstone Kelly* (1959), *Ride the High Country* (1962), and *Hud* (1963). For information about homosexual tensions in *Johnny Guitar*, see Roger Ebert, Great Movie review, "Johnny Guitar," *Chicago Sun-Times*, May 8, 2008, accessed July 7, 2012, http://rogerebert.suntimes.com/apps/pbcs.dll/article?AID=/20080508/REVIEWS08/650962984/1023.

15. James L. Baughman, *The Republic of Mass Culture: Journalism, Filmmaking, and Broadcasting in America since 1941* (Baltimore: Johns Hopkins University Press, 1997), 109; Peter Noble, *The Negro in Films* (Port Washington, NY: Kennikat Press, 1969); Edward Mapp, *Blacks in American Film: Today and Yesterday* (Metuchen, NJ: Scarecrow Press, 1972); and Thomas Cripps, *Slow Fade to Black: The Negro in American Film, 1900–1942* (London: Oxford University Press, 1977).

16. Woody Strode quoted in Davis, *John Ford*, 305.

17. Both quotations can be found in ibid., 296, 299.

18. Two releases in 1949, *The Cowboy and the Indians* and *Daughter of the West*, set the stage for westerns that were sympathetic toward the plight of Indians.

19. *New York Times*, July 21, 1950; Philip French, "The Indian in the Western Movie," in *The Pretend Indians: Images of Native Americans in the Movies*, ed. Gretchen M. Bataille and Charles L. P. Silet (Ames: Iowa State University Press, 1980), 99, 100. See also Frank Manchel, "Cultural Confusion: *Broken Arrow*," in *Hollywood's Indian: The Portrayal of the Native American in Film*, ed. Peter C. Rollins and John E. O'Connor (Lexington: University Press of Kentucky, 2003), 90–106.

20. Examples include *Tomahawk* (1951), *Navajo* (1952), *Hondo* (1953), *Seminole* (1953), *Apache Woman* (1955), *Chief Crazy Horse* (1955), *White Feather* (1955), *The Indian Fighter* (1955), and *Winnetou* (1963).

21. Crooked businessmen or politicians are villains in *Comanche Territory* (1950), *War Paint* (1953), *War Drums* (1957), and *Geronimo* (1962). Racist soldiers or government bureaucrats are to blame in *Arrowhead* (1953), *War Arrow* (1953), *Seminole* (1953), *Pillars of the Sky* (1956), and *The Guns of Fort Petticoat* (1957).

22. Other examples include *Devil's Doorway* (1950), *The Battle at Apache Pass* (1952), *The Savage* (1952), *Apache* (1954), *Run of the Arrow* (1957), *Fort Massacre* (1958), *Flaming Star* (1960), and *The Unforgiven* (1960).

23. See *Broken Arrow* (1950), *Across the Wide Missouri* (1951), *Tomahawk* (1951), *Apache Woman* (1955), *The Indian Fighter* (1955), *The Far Horizons* (1955), *White Feather* (1955), *Trooper Hook* (1957), *Yellowstone Kelly* (1959), *The Unforgiven* (1960).

24. Other examples include *Distant Drums* (1951), *Only the Valiant* (1951), *Flaming Feather* (1952), *The Charge at Feather River* (1953), *Drum Beat* (1954), *The Command* (1954), and *The Searchers* (1956).

25. Sensitive images of Hispanics can be found in *Viva Zapata* (1952), *Man from Del Rio* (1956), *Villa!!* (1958), *The Last Rebel* (1961), and *The Magnificent Seven* (1960). John Ford westerns like *Fort Apache* (1948), *She Wore a Yellow Ribbon* (1949), *Rio Grande* (1950), *The Searchers* (1956), and *The Man Who Shot Liberty Valance* (1962) offer sympathetic portrayals of Irish, Swedes, and other white ethnic groups.

26. Adolescent costars are featured in *Saddle Tramp* (1950), *Shane* (1953), and *Hondo* (1953). Other westerns with youth appeal included *Old Yeller* (1957) and *Savage Sam* (1963). Some westerns used teen idols to attract young crowds, e.g., Tab Hunter in *The Burning Hills* (1956). Emphasizing that a new generation had come to the West, *Young Guns of Texas* (1962) starred the sons of Joel McCrea and Robert Mitchum and Alan Ladd's daughter.

27. Rock stars such as Connie Francis, Frankie Avalon, and Fabian also appeared in westerns. For a list of rock songs about the West, see Richard Aquila, *That Old Time Rock & Roll: A Chronicle of an Era, 1954–1963* (Urbana: University of Illinois Press, 2000), 111–12. The connection between the American West and rock & roll is explored in Richard Aquila, "A Blaze of Glory: The Mythic West in Pop and Rock Music," in Aquila, *Wanted Dead or Alive*, 197–210.

28. For attitudes toward juvenile delinquency, see John Patrick Diggins, *The Proud Decades: America in War and Peace, 1941–1960* (New York: Norton, 1986), 198–201; Barson and Heller, *Teenage Confidential*, 47–49. Movies about delinquents out west include *Run for Cover* (1955), *Gunman's Walk* (1958), *Lone Texan* (1959), and *The Plunderers* (1960). The movie poster for *The Left-Handed Gun* is reproduced in Hardy, *Encyclopedia of Western Movies*, 264.

29. Gene Pitney, "The Man Who Shot Liberty Valance," composed by Burt Bacharach and Hal David (Musicor Records, 1962).

Chapter 7

1. Leone's quote comes from David Gregory, *The Spaghetti West*, a documentary written, directed, and produced by David Gregory (Independent Film Channel [IFC] in association with Netflix; Blue Underground, 2005).

2. George-Warren, *Cowboy*, 201.

3. Clint Eastwood quoted in Marc Eliot, *American Rebel: The Life of Clint Eastwood* (New York: Harmony, 2009), 114–15.

4. Sergio Sollima quoted in Gregory, *The Spaghetti West*.

5. For further information, see Christopher Frayling, *Spaghetti Westerns: Cowboys and Europeans from Karl May to Sergio Leone* (London: I. B. Tauris, 2006).

6. The Ferdinando Baldi interview comes from Gregory, *The Spaghetti West*.

7. Information about the mafia's origins and the tradition of Italian vigilantism can be found in Jerre Mangione and Ben Morreale, *La Storia: Five Centuries of the Italian American Experience* (New York: Harper Collins, 1992), 62–64, 73–74. Similar motives and behavior are exhibited by Don Corleone and other antiheroes in Francis Ford Coppola's Godfather series, beginning with *The Godfather* (1972). While there is no evidence that Coppola's movies were directly patterned on spaghetti westerns, it is interesting that Coppola's antiheroes debuted shortly after spaghetti western antiheroes had become a fixture in the era's films.

8. Hardy, *Encyclopedia of Western Movies*, 302.

9. *Minnesota Clay* (1964) and *Blindman* (1971) feature protagonists who cannot see, while the hero of *The Great Silence* (1968) cannot speak. *Death Sentence* (1967) and *God's Gun* (1976) include gun-toting priests; *Shanghai Joe* (1973) and *The Tiger from the River Kwai* (1975) feature protagonists who are martial arts specialists.

10. Manolo Bolognini interview in Gregory, *The Spaghetti West*.

11. Simpson, *Rough Guide*, 35.

12. Sergio Donati is quoted in Gregory, *The Spaghetti West*.

13. Vincent Canby, review of *Once Upon a Time in the West* (1968), *New York Times*, May 29, 1969, accessed May 14, 2013, http://movies.nytimes.com/movie/review?res=9E01E3DC1E3AEE34BC4151DFB3668382679EDE.

14. Lucia Bozzola, review summary, *Once Upon a Time in the West* (1968), *New York Times*, accessed May 14, 2013, http://movies.nytimes.com/movie/36331/Once-Upon-a-Time-in-the-West/overview.

15. The reviewer was referring to *Dead Men Don't Make Shadows*, *Spaghetti Western Database*, accessed May 17, 2013, http://www.spaghetti-western.net/index.php/Dead_Men_Don%27t_Make_Shadows_Review. Numerous spaghetti western protagonists used special weapons: Django used a machine gun to mow down enemies; the protagonist in Sergio Leone's 1972 film, *Duck, You Sucker* (aka *A Fistful of Dynamite*), was an Irish explosives expert; the hero in *A Man Called Blade* (1977) relies on a weapon not generally associated with cowboys, a sharp ax. The Kyle Anderson review of *Django Kill* is in *Modern Primate*, March 28, 2012, accessed May 17, 2013, http://www.modernprimate.com/a-gay-gothic-horror-spaghetti-western-need-i-say-more.

16. Daniel Krupa, "Combat Fatigue: The Beginning of the End," *IGN* May 4, 2012, accessed May 17, 2013, http://www.ign.com/articles/2012/05/04/combat-fatigue-the-beginning-of-the-end.

17. *Trinity Is Still My Name* (1971) was released as a sequel. Copycat fagioli westerns often mimicked Trinity's divinely inspired name with titles such as *And His Name Was Holy Ghost* (1971) and *Holy Water Joe* (1971). For the reaction of Leone and Corbucci to spaghetti westerns, see "A Man Called Trinity" *Spaghetti Western Database*, accessed May 18, 2013, http://www.spaghetti-western.net/index.php/A_Man_called_Trinity. The comments from Christopher Frayling and Sergio Donati come from Gregory, *The Spaghetti West*.

18. The Leone quote was retrieved on May 27, 2013, from the Enoch Pratt Free Library Website, http://www.prattlibrary.org/calendar/atPratt.aspx?id=78560. See also https://groups.google.com/forum/#!topic/Artmobile-Events/itMu2OmGA5g.

19. Robert C. Cumbow, *The Films of Sergio Leone* (Lanham, MD: Scarecrow Press, 2008), 95. The Leone quote is from "Mio nome è Nessumno, Il," *Spaghetti Western*

Database, accessed May 27, 2013, http://www.spaghetti-western.net/index.php/My_name_is_nobody; see also Henry C. Parke, "Interview with 'My Name Is Nobody' Writer Ernesto Gastaldi," *Henry's Western Round-up*, May 12, 2013, accessed May 27, 2013, http://henryswesternroundup.blogspot.com/2013/05/interview-with-my-name-is-nobody-writer.html.

20. Examples from the United Kingdom include *Captain Apache* (1971), *Hannie Caulder* (1971), *The Man Called Noon* (1973), and *Shalako* (1968). Spain produced *Kid Rodelo* (1966), *The Christmas Kid* (1967), and *White Comanche* (1968); Germany, *Thunder at the Border* (1966); and Argentina, *Savage Pampas* (1966). Among the "red" westerns were *Armed and Dangerous* (Soviet Union, 1977); *The Sons of Great Bear* (East Germany, 1966); *Lemonade Joe* (Czechoslovakia, 1964); *The Prophet, the Gold and the Transylvanians* (Romania, 1978); and *Blood Money* (China, 1974). See David Hofstede, "Red Westerns," *Cowboys and Indians: The Premier Magazine of the West* (September 2012), accessed September 30, 2014, http://www.cowboysindians.com/Cowboys-Indians/September-2012/Red-Westerns.

Chapter 8

1. Good introductions to the New Western History include Richard W. Etulain, *Re-Imagining the Modern American West: A Century of Fiction, History, and Art* (Tucson: University of Arizona Press, 1996), especially 170–81; Gene M. Gressley, ed., *Old West/New West* (Norman: University of Oklahoma Press, 1997); and Limerick, Milner, and Rankin, *Trails*.

2. Examples include *Death of a Gunfighter* (1969); *Butch Cassidy and the Sundance Kid* (1969); *Ballad of Cable Hogue* (1970); *The Last Picture Show* (1971); *Wild Rovers* (1971); *Junior Bonner* (1972); *J. W. Coop* (1972); *Westworld* (1973); *Pat Garrett & Billy the Kid* (1973); *The Missouri Breaks* (1976); *Buffalo Bill and the Indians, or Sitting Bull's History Lesson* (1976); *Shoot the Sun Down* (1978); and *Heartland* (1979).

3. Significantly, this was not the first time Altman dipped into American history for a parable about contemporary America. His box office smash from the previous year, *M*A*S*H* (1970), employed the Korean War as a vehicle to critique the Vietnam War and 1960s America.

4. Other comedy westerns that poked fun at the mythic West include *The Rounders* (1965), *The Hallelujah Trail* (1965), *Sam Whiskey* (1969), *Skin Game* (1971), and *The Duchess and the Dirtwater Fox* (1976).

5. Antiheroes can be found in *Cat Ballou* (1965), *Sam Whiskey* (1969), *Ned Kelly* (1970), *One More Train to Rob* (1971), *Wild Rovers* (1971), *The Great Northfield Minnesota Raid* (1972), and *High Plains Drifter* (1973).

6. Quoted in Robert E. Kapsis and Kathie Coblentz, *Clint Eastwood: Interviews* (Jackson: University Press of Mississippi, 2013), 150.

7. Westerns that spotlighted African Americans include *Major Dundee* (1965); *Death of a Gunfighter* (1969); *100 Rifles* (1969); *Sam Whiskey* (1969); *The Red, White, and Black* (1970); *Buck and the Preacher* (1972); *Man and Boy* (1971); *The Legend of Nigger Charley* (1972); *Blazing Saddles* (1974); and *Boss Nigger* (1975).

8. *Ulzana's Raid* (1972) offered a reassessment of Indian-white warfare. Reflecting modern notions of cultural relativism and conflict resolution, it suggested that in

most cases, neither side is totally right or wrong. Instead, Americans (whether in the Old West or by extension in Vietnam) should take a realistic not ideological approach to the enemy. Other sympathetic treatments of Indians include *A Distant Trumpet* (1964), *The Great Sioux Massacre* (1965), *Hombre* (1967), *Tell Them Willie Boy Is Here* (1969), *Little Big Man* (1970), *A Man Called Horse* (1970), and *Buffalo Bill and the Indians, or Sitting Bull's History Lesson* (1976). Hispanics were portrayed in positive ways in *Villa Rides* (1968), *Death of a Gunfighter* (1969), *Valdez Is Coming* (1971), and *Pancho Villa* (1973). Asian Americans appear as good guys in *One More Train to Rob* (1971) and *Red Sun* (1971). Even white ethnics had their day, e.g., *Cheyenne Autumn* (1964), *Seven Guns for the MacGregors* (1966), and *Alvarez Kelly* (1966).

9. Davis, *John Ford*, 321; Kitses, *Horizons West*, 130.

10. John Ford quoted in Davis, *John Ford*, 326.

11. Strong western women were featured in *Cat Ballou* (1965); *The Hallelujah Trail* (1965); *A Big Hand for the Little Lady* (1966); *Hannie Caulder* (1971); *The Train Robbers* (1973); *Jessi's Girls* (1975); *The Duchess and the Dirtwater Fox* (1976); and *Heartland* (1979).

12. "The Ballad of Josie" (1967) was written by Don Costa and Floyd Huddleston and sung by Ron Dante, who also sang lead on the Archies' number one hit from 1969, "Sugar, Sugar."

13. Some westerns pushed sexual boundaries even further, e.g., *Hot Spur* (1968), *Linda and Abilene* (1969), *Girls in the Saddle* (1969), *The Scavengers* (1969), and *Hard on the Trail* (1972). America's experience in Vietnam influenced how westerns treated the military, e.g., *Major Dundee* (1965) featured military leaders motivated by self-interest; *The Great Sioux Massacre* (1965) echoed the era's antiwar attitudes when it declared that self-serving politicians, military men, and capitalists were to blame for brutal U.S. wars against innocent Native Americans.

14. "Jeremiah Johnson," composed by John Rubinstein and Tim McIntire (Warner Brothers, 1972).

15. Ibid.

16. Johnny Rivers, "Summer Rain," composed by James Hendricks (Imperial Records, 1968).

17. Youth culture glorified Indians as the antithesis of America's conformist society. Emulating Native Americans, many young people wore fringed leather jackets and headbands, practiced mysticism, and tried peyote. They applauded pro–Native American rock songs, such as Buffalo Springfield's "Broken Arrow" (1967) and Michael Murphey's "Geronimo's Cadillac" (1972). And they made best sellers out of books that treated Indians sympathetically, including John Neihardt's *Black Elk Speaks*, Carlos Castaneda's *The Teachings of Don Juan: A Yaqui Way of Knowledge*, and Dee Brown's *Bury My Heart at Wounded Knee*.

Chapter 9

1. Glen Campbell, "True Grit," composed by Elmer Bernstein and Don Black (Capitol Records, 1969).

2. Roger Ebert, review of *True Grit*, *RogerEbert.com*, July 1, 1969, accessed June 29, 2013, http://www.rogerebert.com/reviews/true-grit-1969.

3. Traditional John Wayne films include *El Dorado* (1967), *Chisum* (1970), *Big Jake* (1971), *The Cowboys* (1972), *Cahill U.S. Marshal* (1973), *Rooster Cogburn* (1975), and *The Shootist* (1976). Westerns that glorified the mythic West include *Mackenna's Gold* (1969), *Shoot Out* (1971), *Breakheart Pass* (1975), and *Bite the Bullet* (1975). Colorful western characters can be found in *The White Buffalo* (1977), *Nevada Smith* (1966), *Will Penny* (1968), and *The Cowboys* (1972). Gunslingers and outlaws remained a staple, e.g., *Ballad of a Gunfighter* (1964), *Deadwood '76* (1965), and *Shoot Out* (1971). Indians added excitement to *Fort Utah* (1967), *Red Tomahawk* (1967), and *40 Guns to Apache Pass* (1967). Homesteaders are protagonists in *The Night of the Grizzly* (1966), *El Dorado* (1967), and *Firecreek* (1968). And, of course, rugged lawmen were featured in westerns such as *Law of the Lawless* (1964), *Johnny Reno* (1966), and *Breakheart Pass* (1975). Neotraditional westerns such as *The Undefeated* (1969), *Shoot Out* (1971), *Man in the Wilderness* (1971), and *Bite the Bullet* (1975) continued the notion that the mythic West was a land of opportunity, success, and redemption.

4. Independent women are also featured in *The Shakiest Gun in the West* (1968), *Shoot Out* (1971), *The Train Robbers* (1973), *Pioneer Woman* (1973), and *Zandy's Bride* (1974). Neotraditional westerns glorified Indians, e.g., *Mackenna's Gold* (1969), *The White Buffalo* (1977), and *Grayeagle* (1977); for positive images of Hispanics, see *Return of the Seven* (1966), *Rio Lobo* (1970), and *Bite the Bullet* (1975). *The Legend of the Golden Gun* (1979) features a runaway African American slave (Carl Franklin), who initially speaks in an inarticulate slave dialect. That changes instantly once he realizes that the white man he saved is not a southern sympathizer. Called Book by his friends because of his love of reading and knowledge of the Bible, Shakespeare, and history, the ex-slave becomes a noted author and the film's narrator as he helps the white protagonist succeed.

5. Some westerns starred popular rock & roll singers in traditional roles, e.g., *The Fastest Guitar Alive* (Roy Orbison, 1967); *Gunfight in Abilene* (Bobby Darin, 1967); and *Charro!* (Elvis Presley, 1969). Other westerns spotlighted young people, e.g., *Young Fury* (1965), *Shoot Out* (1971), and *The Cowboys* (1972).

6. Lynn Baker, "A Rainbow Made of Children," composed by Lynn Baker (Warner Bros. Records, 1971).

7. Coven, "One Tin Soldier (The Legend of Billy Jack)," composed by Dennis Lambert and Brian Potter (Warner Bros. Records, 1971).

8. Other neotraditional westerns include *Ride Beyond Vengeance* (1966), *The Magnificent Seven Ride* (1972), *The Master Gunfighter* (1975), and *Breakheart Pass* (1975). Some poked harmless fun at the mythic West, e.g., *The Outlaws Is Coming* (1965), *Texas Across the River* (1966), *The Shakiest Gun in the West* (1968), *Support Your Local Sheriff* (1969), *Support Your Local Gunfighter* (1971), *The Apple Dumpling Gang* (1975), *The Great Scout and Cathouse Thursday* (1976). Others mixed traditional western images with classic horror movies, e.g., *Billy the Kid versus Dracula* (1966) and *Jesse James Meets Frankenstein's Daughter* (1966).

9. In rapid succession came neotraditional films such as *The White Buffalo* (1977), *Grayeagle* (1977), *Comes a Horseman* (1978), and *The Electric Horseman* (1979), as well as comedy westerns like *Goin' South* (1978), *The Frisco Kid* (1979), *The Villain* (1979), and *Wanda Nevada* (1979). There were also traditional TV movie westerns like *Kit Carson and the Mountain Men* (1977), *The New Maverick* (1978), *The Legend of the Golden Gun* (1979), *The Sacketts* (1979), and *The Wild, Wild West Revisited* (1979).

Chapter 10

1. The movie poster for *Urban Cowboy* can be found on *Wikimedia*, accessed July 27, 2013, http://upload.wikimedia.org/wikipedia/en/thumb/6/6b/Urban_cowboy_Poster.jpg/220px-Urban_cowboy_Poster.jpg.

2. Roger Ebert, review of *Heaven's Gate*, *RogerEbert.com*, January 1, 1981, accessed July 26, 2013, http://www.rogerebert.com/reviews/heavens-gate-1981.

3. For the Johnson County War, see T. A. Larson, "Johnson County War (1992)" in Lamar, *New Encyclopedia of the American West*, 577–79; and White, *"It's Your Misfortune and None of My Own,"* 345–46.

4. Other neotraditional westerns include *The Man from Snowy River* (1982), *The Alamo: Thirteen Days to Glory* (1987), *Proud Men* (1987), *Conagher* (1991), *Wyatt Earp* (1994), *Windrunner* (1994), and *The Horse Whisperer* (1998). Remakes of classic westerns also spotlighted the mythic West, e.g., *High Noon, Part II* (1980); *Stagecoach* (1986); and *Red River* (1988). Hollywood also cranked out westerns based on popular TV shows, e.g., *The Legend of the Lone Ranger* (1981), *Maverick* (1994), *The Cisco Kid* (1994), and *Wild, Wild West* (1999). Michael Mann's *The Last of the Mohicans* (1992), based on James Fenimore Cooper's novel, was particularly effective in capturing sounds and images of the mythic West. Set on the colonial frontier, it starred Daniel Day-Lewis as Hawkeye and Madeleine Stowe as Cora Munro. The movie told a familiar tale about a rugged frontiersman who battled Indians and assorted villains as he fought to defend liberty, justice, and of course, a beautiful damsel in distress. Equally important, it featured stunning cinematography that showcased the mythic feel of beautiful mountains, waterfalls, rivers, and pristine wilderness.

5. Ronald Reagan, "State of the Union Address," February 6, 1985, *Specials*, CNN.com, accessed August 25, 2013, http://www.cnn.com/SPECIALS/2004/reagan/stories/speech.archive/state.of.union2.html.

6. Reagan's administration got mixed reviews when it came to environmental policy. See Philip Shabecoff, "Reagan and Environment: To Many, a Stalemate," *New York Times*, January 2, 1989, accessed August 25, 2013, http://www.nytimes.com/1989/01/02/us/reagan-and-environment-to-many-a-stalemate.html?pagewanted=all&src=pm.

7. For information about Billy the Kid, see Gary L. Roberts's essay, "Billy the Kid," in Lamar, *Encyclopedia of the American West*, 100–101. For more detailed coverage, see Robert M. Utley, *Billy the Kid: A Short and Violent Life* (Lincoln: University of Nebraska Press, 1991). An overview of the historical accuracy of the two *Young Guns* films can be found in Marcelle Brothers, "History vs. *Young Guns*," *About Billy the Kid*, accessed August 6, 2013, http://aboutbillythekid.com/young_guns.htm.

8. Jon Bon Jovi, "Blaze of Glory," composed by Jon Bon Jovi (Mercury, 1990).

9. See Janet Maslin, review of *The Mask of Zorro* (1998), "What? A Sign of the 'Z'? The Cunning Fox Is Back," *New York Times*, July 17, 1998, accessed July 7, 2014, http://www.nytimes.com/movie/review?res=9407E3DF1430F934A25754C0A96E958260. Examples of comedy westerns include *Lust in the Dust* (1985), *Where the Hell's That Gold?* (1988), *El Diablo* (1990), *Back to the Future Part III* (1990), *City Slickers II* (1994), *The Cherokee Kid* (1996), and *Almost Heroes* (1998).

10. For example, there was a 3-D western, *Comin' at Ya!* (1981); science fiction westerns like *Timerider: The Adventure of Lyle Swann* (1982), *Alien Outlaw* (1985), and *The Aurora Encounter* (1986); an animated western, *An American Tail: Fievel Goes*

West (1991); and a musical western, *Rustlers' Rhapsody* (1985). TV capitalized on the comeback of traditional westerns with made-for-televisions westerns based on popular TV shows such as *Gunsmoke* and *Bonanza*. *The Cisco Kid*, a popular TV show from the fifties, was remade in 1994 as a movie starring Jimmy Smits as Cisco and Cheech Marin as Pancho. Other traditional westerns made for TV include *The Shadow Riders* (1982); *Louis L' Amour's Down the Long Hills* (1986); and *Last Stand at Saber River* (1997). Singer Kenny Rogers did an entire series of TV westerns in the eighties and nineties based on his hit song "The Gambler." Other singers also got in the TV western act, e.g., *The Last Days of Frank and Jesse James* (Kris Kristofferson, Johnny Cash, and Willie Nelson, 1986); *Pair of Aces* (Willie Nelson and Kris Kristofferson, 1990); and *Outlaw Justice* (Willie Nelson, Kris Kristofferson, Waylon Jennings, Travis Tritt, 1999).

11. Numerous movies offered new views of western characters and history. *Wild Bill* (1995) dealt with the legendary Wild Bill Hickok, focusing on his failing eyesight, sexual escapades, and drug use. *Son of the Morning Star* (1991) was a TV movie based on Evan Connell's revisionist history of Custer's Last Stand. *The Legend of Alfred Packer* (1980) embellished a true story about a man who resorted to cannibalism when he and friends were caught in a snowstorm in the Colorado Rockies. Packer's bizarre tale later became the basis for *Cannibal: The Musical* (1993), written and directed by Trey Parker, one of the creators of TV's *South Park*.

12. For information about Sioux warfare and hunting practices, see Richard White, "The Winning of the West: The Expansion of the Western Sioux in the Eighteenth and Nineteenth Centuries," *Journal of American History* 65, no. 2 (September 1978): 319–43; Robert M. Utley, *The Indian Frontier of the American West, 1846–1890* (Albuquerque: University of New Mexico Press, 1984), 8–11; Hine and Faragher, *American West*, 317–20.

13. See Vincent Canby, review of *Dances with Wolves* (1990), "A Soldier at One With the Sioux," *New York Times*, November 9, 1990, accessed August 19, 2013, http://movies.nytimes.com/movie/review?res=9C0CE6DB1338F93AA35752C1A966958260.

14. The movie poster for *Dances with Wolves* can be found at BlackBoxBlue, accessed August 19, 2013, http://blackboxblue.files.wordpress.com/2010/12/dances-with-wolves_movie-poster-01.jpg.

15. Strong female characters were featured in numerous films, e.g., *Heaven's Gate* (1980), *Rodeo Girl* (1980), *Cattle Annie and Little Britches* (1981), *Plainsong* (1982), *Old Gringo* (1989), *Dances with Wolves* (1990), *The Ballad of Little Jo* (1993), *Even Cowgirls Get the Blues* (1993), *Buffalo Girls* (1995), *Lone Star* (1996), *Cheyenne* (1996), and *Petticoat Planet* (1996). For reviews of *The Quick and the Dead*, see Owen Gleiberman, review of *The Quick and the Dead* (1995), *Entertainment Weekly*, February 17, 1995, accessed August 13, 2013, http://www.ew.com/ew/article/0,,296117,00.html; and Roger Ebert, review of *The Quick and the Dead*, February 10, 1995, accessed August 13, 2013, http://www.rogerebert.com/reviews/the-quick-and-the-dead-1995.

16. Caryn James, review of *Silent Tongue* (1994), "Sam Shepard's Spiritual, Imagistic Vision of the Old West," *New York Times*, February 25, 1994, accessed August 15, 2013, http://movies.nytimes.com/movie/review?res=9A02EFDA1F3BF936A15751C0A962958260.

17. For an analysis of violence in America during the 1980s and 1990s, see Christopher Jencks, "Is Violent Crime Increasing?" *American Prospect*, December 4, 2000, accessed August 13, 2013, http://prospect.org/article/violent-crime-increasing. Horror

westerns include *Eyes of Fire* (1983), *Ghost Town* (1988), *Sundown: The Vampire in Retreat* (1989), *Into the Badlands* (1991), *Mad at the Moon* (1992), *Uninvited* (1993), *Dead Man* (1995), *From Dusk Till Dawn* (1996), *Blood Trail* (1997), *Vampires* (1998), and *Phantom Town* (1999).

18. The *Wagons East* movie poster is available at Movie Poster Shop, accessed August 15, 2013, http://www.moviepostershop.com/wagons-east-movie-poster-1994.

19. D'Vera Cohn, Paul Taylor, Mark Hugo Lopez, Catherine A. Gallagher, Kim Parker, and Kevin T. Maass, *Gun Homicide Rate Down 49% Since 1993 Peak; Public Unaware*, Pew Research Social and Demographic Trends Report (Washington, DC: Pew Research Center, May 7, 2013), accessed August 27, 2013, http://www.pewsocialtrends.org/2013/05/07/gun-homicide-rate-down-49-since-1993-peak-public-unaware.

20. "Clint Eastwood Talks About the Resiliency of Westerns," *Los Angeles Times*, reprinted August 3, 1992, *Seattle Times*, accessed August 26, 2013, http://community.seattletimes.nwsource.com/archive/?date=19920803&slug=1505633.

21. Ibid.

22. Eagan, *America's Film Legacy*, x, 810–11.

Epilogue

1. "Quentin Tarantino, 'Unchained' and Unruly," Terry Gross interview, *Fresh Air*, NPR, January 2, 2013, accessed July 4, 2014, http://www.npr.org/templates/transcript/transcript.php?storyId=168200139.

2. Ibid.

3. Examples of twenty-first-century westerns include *All the Pretty Horses*, *The Claim*, *High Noon*, *Shanghai Noon*, and *The Virginian* in 2000; *American Outlaws*, *The Ballad of Lucy Whipple*, *Cowboy Up*, and *Texas Rangers* in 2001; *Hooded Angels* and *The Outsider* in 2002; *And Starring Pancho Villa as Himself*, *The Last Samurai*, *The Missing*, and *Open Range* in 2003; *The Alamo* and *Ghost Rock* in 2004; *Brokeback Mountain* and *The Proposition* in 2005; *Vengeance Trail*, *The Legend of Tillamook's Gold*, and *Bandidas* in 2006; *3:10 to Yuma*, *The Assassination of Jesse James by the Coward Robert Ford*, *No Country for Old Men*, *September Dawn*, *Seraphim Falls*, and *There Will Be Blood* in 2007; *Appaloosa*, *Lone Rider*, and *The Good, the Bad, the Weird* in 2008; *Angel and the Bad Man*, *The Hunter's Moon*, and *The Only Good Indian* in 2009; *Gunless*, *Jonah Hex*, *Meek's Cutoff*, *True Grit*, and *The Warrior's Way* in 2010; *Blackthorn*, *Cowboys and Aliens*, *The Legend of Hell's Gates*, and *Rango* in 2011; *Soda Springs*, *Ambush at Dark Canyon*, *Dawn Rider*, *Django Unchained*, and *El Gringo* in 2012; and *Gallowwalkers*, *The Lone Ranger*, and *Sweetwater* in 2013.

4. "Ron Howard on 'The Missing,'" Tatiana Morales interview, *The Early Show*, CBS, November 25, 2003, accessed July 2, 2014, http://www.cbsnews.com/news/ron-howard-on-the-missing.

5. Jerry Saltz, "Missing-Persons Posters," *New York Magazine*, August 27, 2011, accessed July 4, 2014, http://nymag.com/news/9-11/10th-anniversary/missing-persons-posters.

Index

Note: This index takes a historical approach to movies. Given that the book covers almost 1,000 films, the index is highly selective. Only those films emphasized in the text are listed. Other movies may be found in the text or endnotes. Some of the more significant characters, actors, actresses, and directors are also included.

Page numbers in *italics* represent illustrations.

About the Author

Richard Aquila is professor of history and former director of the School of Humanities and Social Sciences at Penn State University, the Behrend College. Previously, he taught at Ball State University and at Metropolitan State University of Denver. He specializes in U.S. social and cultural history, particularly the American West, American Indians, popular culture, and recent America. His publications include *Wanted Dead or Alive: The American West in Popular Culture* (1996); *Home Front Soldier: The Story of a G.I. and His Italian American Family During World War II* (1999); *That Old Time Rock & Roll: A Chronicle of an Era, 1954–1963* (1989); and *The Iroquois Restoration: Iroquois Diplomacy on the Colonial Frontier, 1701–1754* (1983, 1997). Aquila has also written, produced, and hosted numerous documentaries for NPR. His weekly public history series, *Rock & Roll America*, was syndicated on NPR and NPR Worldwide.